DEVELOPMENTS in British Social Policy

edited by

Nick Ellison and Chris Pierson

palgrave
macmillan

First published 2003 by
PALGRAVE MACMILLAN
Houndmills, Basingstoke, Hampshire RG21 6XS and
175 Fifth Avenue, New York, N.Y. 10010
Companies and representatives throughout the world

PALGRAVE MACMILLAN is the global academic imprint of the Palgrave Macmillan division of St. Martin's Press, LLC and of Palgrave Macmillan Ltd. Macmillan® is a registered trademark in the United States, United Kingdom and other countries. Palgrave is a registered trademark in the European Union and other countries.

ISBN 1–4039–0020–5 hardback
ISBN 1–4039–0021–3 paperback

This book is printed on paper suitable for recycling and made from fully managed and sustained forest sources.

A catalogue record for this book is available from the British Library.

Editing and origination by Aardvark Editorial, Mendham, Suffolk

10 9 8 7 6 5 4 3 2 1
12 11 10 09 08 07 06 05 04 03

Printed and bound in Great Britain by
Creative Print & Design (Wales), Ebbw Vale

Contents

List of Figures

List of Tables

Notes on Contributors

Rob Atkinson is Urban Research Director in the Cities Research Centre, Faculty of the Built Environment, University of the West of England. His research interests are primarily concerned with cross-national work on urban regeneration, community participation in urban regeneration partnerships, urban social exclusion and European urban policy. He has presented papers and published widely on these issues throughout Europe.

Kevin Joseph Brehony is Senior Lecturer in Education at the University of Reading. He is currently researching 18th-century dissenting academies and the role they played in the cultural formation of the industrial bourgeoisie and intellectuals. Recent publications include 'An "Undeniable" and "Disastrous" Influence? John Dewey and English Education (1895–1939)' *Oxford Review of Education* (1998); 'Montessori, Individual Work and Individuality in the Elementary School Classroom', *History of Education*, 2001; and 'Researching the Grammar of Schooling: An Historical View', *European Educational Research Journal* (2002).

Roger Burrows is Professor in the Department of Social Policy and Social Work and Co-Director of the Centre for Housing Policy at the University of York. He is the author of numerous articles and chapters on housing, health and social aspects of digital technologies and his books include (with J. Ford and S. Nettleton) *Home Ownership and the Risk Society; A Social Analysis of Mortgage Arrears and Possessions* (2001); and (edited with M. Featherstone) *Cyberspace/Cyberpunk/Cyberbodies* (1996).

Philip G. Cerny is Professor of International Political Economy in the Department of Government at the University of Manchester. Recent publications include *The Changing Architecture of Politics: Structure, Agency and the Future of the State* (1990); *Globalisation as Politics: Shaping Structures and Strategies in a Complex World* (2003); and (co-edited with Susanne Soederberg and Georg Menz) *Internalising Globalisation: The Rise of Neoliberalism and the Erosion of National Models of Capitalism* (2003).

Alan Deacon is Professor of Social Policy and a member of the ESRC Research Group on Care, Values and the Future of Welfare at the University of Leeds. He has published widely on welfare reform in Britain and the United States and his most recent book is *Perspectives on Welfare* (2002). He is currently Chair of the Social Policy Association.

Rosemary Deem is Professor of Education at the University of Bristol and Director of the UK Learning and Teaching Support Network Education Subject Centre, ESCalate. She is joint managing editor of *The Sociological Review*. Recent publications include 'Globalisation, New Managerialism, Academic Capitalism and Entrepreneurialism in Universities: Is the Local Dimension Still Important?', *Comparative Education* (2001); and 'Talking to University Managers – Methodological Dilemmas and Feminist Research Strategies', *Sociology* (2002).

Nick Ellison is Senior Lecturer in the Department of Sociology and Social Policy at the University of Durham. Publications include (with Chris Pierson) the previous edition of *Developments in British Social Policy* (1998); a number of chapters and articles concerned with citizenship and welfare; and *The Transformation of Welfare States?* (2003). He is also co-editor (with C. Bochel and M. Powell) of *Social Policy Review*.

Mark Evans is Senior Lecturer, Head of the Department of Politics and Provost of Halifax College at the University of York. He has published widely in the areas of constitutional reform, policy analysis and post-war reconstruction and development. Recent publications include *The New Constitutionalism and the Impact of Spill-over* (2000); *Constitution-making and the Labour Party* (2002); and (with Jim Buller) *Policy Transfer in Global Perspective* (2003).

Dan Finn is Professor of Social Policy at the University of Portsmouth. He is an expert on employment programmes. Between 1997 and 2002, he was a Special Adviser for the House of Commons Education and Employment and then Work and Pensions Select Committee. He was also an 'expert adviser' to the National New Deal Task Force and then the National Employment Board.

Tony Fitzpatrick is Senior Lecturer in the School of Sociology and Social Policy at the University of Nottingham. His work involves exploring the relevance to social policy of environmentalism, new technologies, social democracy and various other contemporary social and political theories. His main publications are *Freedom and Security* (1999); *Welfare Theory: An Introduction* (2001); and *After the New Social Democracy* (2003).

Janet Ford is the Joseph Rowntree Professor of Housing Policy at the University of York. Her research interests focus on sustainable home ownership and the nature of the linkages between housing, the labour market and social security. Recent publications include (with R. Burrows and S. Nettleton) *Home Ownership and the Risk Society; A Social Analysis of Mortgage Arrears and Possessions* (2001).

Robert Geyer has been researching EU social policy, Europeanization and European social democracy since the early 1990s. Branching away from European studies, he began working on integrating complexity theory into the social sciences in the late 1990s. He has been teaching at the University of Liverpool since 1996 and recent publications include *Exploring European Social Policy* (2000).

Caroline Glendinning is Professor of Social Policy, National Primary Care Research and Development Centre, University of Manchester. Among her many publications she is co-editor (with Martin Powell and Kirstein Rummery) of *Partnerships, New Labour and the Governance of Welfare* (2002).

Gail Lewis is Senior Lecturer in Social Policy at the Open University. Her research interests are the dynamics of gender and racialization in the social relations of welfare in postcolonial Britain. Her publications include *'Race', Gender, Social Welfare: Encounters in a Postcolonial Society'* (2000); 'Categories of Exclusion: 'Race', Gender and the Micro-social in Social Services Departments' in Breitenbach, E., Brown, A., Mackay, F. and Webb, J. (eds) *The Changing Politics of Gender Equality in Britain* (2002); 'Racialising Culture is Ordinary' in E.B. Silva and T. Bennett (eds) *Everyday Cultures* (2003).

Jane Lewis is Barnett Professor of Social Policy at the University of Oxford. She has written widely on gender issues, family policies, the relationship between the state and the non-profit sector and the history of social policies. Her most recent books are (edited with B. Hobson and B. Siim) *Contested Concepts in Gender and Social Politics* (2002); *The End of Marriage? Individualism and Intimate Relations* (2001); (with K. Kiernan and H. Land) *Lone Motherhood in Twentieth Century Britain* (1998).

Susanne MacGregor is Professor of Social Policy and Director of Research and Post-Graduate Studies in the School of Health and Social Sciences at Middlesex University London. She is currently Programme Coordinator for the Department of Health's £2.4 million Drugs Misuse Research Initiative, funded under its Policy Research Programme. Recent publications include 'Shifting Images of Poverty and Inequality in Britain 1942–1990: The Political and Institutional Context' in J.P. Revauger (ed.) *Pauvreté and Inégalités en Grande-Bretagne* (2001); and 'The Problematic Community' in M. May, E. Brunsdon and R. Page (eds) *Social Problems and Social Policy* (2000).

Jenny Morris is a freelance researcher. Her publications include *Independent Lives? Community Care and Disabled People* (1993); *Pride Against Prejudice: Transforming Attitudes to Disability* (1991); and *Community Care: Working in Partnership with Service Users* (1997).

Tim Newburn is Professor of Criminology and Social Policy at the London School of Economics. He is the author or editor of 17 books on subjects including policing, private security, criminal justice policy, young offenders and masculinity and crime. He is co-editor of the journal, *Criminal Justice*, and general editor of the *Longman Criminology Series*. With long-time collaborator Trevor Jones of Cardiff University, he is currently engaged in a three-year ESRC-funded study of the relationship between US and UK crime control policies and rhetorics.

Matthew Page is a Senior Research Fellow at the Institute for Transport Studies (ITS), University of Leeds. Recent publications include (with M.R. Tight, A.L.

Bristow and D. Milne) *Transport: A Vision for the Future* (2000); and (with G. Whelan and A. Daly) 'Modelling the Factors which Influence New Car Purchasing' Proceedings of the European Transport Conference. Published by PTRC (2000).

B. Guy Peters is Maurice Falk Professor of Government at the University of Pittsburgh. Among his recent publications are *Institutional Theory in Political Science* (1999); (edited with M. Bovens and P. Hart) *Success and Failure in Public Governance* (2001); and *American Public Policy* (6th edn) (2003).

Chris Pierson is Professor of Politics at the University of Nottingham. He is the author of *Beyond the Welfare State?* (1998); *Hard Choices: Social Democracy in the Twenty-first Century*; and (with Francis G. Castles) *The Welfare State Reader* (2000).

Sue Regan is Associate Director and Head of Social Policy at the Institute for Public Policy Research. She also manages the Centre for Asset-based Welfare based at IPPR. Her research brief includes housing, communities, assets and welfare. Prior to 1998, she worked in Whitehall at the Department of Social Security, her last posting being Private Secretary to the Secretary of State. Recent publications include *Assets and Progressive Welfare* (2001); *Squeezed Out: Choice and Affordability in Housing* (with Ruth Patrick) (2001); and *A New Contract for Retirement* (with Peter Robinson and Richard Brooks) (2002).

Tom Shakespeare has researched and taught sociology at the Universities of Cambridge, Sunderland, Leeds and Newcastle. He is currently Director of Outreach at the Policy, Ethics and Life Sciences Research Institute, Newcastle. He has written and broadcast widely on aspects of disability and genetics. His most recent book (with Anne Kerr) is *Genetic Politics: From Eugenics to Genome* (2002).

Acknowledgements

The author and publishers wish to thank the following for permission to reproduce copyright material:

The Institute for Fiscal Studies for Table 7.3: Brewer, Clarke and Wakefield (2002) *Social Security Under New Labour: What Did the Third Way Mean for Welfare Reform* (p. 33).

The Joseph Rowntree Foundation/Chartered Institute of Housing and the Council of Mortgage Lenders for data used in Table 8.1: S. Wilcox (ed.) (2001) *Housing Finance Review 2001/2002* and S. Wilcox (ed.) (2002) *UK Housing Review 2002/2003*.

IPPR for Table 15.2: Robinson (2001) *Time to Choose Justice*.

The European Parliament for Table 15.3.

Blackwell Publishing for Table 16.1: Geyer (2000) *Exploring European Social Policy* (p. 204).

National Audit Office for Table 17.1: Comptroller and Auditor General, 2002: 22, *Better Public Services Through e-Government*. HC 704-1 2001–2002.

The Joseph Rowntree Foundation for Figure 17.1: 'Housing support.org.uk: social housing, social care and electronic service delivery' by Nicholas Pleace and Deborah Quilgars, published for the Joseph Rowntree Foundation.

Crown copyright material is reproduced with the permission of the Controller of HMSO and the Queen's Printer for Scotland.

Every effort has been made to trace the copyright holders but if any have been inadvertently overlooked the publishers will be pleased to make the necessary arrangement at the first opportunity.

INTRODUCTION

Developments in British Social Policy

NICK ELLISON AND CHRIS PIERSON

It has become commonplace in discussions about 'the state of welfare' to assume that contemporary social policy making is conducted in an atmosphere of permanent retrenchment, if not 'crisis'. If, in many instances, these terms overstate the character of change, and if the reality of welfare state change is often rather less dramatic than they imply, it is the case nevertheless that many welfare regimes in the advanced democracies have had to 'adjust' their welfare systems to meet new demands. Whether in Britain or elsewhere in the economically developed world, rapid change – economic, social, political – is presumed to have undermined the original purposes of the welfare state as these came to be understood in the 'golden age' of the post-war period. During those years, the industrial democracies of the North and West developed welfare systems which, in one way or other, were designed to alleviate the effects of major known risks on individuals. Unemployment, industrial injury, sickness and old age became the subjects of government policy, schemes to defend citizens against these risks being financed either by employers and employees through dedicated social insurance contributions, by the wider population through general taxation, or by a mixture of the two. If that overused phrase, 'the Keynesian welfare state', had any real meaning, it gathered under its rubric those national systems that provided either state-based, or state-regulated, protection to those in need, its accompanying economic and political rhetoric combining Keynesian demand management theories with egalitarian redistributionist ideologies to produce wide-ranging justifications for increasingly expensive forms of welfare provision.

As a vast array of literature about post-war social policy suggests, the different forms of welfare state in Western Europe and elsewhere coped tolerably well with increasingly sophisticated and costly welfare programmes so long as full (male) employment and a healthy balance of payments persisted.

1

However, when these core features of post-war welfare capitalism began to fail, as they did in the 1970s, the political and economic pressures associated with maintaining comprehensive welfare provision rapidly mounted, along with predictions of crisis and (in certain countries) demands for retrenchment. Trigger factors for this sea change are rightly considered to be the collapse of the Bretton Woods system of fixed exchange rates in 1971 and the dramatic rise in oil prices following the Arab–Israeli war of 1973, both of which exposed the underlying weaknesses of certain national economies – notably the United Kingdom's. In the UK's case, these weaknesses had much to do with historically poor industrial relations, low domestic demand and an inability to match the output capacity and export potential of competitor nations – particularly Japan and Germany in the 1960s and 70s – which led to an increasingly unhealthy trade balance and weak currency. These 'local difficulties' need to be understood in the context of 'global' factors which, to varying degrees, have been held responsible for the decline in nation-states' ability to maintain post-war systems of social protection. Among these, Huber and Stephens (2001: 223) number the

> increasing internationalization of trade, internationalization and multinationalization of production, internationalization and deregulation of financial, capital and currency markets, the decline of the industrial and the rise of the service sector, and the decline of Fordist assembly line, semiskilled manufacture and the rise of 'flexible specialization' and skill-differentiated manufacture.

The relative importance of these changes is, needless to say, hotly debated (see for example, Hirst and Thompson, 1999; Mishra, 1999; Hay, 2001; C. Pierson, 2001), and the list itself is by no means exhaustive, omitting consideration of less tangible cultural changes such as the dramatic shift in attitudes towards marriage and the family, and the role of women in society, which hold clear consequences for welfare state organization and the structure of welfare provision. Rather than attempting to organize these factors in causal sequence – an impossible task – what follows will consider the ways in which national governments have responded to the economic and social challenges they represent.

'Globalization', Retrenchment and National Welfare Systems

After a decade or more of academic debate about the significance or otherwise of 'globalization', which at times appeared to generate a good deal more heat than light, the dust is finally beginning to settle. If initially the weight of opinion seemed to be with the 'hyperglobalizers' – those who argued that the combination of the massive expansion of information and communication technologies, highly mobile capital and transnational corporate power had created an economically 'borderless world' beyond the control of territorially bounded nation-states (Ohmae, 1995; Strange, 1996) – the pendulum has swung towards those sceptics who question whether capital is as unconstrained and national governments as economically powerless as first imagined (Hirst and Thompson, 1999; Hay, 2000). A middle way between the hyperglobalization thesis and outright scepticism would suggest that national governments enjoy a 'bounded autonomy' in macroeconomic policy, continually manipulating public spending and interest rates to accommodate the potential mobility of capital, on the one hand, but also prevailing institutional conditions and domestic (voter) expectations, on the other. In this way, as Reiger and Leibfried (1998) point out, different welfare systems set 'limits to globalization' even as they have to take account of the rapidly changing conditions associated with the expanding global economy (see Evans and Cerny in this volume).

This balancing act has certainly affected the character of many national welfare systems. Even in those countries, such as Sweden and Denmark, with a clear and consistent commitment to high public spending and extensive welfare provision, it is possible to discern 'adjustments' to post-war arrangements in core social policy areas. In general these changes take the form of cuts in 'replacement rates' (that is, the value of benefits measured against the average industrial wage), the reorganization of existing mechanisms for social protection, particularly pensions systems, and the greater decentralization, and privatization, of services. Elsewhere, Christian democratic welfare states such as Germany, France and Italy are also cutting back their generous, if highly gendered, social insurance arrangements to take account of labour market and other changes, while, less surprisingly, neoliberal welfare systems in the United States, Canada, New Zealand and the UK have strengthened the role of the market in the organization and delivery of a wide range of goods and services. In the USA, for instance, 'welfare' (as opposed to 'social security' – the US label for old age pension arrangements) can now only be claimed on a temporary basis with some states imposing stringent work tests and expecting all claimants to participate in the marketplace on pain of benefit withdrawal (Holcomb and Martinson, 2002). In the UK, too, New Deal arrangements for the unemployed make certain benefits conditional on the take-up of the education, training or employment opportunities on offer.

Yet to suggest that all welfare systems are somehow experiencing precisely the same 'crisis', and converging on a single market-oriented model as a result, would be to exaggerate. As many observers (Hay, 2001; C. Pierson, 2001; P. Pierson, 2001) have noted, there is little evidence of a wholesale 'race to the bottom', with countries leapfrogging one another in efforts to cut public spending and taxation in order to make their economies attractive to the supposed preferences of footloose international capital – far from it. Indeed, Garrett (1998) and others (see Rodrik, 1998) have argued that capital can accommodate regimes characterized by high social and public spending if these policies lead to economic and social stability, and reduced labour militancy. Moreover, this lack of convergence is not simply governed by movements in the international economy even if it is accepted that this dimension is significant. Certain policy areas may be particularly sensitive to internal, or 'endogenous', changes. While labour markets *may* be relevant in this respect – after all some commentators (Iversen, 2000) argue that the rapid move away from manufacturing towards services is a product of predominantly domestic changes in consumption patterns – others obviously are. For example, although demographic changes are certainly affecting the great majority of advanced democracies, their impact is predominantly domestic because it is *national* pensions systems developed in the post-war period which require reorganization or reform to meet the challenge of population ageing. While there are certain common denominators of change across regimes, it is difficult to discern any real convergence around one set of preferred pensions arrangements. If anything, national governments appear to be making efforts to maintain the broad contours of their existing schemes, with the diversity this implies, while making fairly extensive adjustments *within* these parameters in an effort to accommodate the large numbers of baby boomers approaching retirement (Bonoli, 2000; Myles and Pierson, 2001).

This notion of (occasionally extensive) adjustment taking place within the parameters set by existing forms of welfare provision in different nation-states has been given a theoretical edge by Paul Pierson (1996, 2001), who points out that there seem to be institutionally bounded limits to change. Essentially, Pierson's argument is that once particular mechanisms of service organization and delivery have become embedded as part of the social and political infrastructure, they can be difficult to shift, partly because politicians may be reluctant to pay the price of stringent retrenchment at the polling booth and partly because organized interests – trade unions, business interests, key pressure groups – can take exception to attempts to change the accepted contours of welfare provision in ways that challenge existing institutional norms. Much depends, of course, on the countries involved because party politics and the nature of 'interest group intermediation' differ widely across welfare regimes. The general point, however, is that even as pressures generated by global phenomena (now including conformity to the stringent economic and fiscal conditions demanded of member states under European Monetary Union) increase, they are likely to be viewed through the lens of the domestic policy agenda and the potential alternatives on offer. This formulation does not deny the logic of the thinking behind Cerny's (2000, and Evans and Cerny in this volume) 'competition state', or Jessop's (1994) 'Schumpeterian workfare state', but it places limits on its vision and scope. Put simply, core elements of these concepts – the privileging of markets, antipathy to welfare dependence – will be interpreted differently depending on the country in question, welfare outcomes being more or less generous depending on the particular combination of economic, political and institutional factors involved. In the British case, the social policies of Conservative governments between 1979 and 1997, as well as 'third way' welfare under New Labour, saw the adoption of a decidedly market-oriented perspective, although, in Labour's case, one nevertheless coloured by a more than residual commitment to social inclusion (as many chapters in this volume attest).

British Social Policy in Historical and Contemporary Perspective

The British welfare state formerly was not characterized by such an explicit orientation towards markets. Indeed, the prevailing consensus during the postwar era (1945–75) was that the state, in the form of central and local government, should have primary responsibility for the delivery of welfare goods and services, the voluntary and private sectors being regarded as, at best, residual contributors. This high regard for the state was the product of a number of factors, the most significant of which concern the apparent efficiency of state economic management during the Second World War and the greater degree of social equality that was perceived to have resulted from the state's intervention in a wide range of areas, including medical services, food rationing and childcare. It is not surprising that, by the war's end, there was a widespread conviction – and not only within the Labour Party – that a greater degree of state economic and social management would be both more efficient and equitable than market solutions. This conviction was bolstered by intellectual fashion: Keynesian ideas highlighting the importance of demand management and full employment appeared to endorse the state's economic role, while the ideals for the abolition of 'want, disease, ignorance, squalor, and idleness' contained in the Beveridge Report's (1942) proposal for a system of universal social insurance seemed to herald a new beginning in which the state would act as the champion of greater equality and social justice.

The fact that Labour won the general election of 1945 with a landslide majority clearly suggested a high degree of popular support for the rapid progress towards a 'welfare state' made between 1946 and 1949. It was during these years that the key building blocks of British welfare were developed – a social security system designed to protect the unemployed, the sick and the old, and a National Health Service designed to provide medical care free at the point of need. In addition, Labour implemented the provisions of the Butler Education Act (1944), creating a system of compulsory secondary education for all children to the age of 15.

If it is no exaggeration to say that this extraordinary burst of legislative activity led to the creation of a welfare state very much in Labour's image, it is equally true that subsequent Conservative governments during the 1950s and early 1960s did little fundamentally to alter the collectivist ideals on which British social policy was based. In this way, the period of 'welfare consensus' which characterized the 1950s and 60s, while by no means *entirely* 'consensual' (Ellison, 1996), nevertheless saw general agreement about the role of the state – central and local – in service provision. Although this general agreement was tested by rising welfare costs during the 1960s, particularly in the health service (Glennerster, 1995), the collapse of the Bretton Woods system and the oil price rises of the early 1970s created the economic conditions for a fundamental rethink of the role and purposes of the welfare state. While Labour governments severely cut social spending in the late 1970s, much to the consternation of their supporters, it was left to Conservative governments to reorganize welfare provision by introducing voluntary and private sector services in certain areas, and 'quasi-markets' in others (Bartlett et al., 1998).

Under Conservative governments in the 1980s and 90s, and New Labour since 1997, Britain presents a rare case of extensive welfare state adjustment – more extensive than the majority of the advanced democracies, with the possible exception of New Zealand. The chapters below, particularly those in Part II, will examine changes in key areas of social policy under New Labour. Of more importance here is an overview of the direction of change since 1997 and a consideration of its possible implications, both for those affected and also for our understanding of the nature and likely future development of social policy in Britain.

'Third way' social policy?

Whether characterized as a recasting of left-wing principles or a pragmatic accommodation to Conservative economic and social policies, the 'third way' remains an enigmatic term. For some it is little more than the post-Thatcherite recognition that markets are important but need regulation by accountable public bodies to function efficiently (see the account in Driver and Martell, 1998). For others, third way thinking holds much greater possibilities. Giddens (2000: 65), for example, argues that:

> in the reform of state and government, as well as in economic policy, third way politics looks to respond to the great social transformations of the end of the twentieth century: globalization, the rise of the new knowledge-based economy, changes in everyday life, and the emergence of an active, reflexive citizenry.

Little is to be gained here by entering into complex debates about the theoretical and moral validity of third way perspectives, but it is important to take account of how key aspects of third way thinking have been interpreted by the Blair governments. One thing is clear: New Labour has not returned to the 'tax and spend' economic and social policies of its Old Labour predecessors, adhering instead to two key elements of the third way that have effectively come to define the government's approach to the welfare state. First, Labour has consistently stressed the redundancy of the socialist versus capitalist, state versus market debates of the post-war period, arguing instead that economic and social policies need to be concerned primarily with 'what works'. Labour governments over the past six years appear to have taken seriously the belief that 'education, incentives, entrepreneurial culture, flexibility, devolution and cultivation of social capital' (Giddens, 2000: 73) are the core factors necessary for the successful negotiation of the new knowledge economy and are prepared to enlist the private and voluntary sectors, as well as the state, in their pursuit. Second, ideologically, New Labour has drawn on communitarian ideas (Etzioni, 1995) to argue for the importance of strong communities. In the context of attempting to build such communities, the Blair governments have developed a range of initiatives ostensibly designed to enhance the opportunities of individual citizens, although there are usually strings attached, as will be discussed below.

In one way or other, these two nodal points of the third way have come to inform virtually every area of British welfare in the era of the 'competition state'. In terms of policy making, they have been interpreted by New Labour in three ways:

1. The refusal to be influenced by traditional 'public good, private bad' socialism has allowed the Blair governments to alter *spending patterns* by focusing state spending on core policy areas, ring-fencing certain services while opening others to the rigours of the market.

2. Labour has also developed new *methods* of welfare organization, particularly within core areas of social policy. Public, private and voluntary
   sectors are encouraged to work in partnership with service users to build
   strong, inclusive communities.

3. The stress upon 'community' has led New Labour to alter the conditions
   of *treatment* for certain groups of citizens in certain areas and spaces of
   welfare. This process can relate to specific policy changes such as increased
   means testing, or equally to efforts to modify the behaviour of those
   whose activities and lifestyles are deemed to be wanting.

Spending patterns

Even before winning office in 1997, the Labour Party made it clear that
certain services – education and health being the most important – would
require additional resources, even if money had to be taken from other areas
of public spending. The first, as well as subsequent, comprehensive spending
reviews (CSR), pushed cash into these major areas, while others – particularly
defence, housing and (in the first Blair government) transport – were not so
well served. If there is any doubt about the nature of the government's core
priorities, these should have been dispelled by the 2002 CSR, which is
devoting an extra £40 billion to the health service over five years and an extra
£12.8 billion to education over a three-year period. Indeed, the pre-budget
report of November 2002 made it clear that the Chancellor, Gordon Brown,
is prepared to risk his 'prudent' image and borrow £20 billion over two years
to ensure these spending commitments are honoured, regardless of the
growing prospect of recession.

Whether spending and borrowing on this scale are economically sustainable remains to be seen, particularly as large tax increases are not an option.
National insurance contributions have been raised, to be sure, but third way
thinking broadly dictates that savings should be made by reducing spending
in areas either where state support masks costs that individuals should be
meeting themselves, or where private and voluntary agencies can provide
services more cheaply. As Glennerster (1999a) has indicated, prime candi-
dates in the first category are retirement pensions and higher education. In
both cases the Blair governments have been keen to reduce these expensive
commitments by encouraging private sector take-up where possible – occupational and stakeholder pensions for those deemed able to make their own
provision for retirement, and loans in place of grants for those students from
better-off families entering higher education. In the second category, housing
has come to be regarded as an area which should be left primarily to the

private sector, with private ownership and private renting, supported by some social housing, being the major forms of provision.

Methods of organization and delivery

The most significant issue relating to the new methods of welfare delivery developed by New Labour surely has to be the greater degree of devolution and decentralization that has come to characterize much of British social policy. In one sense 'devolution' has clearly occurred at the constitutional level, with the granting of limited legislative autonomy to the Scottish and Welsh assemblies. Significantly, Scottish policies for the financing of higher education have developed differently from those in England, Wales and Northern Ireland, and there are also growing differences in areas of health care and tax policy. However, although constitutional devolution has taken up a good deal of journalistic space over the past several years, a rather different and no less significant revolution has been occurring in the delivery of welfare at grass-roots level. Following third way ideas about the need to 'democratize democracy' (Giddens, 2000), New Labour has attempted to create decentralized forms of service delivery primarily through the development of 'partnerships'.

Decentralization is in itself nothing new, but the form that it has taken recently differs from that of previous Conservative governments. In the 1980s and 90s, the Conservatives devised various types of quasi-market in an effort to mimic market competition especially in core areas of welfare such as education and health (Bartlett et al., 1998). Labour has followed the spirit but not the letter of this initiative. Outright privatization apart, in a number of areas ranging from health, employment and education to a variety of initiatives within civil society (Hewitt and Powell, 2002), the Blair governments have experimented with forms of provision which, depending on the service in question, encourage new forms of 'welfare pluralism' through the deliberate mixing of public, private, voluntary and 'community' sector resources and expertise in the context of area-based initiatives (ABI). This process has been pushed a long way. There are now 50 ABIs ranging from fairly small programmes such as the Community Chest initiative and Sports Action Zones to the 64 Health Action Zones and the 73 Education Action Zones. Other ABIs include the Sure Start programme, which will shortly be funding 522 locally based schemes covering deprived areas across England. Although much depends on context, there is little doubt that 'the current drive to encourage (and ultimately to compel) partnerships penetrates much further and deeper than previous attempts', as Clarke and Glendinning (2002: 34)

note. Indeed, in Newman's (2001) view, this dramatic expansion of a
'networked governance of welfare' since 1997 effectively defines the third
way perspective on the organization and delivery of social policy.

Treatment: selectivity and conditionality

However goods and services are delivered, the hallmark of a welfare regime
is the way in which its citizens are treated. Social policy under New Labour
distinguishes among citizens in two related ways. First, they can be treated
according to desert and need, with certain vulnerable sections of the population – children and the already-retired for instance – clearly being regarded
as 'deserving', while others are considered less so. Reacting to the Conservative legacy of high levels of child poverty, Labour has identified children
from deprived backgrounds as in need of specific state support through
higher child benefits, the child tax credit and extra services such as preschool
education (Piachaud and Sutherland, 2000). With respect to retired people,
despite, or perhaps because of, the error of allowing the state pension to
increase by just seventy-five pence in line with inflation in 2000, pensioners
have been treated generously ever since, particularly in the form of the
dramatically uprated minimum income guarantee and a number of untaxed
lump-sum payments and allowances (Toynbee and Walker, 2001). Elsewhere,
though, the manner in which citizens are treated has taken a rather different
turn, with benefits not only becoming increasingly means-tested and thus
selective, but also being accompanied by stringent eligibility criteria. Unemployment benefit, where payments are conditional upon jobseekers taking up
the training and employment opportunities offered, is the clearest example of
this trend towards conditionality (Dwyer, 2000).

The second type of treatment relates to the way in which the state under
New Labour has become involved in efforts to alter the actual behaviour of
certain groups of citizens. The use of public money to encourage employment take-up through New Deal initiatives is an example of one method used
to foster an employment-oriented culture, this particular programme
performing the twin tasks of getting individuals into work and providing
'carrot and stick' incentives to keep them there. For Labour, employment is
very much its own reward, not just because it is considered to be the best
method of enhancing social inclusion but because it also helps to create a
trained and disciplined citizenry able to respond to the changing demands of
the labour market. Outside employment, the emphasis on behaviour is a core
feature of the ABIs. Many of these initiatives, perhaps Sure Start in particular,
have been designed specifically to engage with those living in the most

deprived areas in an attempt to alter attitudes to drugs and health-related issues, sexual behaviour, parenting and so on.

Where Are We Now?

This brief overview of New Labour's application of core third way ideas in policy terms needs to be supplemented by an assessment of its impact both on the structure of the welfare state as well as on perceptions of the role and nature of welfare. What, in other words, does the British welfare state now 'look like'? A short answer would suggest that, after six years or so of New Labour rule, welfare provision in Britain is epitomized by a number of apparent contradictions in terms of core funding, delivery methods and treatment which give it a paradoxical character: public *and* private; decentralized *and* centralized; conditional *and* unconditional. The sequencing of these putative opposites describes the fragmented nature of British social policy, where the experience of welfare among deprived groups and classes contrasts increasingly with that of the better-off.

Returning, first, to spending patterns, it seems clear that the prioritizing of health and education in the context of the ongoing marketization of other sectors has not only compounded the shift away from the traditional collectivist foundations of state welfare but contributed to the development of new, or at least 'reformulated', welfare divisions. In this regard, it is surely no coincidence that these main spending 'winners' are highly valued by middle England – that vast mass of middle-class voters who Blair successfully managed to detach from their natural Tory leanings in the mid-1990s and who have yet to return. Of course, others from more deprived groups can certainly be expected to benefit from the dramatic injections of Treasury cash into these services but, inhibited by a legacy of deprivation grounded in class and geography, citizens from these groups are less likely to gain access to services of the highest quality. Where services are marketized, privatization is likely either to benefit, or certainly not to hinder, those who are in a position to make private (or occupational) arrangements for pensions, and fund their own higher education and housing requirements. Those not in this fortunate position will be forced to rely on poorly resourced and increasingly 'residual' state provision.

Where delivery methods are concerned, for all the rhetoric of decentralization, collaboration and empowerment, the shift to partnerships as the preferred mechanism for service provision has been accompanied by a marked degree of centralization. Rummery (2002: 241) argues, for instance, that 'over-prescriptive encouragement of partnership working from central government' has led to 'systems of auditing and measuring results [becoming] important governing mechanisms in the facilitation (or otherwise) of welfare partnerships', the implication being that the various area-based packages of welfare provision come complete with detailed 'instructions for use' from central government. Certainly the overriding concern (some would say obsession) with performance targets, league tables and other monitoring and surveillance mechanisms speaks to a lack of trust between central government and many of the partners engaged in the ABIs. It may be, as Clarke and Glendinning (2002: 43) note, that where partnerships are imposed and regulated by government, as they frequently are, they may better be understood as 'externally managed systems, whose internal dynamics coexist, potentially uncomfortably, with powerful external direction and intervention'.

Turning, finally, to the treatment of individual citizens, it is becoming clear that individuals can be treated differently depending on a range of factors associated with socioeconomic class and locality. There are two aspects to this issue. First, in core sectors, such as education and health, different patterns of decentralization and centralization are emerging in different localities as certain institutions are permitted to alter their relationship with local and central government. Schools and hospitals identified as particularly successful are beginning to be rewarded with greater autonomy (real decentralization?) and extra resources, while failing institutions face penalties in the form of greater monitoring and central control. It is likely, of course, that better-off groups in better-off localities will have access to higher quality, well-resourced and more 'autonomous' services, while deprived groups in deprived areas will have to make do with less favourable provision, the delivery of which will take place under the constant gaze of the state. Second, looking to deprived areas and the ABIs designed to develop and support new services in them, gains in service quality, including community renewal, appear to come at the price of a heightened paternalism that carries certain dangers (MacGregor, 1999). For example, although failing *institutions* – essentially schools and hospitals – may be fair game for government 'hit squads' and other punitive measures, the increased attention to forms of behaviour in failing *communities* is not only potentially intrusive, in a manner which would be resisted by those living in 'better' areas, but could actually *exclude* or stigmatize citizens by treating them as objects for externally imposed 'improvement'. While the idea of partnership and user involvement is no doubt intended to minimize this tendency, offsetting the still-tangible presence of Victorian attitudes towards the deserving and undeserving poor, recent literature on this area does not suggest that it has yet succeeded (Jordan, 1998; Beresford, 2002; Glendinning et al., 2002).

To this extent, it is important for New Labour's reputation, as a party committed to equity (if no longer equality) and social inclusion, that the contradictions outlined above are somehow resolved. The 'how?' implicit in this statement raises issues of enormous complexity which it would be foolish to deal with here, although it is worth acknowledging that progress in this regard is likely to have a good deal to do with reducing central control, particularly in the shape of the debilitating targeting regimes, and risking giving partnerships a freer democratic rein.

Developments in British Social Policy: Looking Ahead

Although Part II of this volume is designed to assess recent developments in the core areas of social policy in Britain, this book also addresses a number of broader themes, concepts and issues which inform the study of contemporary social policy as an academic discipline. Developments in British social policy are not purely related to the practical issues of policy change. How the role and nature of welfare are perceived – how, in other words, change is understood in analytical and theoretical terms – is an integral part of the study of social policy. For this reason, the chapters in Part I engage with a range of analytical and thematic issues, frequently using examples from the areas discussed at greater length in Part II in order to illustrate the relevance of the points being made. Whether the focus is on the complex relationship between globalization and social policy, or ostensibly more practical matters relating to the causes of, and remedies for, social exclusion, or the nature of the balance to be struck between social rights and duties, the chapters here provide theoretically informed analyses that address contemporary concerns about policy making and implementation both in the British context and across the advanced democracies more generally.

Part II concentrates in fairly traditional manner on the core areas of British social policy, each contributor providing his or her account of developments under New Labour's stewardship. While many of the themes addressed in Part I reappear here, the emphasis is upon a detailed assessment of the government's achievements after six years in office. If the various verdicts on New Labour's welfare policies are at best mixed, there seems to be no doubt that the government itself regards social policy as central to the elusive objective of achieving both greater economic stability – through enhanced competitiveness – and greater social justice. Whether this circle can in fact be squared is open to serious question, as many of the chapters in Part II suggest.

Reading the contributions in Part II is sufficient to demonstrate that social policy is not a static area of study – indeed by the time this book is published

elements of its contents will already be out of date! Keeping abreast of legislative and policy change, however, is only one aspect of keeping up with developments in social policy more generally, for the nature of social policy as an
academic subject area also changes as governments and citizens alike are
confronted by new challenges which demand new policy responses. In Part
III, contributors examine dimensions of change that are likely to have a
significant impact on the future nature and conduct of social policy. Some of
these issues, such as the possible methods of 'paying for welfare' in an era of
low taxation, or the growing significance of Europe, are by no means new in
themselves, although changes within these areas mean that they constantly
have to be considered afresh. Other challenges are more embryonic and, in
an effort to take account of these, three rather more speculative pieces have
been included in this volume because they seem to point the way towards a
different and potentially uncertain future, at least in terms of welfare 'governance'. The intention here is to push understandings of social policy beyond
perennial concerns with traditional social divisions of welfare, the major
policy arenas and the theoretical issues and perspectives typically employed in
the analysis of policy making, towards areas where contemporary developments can be expected to lead to different ways of conceptualizing the role
of welfare in the future. If environmentalism is already the subject of growing
interest among social policy commentators, the full impact of technological
advances in genetics and ICTs is only just beginning to be felt, with a range
of complex moral and ethical issues being raised by the former in particular.
Attending to matters of this kind, in the context of a book that ranges widely
across theoretical concerns and core policy analysis, is to argue for an
approach to social policy that conceives it less as a narrow academic discipline
than as a wide-ranging area of study, the sum of which will always transcend
the scope and complexity of its parts.

Partly because of this eclecticism, the conclusion to this volume does not
attempt to 'sum up' the various arguments, approaches and perspectives elaborated by the contributors in detail – they speak for themselves. Instead, it
returns to the main theme of the introduction: social policy as it has developed since New Labour came to office and the successes and failures of the
past six years. In an oft-repeated phrase, 'the verdict is mixed'. It is certainly
the case that Labour has behaved as a party of progress in some areas, as
many of the chapters in this book make clear. In others, however, there has
been a curious reluctance to act radically, the preference apparently being to
work *within* the parameters imposed by exogenous and endogenous
economic, social and political forces. If in some ways this caution is understandable, it is also disappointing: whatever Labour's achievements, there is
no sign of a 'new social politics' here.

PART I

THEMES AND DEBATES
IN CONTEMPORARY
SOCIAL POLICY

Introduction

Social policy is now high on the agenda not just of domestic governments but also of international agencies (such as the UN and the World Bank). But as its salience has increased, so have the arguments about what exactly social policy is and what it is for. Long gone are the days when the business of social policy was just to deliver more public welfare (where 'more' simply meant spending more money). Social policy is now a much more contested (and interesting) field of study and policy endeavour. Various aspects of the changing nature of the social policy process are captured in the contributions in this section of the book.

We begin with one of the biggest and the most broadly contested of these issues – the impact of globalization on social policy. In a wide-ranging discussion, Mark Evans and Phil Cerny identify the essentials of the processes of globalization and its political offspring, the competition state. They show how New Labour's response to the challenge of globalization was to fashion its own variant of the 'post-welfare contracting state'. Focusing on a series of case studies, they show further that the move 'from entitlement to contract' is likely to have quite ambivalent outcomes in terms of the oft-expressed ambition to improve efficiency while fostering 'real equality of opportunity'. In a complementary paper, Guy Peters shows with great economy and clarity how the very process of governing the welfare state has changed in recent years. While the state remains a key welfare player, Peters identifies three sets of recent changes: in policy, in the instruments of policy delivery (with greater involvement of non-state actors) and in a shift in the function of the state from provider to regulator. What emerges from these several changes is a more complex and multilayered web of 'governance'. The new welfare governance is much more market-focused but, at the same time, it can open up the space for citizen initiatives and may even give greater 'voice' to welfare clients (sometimes!).

Susanne MacGregor's chapter unpacks the idea of 'social exclusion', a key term in the lexicon of the 'new' social policy and considers its embodiment in the policy agenda of New Labour. Advocates of the term have seen social exclusion as a way of capturing the multidimensional nature of poverty and deprivation, opening the way for a more active social policy which will enable the excluded to find a way into mainstream society. Critics have tended to see it as a way of obscuring the unpleasant reality of growing inequality and the lack of a public and political will to address it. MacGregor's treatment shows that there is some truth in both these characterizations (among others) and that the logic of social exclusion sits easily with the policy orientation of New Labour (in the promulgation of various New Deals, for example). Social exclusion certainly has something to recommend it as a multidimensional policy focus. The 'hole at its centre' is the failure to recognize the centrality of (the rising incidence of) plain, old-fashioned inequality.

In her chapter, Jane Lewis assesses the changing balance between rights and responsibilities. This has been a key theme of New Labour's social policy thinking. While maintaining a focus upon the traditional idea of welfare citizenship, the advocates of reform argue that the balance between rights and responsibilities (which is at the core of even welfarist notions of citizenship) has become unbalanced, with citizens' rights wholly overwhelming their corresponding responsibilities. This is most clearly seen in the redescription of the relationship between citizen, (paid) work and welfare. It is the responsibility of the state to enable citizens to make themselves 'work ready'. It is the responsibility of the citizen to take work opportunities when they arise. A re-evaluation of rights and responsibilities is also seen in the attempt to foster a welfare regime in which the state helps citizens to take greater responsibility for their own welfare, for example in the legal and taxation infrastructure that underpins occupational and private pensions. The change is two-edged. When does the state's 'empowerment' of those without work (perhaps disabled persons or women with young children) pass over into coercion? Lewis's balanced treatment reflects this ambivalence. But her discussion ends on a warning note. If the responsibility to find paid employment is made paramount, this threatens to make second-class citizens of those who really cannot work.

Gail Lewis's chapter, with which this section closes, deals with an extremely important although sometimes wilfully obscured aspect of the 'new' social policy – that is, the centrality of ideas (and practices) of diversity and difference. Drawing inspiration from what Lewis here calls a 'poststructuralist' approach, a number of radical critics of the past 20 years have come to criticize welfare state orthodoxy in terms of its assumption that there is a universal and unified welfare subject (or client or citizen) to which welfare policy speaks. Characteristically, it has been argued that even self-styled 'progressive' forms of social policy have smuggled in relations of oppression by talking (and/or governing) as if all of the relevant population shared the characteristics of what is presumed to be a normal, natural and sometimes even 'universal' majority. This is a critique which has it social origins in the so-called 'new social movements' among critics of the gendered and racist characteristics of traditional welfare 'universalism'. Helpfully, Lewis distinguishes between 'diversity' (the recognition that in a whole series of ways we are not all the same) and 'difference' (in which power relations are inscribed in the things that are taken to make us different). She also draws a useful distinction between what she sees as the legitimate appeal of universal claims (for example that all should be treated equally or valued equally) and the illegitimate claims of universalism, which ascribe a particular and prescriptive identity to all members of a given population (a universal which can operate only through the principle of exclusion). Through a series of real-world examples, Lewis shows how difference works and why it matters.

CHAPTER 1

Globalization and Social Policy

MARK EVANS AND PHIL CERNY

Probably the thorniest question in public policy at the start of the 21st century is the relationship between globalization and social policy. Globalization has transformed relationships between the international economy, the state and economic policy, creating new parameters – constraints and opportunities – for trade policy, regulating financial markets, corporate governance, industrial policy, macroeconomic policy and fiscal and monetary policy. Governments have been restructuring the welfare state too. Governments of both left and right in Britain and elsewhere have attempted to make social policy more market-efficient along business lines in order to reduce its perceived downside, rooted in the 'stagflation' crisis of the 1970s. This downside to the welfare state included spiralling costs for the public sector through expanding budgetary 'entitlements', a lack of competitiveness for the private sector through internationally high unit labour costs and labour market rigidities, the institutionalization of inflexible bureaucratic practices and the entrenchment of a dependency culture among workers and the unemployed themselves. Since then, a loose neoliberal consensus has developed across party lines on the need to restructure the welfare state along market lines in order to promote the global competitiveness of national economies, not only for business but also for labour and welfare claimants, the biggest beneficiaries in financial terms from government expenditure.

The welfare state has been marketized in a range of ways – the creation of internal markets in public and social services and the sale of those that are thought to be potentially profitable in the private sector, contracting out a range of services and tasks, the introduction of financial performance indicators to day-to-day operations, payments for services and the tying of benefit entitlements far more closely to participation in the workforce (availability for work), job mobility, training and so on. With regard to the last of these, the aim has been to transform benefits from entitlements or 'claimants' rights' into a range of virtual incentives and compensation for more active participation in the labour force. Indeed, there is a close correlation in time and space between globalization and the restructuring of social policy and the welfare state. This chapter argues that globalization has a number of effects, direct and indirect, on this restructuring of the welfare state.

It is much easier to trace the impact of economic globalization on economic policy and policy making than to assess its impact on social policy. Broadly speaking, when nation-states could still be insulated to some extent from international and transnational economic trends during the period of the long boom after the Second World War through the late 1960s, governments could trade off a certain amount of economic inefficiency for a bit more social justice. Most firms were still primarily dependent on national markets and it was possible to protect domestic industries from foreign competition through tariffs (although these were regularly being lowered as the result of negotiations under the General Agreement on Tariffs and Trade). Cheap labour in the underdeveloped world did not yet threaten domestic wage rates or protected, union-negotiated working conditions. Capital controls and fixed exchange rates under the Bretton Woods system prevented 'hot money' from pouring across borders, so interest rates (monetary policy) could be controlled and a certain amount of inflation tolerated. And macroeconomic policy cycles could be fine-tuned domestically through fiscal and monetary policy to maintain and even regularly increase government expenditure on those social policies deemed important. Social policy was seen as a relatively autonomous, inherently domestic issue area that could be debated and dealt with on the basis of a combination of ethics and voter choices. Competing value systems were represented in Britain, for example, by the alternative approaches of the Conservative and Labour Parties, with their contrasting doctrines and electoral constituencies. The domestic Left–Right spectrum, rooted in the late 19th and early 20th centuries and focused on the redistribution of resources among social groups, constituted the fundamental parameters of policy choice.

Globalization has undermined these economic conditions. As international trade has increased and tariffs have been drastically reduced, manufacturing industry and even small businesses have had to become more import-sensitive, export-oriented, multinational and dependent on global financial markets for investment. Multinational capital looks increasingly to trade off capital-intensive, high value-added production in the advanced industrial countries with cheap labour in the underdeveloped world for labour-intensive industries, while technological change (especially the lowering of transport costs and the flexibility of production) and the growth of service industries undermine trade unions' ability to pressurize both employers and governments to protect their members and fragment traditional class identities and political loyalties. The globalization of financial markets and firms has caused interest rates to converge across borders, rewarded hot money and made anti-inflationary policies and a new embedded financial orthodoxy the touchstone of national monetarism. And a consensus on the need for adapting to the 'realities' of globalization has changed the parameters of politics, as more voters vote for lower taxes and see government, as Ronald Reagan put it, as 'the problem, not the solution'. Political entrepreneurs increasingly reject redistribution for its own sake as economically counterproductive and instead seek to capture the benefits of globalization – created by the expansion of internationally successful businesses – in order to reshape their political co-alitions and prospects of power.

In addition to these more direct effects – which add up to imposing a new embedded financial orthodoxy on the state, cutting costs and emulating business models of organization – globalization has two indirect effects. First, it fosters a wider ideology of the *marketization* of public policy and the state apparatus itself. At the heart of the market is the supplanting of what social historians call 'status' by 'contract' as the dominant mode of social relations – in other words, the replacement of customary entitlement to goods and services, based on a priori social position, class or standing, with contracts negotiated between individuals, firms and other group actors to exchange such goods and services among themselves on the basis of both price (what Marx called 'exchange value') and/or reciprocal rights and obligations. Second, this paradigm shift has led political actors across the party spectrum to alter their policy prescriptions, seeking to adapt to what they and voters see as the realities of a more open, globalizing world – not only to make policy more economically 'efficient' but also to reshape their underlying political coalitions as various social groups fragment, shrink and expand in reaction to global constraints. It is the combination of these trends that we call the 'competition state' (Cerny, 2000; Cerny and Evans, 2000).

The Rise of the Competition State

The result of these changes is a new, loosely knit neoliberal consensus on the state's role in a global capitalist economy. Politicians and policy makers are widely seen, across the party spectrum, as having less scope in balancing ideal-type welfare considerations, voter preferences and the demands of domestic group constituencies. The rapid expansion of the social and economic functions of the state in the first two-thirds of the 20th century was too often ad hoc, costly and counterproductive. Along with these institutional constraints came the ideological turn to Thatcherism and Reaganism in Britain and the United States. Economic growth, consumerism and – paradoxically – a new individualism left over from the 1960s led to weaknesses in the welfare state in the recession of the 1970s and early 1980s being attributed to collectivism and social provision in general. Leaders proposed and voters voted for promised deregulation and lower taxes. Political entrepreneurs like Thatcher and Reagan used the triptych of the 'overloaded state', neoliberal ideology and globalization as a powerful strategic weapon in public discourse, enabling them to appeal to voters and publics – even to potential losers – as well as to a new breed of politicians and bureaucrats. They created the competition state, mark I.

Most analyses of globalization see the new global political economy as relatively unregulated and increasingly integrated across borders. The political conclusion drawn from this is that existing domestic structures must be radically altered in order to restore economic (and social) health. Furthermore, an expanding world economy might be seen to provide an alternative economic strategy for promoting domestic prosperity and counteract poverty and other social ills through so-called 'trickle down' from this supposedly dynamic new form of capitalism. Finally, it lays the basis for a political strategy at two levels: a strategy for restructuring the state, to make the state support the market and market forces rather than dampen down or undermine them; and a strategy for rebuilding political coalitions. With the upper class and high finance already globalized, the old blue-collar, working class shrinking, and middle- and lower-middle-class groups fragmented and looking for lower taxes, a sense of ownership of this new world and leadership, they got it first through the vision of the globalizing grocer's daughter.

In this brave new world, globalization became the hegemonic discourse of domestic as well as international politics, especially in Britain and the United States. As the world recovered in the 1980s and boomed in the 1990s, traditional approaches to economic and social policy were left behind, not just because they didn't work – some of them still did, as writers such as Paul Pierson (1994) and Geoffrey Garrett (1998) have argued – but because they didn't fit into the new ideological, social and political realities that had kept Conservative governments in power since 1970. Thus the Left had to build new coalitions too, and it had to do this by accepting the globalization approach. Mrs Thatcher said of her approach that 'there is no alternative'. Therefore the Left increasingly looked to design a political as well as a policy strategy that created an alternative which retained just enough of the traditional welfare ideals of the Old Left but recast and reframed them within an alternative vision of globalization. Thus a start was made at creating the competition state, mark II.

This might have meant a return to Old Left internationalism, a vision of world government, but that option was (and is still) wholly unrealistic. Instead, the Left needed to show how they could capture the benefits of globalization for the losers as well as the winners, building new coalitions to replace the old, and restructuring the *national state* in order to achieve this. The way to do this, a new group of political entrepreneurs believed, was to embrace globalization wholeheartedly and claim that something not unlike 'trickle down' – but now properly regulated and steered through new public management, 'reinventing government' (including social policy) and the 'end of welfare as we know it' (Bill Clinton) – could be made to work for a wider cross-section of society. These leaders, especially Tony Blair and Gordon Brown in Britain in their construction of 'New Labour' and Bill Clinton in the United States with the 'New Democrats', claimed that only the Centre-Left could actually bring about the kind of globalization that would not only make British industry genuinely competitive but would also build a socially responsible and effective alternative. After looking at the British competition state in more detail, we briefly explore three key case studies of welfare reform under the Blair government – the New Deal, pensions policy and the working families' tax credit (WFTC). The chapter concludes with some general observations about what these case studies tell us about the impact of the competition state project on social policy development in Britain.

The Competition State and British Social Policy

The key to understanding the competition state is that while international competitiveness became the touchstone of legitimacy in both domestic and international policy making, its political implications in a liberal democratic society were not simply to eliminate choices but also to construct new kinds of choices to fit the constraints, from the dog-eat-dog, neoliberalism 'red in tooth and claw' of the Thatcher years to what Bill Clinton called 'globalization with a human face'. The Labour government since 1997 has adopted a policy agenda that in its most crucial aspects reflects the continuing transformation of the British state into a competition state. At a broader political level, this agenda includes: the marketization of 'UK plc' through international structures of governance; the wholehearted embrace of embedded financial orthodoxy, or what Gordon Brown calls 'prudence'; arm's-length micro-industrial policy; reform of the constitutional order and the further development of 'new governance'; and, in social policy, turning old claims to welfare 'entitlements' on their heads through the establishment of workfare schemes, revamped pensions policy and financial incentives such as the WFTC – what we call the post-welfare contracting state. Contracting post-welfarism has not only been a key feature of the competition state in Britain but also a rich source of hybrid policy transfer from the United States and elsewhere, adding a further dimension to the globalization analysis – the spread of such practices across borders. First, however, let us look more closely at the competition state model itself.

The competition state is the successor to the welfare state, incorporating many of its features but reshaping them, sometimes quite drastically, to fit a globalizing world. The defining feature of the post-war industrial welfare state lay in the capacity which state actors and institutions had gained, especially since the Great Depression of the 1930s, to insulate key elements of economic life from market forces while at the same time promoting other aspects of the market. This combination, called the 'mixed economy', was seen to maximize conditions for pursuing redistributive policies while protecting national forms of capitalism from 'market failure'. This did not merely mean protecting the poor and powerless from poverty and pursuing welfare goals such as full employment or public health, but also regulating business in the public interest, integrating labour movements into neocorporatist processes to promote wage stability and labour discipline, reducing barriers to international trade, imposing controls on 'speculative' international movements of capital and so on. All these forms of interventionism have one thing in common: they take for granted a fundamental division of function between the *market*, which is seen as the only really dynamic, wealth-creating mechanism in capitalist society, on the one hand; and the *state*, which is seen as a hierarchical and essentially static mechanism, unable to impart a dynamic impetus to production and exchange, on the other (except in wartime). The state is thus characterized by a mode of operation which undermines market discipline, substitutes 'arbitrary prices' for 'efficiency prices' and distorts efficient market exchange. It is at best a necessary evil, at worst inherently parasitic on the market (see Lindblom, 1977, for a full discussion).

The welfare state was therefore based on a paradox. Although it was there to save the market from its own dysfunctional tendencies – even the most liberal of neoclassical economists agrees that if the state did not exist it would have to be invented in order to counteract market failures – it carried within itself the potential to undermine the market in turn. In the context of the international recession of the 1970s and early 1980s, these tendencies would come to have dramatic consequences for the economic policies of advanced industrial states generally.

Chronic deficit financing by governments in a slump period – widely attributed to the rigidities and virtually automatic ratcheting upwards of welfare expenditure in such periods (Joseph, 1972, 1974) – was seen to soak up resources which might otherwise be available for investment, raise the cost of capital and channel resources into both consumption (increasing inflationary pressures and import penetration) and non-productive financial outlets. Nationalized industry and tripartite wage bargaining were blamed for putting further pressure on inflation, while at the same time preventing rises in productivity thus lowering profitability through rigidities in the labour market. Attempts to maintain overall levels of economic activity through reflation and industrial policy were seen to lock state interventionism into a 'lame duck' syndrome in which the state takes responsibility for ever-wider, and increasingly unprofitable, sectors of the economy. And finally, all these rigidities, in an open international economy, were increasingly believed to have significant negative consequences for the balance of payments, the balance and composition of trade, the exchange rate and therefore the government's capacity to hold the ring in the first place. Increased size and volatility of cross-border capital movements also undermined the capacity of governments to maintain a healthy tax base and thereby have sufficient resources to redistribute in the first place.

In attempting to overcome this combination of factors, the neoliberal approach in economic policy turned welfare state policy prescriptions on their heads. Priority in macroeconomic policy would be given to fighting inflation over employment and welfare policies; in particular, monetary policy was privileged over fiscal policy – attempting to reduce deficits and lower taxes at the same time, thus squeezing government expenditure. Deregulation was high on the agenda too, to give businesses more freedom to adapt to global market conditions. Capital controls and financial markets were deregulated first, while more pro-market regulatory structures were designed in a number of economic sectors. More rigorous financial management systems and financially led programmes of privatization in the public sector were adopted too. From the beginning, then, the impetus behind the emergence of the competition state was to adjust the economic policies, practices and institutions of the state to conform to the anti-inflationary norms of the international financial markets in order to prevent capital flight and make domestic investment conditions attractive to internationally mobile capital.

All these shifts reflect key themes of the competition state. The main challenge facing governments all over the world is their capacity to adapt to the exogenous constraints and opportunities brought about by different processes of globalization while maintaining a politically effective domestic policy programme. We identify five key dimensions of this model:

1. **The nature of the state** *The competition state involves both a restructuring and a qualitative disempowering of the state in the face of the processes of globalization and transnationalization. However, it may also lead to the empowering of the state in certain areas.* Although the state

may be losing some of its 'publicness' and be characterized by a process of 'hollowing out' in which direct economic intervention and redistribution are reduced, the roles of the state as pro-market regulator of the economy and promoter of international competitiveness are enhanced and can even lead to an expansion of state activities overall. This involves a shift of state priorities towards what has been called the 'regulatory state' (Moran, 2002).

2. **The nature of agency** *Globalization is not merely a structural imperative imposed from outside but also involves agents making choices within a realigned policy-making field. Domestic actors reinforce, shape and even produce globalization itself.* Rather than attempting to insulate states from key international market pressures, as state actors in the welfare state sought to do, political entrepreneurs in competition states embrace openness and marketization within a restructured, loosely knit neoliberal consensus. This consensus manifests itself in a moral emphasis on personal responsibility, manifested through contracts, an economic and political acceptance of the correctness of market outcomes and a belief in the liberalization of the modes of regulation, intervention and redistribution.

3. **The nature of the policy agenda** *The creation of a competition state involves a policy agenda which seeks to provide the conditions that will help the state to adapt state action to cope more effectively with what they perceive as global 'realities'.* Particular types of policy change have thus risen to the top of the political agenda: an emphasis on the control of inflation and general neoliberal monetarism, reflected in a wider embedded financial orthodoxy; a shift from macroeconomic to microeconomic interventionism; a shift in the focus of interventionism away from maintaining a range of 'strategic' or 'basic' economic activities for the purpose of maintaining economic self-sufficiency towards a policy of *flexible response* to competitive conditions in a range of diversified and rapidly evolving international marketplaces; new regulatory structures have been designed to enforce global market-rational economic and political behaviour on rigid and inflexible private sector actors as well as on state actors and agencies; and a shift has occurred in the focal point of party and governmental politics away from the general maximization of welfare within a nation (full employment, redistributive transfer payments and social service provision) to the promotion of enterprise, innovation and profitability in both private and public sectors.

4. **The nature of policy development** *Policy transfer has become a key mechanism for delivering the policy agenda of the competition state through elite*

structures of governance. This policy agenda is spreading internationally primarily as a consequence of (a) globalization itself in the broader sense of the term, (b) Americanization (especially through bilateral policy transfer), given the US head start in this area, (c) a tendency in times of change and uncertainty for policy makers to look to 'quick fix' solutions to public policy problems which policy transfer can sometimes provide, and (d) the changing institutional pecking order resulting from the first three, for example the enhanced role of central banks, whose power has increased not only because of their location at the crossroads of the national financial economy and the global financial marketplace, but also because governments of both Centre-Left and Right have come more and more to accept that such agencies should be independent and free of supposedly 'short-termist' political pressures in making key decisions on the setting of interest rates, control of the money supply and regulation of increasingly transnationalized financial institutions and markets.

5. **The nature of ideology – the decline of social solidarity and redrawing the boundaries of the political** *As a result of these changes, some consensual, some coercive, the ideological divide between Left and Right comes to lose many of its traditional landmarks.* Imperatives of international competitiveness and consumer choice come to have a higher ideological status than issues of domestic social solidarity. Social democratic and other Centre-Left parties begin to search for policies, which, while adapting to the new constraints, are intended to promote a diluted form of neoliberalism retaining some social content. Furthermore, the restructuring of the political arena forces parties and governments of the Left to redefine their conception of the 'social' and the 'public' away from the traditional confines of the 'modern' state and towards individual and voluntary sector responsibility. In particular, there has been a paradigm shift in British welfarism that has been manifested in an attack on welfare dependency and the bonding of welfare rights and obligations.

New Labour and the Competition State

On the Left, the first response to Thatcherism and the competition state mark I was to revive a belief in increased redistributive state intervention, as exemplified by the Labour Party's alternative economic strategy in 1983. However, the second response, after abject electoral failure, was to accept the bottom line of an anti-inflation strategy and shift the boundaries of the Left instead, beginning with the election of Neil Kinnock as Labour Party leader following the 1983 elections and culminating in Blair's election to that position in 1994. But Blair and Gordon Brown, his main partner and rival, were to go much further than their predecessors in formulating a strategy explicitly targeted on the competition state model. As Blair himself put it in a speech delivered in Washington on 6 February, 1998:

> We on the centre-left must try to put ourselves at the forefront of those who are trying to manage social change in the global economy. The old left resisted that change. The new right did not want to manage it. We have to manage that change to produce social solidarity and prosperity.

Thus although they have clearly deployed different strategic devices and policy instruments for coping with the impact of varying forms of globalization, the degree of coherence across both Conservative and Labour Party economic projects has been striking. Policy initiatives on both sides have represented common themes in contemporary British economic discourse such as: the rejection of Keynesian demand management; the emphasis on promoting economic growth through the introduction of supply-side policies aimed at freeing up markets and expanding choice; close attention to financial management and control of public expenditure; the defeat of inflation; and ensuring the conditions for stability in the private sector's planning environment. Actually, the main contrast between the parties today lies in their respective attempts to operationalize the competition state in the social policy issue area while maintaining the integrity of the overall package.

This process has not always involved a clear, linear trajectory. Over several years preceding the 1997 election, revising party policy focused primarily on a quasi-corporatist critique of British financial markets through emphasizing 'stakeholding' instead of the more market-oriented notion of 'shareholder value' (see Hutton, 1995). However, since the 1997 general election, the government has abandoned the concept of stakeholding. Indeed, Brown has launched five main initiatives that reinforce market-oriented norms in financial regulation and corporate governance:

1. Greater independence for the Bank of England.

2. The adoption of a code for fiscal stability.

3. A new fiscal framework.

4. The creation of a new finance watchdog.

5. Measures to streamline Bank of England operations in currency markets and make them more transparent.

Much of this was already under way under the Tories, of course, leading Will Hutton to observe that 'to his right, there is general acclaim; to his left, general dismay' (*Guardian*, 7 February 1998). Nevertheless, the task of reshaping social policy to fit neoliberal economic parameters, particularly where redistribution is reduced and/or made conditional on workforce participation and performance, remains particularly problematic, especially in the electoral arena and in links with pressure groups, trade unions and the still vocal 'Old Labour' groups within both the national and parliamentary Labour Party.

The acceptance of the need to marketize the state by Blair, Brown and their key advisers, such as Peter Mandelson, may be viewed as the corner-stone of an emerging global policy agenda for the Centre-Left, forged primarily by Clinton and Blair. On 6 February 1998, for example, Blair and Clinton joined teams of British and US advisors and intellectuals in Washington for a 'wonkathon' (after 'wonk', a US slang term for a policy expert), with the aim of forging an international consensus on the goals of the Centre-Left for the 21st century. Earlier the same day Blair had addressed the US State Department, outlining what he termed the 'five clear principles of the Centre-Left', which he argued were common to both New Labour and the Democrats:

1. Stable management and economic prudence because of the global economy.

2. A change in the emphasis of government intervention so that it dealt with education, training and infrastructure and not things like industrial intervention or tax and spend.

3. Reform of the welfare state ('otherwise the right will dismantle it') through welfare-to-work and managed welfarism.

4. Reinventing government, decentralisation, opening up government ('so that what counts is what works').

5. Internationalism in opposition to the Right's isolationism (see *Guardian*, 7 February 1998).

The main difference between the New Labour and New Democrat projects lay in Brown's emphasis on the importance of long-term organic growth and investment, a reflection of Britain's structurally inferior economic position since the end of the Industrial Revolution in the late 19th century. However, an ever-lengthening list of common policy initiatives developed between the two states provides significant evidence of lesson drawing between Blair's and

Clinton's advisors. Prominent examples include education (reduction of class sizes), crime (zero-tolerance, anti-truancy drives), welfare reform (welfare-to-work, redirecting welfare to the most needy, creation of work incentives such as working families' tax credit) and central bank reform. Some of these reforms focus on what the New Labour and Democrat spin doctors have called 'the third way', which in Blair's terms aims at taking 'the hard edges off capitalism without losing its essential wealth creating drive' (*The Times*, 8 February 1998). In practical terms this means fostering job market flexibility, but at the same time ensuring that those displaced by it are continually retrained so that they remain employable. As Brown argues: 'It shies away from stiflingly big government, while rejecting the minimalist state favoured by some British Tories and the Republican right.'

The Post-welfare Contracting State as a Core Feature of the Competition State

> We understand that economic stability is the prerequisite for radicalism in social policy rather than an alternative to it. We must be the parties of fiscal and economic prudence. Combined with it must be reform of the welfare state ... Welfare has become passive; a way of leaving people doing nothing, rather than helping them become active. (Tony Blair, speech to the Party of European Socialists' Congress, June 1997)

The form the competition state takes in social policy – its mode of marketization in response to global realities – is to replace entitlements with contracts. Three features stand out. First, the ideology of welfare itself has changed and lessons have been incorporated directly from the United States. The ideological sea change underpinning the philosophy of British welfarism began in earnest with Sir Keith Joseph's mid-1970s attack on the post-war settlement (Joseph, 1972, 1974), an argument that proved particularly influential in shaping Margaret Thatcher's thinking. However, it was the ideas of American conservative academics, especially Charles Murray and Lawrence Mead, who gave the critique of welfare dependency greater policy expression. It is also possible to trace a change to the discursive construction of British welfarism from this conjuncture. As Alan Deacon (2000: 8) notes:

> their ideas about welfare dependency and the underclass had a profound impact upon all points of the party political spectrum in Britain ... Margaret Thatcher recorded in her memoirs how these ideas reinforced her conviction that there was no conflict between individualism and social responsibility.

The work of these American conservatives also had an impact on New Labour's thinking, especially in relation to their argument that reciprocal rights and responsibilities could constitute mutually reinforcing elements of sustainable welfarism. This challenged the central premise of Labour's post-war conception of welfare entitlements as the key policy instruments for achieving social equality and solidarity. The importance of bonding welfare rights and obligations into a new 'post-welfare contracting state' won the war of ideas in the leadership of the Labour Party. 'No rights without oblig-ations' became 'a prime motto for the new politics' under New Labour (Giddens 1998: 65).

Second, the welfare state has been reoriented more broadly towards becoming a financially rigorous ensemble of bureaucratic structures and a downsized labour force in keeping with New Democrat thinking in the United States and the economic orthodoxy of a competition state. Whether this has led to the kind of increased efficiencies hoped for has been widely debated. Paul Pierson (2001) and others have shown how welfare spending has remained stubbornly high across advanced capitalist countries despite restructuring. Indeed, as Clayton and Pontusson (1998) argue, reform has led to a far-reaching, market-oriented reorganization of public and social services, but without leading to significant cost savings – often merely shifting costs from direct service delivery to new accounting, monitoring and managerial structures instead.

The third feature of the post-welfare contracting state can be identified in the shift towards further integrating people into the private sector workforce through active labour market inclusion, largely based on the American model and largely rejecting the traditional Swedish neocorporatist 'active labour market' model, itself under pressure from globalization. However, note that once again the development of the post-welfare contracting state predates the Blair government. The focus on the need to produce incentives in the welfare state constitutes an appropriation of a key New Right concept from the 1970s and 80s – the need to destroy the welfare dependency culture through getting people back to work rather than keeping them on benefits. This emphasis on the virtues of work has been central to Blair and Clinton's assault on what Thatcher termed the 'evils of welfare dependency'. Despite the considerable differences which exist between the two welfare systems, not to mention political traditions, Blair and Clinton have argued that the two countries share a common problem of welfare dependency, which can be tackled through welfare-to-work.

These characteristics of the implementation of the competition state model in the social policy arena can be illustrated by three key case studies where attempts have been made to introduce contracting practices and reduce or eliminate entitlement-based ones: the New Deal, pension policy and working families' tax credit (see also chapters by Deacon and Finn in this volume).

The New Deal

In 1996 Tony Blair (1996a: 57) wrote:

> I want Britain to be one of the really dynamic economies of the twenty-first century. It is sobering to think that just over a century ago we were top of the league of prosperous nations, we were thirteenth in 1979, and today we are eighteenth. Yet our people, by their intelligence, grit, and creativity, are still a people unrivalled anywhere in the world. We must develop their ability and so make ourselves world leaders again.

The presumed marriage between the imperatives of a competition state and the government's attitude towards work, and by implication welfare-to-work, is no better expressed than in this quotation from Blair's *New Britain – My Vision of a Young Country* (1996a). It illustrates the rationale behind Blair's aim of increasing the aggregate skill levels of British people in order to compete in the international economy. Since coming to power in May 1997, New Labour has expanded the scope of the post-welfare contracting state by ending free higher education and the introduction of 'workfare' (an American concept from the 1960s and 70s) and 'learningfare' as part of a New Deal for unemployed 18–24-year-olds. The Blair government has placed welfare reform at the heart of the competition state project. Five billion pounds has been spent on the welfare-to-work programme, representing by a considerable margin the new government's largest single public spending commitment. In addition, in successive budgets, Gordon Brown has introduced a raft of financial incentives in an attempt to lift people out of the poverty trap. These measures have included the introduction of the working families' tax credit, and the lowering of national insurance contributions and tax levels for lower paid workers.

The Treasury played the key coordinating role in the development of the New Deal proposals as the centrepiece of the government's welfare-to-work strategy. The official reason why the Treasury led the project rather than the Department for Education and Employment (DfEE), although the latter was represented in deliberations, was that the former symbolized the broader movement of employment policy away from training. However, it may also be argued that Treasury leadership reflected Brown's desire to maintain control over welfare reform in order to steer the competition state. As a senior Treasury official puts it:

everybody knows that this is about the marketization of the state, that's why Brown's so involved. What we don't know is whether he really thinks that it can have some redistributive effects. (personal communication)

The reason why ideas and developments in the United States have been so influential on the British welfare reform debate has already been mentioned and has also been well documented elsewhere (see Deacon, 2000). Suffice to say that history, language, ideology and a shared belief in the competition state project (in particular, macroeconomic analysis) have all played a role. However, to term this an 'Americanization' of the British welfare debate would be a slight exaggeration (see Walker, 1998). As a senior DSS official observes:

Apart from the ability to communicate more easily (and this isn't always the case I can assure you) there is really no compelling reason why America is always our first port of call for welfare ideas. After all they have such a different welfare tradition to ours. (personal communication)

Indeed, there is plenty of evidence to suggest that the Treasury has also been influenced by initiatives in Australia ('lone parents and partners', 'working nation' and 'single gateway/one-stop shop' programmes), Sweden ('working nation'), the Netherlands ('single gateway/one-stop shop' programmes) and Canada (the 'making work pay' scheme). In addition, institutional memory (for example 'jobseeker's allowance' and 'Restart' schemes from 1988 and 1996) has also been influential. Nonetheless, the United States remains the pioneer in ideas about welfare-to-work programmes and in particularly issues of policy presentation.

It was therefore unsurprising that the Welfare-to-Work Unit in the Treasury should focus their search for ideas on the United States, the Commonwealth and certain European exemplars such as the Netherlands and Sweden. In an important sense this focused enquiry on easily accessible exemplars where programme success was easily demonstrated through sophisticated forms of programme evaluation. From its inception, the Welfare-to-Work Unit established close relations with public organizations in the United States who were responsible for delivering and evaluating welfare-to-work programmes such as the Department of Labor and the United States Office of Personnel Management. In addition, the expertise of several high-profile American academics with considerable experience in the welfare-to-work field such as Richard Layard (1997) was also sought. Contact was also made with the architects of 'best practice models' in local experimentation such as 'GAIN' in Riverside, California, 'Florida Wages' and 'Wisconsin Works' (see

House of Commons Social Security Committee, 1998). As a Treasury official notes (personal communication): 'these cases were of interest and influence because of their emphasis on work and not training and because they were all demonstrably successful.'

The Welfare-to-Work Unit held several bilateral meetings with their American counterparts in order to develop more detailed information on delivery and evaluation issues. As one former official who played a search role in the Treasury welfare-to-work nexus recalls:

> for what seemed like months I spent more time with our American counterparts than with my husband. I stayed in regular contact through email and continue to do so in my new job ... the main lessons that we got from the States were about how to join up services across a devolved structure. (personal communication)

The British team was struck by the quality of research conducted in the United States on welfare-to-work programmes. As the same official observes: 'They are really brilliant at the evidence-based evaluation stuff and to be honest we're very poor at it.' This conclusion was also reached at the 530th Wilton Park Conference in New York entitled 'Welfare and Work in Britain and America'. The conference was funded by the Rockefeller, Charles Stewart Mott and Nuffield Foundations with additional financial assistance from the DfEE, DSS and HM Treasury and was held in July 1998. The conference report concludes that:

> research in the UK is not done over long-term evaluation periods, as in the US, with important consequences ... In the UK, there is not the same tradition of non-profit research evaluation. It is dependent on the Government, which is not very good at it, and does not always like the results. (see www.wiltonpark.org.uk/conferences/)

The New Deal was financed through the 'windfall tax' on the privatized utilities to the tune of £4 billion. The final proposals added an element of compulsion to incentivization and were aimed primarily at the young unemployed. It offered four options including subsidized employment and education and in line with Labour's intention to increase overall participation in the labour market, the New Deal was also extended to disabled people, carers and single parents. Although the involvement of these groups is not yet compulsory, a significant step in this direction has been taken with the announcement that they will be required to attend interviews. The issue of compulsion, taken for granted in the United States, is now a feature of the New Deal for 18–24-year-olds. It is judged to be politically acceptable for this age group, but the impact of compulsion for older age groups is open to discussion, and there is an enduring political reluctance to adopt compulsion for lone mothers. Indeed the imposition of welfare time limits or other policies that might cause severe hardship has not been adequately debated in the UK. As a senior Treasury official puts it:

> everybody knows that this is about limiting state commitments and marketizing the state. All you have to do is look at the first page of the New Deal website for the evidence. (personal communication)

The website reads:

> New Deal is a key part of the Government's Welfare-to-Work strategy. It gives New Deal jobseekers aged 18–24, 25 plus, 50 plus and those with disabilities a real chance to develop their potential, gain skills and experience and find work. In addition, New Deal for Lone Parents and New Deal for Disabled People offers the opportunity to lone parents and disabled people on other benefits to explore work options. It's also a great opportunity for businesses to make use of the untapped energies and talents of a new labour force. More than 83,200 companies have signed New Deal employer agreements so far.

In the case of the New Deal, there can be little doubt that a favourable economic climate combined with its compatibility with the broader competition state project allowed the New Deal policy agenda to gain ascendancy. As one senior Treasury official argues:

> Let's face it, if we were suddenly hit with a recession, and one seems likely over the next year or so, much of this would collapse. Why? Because the left is waiting for a chance to reassert itself and Brown has been foolish in resurrecting the language of full employment in a period of economic stability. A recession would provide them with a set of opportunities to fight for more direct intervention into the economy. (personal communication)

Pensions Policy

Pensions policy is a particularly interesting arena in which to explore the impact of broader processes of globalization on the nation-state. Over the past 20 years, there has been a fundamental shift from public to private sector pension provision, and, in keeping with the policy goals of the competition state, this process has been further accelerated under the Blair government. This was first given policy expression in the Green Paper, *Partnership in*

Pensions (DSS, 1998b), which mapped out the government's plans for pension reform. Its main proposals included:

- increasing the basic state pension in line with inflation

- introducing a means-tested minimum income guarantee (MIG) through income support for all pensioners with a full working record

- replacing the state earnings-related pension scheme (SERPS) with a flat-rate state second pension which aims to provide people on incomes of £9,000 or less per annum twice the amount that SERPS provides

- creating stakeholder pensions targeted at middle-income groups (those who earn between £9,000 and £18,500 per annum) who will be encouraged to opt out of the state second pension

- providing tax relief on contributions into stakeholder pensions of up to £3,600 per annum

- regulating the sale of stakeholder schemes through the creation of a Financial Services Agency and regulating the operation of these schemes through an Occupational Pensions Regulatory Authority (see also Royal Commission on Long Term Care, 1999).

This programme was the first explicit recognition by a Labour government that the provision of adequate universal state pensions was a pipe dream and that British people should take greater responsibility for their retirement plans. There are presently three tiers of pension provision in the UK: the basic state scheme which pays a flat-rate pension; the state second pension, which replaced SERPS in April 2002 and is linked to the employee's average earnings over her/his working life; and voluntary private pension provision of two types – occupational and personal pension schemes. Of the British working population, 80 per cent now have access to second- or third-tier pension schemes, although this does not necessarily mean that there is adequate coverage. However, this push towards what Hills and Lelkes (1999) have termed 'selected universalism' under the Blair government has often been tempered by domestic political constraints.

While the long-term aim of the UK government is to pass increasing responsibility for pension provision to the private sector, there has been some short-term retrenchment on this policy in order to meet problems of pensioner poverty which were exposed by the Rowntree Commission on Income and Wealth (Joseph Rowntree Foundation, 1995). The majority of pensioners receive a flat-rate basic state pension which is paid to all those with adequate national insurance credits. By April 2003, the basic state pension is projected to stand at about £77 per week for a single person and £124 for couples (see Clark, 2001). Since the early 1980s, however, this pension has been indexed in line with prices and has fallen behind wages, providing a poor standard of living for pensioners. The current government has attempted to improve the situation by targeting extra resources to pensioners through the MIG. The Blair government has significantly increased the MIG for pensioners on low incomes from £68.80 for a single pensioner and £106.60 for a couple in 1997 to £92.15 for a single pensioner and £154 for a couple in 2001. The MIG is to be set at £100 (£154 for couples) from April 2003. The government hopes that the MIG will rise with earnings, whereas the basic pension will only rise with prices. However, the growing gap will mean that a large number of people will find their income levels inadequate.

In sum, pensions policy has been developed in the UK to ensure that citizens take greater responsibility for their own retirement provision. This will allow for an economically sustainable pension regime in an era characterized by an increasingly ageing population. At the same time the reduced economic burden in terms of state provision should allow the government greater room for manoeuvre to target pensioner poverty more effectively. This remains the key difference between the Blair government and its Conservative predecessors. Pensions policy provides a good example of the capacity of the Blair government to adapt to the exogenous constraints and opportunities brought about by different processes of globalization and marketization while maintaining a relatively effective domestic policy programme.

Working Families' Tax Credit

Working families' tax credit (WFTC) is a tax credit payable to working families, depending on their circumstances, which is administered by the Inland Revenue but is normally paid directly through the pay packet (see www.inlandrevenue.gov.uk/research/wftc6rb.pdf). It has been designed to help meet the challenge of the main policy dilemma in the design of welfare systems:

> to balance the desire to raise the living standards of low income households with that of encouraging self-sufficiency through the promotion of work incentives, and, reducing government expenditure. (Blundell and Walker, 2001: 1)

WFTC is an in-work benefit that has been used in the UK and the US in different forms for some years. For example, in the UK, family income supplement (FIS), which provided an earnings supplement for those families with at least one full-time worker, was introduced in 1971. In the US, the earned income tax credit (EITC) was introduced in the 1970s as a way of introducing a negative income tax for low-income working families. These systems operated differently: the FIS had a full-time work requirement with a 50 per cent reduction rate, whereas the EITC provided a tax credit supplement for all earnings until a maximum income limit was reached. In the US, the EITC played a key role in welfare policy as a mechanism for encouraging work by supplementing the working wage for low-wage workers. In 1988, the UK benefit system was extensively reformed as a response to the changing composition of low-income households. The FIS was replaced with family credit and the structure of housing benefit and income support was also changed. The eligibility criteria for family credit initially required full-time work of at least 24 hours per week but this was decreased to 16 hours per week in 1992. The Blair government is convinced of the ability of in-work credits such as family credit to shift income towards low-income families and influence decisions to work. Hence, the central focus of the WFTC when it replaced family credit in 1999 was its role as a mechanism for encouraging work by supplementing the working wage for low-wage workers. In practice, the WFTC has reduced the tax bill of around one million low-paid families by £20 per week. In addition, the children's tax credit is the equivalent to a 2.5 per cent tax cut for the average family.

The policy debate is now firmly fixed on the role that the WFTC can play in providing work incentives and in activating labour markets. However, opinion remains deeply divided on how effective this strategy can be. Richard Blundell and Ian Walker (2001: 4) note that:

> the evidence from existing reforms across a number of countries suggests that careful design of these programs can significantly increase the incomes of low income families while still providing reasonable incentives for parents to work.

The Institute for Fiscal Studies is more sceptical about their worth:

> in general most of the changes are just presentational. The WFTC is much the same as the old family credit. It's just paid in a different way. And tax discounts are not much use unless you're in work and paying tax. (*Guardian*, 1 May 2001)

The National Association of Citizens' Advice Bureaux has also argued that many families have lost out on other benefits such as free school meals and help with rent and council tax in order to claim WFTC. There has also been some criticism of the discriminatory nature of the payment of children's tax credit to the family's highest rate taxpayer, generally the father. This has proved embarrassing for a government that has pretensions to gender blindness. This problem will be partly resolved by the introduction of a new integrated children's credit in 2003 payable directly to a child's main carer. There is still work to be done on whether this form of contractualization is as effective as claimed.

Social Policy in a Competition State

What do these case studies tell us about the impact of the competition state project on social policy development in Britain?

1. Social policy has been incorporated into the economic orthodoxy of the competition state through its emphasis on reducing welfare dependency and removing any potential obstacles to the control of inflation. In Gordon Brown's words, this calls for 'balanced budgets', 'tight control of interest rates', and the need to deal with unemployment through the marketplace and not government intervention.

2. These initiatives inherited much from the Thatcher and Major governments and personify a longer term paradigm shift in the philosophy of welfarism. The front page slogan on the New York welfare-to-work website sums up this shift in thinking perfectly. Here the slogan 'Welfare-to-work is a programme that creates independence' is superimposed over the words 'Welfare creates dependence'.

3. It is evident that a policy-making elite has emerged which shares a commitment to the common value system of the competition state. Indeed it is here that Treasury officials are seen to be playing a central coordinating role in promoting the competition state project and new forms of complex globalization in the attempt to adapt state action to cope more effectively with what they see as global realities.

4. The battle for the hearts and minds of the British people is a key problem for the competition state, as many of its key reforms rest on changing norms and values and challenging the dependency culture of the post-war settlement (for example New Deal, pensions, student loans).

These reforms dramatically symbolize a move away from the norms of labourism – from collective to individual bargaining, from public to private ownership, from entitlement to contract, and towards consumerist rather than productionist values. In the same way that Thatcherism operated as a discourse which situated subjects, made sense of their experiences, mobilized support behind particular projects and established the basis for political, intellectual and moral leadership (see Hall, 1985; Jessop et al., 1988), New Labour attempts to sell itself as 'globalization with a human face'. In particular, the policy agenda of New Labour attempts to change individual and group attitudes to entrepreneurship whether through welfare-to-work, pensions policy, student loans or central bank reform.

In a world where national competitiveness is seen – not only by businessmen, economists and conservative social theorists but also by political entrepreneurs and even voters – to require marketization and liberalization, convergence on the neoliberal paradigm reflects both the real and the perceived constraints of global realities. The restructuring of the welfare state around the principles of market efficiency, individual responsibility and reciprocal contractual rights and responsibilities has proved far more significant than mere cost accounting or embedded financial orthodoxy. Paradoxically perhaps, the ideology of the competition state, rooted in globalization, has not saved the taxpayer money or made social policy more economically efficient, so much as it has restructured the basic social bonds between policy and publics, between state and society.

Further Reading

Clayton, R. and Pontusson, J. (1998) 'Welfare-State Retrenchment Revisited: Entitlement Cuts, Public Sector Restructuring, and Inegalitarian Trends in Advanced Capitalist Societies', *World Politics*, **51**(1): 67–98.

Deacon, A. (2000) 'Learning from the US? The Influence of American Ideas upon "New Labour" Thinking on Welfare Reform', *Policy and Politics*, **28**(1): 5–18.

Esping-Andersen, G. (1996) *Welfare States in Transition: National Adaptations in Global Economies*, London: Sage.

Hirst, P. and Thompson, G. (1996) *Globalisation in Question*, Cambridge: Polity Press.

CHAPTER 2

Governance and the Welfare State

B. GUY PETERS

The welfare state, as a set of normative and political commitments on the part of government to its citizens, has become embedded deeply within the institutional structure of contemporary political systems. Having been in existence in some form or another for decades, and playing major roles in the legitimation of the state, the programmes of the welfare state are the central elements of the public sector in most industrial democracies (Myles and Quadagno, 2001). The institutionalized position of these programmes is supported by a number of political forces. First there is the clientele of the programmes who are concerned about the continuation of their benefits. When the design and administration of social programmes are linked directly with 'social partners', meaning for the most part trade unions, that political support is even more apparent and more important (Marier, 2002). Also welfare state programmes are supported by the public employees responsible for delivering the programmes, meaning both senior bureaucrats who may have had a role in fostering the conceptions of the programmes,[1] and the substantial and well-organized body of rank-and-file employees who administer the services directly. The power of these lower echelon public employees is especially apparent for programmes such as health care that are extremely labour-intensive.

From the perspective of the historical institutionalists, the programmes of the welfare state should be, if not immune from change, at least resistant to change. To some extent the 'path dependence' (Thelen and Steinmo, 1992) assumed in historical institutionalism has been quite evident in social policies, and most of the programmes formulated during the 1950s and 60s, or even before, continue in quite recognizable forms into the new century (see King, 1995). That having been said, however, programmes that have maintained predominately stable purposes and goals may now be administered in rather different ways, and may have their effective goals, if not their stated goals, somewhat modified through those reforms. Further, changes in political ideologies have produced new types of social programmes which depend less on conventional formats for service delivery than do the fundamental programmes of the welfare state.

This chapter will examine the changing forms and formats for delivering social services in contemporary governments. In general the changes that have been implemented in the methodology for service delivery during the past several decades can be discussed in terms of 'new governance' (Salamon, 2002), moving from direct command and control over services through the public sector hierarchy towards more indirect mechanisms for achieving the same policy goals. A good deal of this discussion about adopting the instruments of new governance in delivering public policies has been concentrated on the role of the market as the source of ideas for change (see Bartlett et al., 1998; Braun and Busch, 1999), but the ideas of governance go further in shifting the manner in which the programmes of the welfare state are delivered.

There certainly have been a number of market-based reforms implemented but there are also other ideas at work, and other styles of change in social policy.[2] The principal alternatives to market ideas as a basis for modifying programmes also involve more indirect means of service delivery. The difference is that the same changes in service delivery are justified less by economic efficiency and more as being more humane, more flexible and more responsive to the demands of clients. However, if there is a single dominant idea about social policy it is that business as usual in the public sector is not an acceptable option.

The adoption of these policy reforms[3] is more difficult to predict on the basis of partisan affiliations or ideological predispositions than might be expected. Certainly some of the more extreme changes imposed on welfare state programmes have been associated with the political Right. There are, however, a number of ideas 'in good currency' about governance in general, and social policy in particular, and governments are willing to pick among those ideas based upon a variety of factors, not least of which is the political appeal of any change for the government of the day. As there has been some general shift towards a more neoliberal perspective on the role of government and the way in which governments should deliver their programmes, parties of the political Left have become at least as enamoured as the political Right in producing managerial and substantive changes in governing. In fairness, proposals for the same, or at least similar, changes have been justified by quite different political ideologies, with traditional hierarchical forms of service delivery seen as demeaning and rigid. That having been said, the dominant policy shift has been towards neoliberal ideas, often dressed up as the 'third way' between strictly market ideologies and the (now) old-fashioned socialist ideas associated with the political Left.

While we will be concentrating attention on issues of service delivery, the role of the market in changing the welfare state extends well beyond simply changing patterns of service delivery. The fundamental logic of these programmes has been affected, so that the purpose of social programmes increasingly is to underpin the market and create greater competitiveness rather than to compensate for the social problems created by the market (Scharpf and Schmidt, 2000). That is, the fundamental purpose of the welfare state is moving towards getting people back into work, rather than providing social protection against unemployment, illness and other socio-economic problems. Competitiveness as a value in public policy has been spurred on by globalization and the power of the international marketplace in domestic policy making, as well as by the more general changes in the climate of ideas.

The impact of the hymns of praise to the market concerning social policy has become rather pervasive. For example, the rather trendy concept of 'social exclusion', that might possibly be conceptualized as a means to extend the umbrella of social protection, appears to have been utilized in some circumstances to argue that being out of work is the most fundamental basis of social exclusion in capitalist economies. Operating from that premise, the purpose of social programmes becomes employment rather than amelioration of social deprivations. That being out of work is a basis for social exclusion is in some ways a truism, but the drive for employment possibilities appears to have a much closer connection to the design and implementation of social programmes than in the past.

The most common market-based concept for reforming the welfare state is the substitution of 'workfare' for the more traditional 'welfare' programmes which were designed to cope with the economically and socially deprived. These programmes have been the source of the majority of the critiques of welfare state programmes, from both the political Right and Left. In the 1990s, these critiques came to be acted upon, interestingly often by governments of the political Left. The most obvious example of this type of change was the welfare reform implemented during the Clinton administration in the United States.[4] This policy idea was soon dispersed widely, even to countries that might have been expected to retain a stronger public sector role in social policy and a more redistributive set of outcomes from their intervention.

Changes in the Welfare State

The shifts in the welfare state can be grouped into three broad categories. These categories are to some extent interconnected, but yet the logic for making the change and the nature of the changes have important analytic differences, as well as important differences for the recipients and providers of the programmes. These three types of change are:

1. **Policy**. Although not the central focus of this chapter, there have been fundamental shifts in the policies being delivered by government. In particular, governments have been tending to search for alternatives to their traditional commitments to providing social services directly through the public sector (see Walsh and Stewart, 1992). The market is the most logical alternative to these long-standing commitments. In particular, governments have been searching for, and implementing, programmes that depend more upon individual participation in the private economy than upon direct government grants to needy individuals. The public sector may still be involved in making labour force participation more feasible, for example through subsidizing childcare and transportation, but the central focus of workfare programmes is just that – work.

    For pension programmes the market shift is, as we will point out below, towards moving some part of the activity directly to market actors, but even when the programmes are not moved to the market they may have more market principles attached. In particular, public pensions are tending to become more actuarial in the way they link contributions and benefits so that the potentially redistributive elements of pension programmes are being de-emphasized. That shift in turn will influence their administration and their connection with social and political actors.

2. **Instruments – the use of social actors**. Governments have been actively changing the instruments that are utilized to deliver their social programmes. One of the most important of these changes has been increasing involvement of non-governmental actors in the delivery of public services. As we will point out below, there are a variety of actors of this sort being used, ranging from for-profit organizations to the clients of the programmes themselves. As we will note below, one of the standard critiques of social programmes has been that they are excessively bureaucratic, so the use of social actors not only saves public money, it also may enhance the acceptability of the programmes to their clients and the public in general.

The use of social actors is done largely to enhance the governance capacity of the public sector, but this shift also has important democratic implications. As well as a market ethos that is important in the contemporary period, there is also a democratic ethos that attempts to provide more opportunities for citizens to influence the choices made by the public sector. The involvement of social actors in social programmes may be based largely on organized groups and/or client groups but there is still some involvement.

3. **Instruments – the regulatory welfare state**. A second change in the instruments used to deliver social programmes is to shift from direct provision of those services to regulating their provision from other actors. This is to some extent a natural reaction to the use of the private sector rather than direct public provision. In some instances, however, the choice of the regulatory instrument goes further and government seeks to provide new services, or at least to require the creation of new benefits, which were not part of the range of benefits previously provided. For example, benefits such as maternity leave, childcare and even the minimum wage have been expanded substantially through regulatory means, providing a range of benefits that are funded primarily through private action rather than taxing and spending.

There is a second, and less benign, aspect of the turn towards a regulatory welfare state. This negative aspect of regulation as an instrument is that the programmes may be used increasingly to control the behaviours of recipients. In the United States, means-tested benefits such as the former aid to families with dependent children (AFDC – 'welfare') have had some regulatory impact for some time (Piven and Cloward, 1972). In Europe, however, the shift towards programmes such as workfare has tended to involve more attempts by government at regulating the behaviour of clients, for example demanding greater efforts at training or work if benefits are to be maintained (see Ross, 2002). This shift involves simply developing control over clients through the threat of withdrawal of benefits, even including 'encouraging' marriage for recipients.

These shifts in the provision of government social programmes have not been undertaken simply for the sake of change, but rather reflect a series of perceived deficiencies in these programmes. These deficiencies are both substantive and procedural, and often address the fundamental performance of state programmes.

The Logics for Changing Social Programmes

Policy change comes from the exercise of political power, but that power is generally more palatable if it is backed by some logical justification for the changes. Given the entrenched nature of programmes, whether social, defence or whatever, any movement from the status quo tends to require political mobilization, and that political mobilization in turn generally requires some basis of ideas and theory that helps to legitimate the policies. The welfare state was created out of one dominant set of ideas for change, albeit interpreted somewhat differently in different political systems (Esping-Andersen, 1990; Goodin et al., 1999; de Menil, 2002). Contemporary changes have some systematic ideas, but also reflect a series of more empirical critiques of the existing set of programmes.

The critiques of social programmes, especially means-tested programmes, are numerous and often quite intense. The most familiar are the critiques from the political Right that these programmes are expensive, produce little benefit for the society and encourage indolence and dependency on the part of the recipients. Even social insurance programmes such as public pensions have been criticized as being poor investments for the participants and as disincentives for savings and investments in the economy as a whole. These neoliberal critiques have been most common in some of the Anglo-American countries (Fawcett, 1995), but also have become increasingly prevalent in Continental European countries, even in those countries with extensive commitments to the welfare state and *services publics*. The welfare state has been a powerful shibboleth for decades, but has now lost some of its appeal and any deficiencies have become more central to political debate.

Another critique of the welfare state comes from quite the opposite direction politically, although in some instances the implications for changing programmes may not be very different from those of the conservative critiques. The critique, often expressed by the political Left, is that the programmes of the welfare state, again especially means-tested and categorical programmes, are excessively bureaucratic. Both the criteria of eligibility and particularly the style of administration are perceived to demean the recipients of these programmes and prevent their development as human beings. As such they may perpetuate dependency rather than help to alleviate it. With the redefinition of many problems addressed by social programmes under the rubric of 'social exclusion', the hierarchical and bureaucratic nature of conventional programmes may widen the gulf between the mainstream of society and the excluded.

The administrative style of most conventional social programmes has been hierarchical and has focused on the role of public sector organizations – the hierarchical character of these programmes makes them less humane, and even less effective, than they should be. As a consequence, welfare state programmes often ignored the importance of civil society organizations in the development, and particularly in the implementation, of services. This was true whether the possible civil society providers in question were those involving clients or complementary providers of services such as voluntary organizations. Stated differently, the instruments used for the delivery of most social programmes have denied clients any effective involvement in, and any real choice about, the programmes that they depend upon.

A third direction of critique of welfare state programmes is less ideological and is concerned more strictly with the policy issues raised by this set of programmes. One of the most important of these analytic critiques of social programmes is that individual social programmes are often developed in isolation from allied concerns such as health, employment or education, or even from other social service programmes (see Bardach, 2000). The absence of effective coordination of social programmes provides suboptimal services to the clients, creates unnecessary expenditure demands and, perhaps most importantly, means that these services are less effective than they might be. Stated differently, welfare state programmes as they have been developed often take very narrow views of the needs of their clients and therefore place the burden of obtaining a full range of services on the clients. This need for more integrated services has been exacerbated, at least in its political relevance, by the greater visibility of groups such as the elderly, women, children and immigrants who have a variety of needs which cut across conventional programme lines.

These issues concerning social programmes are hardly new, and some of these critiques have been made from the inception of the welfare state. Even before these programmes were adopted, the political Right issued dire warnings about the negative consequences of sheltering individuals from the pressures of the market. Likewise, the impersonal and demeaning treatment provided to their clients by many social programmes has been critiqued any number of times.[5] And inadequate coordination is one the most persistent critiques of all public programmes, whether directed at social problems or not (Peters, forthcoming). Social programmes are one of the major expenditure areas of government and it is not surprising that there are constant pressures to make them 'work better and cost less'.[6]

Delivering Public Programmes: Transformations in Instruments

What is different about the contemporary round of critiques of the welfare state is that they are occurring when the delivery of public services, whether these are social programmes or not, is also being transformed. The period from the 1980s onward has been one in which the conventional structures and procedures of the public sector have been reformed more extensively than perhaps at any time since the creation of the modern nation-state (Raad-schelders and Toonen, 1999). The bureaucratic, hierarchical pattern of service delivery that was central to the operation of the state has been transformed dramatically across the whole range of public programmes. As already noted, those reforms have included a wide variety of mechanisms by which the state may achieve its purposes.

In line with the general changes in governance already outlined, there have been fundamental patterns of change in public programmes, including social programmes, that have enhanced participation within them. In the case of social programmes, and to a lesser extent other programmes, participation has implied not only the clientele of the programme but also the lower echelon workers in government. The logic of permitting greater participation by the lower echelon workers is that, at an organizational level, these are the personnel who are in the closest contact with the clients of the programme. These are, therefore, the members of the programme who will have the greatest amounts of information about the needs and wishes of those clients.[7] That having been said, these lower echelon workers often have the greatest sympathy, or at least empathy, for the demands of the programme's clients and therefore may be more willing to provide benefits to the clients. Thus, while this change in the delivery of public programmes may make the workers within the programmes more satisfied with their level of influence over the outcomes of their programmes and their level of involvement, that involvement may alter some of the programmes as they are implemented and produce additional costs on the public purse.

The logic of enhancing participation by the clients of social programmes is somewhat different. One argument on behalf of enhancing this dimension of participation is that, like the street-level bureaucrats, the clients have a great deal of knowledge about their needs and about the real social conditions under which they live. These clients are hardly objective sources of information about their own programmes, but they can provide one source of experiential data that most social programmes have difficulty gathering, or even processing. Further, part of the managerialist changes in administering government programmes mentioned above is that client satisfaction is an important dimension of any assessment of programmes, and this is to some degree true for the clients of social programmes as well as those of more middle-class programmes.

In addition to their utility simply as a source of information for improved policy making, the clients of social programmes can be employed to administer their own programmes, and (presumably) also to administer the programmes in ways that will benefit the recipients. For example, the clients of housing programmes can be used to manage their own housing projects (Sorenson, 1997), and parents can be used as part of the management of local schools, reducing the managerial demands for school boards and so on and also providing for greater diversity in schools' offerings. This shift in administrative styles assumes that uniformity is no longer as important for good public service as conventional wisdom had made it.

These reforms involving self-management are also important as a means of enhancing democracy in administration and in the performance of public tasks. In addition to simply providing the information about their perception of the problems (in the programmes as well as in society), clients of social programmes may be assigned legitimate rights in the design and implementation of their programmes. Beginning perhaps with the concept of 'maximum feasible participation' in American urban programmes (Moynihan, 1969), the logic of social policy has been moving in a rather corporatist direction, providing the clients of programmes the opportunity to participate, and even fostering the capacity for participation that may have been severely underdeveloped among those populations.

Although involving clients in delivering social programmes has had some advantages, it has not been an undivided blessing. At the same time that involvement brings many disadvantaged people into the political process, this process has also made programmes more difficult to control, and has presented consequent problems of accountability. In some cases, client involvement has left the communities in which programmes are located worse off, as the leadership becomes coopted and leaves the community. Thus, like all reforms of the public sector, moving towards a more powerful position for clients of social programmes must be considered carefully before being implemented, and is far from a panacea for all the problems of the welfare state.

Patterns of Involving Private Sector Organizations

As well as opening social programmes to greater participation by workers and clients, changes in the instruments of these programmes have opened a variety of arrangements with private sector organizations – for-profit and not-for-profit alike – in the delivery of programmes. Some of these arrangements are simple contracts through which the public sector pays for provision of a certain public service for a specified period at a specified price (Greve, 1999). The contract is a very familiar relationship between the public and private sector, but it also is being affected by the drive towards greater use of the market in government. In particular, contracts are becoming substantially clearer about the standards of performance that will be required of the contractor, and a link between these standards and the payment of the vendor.

The development of stricter performance contracting in the relationship between government and the private sector may have the perverse consequence of actually reducing the quality of the services delivered. To be effective in other than a cursory manner, many social programmes require something other than a quick, and perhaps anonymous, contact between the service provider and the client. Contracts are appropriate for specifying measurable and generally rather simple aspects of programmes, but they are often inadequate for specifying the more subtle aspects of service required in the personal social services. Mechanisms such as relational contracting (Williamson, 1985) may be used to provide a less severely constrained relationship between the actors involved in the process, but that type of contracting may require developing trust and a longer term commitment than is possible with contemporary conceptions of good public management.[8]

The public and private sectors also can become linked through softer mechanisms such as partnerships and networks when providing social policy (Powell and Exworthy, 2002). This style of relationship may be thought of as a form of relational contracting, given that the two sides enter into a long-term and generally thinly specified relationship around delivering particular types of service. Partnership arrangements are hardly novel, in the past they have been more common for programmes such as economic development than for social services. Social programmes have been thought of as something government should do itself. With declining resources, governments have sought to some extent to use partnerships with other sectors as a means of continuing benefits while restraining the growth of expenditure.

By choosing to use partnerships as part of their strategy for delivering public services, governments are accepting a variety of benefits for the delivery of their programmes. First, regulation enables government to lower the costs of programmes. Second, the public sector is able to tap into a good deal of knowledge about the service area that it may not possess itself. This access to information is especially significant when the partnerships are with community-based organizations which tend to work from the grass roots and thus develop a type of local knowledge and acceptance among clients. The more top-down public bureaucracy might never be able to develop those connections with local communities. Finally, with voluntary organizations, governments often are able to tap a reservoir of goodwill and skills that again would be difficult to obtain from other sources.

Partnerships are not an undivided benefit, and there may be some important problems for government (as well as the private sector organization) in these relationships. For government the principal problem arising from the use of partnerships is the loss of control over the delivery of programmes being administered in its name. Some individuals may regard this loss as a benefit rather than a cost, given that the administration of programmes through private organizations is likely to be less bureaucratic, in the pejorative sense of the word, than it would be within government. That having been said, however, government may be left having accountability for the programmes (at least in the eyes of the average member of the public) but with little real control over the conduct of those programmes. Further, given that many of the programmes which are administered through public–private partnerships are in the personal social services – programmes that require greater levels of judgement than simply deciding eligibility for benefits – the accountability gap may be more pronounced.

For the private sector members of partnerships in social policy, the problems may be even more compelling. Involvement in a partnership with government, even when well-intentioned on both sides (as most are), does involve the loss of some autonomy for the private organization. This has arisen most strongly with respect to two types of involvement of the private sector with government. The first has been the movement towards 'faith-based' programmes in the United States, in which the Bush administration sought to administer a significant share of social services through Church-based organizations. Civil libertarians objected to this initiative on the basis of its apparent attack on the 'wall of separation' between Church and state, as well as its placing clients in the position of being proselytized in exchange for benefits. Many Churches opposed the plan as vigorously, if not more so, arguing that increased involvement would almost certainly mean bureaucratization of their programmes, and the loss of the very character of the programmes that had made them more successful than some public programmes (Hutcheson, 2001). Even when there is not a question of Church and state involved, the involvement of voluntary organizations with government can be problematic for those organizations. With money goes control (Harris and Rochester, 2000) and the displacement of the goals that had been the foundation of the organizations.

The second dimension of involvement of private actors in partnerships with government that may prove problematic is the 'user movement', in which clients of programmes become heavily involved in the delivery and evaluation of programmes (Beresford, 2002). Just as with the faith-based initiatives, there is clear threat of the loss of autonomy for private actors, and of creeping regulation by government, in close linkages between user organizations and social programmes. This is especially the case when the groups involved have been established largely in opposition to the bureaucracies in question, for example in the field of disability. Involving groups in partnerships then is a less than subtle form of cooptation, and may be a threat to the very values which made these groups successful for their members in the first instance.

The Use of Regulation

The power of the state to regulate is an important means of intervention into the economy and society that is often forgotten when discussing the welfare state. The use of regulation as a means of addressing social problems, or indeed any other problems faced by government, has several advantages for the public sector. The first is that it is less visible to the public, even though it may be effective in moving resources around in the society. Thus, in a period in which the public is rather critical of government, the use of regulation may facilitate reaching goals with a minimum of political reaction.

Just as it is less visible, so too is regulation less expensive for government, as creating benefits by regulation involves relatively little public money. For example, government can address the problems of low-paid employment in the private sector by developing a series of programmes for housing supplements, income supplements and so on, all of which would involve taxing and spending. The same problem could be addressed by mandating a 'living wage' in the economy. This might have other residual impacts, for example reducing the level of employment, but the immediate problem could be ameliorated, if not eliminated, simply by the application of the power of law rather than money.

Regulation can also be utilized to develop a range of services that might be difficult for government to fund directly. For example, government might find it expensive to create daycare for all children or pay for maternity leave for employees, but it can do so readily by mandating provision of these services by the private sector. Although the state is involved in creating these benefits by its political power, the winners and losers in the process are less visible than would be the case if the services were delivered directly by government. The capacity to disguise winners and losers is crucial for the political palatability of these regulatory programmes, and also contributes to the capacity to fly beneath the political radar.

As applied directly to the several problems confronting the welfare state, regulation has become increasingly crucial to the success of these programmes. Given fiscal crisis and the general decline in public confidence in government, the capacity to produce behavioural and programme change through regulation is often a significant factor in programme success. Not only is regulation capable of creating services and benefits at low cost, it is also capable of creating environments in which private, market-based social activity is possible. For example, if private pensions are to become important complements to, or perhaps substitutes for, public sector pensions, then the risk to individual investors must be minimized (see VanDerhei and Copeland, 2002).

Unfortunately the regulatory capacity of government in social policy appears less well developed than in economic policy, and several attempts to regulate pensions have been less than successful. Although the United States regulates company pensions under the Employees Retirement Income Security Act, the recent collapse of Enron and loss of pensions demonstrated the weakness of those regulations and the need to develop a means of collecting information and assessing risk in privately provided social programmes.[9] In a related field, the regulation of health insurance and providers such as health maintenance organizations also has proven rather unsuccessful in reducing costs and ensuring access. Previously, there had been several problems of pension losses or downgrading in the United Kingdom. These problems may be expected to become more common as private pensions become more widely used in other industrial countries.

Social policy is perhaps more difficult to cope with through regulatory instruments than are economic issues (May, 2002). This difficulty is in large part a function of the greater difficulty in defining and measuring the behaviours being regulated than is true for economic variables such as prices that are the usual target of regulation. In addition, attempts to impose tight controls over many aspects of behaviour may be considered excessively intrusive by societies that have ceased to accept social controls over many aspects of behaviour, and see no reason why individuals receiving social benefits should be treated much differently.

Conclusion

Governments continue to be heavily involved with social policy programmes, despite the changes in priorities within the public sector. Governments remain deeply involved in social policy, but are involved in rather different ways than in the conventional conception of the welfare state. The social programmes that now are being implemented are more closely linked to market logics than in the past, and are designed to be linked more closely with the market than were the more conventional programmes. Further, the instruments through which programmes are being delivered are based even more clearly on market concepts of good administration than the programmes that are being developed.

We should not, however, be totally absorbed by the importance of market ideas in the governance of social policy. At the same time that government is employing market mechanisms, it is also involving a range of more democratic forms of relating to the society that they are meant to be serving. These forms of involvement of the surrounding society in the delivery of programmes are a means of permitting recipients to have some influence, as well as a means of permitting social organizations concerned with the policy to exert some influence. This may be an imperfect form of democracy, but may still be a more democratic means of administration than the conventional forms of service delivery.

Further Reading

Glendinning, M., Powell, M. and Rummery, K. (eds) (2002) *Partnerships, New Labour and the Governance of Welfare*, Bristol: Policy Press.
Peters, B.G. (2001) *The Future of Governing*, 2nd edn, Lawrence: University of Kansas Press.
Salamon, L.M. (ed.) (2002) *Handbook of Policy Instruments*, New York: Oxford University Press.

Notes

1   The most well-known example of this role for bureaucrats is found in Heclo's (1974) discussion of the diffusion of ideas concerning the welfare state.
2   For a general discussion of the alternative styles of reform in contemporary government see Peters (2001).
3   See Note 1 above.
4   This legislation had the rather ideological title of the Personal Responsibility and Work Opportunity Reconciliation Act.
5   T.H. Marshall's observation that social citizenship would not be complete until the man in line for the dole was treated the same as the man in line for opera tickets remains one of the most telling critiques of this sort.
6   This was the goal for all public programmes issued by the National Performance Review (Gore Commission) in the United States.
7   This is the familiar characterization of street-level bureaucracy and its close ties with the public that it serves. See Lipsky (1980) and Vinzant and Crothers (1998).

8 Rather perversely, the public sector tends to be less successful in using relational contracting than does the private sector, even though the goods and services being purchased in the public sector often are more difficult to specify than those in the private sector. Combining the legal idea of contracts with the accountability culture of the public sector tends to produce an excessively rigid use of the instrument.

9 Conventional company pensions (defined benefit programmes largely) are protected through the Pension Benefit Guarantee Corporation, but the investment-based, 401(k)-type plans at Enron are not guaranteed, and that corporations have more control over the plans, in hindsight, appears desirable.

CHAPTER 3

Social Exclusion

SUSANNE MACGREGOR

In the 1990s, the phrase 'social exclusion' gained prominence in the political lexicon. It began to be used so often and so variously that some questioned whether it had lost all meaning or value. But this very elasticity made it especially useful, as new directions in politics and social policy were being pursued. What had once seemed to be merely a rather infelicitous construction, a product of technical debate in European social policy circles, became part of a general common-sense understanding of the social world at the turn of the century. As such, it was by definition 'fragmentary, incoherent and inconsequential' (Gramsci, 1971: 419).

The story of this chapter is of a battle of ideas in a period of change and transition. A complex dance is observed where social philosophies, ideologies and common-sense views interlink with social scientific theories and empirically derived findings to shape the design of new social policies. How far these build to a new paradigm or result in an inchoate mix of reactive proposals will be a key issue to reflect upon.

Discourses of Social Exclusion

A focus on social exclusion draws attention to the boundaries of the social world. Who belongs and who is outside? What distinguishes the excluded from the 'hard working ordinary people' with whom they are contrasted? In contemporary British social politics, discourses of social exclusion refer to a collection of different categories of people, whose social position and belonging is contested, challenged, under observation and scrutiny – whose membership of British society is at best conditional. These include asylum-seekers, economic migrants and refugees, drug addicts, young criminals, the homeless, truants, violent and disruptive schoolchildren and persistent offenders – an array of groups whose behaviours are thought to threaten normality, social cohesion and well-being.

Social exclusion and poverty are often discussed together but the link between them is a confusing one. As the term 'social exclusion' followed a journey from its invention in social policy circles Europe to its central location in New Labour's social policy armoury, it lost some of its concern with the link between material poverty and the ability to participate fully in society. This original conception had usefully looked at the processes that lead to exclusion, drawing attention to the decisions and behaviours of 'normal' people – those who are doing the excluding. Over time, more attention was paid to the behaviours of the excluded, linking these new words to the more recently dominant concept of 'the underclass'.

Social exclusion, as used in international and European social policy discussions, is closely linked to core concepts of poverty, deprivation, change, development, participation, marginalization, rights and social justice. A key assumption is that societies are in the process of being transformed, with a deepening of social inequalities, labour market segmentation and changes in the quantity and quality of jobs (Gopinath, 1995: v). Economic changes are producing instability and disintegration in both developed and developing societies. Policy responses here are characteristically anti-poverty strategies. Combating social exclusion became an EU policy priority, especially through interventions to reduce long-term unemployment and encourage reinsertion into labour markets.

The European Commission placed the concept at the centre of its social policy, linking it to the idea of an inadequate realization of social rights. The Observatory on National Policies to Combat Social Exclusion defined social exclusion 'in relation to the social rights of citizens ... to a certain basic standard of living and to participation in the major social and occupational opportunities of the society' (Room, 1992: 14).

A different approach is evident in tabloid discussions in Britain. Lynda Lee-Potter commented on an attack on a 77-year-old lady who went to her local fish and chip shop and on the short walk home was attacked by a young boy: she suffered broken ribs, broken shoulder, facial injuries and eventually died. Lee-Potter contrasts the old lady who came 'from the old stock of working class people – proud, indomitable and disciplined' with her presumed attacker, one of the new breed of the poor:

He'll be a feral child, untamed, wild, brutish and without any conscience ... Almost certainly he will be one of several children ... he'll live in a grim, filthy home where he's more likely to get clouted than protected. Probably the television blares out all day and his mother's main journeys of the week are to the welfare and the pub ... He'll be ... no stranger to drugs and drink ... There are thousands like him around Britain today, born to feckless unemployable parents who know that the state will always feed, clothe and house them so why should they make any effort? They appreciate only their rights not their responsibilities. (*Daily Mail*, 17 April 2002: 13)

Some of these ideas are present in the New Labour discourse. The election of New Labour in 1997 did not signify a year zero in which people suddenly saw the world differently. The common sense that had developed over the previous 20 years, criticizing the welfare state and condemning the behaviours of the adult poor and their children, did not disappear overnight. To retain its popularity New Labour had to appear responsive to many of the real concerns that underlie this rhetoric.

Between these two positions – the rhetoric of social justice and the rhetoric of the underclass – lies a third way. This discourse emphasizes a tough concept of community where rights and responsibilities go hand in hand. Everyone should have a stake in society and no one should be excluded from it (Mandelson and Liddle, 1996: 19). The abolition of long-term unemployment would be central to realizing this aim. The breakdown of law and order was seen as linked to the break-up of a strong sense of community, linked in turn to the breakdown of family life (Mandelson and Liddle, 1996: 48). The solutions would lie in strengthening the family, strengthening ties between generations, rebuilding communities and fighting crime, a new contract between society and young people, and a reformed welfare state (Mandelson and Liddle, 1996: Ch. 5).

The third way approach to a new politics was outlined by Tony Blair:

a modernised social democracy, passionate in its commitment to social justice and the goals of the centre-left, but flexible, innovative and forward looking in the means to achieve them … a *third* way because it moves decisively beyond an Old Left preoccupied by state control, high taxation and producer interests; and a New Right treating public investment, and often the very notions of 'society' and collective endeavour, as evils to be undone. (Blair, 1998a: 1)

The aims of social policy would be to

seek a diverse but inclusive society … an inclusive society imposes duties on individuals and parents as well as on society as a whole … Strong communities depend on shared values and a recognition of the rights and duties of citizenship – not just the duty to pay taxes and obey the law – but the obligation to bring up children as competent, responsible citizens, and to support those – such as teachers – who are employed by the state in the task. (Blair, 1998a: 12)

The Third Way recognises the limits of government in the social sphere, but also the need for government within those limits to forge new partnerships with the voluntary sector. (Blair, 1998a: 14)

In December 1997, the Social Exclusion Unit was set up at the heart of the Whitehall machine, designed to work under the Prime Minister's direct patronage. Earlier in 1997, after only one month in power, Tony Blair had visited the Aylesbury Estate in Peckham, southeast London (conveniently situated a short car journey from Westminster and thus the location for a number of press conferences). The promise that day was 'no forgotten people and no no-hope areas' offering a new social contract between comfortable Britain and the poor. The socially excluded would be brought back into society mainly through welfare-to-work programmes. Alongside a number of policies to deal with youth offenders, unemployment, teenage pregnancy and more was a commitment to abolish child poverty in 20 years.

Social exclusion thus forms a key concept within a new language of political debate. Levitas has argued that what has developed has been a 'language about social cohesion, stakeholding, community, social exclusion and inclusion' which was central to the creation of a centre-left consensus on which New Labour's electoral success was based (Levitas, 1998: 2). She categorises the different discourses of exclusion as RED, MUD and SID. RED is a redistributionist discourse, in which social exclusion is intertwined with poverty; MUD is a moral underclass discourse which uses the language of social exclusion but is merely a reinvention of the underclass discourse; and SID, a social integrationist discourse, sees inclusion primarily in terms of labour market attachment. For her, social exclusion is an essentially contested concept (Levitas, 1998: 3).

Theories of Social Exclusion

Social exclusion has also increasingly attracted the attention of the social sciences. Theories of social exclusion appear in economics, geography, sociology, political science, criminology and psychology, as well as in social policy. Partly this demonstrates the way that academic social science follows government agendas, influenced by the availability of funds and the need to appear to be relevant. But not all the explanations take for granted the assumptions of common sense and political rhetoric: some have seen their role as being to challenge these orthodoxies.

A valuable feature of contemporary social scientific discussion of social exclusion has been to bring together sets of observations and explanations which derive from separate disciplines. Some of the best theories draw inter-connections between urban studies, criminology and social policy, fields too often still dealt with as though in separate universes. A few examples will illustrate key themes.

In *The Exclusive Society* (1999), Jock Young stresses that there are real-world constraints creating the conditions in which social exclusion has become an important fact of contemporary life. He emphasizes the rapid unravelling of the social fabric, the rise of individualism and the slow but steady erosion of deference. He describes

> a movement from an inclusive society of stability and homogeneity to an exclusive society of change and division. In this late modern world, exclusion occurs on three levels: economic exclusion from labour markets, social exclusion between people in civil society and the ever-expanding exclusionary activities of the criminal justice system and private security. (Young, 1999: vi)

He goes on to suggest that:

> We live now in a time where there has been massive structural change: where there have been fundamental changes in the primary and secondary labour markets; where the employment patterns of women have radically changed; where structural unemployment has been created on a vast scale; where communities have disintegrated; where new communities have emerged in a multicultural context; where patterns of leisure have been manifestly restructured; where patterns of social space have undergone redefinition; where the agencies of the state have undergone systematic transformations and reappraisal by the public. And these structural changes have been accompanied by cultural changes no less dramatic ... all of this ... must be related to the quantum leap in crime and inci-vilities and to the debate over rules and standards which we now experience. (1999: vi)

Underlying all this is an ever-present sense of insecurity among 'ordinary people': precarious anxiety among the better-off breeds intolerance and puni-tiveness towards the law breaker (Young, 1999: 8). The rise in crime is the central motor of change. The total recorded crime rate for England and Wales in 1995 was 11.5 times that in 1955, the rate of violence was almost 20 times. In a reassertion of the insights of Robert Merton, Young empha-sizes the role of values in society over and above the simple availability of work and adequate income:

it is not material deprivation per se, nor lack of opportunity which gives rise to crime but deprivation in the context of the 'American Dream' culture where meritocracy is exhorted as open to all. (Young, 1999: 81)

Meritocracy and consumer culture conspire together to create the contemporary phenomenon of social exclusion.

David Byrne similarly has combined insights from separate disciplines to present an analysis of social exclusion. He places

very considerable emphasis on both the multidimensionality of exclusion, understood in terms of the complex dynamics of life trajectories, and on the significance of spatial separation within the urban areas of advanced industrial societies. (Byrne, 1999: 2)

With Young, he sees the obsession with social exclusion as being principally driven by concerns for social order. He places contemporary urban and social policy at the core of his analysis, showing how social policies themselves create contemporary forms of social division. He too identifies the insecurities and anxieties of the 'squeezed middle' as part of the explanation for the exclusion of the poor. Importantly, he notes that mobility may be closing down in postindustrial societies, affecting chances of both social and spatial mobility. In contrast to Young, he sees the central dynamic leading to social exclusion as emerging from the characteristics of 'capitalist' rather than 'late modern' societies. 'Advanced industrial societies are converging on a norm of social politics organised around a flexible labour market and structural social exclusion' (Byrne, 1999: 70).

An important feature of contemporary social exclusion is the relationship between social and spatial segregation. Geographical theories emphasize that the processes of unemployment and social exclusion have an important local level of operation: labour market dynamics are in part locally constituted (Lawless et al., 1998: 10). People are pushed out of mainstream society and into neighbourhoods which form pockets of poverty and deprivation. It becomes difficult to extract oneself from these neighbourhoods.

David Sibley (1995: ix) stresses that 'power is expressed in the monopolisation of space and the relegation of weaker groups in society to less desirable environments'. Urban policies have acted to separate out groups in the city and keep the underclass at a distance. Exclusion has its source in institutional practices. So an understanding of social exclusion should begin by identifying what it is in current social policies that acts to create communities of the excluded. Urban policy, criminal justice policy, employment policies, educational policies, welfare policies – all can be seen to play their part. At a minimum, they exacerbate conditions created by wider forces in the economy, politics and culture. Beyond this, they may also directly encourage these conditions.

Many of these studies see politics at the root of social exclusion. The powerful and the privileged appropriate what opportunities they can from the market. The increased stress on competition as the driver of dynamic economies necessarily brings with it a 'winners and losers' society. Widening inequalities create layers of disadvantage. Among these are immigrant groups such as 'guest workers' granted residence but not citizenship rights. Others are excluded on individual grounds. It is notable that the relation between these two layers of the excluded is emerging as a key feature of contemporary European politics. The tensions between them, especially where overlain with racist separations, increasingly form the focus of protests and discontent and may be the flash point for wider changes.

Political economic theories identify the character of contemporary societies as 'post-Fordist', involving a new toughness on welfare, increasing poverty and increasing hostility to outsiders (Kennett, 1994). Another important feature of contemporary exclusion identified by some commentators is the feminization and racialization of poverty (Jordan, 1996). These accounts emphasize the interaction between the grand transformations taking place in social regimes and the creation of particular forms of exclusion. The mass solidarities established through welfare states have broken into narrower mutualities: the end of the Keynesian–Beveridgian welfare state regimes and dominance of neoliberalism has created increasing fragmentation, inequality and polarization.

Alongside this transformation, social science itself has been transformed, in particular the discipline of social policy which grew up with this formation. 'Today's social policy is at once more heterogeneous in its approaches and objectives and more wide-ranging in its concerns' (Jones, Finer and Nellis, 1998: 1). A review of theories of social exclusion supports this perception. As social policies are transformed so the discipline of social policy itself is in the process of reconstruction. In particular:

> the control of delinquency by one means or another has become central to the credibility of the new social policy, which is itself more about managing insecurity than guaranteeing security. (Jones et al., 1998: 1)

There are of course major continuities in discussions of social exclusion, linking back to theories of the dangerous classes, problem families and the underclass as John Macnicol (1999) has repeatedly reminded us. There are continuities in the organisation of societies from the 19th through to the 21st century. But social science also attempts to explain the nuances and differences within grand epochs. Social scientific theories of social exclusion focus on the changes that have taken place in the societies, cultures, economies, politics and geographies of societies and state formations variously described as late modern, consumer capitalist or post-Fordist. Social exclusion is thus not a residual matter rooted in individual pathologies but is endemic to these new formations. The logic is that to deal with it effectively would require fundamental changes in social organization.

Researching Social Exclusion in Britain

A rather different stream in social science emphasizes the value of social investigations. Social reporting has long been an important aspect of British sociology. In particular, counting the numbers of the poor holds a venerable place in the British approach to social science. Under the New Labour government after 1997, social research came into its own and large amounts of money became available to research the important social questions of the day. Among these, social exclusion and related social problems figured prominently. Research on topics such as crime, youth offending, drugs and teenage pregnancy flourished.

Academic research on social exclusion initially located the issue firmly within a context of poverty and inequality. From the mid-1980s onwards, a series of studies had mapped the contours of growing polarization and deprivation in Britain (for example Faith in the City; Dahrendorf Report; Commission on Social Justice). The Rowntree research programme on income and wealth had revealed a widening gap between rich and poor (Hills, 1995). The European poverty programmes from the mid-1970s to 1994 had introduced the concept of social exclusion to this stream of research, partly via the Social Exclusion Observatory.

The Observatory faced the task of arriving at an operational definition of social exclusion. The concept had to be distinguished from related concepts such as poverty and marginalization and it needed to be identifiable empirically by means of well-defined indicators. The approach adopted was to define social exclusion in terms of the denial or non-realization of social rights. In tracing the effects of exclusion from these rights, the Observatory collated information on multiple, persisting and cumulative disadvantage. The focus was emphatically on disadvantage and evaluations of policy effectiveness, on the institutional factors leading to exclusion.

In Room's (1995) account, the phrases 'poverty' and 'social exclusion' are used together. Combating unemployment and promoting reinsertion into work were seen in EU social policy as the most important elements in efforts to combat social exclusion (Room, 1995: 8). Adapting to these contextual changes, research was also refocused. Attention to disposable income and expenditure continued to be emphasized. But greater attention was given to multidimensional disadvantage. More attention was paid to processes and developments over time rather than simply static assessments at one moment in time. And more attention was paid to the disadvantages of local communities as well as individuals and households. Data on education, employment, working environment, health, housing and social participation were collated and newly collected.

As a result of these trends, over time the concepts of poverty and social exclusion became more clearly distinguished. Poverty is about the lack of resources available to an individual or household and the resulting low level of consumption (Room, 1995: 243). By contrast, social exclusion has to do with relational issues – inadequate social participation, lack of social integration and lack of power (Room, 1995: 243). Or as Walker and Walker (1997: 8) put it:

> poverty is about a lack of the material resources, especially income, necessary to participate in British society. Social exclusion refers to the dynamic process of being shut out, fully or partially from the systems which integrate a person into society – in effect the denial of citizenship rights.

However, as research began to pay attention to indicators of social exclusion distinct from poverty per se and analyses sought to explain the process of exclusion over time, the question arose of why some people experiencing poverty also experience social exclusion while for others this is not the case? Why do some people escape from poverty or while remaining in poverty manage to avoid being pushed out to the edge while others become locked into social exclusion? The answer increasingly seemed to lie with the behavioural characteristics of the excluded. This harks back to old issues in poverty analyses where explanations were thought to lie in differences between primary and secondary poverty and the deserving and undeserving poor as well as with poverty and unemployment traps.

With the growth of attention to social exclusion in Britain in recent years, the balance between the European institutional approach and an approach (dominant in USA) which gives more emphasis to behavioural causes of exclusion has shifted. For example, John Hobcraft, in an influential study emanating from the LSE's Centre for the Analysis of Social Exclusion (CASE) (an ESRC research centre), looked at intergenerational and life course transmission of social exclusion. His account paid attention to influences of childhood poverty, family disruption and contact with the police (Hobcraft, 1998). The study used data from the National Child Development Study to examine how experiences during childhood are linked to a wide variety of outcomes in adulthood. The goal was to examine the extent to which social exclusion and disadvantage are transmitted across generations and across the life course. For example, by 16 years old, 44 per cent of the poorest boys had contact with the police compared to 13 per cent of the non-poor; anxious children experienced more malaise as adults; children born out of wedlock were more than twice as likely as others to have extramarital births themselves. Men whose parents were divorced were more likely to have multiple partnerships themselves. And boys with step-parents were nearly three times as likely to be homeless in their twenties. Care and fostering had a devastating effect on most adult outcomes for females.

The volume of research on social exclusion in Britain is such that it is impossible to review it all here. However, it is possible to characterize the broad themes. Some research has focused on issues relating to employment opportunities; some studies have paid attention to causes of social exclusion lying in early experiences and behavioural patterns; while other studies have looked at geographical and community influences, focusing on neighbour-hoods, housing and the area bases of social exclusion and the politics of place.

In social policy departments around the country, a range of research work has gone on, often funded by the Joseph Rowntree Foundation, aiming to describe and explain the paradoxical emergence and continuance of social exclusion in a society three times richer than when the 1940s' welfare state was established. Older and continuing causes of social exclusion are identified such as poverty and inequality, especially relating to unemployment and long-term unemployment, and the gaps between work-rich and work-poor house-holds and those with educational qualifications and those without. Differences become entrenched between those on benefits and those in the labour market, those who are healthy and those with a long-standing illness and those who are white and those who are Pakistani or Bangladeshi, and between those owning their homes and those in rented accommodation. These are exacer-bated by policy developments such as changes in social security entitlements, inadequacies of housing policy and management, deteriorating public trans-port and poor educational experience. Social changes such as the rise in the number of lone-parent families and deindustrialization are linked to the increased concentration of poverty in distinct neighbourhoods and areas – especially large urban areas, particular estates and older industrial regions. Other social changes create newer forms of exclusion such as exclusion from the information society – lack of access to a computer or telephone – and financial exclusion becomes increasingly important in a society based on credit and organized around consumerism. The increased use of league tables and performance measures increases the gap between the winners and the losers, stigmatizing the unlucky people, areas and institutions and permanently marking them as failures.

One wonders if there is a need for more social research since the explanations of poverty and social exclusion seem so well-established and familiar. But research is needed to play a part in arguing and persuading that the problem remains. Poverty was banished from the lexicon in the Thatcher years and had to be rediscovered anew by a new wave of social research utilizing the terminology of social exclusion. Politicians and civil servants need to be persuaded but more important is to persuade the public.

From varying angles and in different styles and languages, evidence accumulated on social exclusion, pointing quite clearly to the need for policy change and intervention. In addition to the research of social policy analysts and journalists, another powerful group influencing the agenda were the applied economists who focused their attention particularly on exclusion from the labour market and proposed remedies to deal with this. Most influential among this group were Richard Layard and a group of colleagues at the LSE in the Centre for Economic Performance.

Research in the 1980s and 90s had built up a picture of the social impact of economic change. The evidence pointed strongly in the direction of a process of cumulative disadvantage. Those in insecure labour market positions suffered from a series of major disadvantages in terms of personal welfare.

> The unemployed, the insecure low-paid and the insecure non-employed stood out from other groups in the degree of financial difficulty they confronted and in the extent to which they had been forced to cut living standards. (Gallie and Vogler, 1994: 334)

There were clear links to their quality of housing and their psychological and physical health. The policy implications increasingly were recognized as the need to increase employment opportunities, although less attention was paid to the quality of the work that would be available – whether poor work is better than no work would remain a serious question for debate.

The argument was taken forward by Richard Layard who, in *What Labour Can Do* (1997), presented an account lauded by Gordon Brown as a 'clarion call for change'. In a chapter entitled 'From Welfare to Work' he set out the dimensions of what would be the new policy approach. For most poor people, the way to a better life would be to work and earn. The basic strategy for dealing with want is to get people from welfare into work. The priority should be to reintegrate the long-term unemployed into the workforce:

'"Inclusion" must be the guiding principle' (Layard, 1997: 57). The hand-out should be replaced by the hand up. Three main alternatives – the recruitment rebate, the job creation project and education – would be a suitable solution for every long-term unemployed person. To make sure work pays, he argued for a minimum wage and in-work credits. He set out his proposals in detail and concluded that the

> welfare to work strategy must be the centrepiece of any attack on poverty. It will not only raise incomes while people are of working age. It will also help to raise their pension contributions so that they can have a decent old age. (Layard, 1997: 77)

These ideas would form the core of New Labour's approach to social exclusion when in power from 1997.

New Labour Policies on Social Exclusion

The new Labour government adopted a distinctive approach to the understanding of social exclusion. This was based on a social democratic analysis of what happens when work disappears (Wilson, 1996). Loss of manufacturing jobs leads to the collapse of old working-class communities and with this a change in cultures and values. Policies to address this situation would need to be wide-ranging, principally focusing on building a dynamic economy and reducing unemployment. Alongside these would be alterations in social security to encourage people into work and in particular tackling child poverty. But all departments of state would need to be involved and work together in devising imaginative policies to deal with the human and cultural effects of social fragmentation and social breakdown. Social exclusion is a wide-ranging phenomenon representing systemic malaise which would not be solved just by the provision of income or jobs. Education would have a key role to play in improving the skills and aptitudes of the workforce, suiting them for the new jobs which would become available in the knowledge economy. Initiatives such as Sure Start would tackle those disadvantages which start early in life so that all children would have the same opportunities to benefit from education and training. Health initiatives would tackle deep-seated inequalities. Special initiatives to tackle drug taking and youth offending would encourage those affected to seek treatment and benefit from rehabilitation schemes.

The New Labour approach to social policy would be based on evidence. It would be pragmatic not ideological. Coordinated, working together across departments would be the order of the day, with an emphasis on developing 'joined-up' solutions. The emphasis would not, however, be on process but on outcomes. 'What works?' would be the key question in devising policy, not automatically adopting the traditional solutions proposed by unions, local authorities, professional bodies or civil servants. Indeed, these old solutions were seen as part of the problem and the voices of these groups tended to be dismissed as simply representing old provider interests. New groups were encouraged to enter into partnership with government in tackling the new agenda, especially representatives of the voluntary sector, churches, faith groups, charities and community groups. These latter were thrilled and enthusiastic at last to be invited into the places where policies were devised and they held out great hope for a new beginning.

On the economic front, key policies were the national minimum wage, the various New Deals and alterations to taxes and benefits. These changes, announced in successive budgets, focused especially on attacking child poverty, increasing the incentive to enter the labour market through tax-credit schemes and support for childcare. It was recognized that more needed to be done to plug the gap between nursery provision and childcare in order to make it easier for parents to go out to work. In 2001, plans were announced for 45,000 new childcare places in 900 new neighbourhood nurseries over the next three years. Budgets also contained some redistributionist measures through a series of what were termed 'stealth taxes', which tended to hit middle-income groups, to provide more cash for the poor – abolition of mortgage tax relief and the married couple's tax allowance, for example.

The government had pledged to eradicate child poverty by 2020, reducing it by half by 2010. The government committed itself to annual reporting on its anti-poverty strategy in *Opportunity for All* (DSS, 1999) and adopted 30 indicators to monitor the effectiveness of its policies including literacy and numeracy, health outcomes and teenage pregnancy. The approach would build on four strands:

1. More support for family finances.

2. Giving priority to children's services especially in health and education.

3. Offering support for parents.

4. Pursuing a partnership with the voluntary and community sectors.

On the whole, the government's initiatives on child poverty were welcomed by those involved in child policy, although they felt that more could have been done in the first term of office.

At the centre of government policy on jobs was the New Deal, with its various special programmes for distinct groups. The New Deal was lauded as the best concrete example of the rights and responsibilities approach to social problems. While opportunities were offered through the New Deal, there was no fifth option of a life on benefit. Through the New Deal, 32,000 people had been sanctioned – it was a tough approach but it worked:

> A decent education and a job are the best anti-crime policy; the best anti-welfare spending policy; the best strong community policy; the best anti-poverty policy we can have. (Blair, 2000)

The work of the Department for Employment (DfEE/DfES) is of central importance here, along with the Treasury, in affecting supply-side issues in the labour market. But where problems were more entrenched, other agencies and policies would have to be drawn in. The other key prong in the government's strategy was the setting up of the Social Exclusion Unit (SEU). The SEU has been seen as one of the success stories of the New Labour government, especially because of the energy and drive it devoted to its task. The SEU was meant to be a force for change. It would ginger up all government departments and get them to focus on the issue of social exclusion and promote new ways of working in partnership across government and between government and non-statutory bodies. Its approach was to gather evidence on a problem from a range of sources then make recommendations on what should be done. In some areas, for example with regard to teenage pregnancy and neighbourhood renewal, the SEU reports can be seen to have directly shaped ensuing policy strategies.

Eighteen Policy Action Teams (PATs) were set up by the SEU, following its report on neighbourhood renewal, which worked on policies aiming to get people back to work, improve housing and the environment, build a future for young people, improve access to services and improve governance. The PAT on Jobs, for example, included representatives from a range of organizations involved in delivering training or employment services, representatives from ethnic minorities, academic experts, officials and business people. It took evidence in the form of research, reported experiences and observation and made 60 recommendations. This way of working was typical of the work of the PATs and formed a distinctive aspect of the work of the SEU. The SEU represents a new approach to policy making. Where the old style would involve select committee reports, Green and White Papers, the new approach involved special advisers and adopted a think-tank style, bypassing parliament and the traditional civil service to produce policy statements and aimed at rapid implementation.

The other key area to highlight in addition to the New Deals and the work of the SEU is that of criminal justice policy (see Newburn in this volume). Here huge sums of money were made available for prisons to introduce counselling, drugs programmes, anger management and various other cognitive-behavioural courses. This has developed in parallel with an apparent inexorable rise in the prison population. Measures introduced linked to the social exclusion agenda include parental control orders and curfew orders. Antisocial behaviour has risen up the agenda with antisocial behaviour orders being encouraged. All these are thought to emphasize an exclusionary rather than an inclusionary ideology (Hoyle and Rose, 2001: 79). Hoyle and Rose (2001: 80) comment on the

> contradiction between zero tolerance and criminalizing antisocial behaviour on the one hand and the welfarist, rehabilitative philosophy underlying some of the government's youth justice and prison policies. (2001: 80)

The same contradiction can be observed in drugs policy with one hand aiming to improve treatment and care and the other emphasizing harsher penalties.

Terence Morris (2001: 358) also sees New Labour policy in this area as 'driven less by original thinking than by the necessity of being reactive to public opinion'. Similarly, Home Office policy on immigration 'has not discernibly diverged from that of its predecessor, being based upon the assumption that application for such status is bogus unless proved otherwise' (T. Morris, 2001: 365).

Evaluation of New Labour Initiatives on Social Exclusion

The minimum wage, the various New Deals and Sure Start have received early if modest endorsements of their effectiveness. Glennerster quotes estimates which suggest that youth unemployment is perhaps 40 per cent lower than it would have been without the New Deal (Glennerster, 2001a: 387; also Finn in this volume). The investment of substantial additional resources into services, benefits and tax credits ought to have observable effects. Child poverty rate reductions have been contested but look likely to be on course, even if the target is an ambitious one. Reductions in unemployment appear emphatic, although some still refer to the problems of measurement; however, whether New Labour policies were themselves the cause of these reductions has also been questioned. There have been impressive increases in benefit payments, especially to children and pensioners. A real achievement has been 'bringing the issue of poverty into the policy arena and being explicit about the responsibility of government to tackle it' (Taylor, 2001: 8). Another has been the attempt to achieve joined-up government through the SEU, Sure Start, zones and local strategic partnerships. Here there has been an impressive generation of new ideas but less success in changing practice.

The stress on community involvement which runs through many of these policy developments is problematic. Communities themselves are not necessarily inclusive or tolerant of outsiders such as asylum-seekers, recovering addicts, travellers or other groups. It is odd that community breakdown is seen as the cause of problems, while at the same time communities are invoked as the solution. At worst, this rhetoric can serve as a cloak to hide the retreat of the state from service provision. Partnership is a common theme in many New Labour policies but it should be recalled that a long-standing criticism of this approach has been that of the requirement to involve communities without providing either the time or the resources for this to be effective. Most communities still feel on the margins of decision making.

Another key feature is the stress on joined-up policy making. But, in practice, in spite of the rhetoric, there is not much evidence of government departments at the centre sharing budgets or giving up mainstream resources to new units. For example, the responsibility for drugs – one of the first areas to attempt a joined-up approach under the command of a drugs tsar and located initially in an anti-drugs coordinating group in the Cabinet Office – has moved back into a mainstream department, the Home Office, which is now leading on drugs strategy.

While the evidence base on social exclusion and social policy is much improved, the major worry is 'that the key policy instruments are not strong enough to address the root causes of exclusion in the face of long-run international forces' (McCormick, 2001: 94). 'Deciding whether the goal is greater equality or greater inclusion or both is not the only important question facing Labour but it cannot be avoided indefinitely' (McCormick, 2001: 95). The contradictions in policies operating in different areas has been commented on by a number of people, particularly in referring to the harshness of criminal justice policy contrasting with the rhetoric on social inclusion. In this area, respect for evidence appears much weaker and the demands of populist politics greater.

Conclusion

Bauman's analysis of contemporary society provides the most fundamental critique of the third way approach (Bauman, 1998). He argues that it is not work which is the means of integration, it is money. This gives you the means to participate in consumer society. So those who cannot work and low-paid workers are the ones who are actually excluded, since they cannot buy into acceptable styles of living. Also missing from discussions focused on the new urban poverty are a whole range of people who are actually disadvantaged – such as disabled people, some older people, low-paid workers and some ethnic minorities.

The intrinsic problem with the term 'social exclusion' is that it 'represents the primary significant division in society as one between the included majority and the excluded minority' (Levitas, 1998: 7). Attention is drawn away from the inequalities and differences among the included. Inequality and poverty are seen as pathological and residual rather than endemic (Levitas, 1998: 7).

The attention given to social exclusion in Britain at the turn of the 21st century has been primarily about redrawing the boundaries between acceptable and unacceptable behaviour. But this effort has focused almost entirely on distinguishing the genuinely unemployed from those who are not, the genuine asylum-seeker from the economic migrant, the disreputable from the respectable poor. This concentrates on bad behaviours among the poor, ignoring the drug taking, infidelities, frauds and deceptions and other human frailties found among the rich, the better-off and the not-quite-poor. Attacks on the disreputable poor have always been as much about disciplining the majority, by warning of the dangers of deviance and failure (Matza, 1971). In a meritocratic winners' and losers' society, this function is even more important. What happens to those who do not reach the required standards, in particular those who cannot pay their way, sends a clear message to the majority to keep in line or suffer the consequences.

Levitas sees the SEU as strongly imbued with MUD, with its conception of social exclusion as having largely to do with questions of social order. She worries that the constant stress that exclusion was about more than poverty would become a justification for not addressing poverty directly. Too much attention was paid to issues such as low educational achievement, truancy, drug abuse, worklessness, poor health and poor housing and not enough to low income.

In this new social politics, a striking phenomenon is that of the existence of parallel universes. Different narratives are presented to different audiences, and a gap appears between the rhetoric shouted loud in popular politics and the reality of more reasoned policies being devised and implemented behind the scenes. In an era where politics and policies are defined on the axis of the relations between professional politicians and the mass media, social policies and ideologies seem to veer erratically between different poles, as they aim to both reflect and shape popular understandings.

The gap between rhetoric and reality is an old one in social policy. The difference between design and implementation has often been noted, usually influenced by issues of cost as well as feasibility, which explain inconsistencies. Now the gap is a rather different one – that of parallel universes. With the end of ideology in social politics, the role of government is very much one of balancing and managing different views in a context of pluralist politics. So some New Labour policies on social exclusion could be characterized as progressive and liberal but these tend to be hidden from the *Daily Mail* reader. The sensible, well-informed clarity of the proposals of the Policy Action Teams, for example, contrasts with the more strident, harsh voices heard most markedly just before elections. Even before local elections, election broadcasts and other statements contain tough talking about crime, immigration and antisocial behaviour.

Does this represent a new paradigm in social politics? Levitas presented us with three discourses on social exclusion – RED, MUD and SID. Applying these as heuristic devices to help evaluate New Labour policies, we can see that a bit of each is present. There has been some redistribution, if by stealth, especially via Gordon Brown's Treasury policies and budget statements. Social reintegration through participation in work is of course strongly emphasized in many areas, especially through employment and labour market policies including the New Deals. But the underclass, with its distinctive behaviours, also takes up a large share of attention and is a clear theme in many social policies. However, the underclass is not seen necessarily as irremediable as it was with the radical Right. With rehabilitation, support and guidance, some may change their ways. For those who fail to reform, however, the punishment will be heavy.

This eclectic mixture of ideas and approaches is only a problem for those who want a consistent and clear ideological framework to guide policy. But this is an essentially non-ideological government: 'when people look at this government, they do seem to see themselves: practical, sentimental, well-meaning, resolutely non-ideological and more than a little hazy on detail' (Bagehot, *The Economist*, 4 May 2002: 38).

New Labour offers post-ideological politics for a post-ideological age. A key claim has been that New Labour policy is evidence-based – it is the 'what works?' approach. The third way, rather than being a distinctive path between different trajectories, is instead a pick-and-mix assortment of different ideas.

For public policies in general, constrained by events and buffeted by tabloid headlines, lack of vision has at times been a problem for the third way. Policies have seemed to be mainly reactive, manoeuvring through complex problems, rather than striking a clear path ahead. But policies on social exclusion have been relatively coherent and consistent. Paradigm would be too grand a word to describe them, being as they are a mix of common sense, straight talking and good intentions. The hole at their centre, however, is the failure to question the deep and rising inequalities which determine, above all else, the values and opportunities shaping British society in the early 21st century.

Further Reading

Giddens, A. (1998) *The Third Way: The Renewal of Social Democracy*, Cambridge: Polity Press.

Gordon, D., Adelman, L., Ashworth, K. et al. (2000) *Poverty and Social Exclusion in Britain*, York: Joseph Rowntree Foundation.

Hills, J., Le Grand, J. and Piachaud, D. (eds) (2002) *Understanding Social Exclusion*, Oxford: Oxford University Press.

CHAPTER 4

Responsibilities and Rights: Changing the Balance

JANE LEWIS

The idea that 20th-century welfare states have engaged in the development of social rights has been a major thread running through the post-war analysis of social policy. The major reference point has been T.H. Marshall's *Citizenship and Social Class* (1950), which offered a neat linear account of the acquisition of rights, from civil rights in the 18th century, to political rights in the 19th and social rights in the 20th century. It is all too easy to knock holes in Marshall's schema, for example women gained social rights in the form of protective labour legislation – regulating hours and conditions of work – in the 19th century in many European countries, but had to wait until the 20th century for political rights in the shape of the franchise. Nevertheless, the notion that modern welfare states have increasingly provided benefits and services 'as of right' has proved a powerful one. Indeed, Marshall has often been criticized for not paying due attention to obligations. This is not quite fair. In a little-quoted passage, he stressed the importance of obligations and reflected on the difficulty of enforcing these: 'It is no easy matter to revive the sense of the personal obligation to work in a new form in which it is attached to the status of citizenship' (Marshall, 1950: 79).

In so far as the core programme of modern European welfare states, with the exception of the UK, has been social insurance (in respect of unemployment, sickness and old age), it is easy to understand the pull exerted by the language of social rights. Influential comparisons of welfare states have focused in the main on insurance programmes and the nature of 'entitlements' (Esping-Andersen, 1990). The idea that an individual paid in so much to a social insurance programme and had the concomitant 'right' to then claim so much appeared inviolable. Yet, in the early 1980s in the UK, the Thatcher government 'rolled back' the right to insurance-based state pensions and met with very little by way of public protest (Glennerster, 1995). For while a social right attaches to the individual, its existence

75

depends on some kind of collective sanction as well as political will and, in the 1980s, attitudes, norms and values regarding the desirability of social provision changed.

The argument from neoliberal New Right thinking that proved so influential during the 1980s was threefold: first, it viewed the idea of social rights as antithetical to the exercise of individual freedom; second, it questioned whether there could in practice be any such thing as a social right, and third; it said that there had been too much emphasis on 'rights' during the post-war period and insufficient attention paid to 'responsibilities' (Murray, 1984; Mead, 1986). The first and the second strands of the argument were closely linked via the debate over taxation and the financing of benefits and social services. It was held that the individual both had the right and indeed was the best person to decide how to spend his or her money, which called into question state financing for social welfare programmes. The issue of public expenditure also makes the very existence of social rights appear fragile, for a right can only *be* a right if the person in possession of it can exercise it. A central problem relates to the fact that social rights are fiscally conditioned. Thus, if my local hospital Trust runs out of money, my right to medical treatment may be postponed indefinitely. In face of the political Right's hostility to the concept of social rights, the Left attempted a defence. Plant (in Plant and Barry, 1990) argued that even the defence of individual liberty required the commitment of resources. But often, even after the construction of lengthy and sophisticated arguments, the only rights that proved justifiable were frankly minimalist ones which in practice amounted to little beyond the old Poor Law (for example Goodin, 1985) – the relief of the destitute – that would provoke no opposition from opponents of state welfare.

Critics of state welfare have also insisted that it is too easy to get something for nothing, that social rights exist without concomitant responsibilities. In fact, all social provision has been conditional and very few programmes have been conditional only on citizenship in the sense of residency. Social insurance systems were attractive because the conditionality appeared to be automatic, the payment of benefits depended on the payment of contributions. In social assistance schemes, the payment of benefits was dependent on a means test and a more or less tightly defined and enforced requirement to seek work. These benefits were deemed to be benefits 'as of right' by the claimants' movements of the 1970s, and eligibility was determined more by means testing than by steps to ensure labour market activation (and for this reason were subsequently labelled 'passive'). Such social programmes were redistributive and could therefore be argued to be fundamentally more generous in respect of entitlements than they were strict in the enforcement of duties by the individual; albeit that Falkingham and

Hills (1995) have concluded that social insurance redistributes mainly over the individual's own lifetime.

The case for social rights has always involved moral arguments, and these are vulnerable to attack and change in face of shifting norms (Lewis, 2001). One of the most powerful attacks on post-war social provision came from Charles Murray (1984) in the mid-1980s, when he suggested that poverty programmes in the United States and in particular the means-tested assistance offered primarily to lone-mother families via aid to families with dependent children had succeeded only in exacerbating the problem it had set out to solve, the proof being that the numbers of lone-mother families had increased dramatically. He concluded that the moral hazard of such programmes had become too great and the only solution was to withdraw such benefits entirely (Murray excepted social insurance programmes which in his view operated a more balanced system, setting the right to benefit against the responsibility to contribute). A less draconian solution was reached by Lawrence Mead, also in the mid-1980s. He suggested that a way must be found to match all rights to cash benefits by responsibilities, and in the case of means-tested benefits the primary responsibility should be to engage in paid work.

What began to happen in the 1980s was an insistence that the balance of rights and responsibilities be met by each individual, and increasingly that the individual rather than the collectivity should bear more responsibility for his or her own welfare. Social insurance is properly conceptualized as an inter-generational contract, but even this was subordinated to the concern to make sure that the individual was made more directly aware of his or her responsibilities, to provide for a pension, for example, and of the rights that would follow there from. Thus the overwhelming concern of policy makers became that of enforcing a balance between social rights and responsibilities in the behaviour of each and every citizen. This was the basis of a new 'contract-ualism' and, as Stuart White (1998) has pointed out, it is by no means clear that it is based on a 'fair reciprocity'.

The focus of attention over the last decade in most Western welfare states has been responsibilities rather than rights, and the definition of respons-ibilities has been overwhelmingly on the duty of the individual to engage in paid work. As Carole Pateman (1988) has pointed out, this is likely to be defined as the individual's citizen-duty in modern states (although the bottom line may still be the obligation to fight for country in the case of men, and, more controversially still, to reproduce in the case of women). Employment provides the route to independence for the modern citizen and, in respect of the kind of welfare state restructuring that has gone on over the past decade, has been made central to welfare reform. Thus, much more emphasis has been placed on the benefit claimant's responsibility to look for work, train, and/or take whatever might be offered by way of a job. The importance attached to responsibilities does not stop at the obligation to work, for example parents have been required to account for truanting and delinquent children, but it is the axis around which a new model of welfare has emerged over the last ten years. This in turn raises questions about what happens to rights in the new contractualist model. What is promised in return for the responsibility to engage in paid work is an opportunity structure designed to make entry into the workforce possible. But in such a welfare model, those who do not enter the labour market, for whatever reason, may run the risk of becoming second-class citizens, even though they may be conceptualized in terms of a socially approved 'rights-bearing' category. In any case, they are likely to be disadvantaged in a system that demands that the individual takes more responsibility for his or her social provision. In what follows, we first explore a little more the reasons for and the nature of the new-found stress on responsibilities and then pursue by way of example two groups of people for whom the emphasis on the importance of paid work has proved difficult and for whom it is doubtful that a fair reciprocity has been achieved: women and those with disabilities.

The Emergence of a New Welfare Model

When commentators first attempted to identify the core principles of New Labour's so-called third way, all identified responsibility as a key component (Le Grand, 1998; Lister, 1998; White, 1998). The link to opportunity structures was also made clear, for example in the 1998 Green Paper on welfare reform:

> The welfare state now faces a choice of futures. A privatised future, with the welfare state becoming a residual safety net for the poorest and most marginalised; the status quo, but with more generous benefits; or the Government's third way – promoting opportunity instead of dependence, with a welfare state providing for the mass of the people, but in new ways to fit the modern world. (DSS, 1998a: 19)

The obligation to engage in paid employment was made clear:

> It is the Government's responsibility to promote work opportunities and to help people take advantage of them. It is the responsibility of those who can take them up to do so. (DSS, 1998a: 31)

The association of benefits with dependence and of employment with independence was thus also made clear. Howard Glennerster (1999b) has expressed the view that we may now be seeing the emergence of a new kind of welfare state altogether in the UK, where we see a strong commitment to basic welfare services alongside an acceptance of the low-wage, flexible labour market that was created by successive Conservative governments, together with a commitment to both in-work subsidies (first via the benefit system and now via taxation) and labour market activation programmes (the so-called New Deal). Welfare benefits have been tied to work via policies to get people into employment and to make work pay, with welfare services, especially health and education, then being justified in terms of social investment. The key linkage is between social and economic policy and the key mechanism is the recasting of the work/welfare relationship via the emphasis on responsibility and opportunity.

Sources of the emphasis on responsibility defined in terms of employment

It is no easy task to identify the factors pushing the emergence of such a model. Jordan (1998) has pointed out that the new framework takes the moral high ground in seeking national regeneration, ethical principles and the common good, cohesion and self-discipline, all of which are felt to be embodied in a commitment to the work ethic. This has arguably been most strongly articulated in the English-speaking countries, although the 'Dutch miracle' (Visser and Hemerijck, 1997) and the joint Blair–Schroeder (1999) document on the third way are evidence of similar thinking elsewhere. In the American debate, the emphasis on securing greater labour market participation was about securing a greater balance between social entitlements and responsibilities, and about removing people from the welfare rolls. Welfare-to-work programmes were implemented in a more (for example Wisconsin) or less (for example Oregon) draconian fashion. The road to competitiveness took the form of a low-wage, flexible, full-employment economy, in which all adults were expected to participate. Alan Deacon (2002) has emphasized the extent to which American ideas about the responsibility to work influenced UK governments.

In Europe, the stress on the responsibility to participate in the labour market took a somewhat different tone. 'Labour market insertion' has been viewed as the means to combat social exclusion. The idea of 'active' citizenship has been grounded in the responsibility to work, seeking to avoid both the stress on entitlements and the stress of neoliberalism on the individual pursuing his or her self-interest, which arguably results in a 'dutiless individualism' (Plant, 1998). Nevertheless, Ruth Levitas (1998) has drawn attention to the extent to which a 'social integrationist discourse', stressing inclusion via participation, above all in the labour market, has taken priority over a 'redistributive egalitarian' discourse.

It is also possible to link the emergence of a new welfare model and the emphasis on the responsibility to work in particular to globalization, but the precise nature of the effects of increasingly open markets and growing competition is hard to pinpoint. It may be that the most significant effect has been the way in which it has influenced change in the whole approach of governments to social provision, rather than in actually forcing a 'race to the bottom' in terms of cuts to social spending. David Piachaud (2000) has underlined the influence achieved by the 'Washington consensus' in prescribing for social policies private rather than public provision, allocation by markets rather than on the basis of need, targeting rather than universal provision, charging rather than tax-based finance and decentralization rather than central planning. The effects of globalization on the *principles* informing the restructuring of welfare systems in the 1990s have thus probably been more dramatic than on cuts in social programmes. The increased demands for competitiveness have justified a tougher approach to cash benefits, with a call to match entitlements to benefit with concomitant responsibilities to train or to work, as well as lending support to major welfare state services that can be perceived as increasing human capital (chiefly health and education).

The globalization thesis directs the attention of governments to labour markets and competitiveness and this discourse is dominant, with economic policy dictating social policy formation. European Commission documents show this clearly. The Commission has stressed the importance of adult labour market participation in order to increase competitiveness (CEC, 1993, 1995, 2000a, 2000b). Both the EC (CEC, 2000a) and the OECD (2000) have emphasized the importance of policies to 'make work pay' and, in the words of the EC, of strengthening 'the role of social policy as a *productive* factor' (CEC, 2000a: 2, emphasis added).

In addition, there is a closely allied set of arguments emanating from the US and New Zealand that wraps up concern about internal demographic challenges in the form of low birth rates and ageing populations into a notion of intergenerational conflict (Thomson, 1991; Kotlikoff, 1992). The conclusion from this work on 'generational accounting' is that current levels of social provision, particularly in respect of pensions, are unsustainable, thus justifying privatization and making the individual responsible for providing a larger proportion of his or her pension. At this point, the notion of a new balance between rights and responsibilities is cast into doubt. Not only is the responsibility to work being linked to any claim that is made on the state, but the individual is also being told that he or she will have to be more self-reliant in future. Individual responsibility is being stressed as an alternative to collective responsibility.

Welfare reform and responsibilities in practice

The emphasis on responsibilities and paid work as the key obligation of adult citizens has increasingly characterized welfare reform in many Western European social democratic states, where the work/welfare relationship has been recast so as to tip the balance of priorities towards enforcing the responsibilities of claimants (Lewis, 1999; Goodin, 2001; Green Pedersen et al., 2001). Goodin (2001: 9) has emphasized the importance of the emergence of 'a new constellation of work-and-welfare variables'. Broadly speaking, the emphasis in these countries is on so-called 'active' rather than 'passive' welfare, albeit to different degrees[1] and with very different implications, depending on the existing policy logic of the particular welfare regime and the conditions on which employment is promoted.

The emergence of a new welfare model is clearest in the UK, the Netherlands and Denmark. Welfare state change in the Netherlands has been explicitly based on labour market activation and flexibility, alongside wage moderation (Visser and Hemerijcke, 1997). In Denmark, the workfare measures which were introduced in the 1990s focused again on activation, eschewing cuts in benefits and the minimum wage (Torfing, 1999). Unlike Sweden, Denmark had a tax-based, universalist 'passive' welfare system. In many respects, the way in which Denmark has recast the work/welfare relationship brings it more into line with its Scandinavian neighbour, whose welfare model has long rested on 'active citizenship' and the notion of an adult citizen worker who is granted permission to leave the labour market for a cause. Green Pedersen et al.'s (2001) discussion of Denmark and the Netherlands has emphasized the extent to which it is possible to observe a coherent set of supply-side changes in the form of job creation, labour market activation policies, high labour market participation, wage moderation and macroeconomic stability, to which may be added a commitment to invest in human capital, particularly in respect of children and particularly via education and health services. The goal in these countries was to preserve the post-war commitment to social provision and social solidarity – a priority has been to ensure that more flexible labour markets have been accompanied by a measure of security (Kvist and Thaulow, 2001; Van Oorschot, 2001).

The case of the UK has been somewhat different, in that under successive Conservative governments the insistence on the responsibility to work was accompanied by an effort to reduce collective responsibility and increase the responsibility of the individual for his or her welfare. Certainly, during the 1980s, the UK government opted for adversarial rather than consensual politics, aimed at reducing the power of organized labour as a prelude to creating what amounted to a low-wage, flexible, labour market on the US rather than the European social integrationist model, with workers priced into employment, not least by substantial cuts in benefits. However, post-1997, the UK model for promoting welfare-to-work has begun to resemble that of other social democratic European countries, with the Labour government's introduction of the New Deals (labour market activation programmes for different groups in the population) and policies to 'make work pay', including a minimum wage and generous wage subsidies. The policy goal is no longer to abandon as much of social protection as is feasible, but rather to promote social inclusion as *per* the European model. Nevertheless, there remains a huge difference between the UK's low-wage, low-skills equilibrium and the production regimes of its Continental neighbours (Soskice, 1999). In addition, the large amount of surveillance that characterized the late 1980s' and early 1990s' reforms of the social security system still shapes arrangements now. Thus, the terms on which the new-found emphasis on responsibilities translates into 'activation' and the policies embodying the new principles will look very different in different countries.

Responsibility as Opportunity

No matter what the terms of implementation, the recasting of the work/welfare relationship in this way is likely to throw up problems. We will briefly identify three of the most important in the UK context.

First, it is noteworthy that the UK government's Green Paper on welfare reform (DSS, 1998a) said nothing about a major issue of concern in the UK context, the adequacy of benefits, nor does it make clear what future there is for social insurance in the British social security system (almost certainly very little). The new tax/benefit strategy and increases in child benefit and the child element in social assistance payments have resulted in a substantial reduction in child poverty since 1997. Nevertheless, the focus on the importance of work, which for many groups has been positive, has been paralleled by a more negative approach to benefits for adults. The preoccupation with the creation of work opportunities has overridden concern about benefit adequacy.

Second, alarm has been raised about the exclusionary potential of a social inclusion strategy based on employment opportunities. There will, after all, always be some who *cannot* engage in paid labour (see below). This was acknowledged in New Labour's welfare reform Green Paper (DSS, 1998a: 29), where Tony Blair's introduction said: 'We want to rebuild the system around work and security. Work for those who can; security for those who cannot.' However, as Hills (1998: 28) noted, the post-war Beveridgean position would have been 'security for all'. The TUC (1998) calculated that only a minority of benefit claimants will be able to move from welfare to work; and Alan Marsh (2000) reported that as many as 35 per cent of unemployed lone parents experience serious ill health. Furthermore, as A.B. Atkinson (1998: i, 9) has observed:

> Unemployment may cause social exclusion, but employment does not ensure social inclusion; whether or not it does so depends on the quality of the work offered. 'Marginal' jobs may be no solution.

Labour's strategy has relied on a supply-side policy, intended to increase people's 'employability', rather than on the demand side and 'employment'.

There is also the issue of how far government is prepared to go in forcing individuals to be responsible, which, as Desmond King (1999) has argued, is a hallmark of 'illiberal social policy' in liberal states. In the US, Mead (1997) has identified the trend towards enforcing personal responsibility as 'the new paternalism'. In New Labour's imagination, responsibility probably has more resonance with George Orwell's hankering after 'decency', a very 'English' concept that is hard to define, but which almost certainly involves 'doing the right thing'. Certainly, the Labour Party is determined to strive for a balance between rights and obligations. The approach is more fearful than punitive, although it is still paternalistic in that the aim is to change behaviour.

The overarching assumption is that work = activity = good, while receipt of benefits = passivity = bad. However, this simple, dichotomous view not only narrows the concept of social security, but also threatens to lose sight entirely of its meaning in terms of prevention, restoration and compensation (Sinfield, 2001). And yet, taking the 'right to work' seriously is crucial for citizenship in modern states.

A New Welfare Model – Work for All?

The equation between responsibility and paid work in the new mechanisms designed to harness the cash benefit system to the labour market raises most questions about those groups who may have difficulty in complying. In the case of women, the main issue is the extent to which responsibility is linked only to paid work, ignoring other forms of 'activity', particularly the unpaid work of care. In the case of disabled people, the main issue is lack of access and/or incapacity to work. Do these groups retain the 'right' to remain out of the labour market and, if they do, do they also tend to become second-class citizens, especially given the accompanying assumption that individuals will increasingly 'self-provision'?

Women

The first point at issue with the recasting of the work/welfare relationship arises from the narrowness of the definition of what constitutes 'work', given that the responsibility for the unpaid work of care continues to be carried out disproportionately by women. The second point concerns the extent to which the responsibility to enter the labour market is also linked to the assumption that the individual will do more to provide for her own welfare.

Labour force participation rates for the past 20 years show women's participation rising, and rising relatively steeply in most European countries, and men's participation rates falling. Cursory inspection would thus conclude that individualization is more and more a reality, which may also fit with a superficial reading of the statistics on family change, which reveal high divorce rates, high rates of lone parenthood and increasing numbers of single-person households. But, in the Netherlands and the UK, virtually the whole post-war expansion of female employment has been part time. Indeed, almost a quarter of British women with children under ten worked 15 or fewer hours per week in the late 1990s (Thair and Risdon, 1999), and 24 per cent of all female employees worked under 20 hours a week (Rubery et al., 1998). The vast majority of Dutch women work part time, 80 per cent in 1994; 33 per cent work less than 20 hours a week (Hooghiemstra, 1997).[2]

During the last quarter of the 20th century, research revealed the extent to which the male breadwinner system no longer described behaviour for a significant proportion of families (Crompton, 1999; Lewis, 2001). But nor have families become fully individualized, with both partners, or a lone mother, engaged in full-time work and economically independent. The male breadwinner model has eroded but the social reality is still far from a family comprising self-sufficient, autonomous individuals. While women's behaviour has changed substantially in respect of paid work, they still perform the bulk of unpaid care work, which was their obligation under the old work/welfare model. Men have changed much less in respect of the amount of either the paid or unpaid work they do (for example Laurie and Gershuny, 2000). The pattern of paid work between men and women in households is now much more difficult to predict, but patterns of unpaid work have not changed so much, although the mix of provision in respect of unpaid work (from market, third sector and public sources) which accompanies unpaid informal provision varies between countries and according to both the hours of paid work carried out by women and their partners' earnings (Lewis, 2000; Warren, 2000).

The social reality in the UK, which has historically operated on the assumption of a strong male breadwinner model, amounts to a one-and-a half-earner model. Furthermore, close examination of some of the new policies associated with welfare reform reveal an ambivalence about full individualization (Lister, 1998). For example, the effect of working families' tax credit (WFTC) on women with partners may be equivocal because it is administered on the basis of joint earnings and may thus reduce the incentive for partnered women to enter low-paid jobs (Rake, 2000; McLaughlin et al., 2001). Both increased means testing and the move towards tax/benefit integration work in the opposite direction to individualization and the promotion of an adult worker model. Thus, the New Deal for the Partners of the Unemployed (mainly women) treats them both as having an independent relationship to the labour market and as dependants. Their access to the programme is dependent on being the partner of an unemployed man. Thus, while ideas about individualization are clearly expressed, it is still assumed that married women can depend on their husbands as and when necessary. In regard to lone parents attending an initial New Deal interview, by December 1999 only just over half came from the target group of women with school-age children, who are seen as the most likely to enter the labour market (Millar, 2000). Duncan and Edwards (1999) have argued that this is likely to reflect the fact that women themselves continue to put caring responsibilities first. As Evans (2000: 26) has remarked, the incentive structures of the British system 'prioritize the move into work and reinforce the view that welfare-to-work is a single point transition'. But this is unrealistic, given the nature of many of the jobs on offer and the care responsibilities that women in particular bear.

The emphasis on the responsibility to engage in paid work thus ignores care in a number of different ways. First, it ignores the fact the women are not necessarily 'passive', whether as benefit recipients or dependants on a male wage, but are usually engaged in some form of unpaid care work. The middle-aged woman who gives up her job to look after an elderly mother and becomes 'passively dependent' on state benefits does so in order to help her mother remain independent. The problem of conceptualizing the balance of rights and responsibilities as existing within the confines of a single individual's life becomes immediately clear.

Second, the new vision of an adult 'citizen worker' pays insufficient attention to the way in which care work will be done. The expectation that women would be in the labour market was accompanied by the first post-war effort in the UK to make collective provision for childcare via the 1998 national childcare strategy and the childcare tax credit. However, the coherence of policies in regard to care is markedly less than those delineating the new work/welfare relationship, and the monies allocated to care are considerably less than those allocated to programmes designed to get people into work and to make work pay. This becomes especially important in respect of the elaborated meaning of responsibility in the sense of individual rather than collective responsibility for social provision. The shift towards an expectation that women will be in the labour market and towards the idea that people must shoulder more individual responsibility for their own welfare, for example in respect of pension provision, means that the new welfare model may well disadvantage women, just as did older assumptions that women would be dependent on a male breadwinner.

Thus, in the case of women, the new-found emphasis on responsibilities fails to recognize that women's opportunity structure for entering the labour market is substantially different from that of men, due mainly to the gendered division of paid and unpaid work. The simple dichotomy of (paid) work/welfare is particularly inappropriate in the case of women, whose relationship to welfare tends to be more complicated than that of men, involving as it does their position as paid workers and unpaid carers. The recasting of the work/welfare relationship is in danger of ignoring the way in which the need for 'social security' is gendered and, given women's responsibility for care, does not offer a 'fair reciprocity'. Furthermore, when it comes to the call for individuals to bear more responsibility for their own social provision, women's short hours, low pay and low-status employment is bound to disadvantage them. Nevertheless, an individualized model has the potential to offer more to women than the old male breadwinner model, which, while it made provision for care work, did so at the expense of making women economically dependent on men. The point is that the responsibility to engage in paid work must be accompanied by measures that ensure a fair reciprocity, which means in turn that adequate provision is made for care work. Only then will there be a genuine opportunity to work. However, the issue as to whether other forms of unpaid work should be recognized and valued will remain.

Disabled people[3]

In some respects, the emphasis on the individual's responsibility to engage with the labour market also has the potential to offer more to disabled people too. The Labour government's principal objection to the 'all work test' for invalidity benefit was grounded on the fact that the test 'focuses exclusively on what people *cannot* do and provides no assessment of, or information about, the capacities and abilities of people with a long-term illness or disability' (DSS, 1998a: 16). The emphasis on work as a means to social inclusion and on disabled people as active, dynamic individuals too often denied the opportunity to participate and 'consigned to a life on benefits' (DSS, 1998a: 1) chimes with the language of empowerment long used by campaign groups. However, the reform of disability benefits is also designed to distinguish between those who can and those who cannot work. In effect, the new-found stress on the responsibility to work has firmly stratified the population of disabled people,[4] separating those who will be given 'the opportunity' to work from those who will retain the right to benefit.

Discussion of those with severe disabilities in the policy documents acknowledges their need for care and that they 'depend on benefits', but in so doing inevitably condemns them to the status of 'passive' benefit recipients. Severe disability necessarily becomes abnormality, signalled by the definition of impairment as something affecting 'normal day-to-day activities' (DSS, 1998a: 11). The test of disability is now oriented less towards the needs arising from incapacity and more on the extent to which incapacity is a barrier to work. The right to benefit of those deemed incapable of employment is assured, but so is their exclusion from the activity that is held to be central to modern citizenship, notwithstanding the pledge to ensure that they have the wherewithal to 'live independently and with dignity' (DSS, 1998a: 9). It is difficult to see how those who are unable to respond to the new opportunity structures designed to promote labour market participation and who therefore exercise their right to financial support by the collectivity can avoid second-class status in this model which is tipped towards an emphasis on responsibilities.

The new policy logic structured around the responsibility to work has resulted in significant changes to the way in which disabled people are treated. Changes to the severe disablement allowance (a non-contributory benefit that was available to people of working age who had been unable to engage in paid work at all, or sufficiently to be able to qualify for the contributory incapacity benefit) mean that it has been restricted to those who have claimed it before the age of 20, the rationale being that those who become severely disabled after the age of 20 have had the opportunity to work and qualify for incapacity benefit. Those wishing to claim the non-contributory disability living allowance, designed to meet the extra costs faced by people with disabilities and those finding themselves unable to continue in paid work owing to a disability and therefore seeking invalidity benefit, must undergo more rigorous and more medicalized assessment (Oliver, 1999). The context in respect of invalidity benefit is the huge rise in the costs of these benefits over the past 20 years (Berthoud, 1998; Burchardt, 1999), which makes it additionally difficult to accept any simple notion that the reforms are designed solely to enable disabled people to attain economic independence. The desire to make a primary distinction between those who are capable of work and those who are not is as much to do with enforcing the responsibility of the individual to work as offering the individual the opportunity to gain access to an independent income. *But* opportunity/empowerment structures are nevertheless a part of the story. The New Deal offers disabled people a means of finding work and the disabled person's tax credit is part of the government's policy to make work pay.

The responsibility to work presented as the right to the opportunity to work resonates powerfully with much campaigning around disability issues, but the discrimination faced by disabled people in the labour market makes the language of empowerment additionally questionable. Just as in the case of women where the issue of unpaid care work has by no means been ignored, so discrimination has been addressed by the establishment of a Disability Rights Commission (DRC, 2002). But, just as the expenditure on care policies has been relatively small compared to that on activation policies and policies designed to make work pay, so equal opportunities legislation is inadequate to the task of tackling discrimination, relying as it does on the individual to seek redress, which may prove a well-nigh impossible burden for people with physical or mental disabilities.

Conclusion

The shift towards an emphasis on responsibilities has two main dimensions: the insistence that each individual has the responsibility to seek employment, and the importance attached to the responsibility of the individual to do as much as possible to meet his or her own welfare needs. The policy goal has been to ensure that claims made on the state by individuals are matched by the responsibility to work or train, and to increase individual responsibility for welfare at a time when the proportion of dependent people is increasing and state welfare is no longer expanding. But the new model of welfare based on the recasting of the work/welfare relationship should not be seen simply as a rolling back of rights in favour of responsibilities. For the favouring of responsibilities has been couched in the language of opportunity, with the state undertaking to provide the opportunity to work. If wages are the best, or at least a very important, component of welfare, the 'right to work' must also be important. Rights are therefore written back in *via* responsibilities. However, such an approach does pose considerable difficulties for many groups and individuals. Paid work is not the only socially desirable form of participation in society. Furthermore, the way in which the new approach has made it so central threatens to make those who cannot work, as well as those who will not work, into second-class citizens.

Further Reading

Blair, T. and Schroeder, G. (1999) *Europe: The Third Way – die Neue Mitte*, London: Labour Party and SPD.

Deacon, A. (2002) *Perspectives on Welfare: Ideas, Ideologies and Policy Debates*, Buckingham: Open University Press.

Goodin, R.E. (2001) 'Work and Welfare: Towards a Post-productivist Welfare Regime', *British Journal of Political Science* 31: 13–39.

Plant, R. and Barry, N. (1990) *Citizenship and Rights in Thatcher's Britain: Two Views*, London: Institute of Economic Affairs.

Notes

1 Gallie and Paugam (2000) and Lodemel and Trickey (2000) both offer data for 1996 and 1999 respectively, but the figures for spending on active labour market programmes are very different. The degree to which such programmes serve to increase skill levels also varies markedly.

2 I am grateful to Trudie Knijn for this reference.

3 I am grateful to Carolyn Birt for research assistance on this topic.

4 Esping-Andersen (1990) insisted on the capacity of welfare states to socially stratify.

CHAPTER 5

'Difference' and Social Policy

GAIL LEWIS

At the beginning of the 21st century, British social policy is faced with a major challenge. It is charged with the task of devising an ensemble of strategies, entitlement criteria, organizational forms and systems and professional practices which have the capacity to foster social solidarity and inclusion, while also recognizing difference and multiplicity. These issues impact upon an area of traditional concern in social policy – that of social justice – since ways to reconcile these two demands must be found that do not lead to a simple reinscription of existing social inequalities. Moreover, while the question of social justice may be well established in social policy, questions of difference, multiplicity and fragmentation imply that established ways of attempting to promote social justice are no longer possible or socially legitimate. In this chapter we will explore some of the ways in which social policy has responded to social difference and suggest that some issues of concern remain. The term 'social policy' is used to refer to both the academic discipline and the array of policies, agencies and professions involved in the production and delivery of welfare services and benefits. Social policy is then both a field of study and analysis and a set of social practices and organizational forms, ranging from the social security system, hospitals, primary care or mental health trusts, to social housing and the education system.

It is not possible to attempt a negotiation of these rocky waters without paying attention to the array of critiques, claims and counter-knowledges that have been put onto the agenda by what have become known as 'new social movements' (NSMs). Nor is it possible to forget that the voices of these NSMs have added to, rather than replaced, class-based knowledges and the critiques and claims expressed in terms of class inequalities. However, this augmentation of the social inequality agenda has meant that class-based critiques of welfare state practices have to be rethought as pointing to one *among a range* of inequalities attached to the constitution of social differences. In this sense, the various forms of social difference and inequality have been conceptualized as connected but not reducible to class. That is, no one form of inequality is conceived as the primary form of difference and inequality from which all other forms spring.

This chapter explores some of the dimensions of these 'new' ways of thinking the connections between social differences, social inequalities and social policy and points to some of the issues that arise from the challenges facing contemporary British social policy. We begin with a brief discussion of terms, and then identify the ways in which the term 'difference' is used, in particular the distinction between diversity and difference. We move to a consideration of some of the political and theoretical factors that have led to the issue of difference becoming an explicit concern for social policy. This is followed with a section sketching the predominant social policy approaches to differences of gender and ethnicity. We also suggest some limitations of these orthodox approaches and suggest that difference, like 'similarity', should be thought of as a *process* structured in and through social practices. Building on arguments raised earlier in the chapter, we suggest that difference always underwrites constructions of 'the universal', or that which is positioned as if it is without difference or particularity, that is, as standing for a generalized human condition. The argument is located specifically in the terrain of the provision of welfare services, rather than the distribution of welfare benefits, and shows that difference – of gender and ethnicity – is an outcome of organizational and professional practices as well as wider social processes.

Clarification of Terminology

The words 'diversity' and 'difference' are now commonplace in the language of social policy. From government White Papers, to policies governing specific welfare services such as social services or the NHS, to professionals' understanding of the issues relevant to their work, through to academic social policy texts, these two words recur with increasing frequency. Often they are used interchangeably and in connection with policy or practice issues related to those areas defined as 'inner city' or 'metropolitan'. In connecting diversity or difference with specific localities, there is an implicit coding going on in which diversity/difference comes to stand for ethnic and/or religious diversity. Diversity and/or difference here often becomes a code for something called 'multiculturalism', which itself is understood in a descriptive sense of people with numerous cultural heritages living side by side in parts of Britain. In contrast to this approach, we want to suggest, first, that a distinction be made between diversity and difference. Second, that both terms be thought of as signalling more than just ethnic plurality. Third, that a central element underwriting the distinction between them is their connection to issues of inequality.

Both diversity and difference refer to numerous variations in aspects of social life – ethnic pluralities are included but so too are diverse sexual identities and practices, forms of family and household arrangements, gender identities and practices and diversity of class and religion. This plurality of identifications and ways of living may be thought of as signalling social diversity in so far as they are conceived as emerging from a level playing field or a dynamic of equality. Or to put it in opposite terms, 'diversity' is the term used to signal social plurality when such plurality is conceived outside the dynamics of power and inequality.

Once we conceive of social plurality through a concern to understand its relation to dynamics of power and inequality, then the term 'difference' is more appropriate yet distinct from that of diversity. In this approach, difference becomes inseparable from the issue of power and inequality. As a consequence, the multiple forms of social difference in relation to class, ethnicity, gender, age, (dis)ability, religion and sexuality become inflected through dynamics of power. In this case, analysis of the constitution and practice of social differences becomes an analysis of the workings of, and resistance to, power and the inequalities that result from it. Finally, from this perspective diversity becomes a project to be achieved – linked to the pursuit of social justice – rather than a description of existing social relations of welfare or British society more generally.

New Social Movements and the Issue of Difference

At its most basic level, difference can be thought of as emerging from a process of classification in which social groups and individuals come to be identified – or identify themselves – on the basis of a selected number of characteristics. In this sense, to speak of difference is to speak about boundaries and their formation and the impact of this process of boundary formation on subjectivity, identity, experience, opportunity and expectation. The development of concern within social policy (in both senses identified earlier) about the links between difference and opportunity, expectation and experience was associated with the demise of class as the dominant lens through which social inequality was measured and analysed. To some extent, changing demographic and social patterns provided the context for this shift in focus. Factors such as the increasing multicultural profile of the population; changes in patterns of household formation; shifts in gender and sexual relations; and major industrial restructuring all had some influence on the demand for and distribution of welfare services and benefits. However, more specifically, the concern with difference and its importance for questions of social policy arose as a result of the challenges and claims made by a range of social actors who were pointing to other, interconnected forms of social inequality, both generally and in the social relations of welfare.

This range of new political constituencies were convened around the formation of identities and solidarities in relation to social differences of gender, race/ethnicity, sexuality and disability. There were also challenges made to social policy on the basis of forms of consciousness about the relationship between human beings and the natural world, for example ecological movements. These new political solidarities came to be known as new social movements (NSMs) which, at the most general level, can be defined as an organized effort, outside the formal political system, to promote or resist change in a major aspect of existing social relations and institutional practices. Alain Touraine (1981), a key theorist of NSMs, has identified them as signifying and expressing a distinctive type of social conflict, in that they articulate a new political, cultural and social vision as they contest and challenge a range of social subordinations and inequalities that lie beyond the domains of production relations. Touraine conceives these movements as more than simply operating in settings beyond the formal political process, rather he sees them as representing an alternative to it.

This understanding is captured by Melucci (1980: 2) when he says that in so far as these movements represent 'the defence of identity,' the 'continuity and predictability of personal experience is beginning to constitute the substance of new conflicts'. Melucci points to a second feature of social movements that has important implications for the ways in which we might think about the tensions that have arisen in social policy as a result of attempts to incorporate difference into a widened remit of social justice. Or to put it another way, the tensions between the universalist principle and particularistic claims in social policy. This is their concern with *the body*. Thus, black, gay and lesbian, disabled rights and women's movements have all sought to reject or challenge the dominant meanings attributed to bodies (Gilroy, 1987). They have attempted to resignify bodies as sites of autonomy, desire and resistance. In social policy terms, these 'struggles' over the meaning and control of bodies necessarily involve challenges to established welfare practices and their normative evaluations about those who inhabit 'subordinated' bodies. NSMs, then, have come to define issues of difference and identity around social meanings about, and practices of, the body (Lewis et al., 2000). This has had implications not just for how we conceive and practise forms of democratic politics but also for the principles that underlie the organization of social welfare.

In relation to the argument here, there are two issues of particular relevance. First, their emphasis on bodily autonomy, integrity and identity has had a dual effect. On the one hand, it has meant that analytic attention has focused on links between inequalities inside production relations and inequalities in other social domains such as the family, community and civil society more generally. On the other hand, this has resulted in a call for an extension beyond participation in the labour market as the basis on which social rights are accorded. As will be shown later, it is not strictly accurate to suggest that the call for an expansion of the criteria on which social rights are accorded was voiced only in the late 20th century. For example feminists made this claim in the mid-1940s in response to the Beveridge proposals. It is more accurate to say that the social base of this call widened significantly and became increasingly vocal with the rise of the NSMs.

There has been a second effect of the analytical focus on the links between the body as an indicator of social difference and the legitimation of gendered, racialized and other forms of (non-class-based) social inequalities. This has been the shift from a predominant concern with inequalities in the benefits system, or those aspects of welfare concerned with the (re)distribution of material goods. Recognition of other forms of inequality has widened the analytic horizon to take in welfare services and relations between users and professionals in order to explore and challenge the ways in which practices of service delivery are premised upon and produce patterns of inequality and social difference. In particular, feminists, anti-racists, and disabled rights and gay and lesbian activists have sought to analyse and expose some of the ways in which welfare services contribute to the formation of structured inequalities and the hierarchical ordering of difference (Harrison, 2001).

Developments in Social Theory: The Production of Social Difference

Alongside these activist challenges and claims, the impetus that has led to a concern with social difference – and the inequalities attached to its numerous forms – has come from developments and shifts in social and cultural theory. Grouped under the umbrella term 'poststructuralism', these new perspectives have widened the terms of debate and inquiry within social policy beyond a focus on issues of the production, distribution and administration of welfare resources; and beyond a concern with the patterns of access or participation of particular groups. The rise of poststructuralist perspectives in the social sciences generally and their entry into social policy has meant that new questions, objects of enquiry and dimensions of analysis have emerged. While retaining a concern with the dynamics of power embedded within and (re)produced by the system of social welfare, poststructuralist approaches shift attention away from a sole focus on the state, the logic of capital or patterns of class inequality as the objects of analysis in social policy. 'Power' remains a concept central to any poststructuralist understanding of the social practices of welfare, but in new and multifarious ways. One way of expressing the new dimensions added by poststructuralist approaches is captured by O'Brien and Penna (1998: 8), when they write that

> social welfare can [also] be conceptualized as a discourse ... a 'discourse of social welfare' comprises an organization or matrix of knowledges – a culturally constructed and politically sanctioned framework defining experience and for realizing definitions in practice. A discourse of social welfare gives definition to the world in both the conceptual and material senses of this term.

The effect of this has been to call into question the categories and assumptions standing at the very heart of social policy as both academic subject and welfare practice. This approach requires some explanation and it is appropriate to begin with the notion of 'the subject'. One feature of the many theoretical approaches grouped under the umbrella term 'poststructuralism' is their emphasis on language and meaning. In these approaches, language does not simply describe things that pre-exist society and culture. Rather language is conceived as an active force that brings into being – or constitutes – that which it apparently describes. In this sense, the meaning of something arises from the workings of language itself. Meanings occur in an organized system and act to position people and things in a regular system of relationships. For example, the binary pair man/woman places people called one or the other in a social relationship that has some regularities within specific systems of meaning. This process is what O'Brien and Penna are referring to in the quotation cited above. So what we call something, the name we give it, signals a whole field of social meanings, thereby making the thing named socially intelligible. This system of organized meaning is referred to as 'discourse'.

Discourses have a number of features. They involve statements about a topic; they govern what is sayable or knowable about a topic; they produce certain types of people – or subjects – who are then seen as 'authentic' or the 'real' thing. Some discourses become the hegemonic way of understanding a topic or category of person and achieve the position of 'truth'. As a result, they prescribe what can and should (or cannot and should not) be said or done about something. That is, they define what is appropriate institutional or professional practice, for example, of the school/teacher, social security agency/benefits worker, the social services department/social worker and so on. However, discourses also change in different historical moments and are open to contestation. Discourses, then, are fields of knowledge which define what is knowable about a topic/category of person and subordinate or silence other forms of interpretation.

Because one effect of discursive power is its capacity to constitute – or bring into being – particular types of people, or 'subjects', discourses are central to the constitution of social difference. Take, for example, the categories 'mother' or 'ethnic minority'. Each of these names is apparently self-evident, referring to individuals or groups defined by some biological or cultural characteristics – they are seen as naturally occurring. However, the poststructuralist suggestion that these names do not describe any property inherent to these categories implies that these names refer to social not natural categories. The term 'subject' refers to the ways in which people or groups are 'formed' or constituted through the meanings attached to particular names or labels. This is referred to as the 'discursive constitution' of the subject (Hollway and Jefferson, 2000).

The example of a recipient of welfare benefit provides an illustration of this process. One feature of the restructuring of welfare in the UK which began in the 1980s was a profound change in government, and to some extent public, attitudes to unemployment and social security benefits. This change expressed a shift away from the post-war ideas that such benefits were reflections of citizenship rights and commitment by the state to guarantee minimum income levels. In place of this, a new idea came to top the government's (and others') agendas and this was that such benefits encouraged dependence and eroded individual responsibility and enterprise (Hughes and Lewis, 1998). The result was the renaming of unemployment benefit as 'jobseeker's allowance', and a change in the name of the recipient from unemployed claimant to 'jobseeker'. Such a name change reflected the emergence of

> three premises: that social security had to be adapted to meet the needs of a flexible labour market; that employment provided the best defence against poverty; and that social security policies should be active rather than passive. (Walker and Howard, 2000: 40)

A new 'subject' had been created in the process and was formed now in the image of employment and personal responsibility rather than citizenship and collective responsibility.

This approach to the production of social knowledge has profound implications for social policy and the issue of difference. It represents a radical departure from the empiricism of much social policy orthodoxy, which is premised on the idea that welfare needs are simply there to be discovered through the application of research instruments such as the social survey or, more locally, by the client questionnaire or assessment form. In this context, the duty of social policy and welfare agencies is to meet these needs through the application of rational, objective and bureaucratic or managerialist procedures.

However, in arguing that 'knowledge' is a socially constituted category through which power is manifest and deployed, poststructuralist approaches destabilize the notion of a universal human subject whose needs can be known through the application of rational, bureaucratic procedures. In this sense, the ontological status of 'the universal subject' of Fabian or social democratic welfare is opened to deconstructive scrutiny. So too are the methods of categorization and description of such subjects. At the same time, the assumptions of the 'rational actor' within the bureau-professional machine of welfare provision are called into question.

Poststructuralism's positive effect has been to place the issues of difference, identity and particularity onto the social policy agenda. This is achieved by the insistence on exploration of categories, practices and relations that were previously assumed or taken for granted. Some examples are: questioning the naturalness of the social relations of care and their gendered dimensions; challenging the idea that welfare professionals have a superior knowledge of service user needs and how to meet them, in, say, relation to children or people defined as disabled; or that there are specific pre-social groups called 'ethnic minorities' who have specific cultural needs. This has a number of methodological implications that are relevant to social policy. As already mentioned, the refusal to treat social differences as pre-social or as essential characteristics of particular groups or individuals draws attention to them as the outcomes of processes of *subject formation*. Pushed by the political challenges of NSMs, the emerging poststructuralist social policy is seeking to understand the relationship between the knowledges and practices of social welfare and the production of a wide array of social differences, including those of ethnicity, gender, class and sexuality. Centrally, exploration of this link involves conceptualizing *difference as a set of social practices*. As Himani Bannerji (1998: 289) puts it, difference should be thought of in terms of the 'social relations of power and ruling, not as what people intrinsically *are*, but what they are ascribed as in the context of domination'. The convergence of new forms of social activism, on the one hand, and intellectual developments, on the other, have had two main effects. First, they have led to the issue of social difference becoming an increasingly important concern for social policy. Second, they have demanded that a wider set of inequalities be recognized and addressed and the developments in theory have offered alternative ways of understanding how social differences and their inequalities are socially constituted. Differences once seen as natural, even if encumbered with inequality, are now potentially understandable as the product or outcome of the social dynamics of power and meaning.

In the attempt to challenge and dislodge the forms of inequality connected to social differences, new social identities and political constituencies have been convened around dimensions of difference. In this sense, we can say that social differences also emerge from the challenges to domination and inequality and the struggle for self-defined identities. Thus social differences are formed in the dynamic interplay between domination and the struggle against it; between the attempt to establish the boundaries of the normal and attempts to dislodge and/or expand those boundaries; between the attempts to limit the criteria of access to resources (including those of welfare) and the struggle to breach or replace those criteria. The result of all this is that previously unrecognized social divisions and identities, such as those formed around subordinations or exclusions attached to race, disability, age and gender difference, have reconfigured the social policy agenda.

Approaching Social Differences of Gender and Ethnicity: The New Orthodoxies

So far we have argued that the issue of social difference became a concern for social policy, in both its senses, because of the combined effects of the claims made by a diverse array of NSMs and new ways of theorizing social life and systems of meaning. The impression given of these two forces as separate is to some extent false. It presents an artificial picture because part of the way that claims were made was in the form of analyses of the inequalities embedded in the welfare state and the assumptions that underpinned it. These analyses resulted in the development of theoretical explanations of the welfare state as structured through forms of gendered, racialized, heteronormative and disablist inequalities.

These critiques and claims for greater equality resulted in their turn in an attempt by welfare agencies to understand and rectify how their modes of operation were reinforcing inequalities. Through the adoption of things such as equal opportunity or diversity strategies, agencies were attempting to respond to the newer understandings about the dimensions and sources of inequality and promote greater equality of access and experience for an array of service users defined through their difference.

Important as these were, we want to point to a significant limitation in the way in which social differences were conceived and responded to. The core of the argument here rests on two propositions. First, that despite recognition that social policy operates in the context of highly differentiated populations, there is still a tendency to conceive multiple dimensions of difference as singular and mutually exclusive. For example, both gender difference and inequality and racialized difference and inequality are treated as if they are unconnected. One problematic effect of this is that gender is deemed to reference women – as opposed to women *and* men – and, in the discourse of universalism which still prevails in social policy these women are assumed to be white. This process of excluding men, masculinity and racialization from strategies to deal with gendered inequalities is the result of two, interconnected processes. There is the idea that because concerns with gender emerged as part of an agenda to promote greater equality, the focus had to be on those who were positioned as subordinate. This necessarily excluded men – and practices of masculinity – because, collectively these were privileged in the current social relations of welfare. More recently, there has been a greater awareness of gender as a relational category and this has led to the recognition that equality strategies need to pay attention to the relation between the subordinate and the dominant. At the same time, race and ethnicity have tended to be conceived as relevant only to black, Asian or other people positioned as minority ethnic. Whiteness – and therefore the people discursively positioned as ethnic majority and the universal norm – is seen as outside the remit of a strategy to address racialized inequalities. This is because of a logic similar to that operating in relation to gendered inequalities.

The second proposition central to the argument here is that despite the emergence of a more complex understanding of inequalities in social policy, there is still a proclivity to maintain a binary divide between the universal and the particular (universality and difference). This issue is considered in more detail in the next section. In the rest of this section, we consider further the issues raised above.

The problem with approaching gender, race and ethnicity as separate modalities or spheres of difference has both an empirical and a theoretical dimension. Empirically, gendered subjects are always also racialized or ethnicized subjects, just as racialized and ethnicized subjects are always also gendered (just as they are classed and aged). In policy discourses, these correspond to categories such as 'white male', 'white female', 'Jewish woman', 'black male' or 'African-Caribbean woman'. Similarly, as embodied welfare subjects, such persons engage with the organizational structures and practices of welfare agencies and are greeted through the discursive spectacles that dominant knowledges construct around social differences. For example, the assumption that issues of ethnicity would not be relevant to a service user who is white-skinned and speaks fluent English.

Theoretically centring the intersectionality or mutual constitution of differences of gender, race or ethnicity is also essential; for it is not possible to understand or analyse the *processes* by which categories of difference are constituted, or the subjects they interpolate, if they are conceived as distinct and separable theoretical or empirical dimensions. Avtar Brah (1996) uses the example of ethnicity to capture both the relational character of social differences and their intersection or mutual constitution in this way:

> Ethnicity is not about communicating a pre-given, already existing cultural difference. Rather, it is the process whereby one group seeks to distinguish itself and mark its own distinctiveness from another, drawing upon a variety of historically variable criteria. (p. 237)

> it is important to stress that both black and white people experience their gender, class and sexuality through 'race'. Racialization of white subjectivity is often not manifestly apparent to white groups because 'white' is a signifier of dominance, but this renders the racialization process no less significant. It is necessary, therefore, to analyse the processes which construct us as, say, 'white female' or 'black female', as 'white male' or 'black male'. This is necessary if we are to decipher how and why the meanings of these words change from plain descriptions to hierarchically organized categories under given economic, political and cultural characteristics. (pp. 105–6)

The emphasis here is on *process* and *relationality*, that is, forms of social difference come about in interaction with each other and in concrete social, economic, cultural and, we would add, organizational situations and relationships. However, this mutually constitutive relation tends to get lost in both academic analyses and policy formulations.

For example, feminist theory and practice are aimed at revealing and challenging the inequalities rooted in ideologies of biological variations of sex, including how such ideologies have affected forms of social welfare. In the wake of debates within feminism between middle-class and working-class, black, Asian and white women, lesbian, bisexual and heterosexual women, to name a few, there has been an increasing understanding that there is no single or unitary category of 'woman'. Instead, many feminists now recognize multiple 'womanhoods' that reflect differences in social condition which are themselves linked to inequalities of class, racism or heterosexism. Such differences in social condition mean that there are multiple ways of experiencing and identifying with what it means to be a woman. Such variation affects all aspects of social and psychic life including position within and experience of social relations of welfare. However, despite this growing understanding of the multiple ways in which gender difference is lived, much of the feminist social policy written by white women proceeds as if there is a single binary divide between women and men. One example is the literature on care, where, despite notable exceptions (Graham, 1991; Meyer, 2000), the tendency is to homogenize the category 'women' and pay no attention to variations of class, racism or other dimensions that produce differences of social condition (for one example, see Daly and Lewis, 1998).

In relation to the policy universe, many contemporary policy documents emanating from diverse welfare agencies appear to have recognized this complexity of the dynamics of difference. However, upon closer examination, it is apparent that there is still a tendency to treat dimensions of difference as discrete and even as naturalized, pre-given categories and behaviours. The following series of quotations, taken from a tool kit aimed at helping to create cultural sensitivity in NHS mental health organizations in order better to meet the particularistic needs of ethnic minorities, illustrates this process:

> The NHS was conceived with the fundamental principle of equality of service provision for all. However it has been acknowledged that there are major variations in the service delivery and treatment (health outcomes) for some groups. Delivering effective services to meet the mental health needs and concerns of minority ethnic communities in Britain has long been recognised as problematic. For example, suicide rates are higher for Asian women and young black men, and schizophrenia diagnosis rates are higher for African and Caribbean men (especially second generation). ... Undoubtedly, there are inequalities in health service provision.
>
> ...
>
> A number of key health policy documents highlight issues relating to minority ethnic groups, such as fair access to services. The *NHS Plan* notes that people in minority ethnic communities are less likely to receive the health services they need. The *National Service Framework (NSF) for Mental Health* emphasises existing services' insensitivity to people of African and Caribbean ethnicity and notes that assessment procedures are inadequate for Asian communities. The NSF also stresses that minority ethnic groups (including refugees) suffer from social exclusion that compounds their mental health problems.
>
> ...
>
> Measuring cultural sensitivity is important for meeting national requirements and providing excellent services. An audit tool can provide performance indicators to show evidence that, for example, people from minority ethnic groups have been properly assessed and cared for, and that assessment and care are improving. It can be used to elicit users' views. (Sainsbury Centre for Mental Health, 2001: 3–4)

These excerpts make it clear that providers of welfare services are concerned to meet particularistic needs of groups demarcated by some form of social difference. They also show that there is a degree of recognition that specific needs may also be linked to more than one dimension of difference. In these examples, mental health patterns seem to be linked to both gender and ethnicity. However, the policy approach also illustrates some of the conceptual weaknesses discussed above. Both ethnicity and gender are apparently conceptualized as pre-given – a user is straightforwardly 'an Asian woman' or an 'African or Caribbean man'. The way to understand the significance of these factors for the mental health services that such individuals require is to be culturally sensitive and this in turn requires becoming familiar with a set of pre-given cultural characteristics associated with these groups.

Such an approach is problematic because, while aiming to create greater equality, it fails to see that modalities of social difference – and the inequalities attached to them – are produced relationally; that is, through concrete social relations and interactions such as the process of assessment for mental health, physical health and social care or the dynamics of daily life in the classroom or lecture theatre. It is this process of simultaneous and continual restatement and production of social differences that is meant when we say that ethnicity and gender are contingent forces and categories. However, to say that they are contingent is not to say that their enactment and reproduction do not take identifiable forms or patterns of inequality. It is, though, to say that attempts to tackle such inequalities need to be grounded in an understanding that they are social and relational categories, not pre-given, asocial or static ones that simply interact with wider social processes.

There is a second, connected and perhaps even more profound problem summoned by the approach conveyed in the policy cited above. This is the unspoken assumption of a universal, unspecific subject that apparently stands at the heart of current methods of service delivery. It is this issue that we discuss in the following section.

Rethinking the Universal

Having suggested that the issue of difference entered the social policy agenda on the cusp of the 20th and 21st centuries, we now want to qualify this claim in order to restate it. This qualification and restatement has two objectives. First, by qualifying this claim, we suggest that issues of difference have, in fact, been central to social policy and social welfare throughout the 19th and 20th centuries. For the 20th century, we will illustrate this with a brief consideration of the 1942 Beveridge Report on *Social Insurance and Allied Services* (for evidence of the centrality and operation of some of the ways in which notions of difference were central to 19th-century practices of social welfare, see Lewis, 1998). The second objective is to use this qualification as the conduit to the restatement. Here the focus will be on a consideration of how we might use the enriched understanding of difference that we now have to distinguish between universal rights of access and equality of experience and universalism as implying a normative subject against which a series of particulars emerge.

Ellison (1999) has reminded us that a commitment to a universalist ethic was a founding principle of the welfare state inaugurated in the Beveridge reforms of the 1940s and inscribed in T.H. Marshall's (1950) theory of social citizenship that these reforms instantiated. The universalist principle connected citizens, welfare and the state by according all those belonging to a given polity – here the nation-state of the UK – the right to a state-guaranteed minimum standard of living. It was universal because it was the status of citizen that accorded this right regardless of other sectional interests or disparities between social groups. There were three principles underlying the recommendations on social security in the Beveridge Report. These three principles reflected a vision of a wide-ranging social policy that transcended sectional interests and connected state and individual:

> The plan for Social Security set out in this Report is built upon these [three] prin-
> ciples. It uses experience but is not tied by [specific] experience. It is put forward
> as a limited contribution to a wider social policy, though as something that could
> be achieved now without waiting for the whole of that policy. It is, first and fore-
> most, a plan of insurance – of giving in return for contributions benefits up to
> subsistence level, as of right and without means test, so that individuals may build
> freely upon it. (Beveridge, 1942, paragraph 10)

This report was, of course, a set of recommendations about how to secure the citizenry against want and, in declaring this as one of 'five giants', it explicitly recognized that there were other dimensions to social policy that needed tack-ling. But the universalist principle was to prevail across each of them.

As we have already seen, the universalist ethic was subjected to serious chal-lenges from the mid-1970s, as political constituencies outside the labour movement became increasingly vocal and effective in challenging the social politics of welfare and as economic recession and welfare retrenchment under-mined the welfare state's economic base. And as we have also seen, it was in the context of this contradictory pincer movement that the issue of social difference entered the social policy agenda. However, even prior to the chal-lenges that arose after the mid-1970s, the way that difference, especially gender difference, was scored through the universalist ethic was apparent. Again the Beveridge Report illustrates the point, making it clear that as a policy aimed at insuring against want, the contract was between those in employment, and therefore making contributions, and the state. However, it also makes it clear that a strategy against want must acknowledge two social facts: the position of married women and variations in family size:

In any measure of social policy in which regard is had to facts, the great majority of married women must be regarded as occupied on work which is vital although unpaid, without which their husbands could not do their paid work and without which the nation could not continue. In accord with facts the Plan for Social Security treats married women as a special insurance class of occupied persons and treats man and wife as a team. (Beveridge, 1942: 52)

In relation to variations in family size, the plan sought to build into its policies a system of providing allowances for children. During times of unemployment, the plan proposed that levels of allowance should take into account differential family size. Alongside this, the policy also provided for allowances for children at times of employment. Thus the system of social insurance would have built into it a mechanism for adjusting income to family size:

Without such [children's] allowances as part of benefit or added to it, to make provision for large families, no social insurance against interruptions of earnings can be adequate. But, if children's allowances are given only when earnings are interrupted and are not given during earnings also ... evils [of want] are unavoidable. (Beveridge, 1942: 8)

What is clear from these extracts is that family units are assumed and that the family member who is socially insured – assumed to be the man – would be the conduit to income security for his dependants.

A plethora of feminist scholarship since the 1970s (Wilson, 1977; Land, 1980, Lewis, 1983; Lister, 1990; Pascall, 1993) has pointed to the profound gender inequalities that resulted from this assumption about a heteronormative gender division of labour. But even when the report was first published, contemporary feminists were pointing to the ways in which it institutionalized women's dependence and thereby undermined their status as autonomous citizens. For example, the Women's Freedom League (1943) argued that:

men and women should in marriage not be treated as a 'team' but as individuals each paying equal contributions and receiving equal benefits; and that in every case men and women should pay the same and receive the same benefits.

And a pamphlet by Abbott and Bompass (1943: 3) stated that:

It is where the Plan falls short of being really national in character. Where it shuts out or exempts from all direct participation over nine million adult women, where it imposes special financial burdens on men alone, instead of spreading them equitably over all, that it fails ... The error – an error which lies in the moral rather than the economic sphere – lies in denying to the married woman, rich or poor, house-wife or paid worker, an independent personal status. From this error springs a crop of injustices and complications and difficulties, personal, marital and administrative, involving in the long run men both married and unmarried and the unmarried as well as the married woman.

What this points to is that difference is already a constitutive principle of a universalist social citizenship. To be a citizen – with universal rights – presumes an ability to adopt or meet the criteria that define the universal, including the capacity to participate in what is deemed to be the common culture (Marshall, 1950). As Yeatman (1994: 85) points out, such persons are 'those who can achieve independent status as freely contracting individuals via market activity', and in relation to the universal principle inscribed in Beveridge, it is labour market activity. The 'others' of this citizen, as Yeatman (1994: 84) argues, are all those who

by the assertion of a disembodied, rationalist principle of generality (whether this is that of the rational state or of market transaction) are excluded from this ideal. These others include all whose bodies require special provision – who are consti-tuted as dis-abled in respect of the norm – and all who are regarded by their occu-pational placement or culture as unable to attain the impersonal, rational and disembodied practices of the model citizen.

The force of feminist critiques such as these lies in the ways that they point to the exclusionary effects of the universalist ethic embedded in the post-war welfare state. Whether this be the result of the gendered assumptions of the male breadwinner or the construction of the welfare subject in disembodied and rationalist terms, the discourses and practices of social welfare have been and are profoundly implicated in the production of social differences and inequalities.

The critiques and claims of feminist, anti-racist, gay and lesbian, and disabled rights activists and other constituencies of users point to a significant theoretical tension within the principle of universalism. This is the distinction between, on the one hand, the universalist principle of equal access to, and quality of experience of, welfare services and, on the other, the construction of a universal or normative subject positioned at the heart of the social rela-tions of welfare. The emergence of the question of difference as a key issue facing social policy makes it clear that both these dimensions have to be addressed if the goal of greater equality and social justice is to be achieved. However, it is also clear that a theoretical distinction between them must be maintained in order that the organization and delivery of social welfare does not simply reproduce a set of social differences and inequalities. Devising and implementing a system of universal access to the whole range of welfare benefits and services is itself a complex task (as the post-war history of welfare shows) and involves thinking about how differences in social condition should or could influence criteria of access. Issues that need to be considered include the following. To what extent and in what areas of welfare should material wealth determine access to benefits or services? To what extent should residence in a particular nation-state be the criteria of entitlement to the full range of services and benefits as opposed to legal citizenship? Should involvement in paid employment be regarded as the primary condition determining the degree of entitlement?

There are many more issues. But conceptualizing welfare through the lens of difference makes it clear that it is equally important to dismantle the notion of a universal subject who stands above the particularities of social differences and instead conceive the population of welfare users as *all* equally constituted through particularity and difference. In this way, even the middle-class, white, English, Protestant, nuclear family that is currently positioned as the model welfare subject is incorporated as one kind of particularity reflecting difference of social condition. Instead of those defined through difference being hierarchically positioned in relation to an apparently transcendent (and normative) universal, social policy's project will be reconceived as one of how to promote social justice for a highly fragmented population of users and recipients. In this approach, difference itself becomes the universal condition. Rather than attempt to accommodate a range of differences while maintaining the inequalities that facilitate the making of a normative universal, social policy would be charged with seeking the mechanisms to devise equality of access and experience in the field of diversity.

Further Reading

Brah, A. (1996) *Cartographies of Diaspora*, London: Routledge.
Harrison, M. (with Cathy Davis) (2001) *Housing, Social Policy and Difference*, Bristol: Policy Press.
Isin, F., Engin, F. and Wood, P.K. (1999) *Citizenship and Identity*, London: Sage.
Lewis, G., Gewirtz, S. and Clarke, J. (eds) (2000) *Rethinking Social Policy*, London: Sage.

PART II

EVALUATING NEW LABOUR'S SOCIAL POLICY

Introduction

Contributions to this section examine recent developments in the core areas of British social policy. Drawing on many of the themes discussed in Part I, the chapters here provide accounts of New Labour's 'progress to date'. Verdicts are, at best, mixed. On the positive side, Finn, for example, acknowledges that some of the New Deal programmes have had a beneficial impact on levels of unemployment, while the 'single work-focused gateway' to the benefit system, the introduction of personal advisers and so on have gone some way to realizing Labour's vision of an 'employment first' welfare state, embedded in a welfare culture characterized by a strong emphasis on 'rights and responsibilities'. Further evidence of successful policy making is provided by Newburn, whose examination of reforms to the criminal justice system suggests that progress has been made in regard to the treatment of young offenders, particularly in relation to the shift away from the essentially punitive nature of the previous regime to one which attempts to incorporate elements of 'restorative justice'.

These positive judgements are reflected in many of the other contributions. Deacon, for instance, notes the beginnings of a decline in child poverty, for which the new tax credits for those in work are partly responsible, while Ford suggests that the government has done much to improve housing conditions and create more effective housing management. Morris argues that with the creation of the Disability Rights Commission, use of direct payments and recognition of the importance of service user involvement, New Labour has rightly acknowledged the kind of support required by people with disabilities for truly 'independent living'.

This picture of New Labour's record on welfare is undermined, however, by failures in other directions. Many contributions mention the tendency to stick too closely to unpopular or discredited Conservative policies. Finn states that Labour has continued with, and indeed increased, benefit sanctions for those failing to participate in employment programmes, while Deacon refers

107

to the continuation and enhancement of means testing in relation to social security, especially old age pensions where there are persistent problems of benefit 'take-up'. Ford notes that the basic market-oriented philosophy and approach to housing policy during the Conservative era have been maintained, with the private sector making further inroads into social housing. According to Brehony and Deem, however, it is in education that Conservative policies have not only been sustained but extended. They comment on the new emphasis on selection in the state secondary school system, as New Labour increasingly encourages a 'diversity' of schooling at this level, while also noting that greater reliance is being placed on the private sector as a way of 'revitalizing public policy' in this area. Looking to other areas, Atkinson refers to the numerous urban regeneration initiatives which have been developed by the government and comments on the failure to create the 'joined-up', coherent approach to urban policy originally envisaged when New Labour came to office. His main point is that the government has fallen victim to a certain narrowness of vision, which owes a good deal to previous Conservative administrations. There is too much stress on the employment aspects of regeneration and the seemingly constant changes, which have become such a notable feature of urban policy, are not only confusing but frequently ignore local conditions in favour of a more centralized model of social control.

'Centralization' is an important theme in this section, not least because of New Labour's oft-stated concern with *decentralization* through partnerships and other forms of local participation. Judging from the chapters here, it appears that the government is finding it difficult to strike the right balance between central and local control, leaving too little to local discretion in some areas and too much in others. In health policy, for instance, Glendinning argues that, certain continuities with Conservative policies apart, New Labour has made far-reaching reforms in the NHS, particularly in relation to GPs and the new primary care groups. GPs are now directly accountable to NHS management systems, which Glendinning regards as one example of 'the strengthening of central control under a cloak of devolutionary rhetoric'. Elsewhere, Newburn refers to the fact that the much-needed reforms to the youth justice system were accompanied by the creation of a 'powerful and controlling bureaucracy in the centre in the form of the YJB' (Youth Justice Board), which imposed central directives and performance measures on the new Youth Offending Teams, so depriving them of an important degree of local autonomy.

Conversely, it seems that in two policy areas, positive benefits could be gained from *greater* central control. Morris suggests that, in community care, a degree of centralization in the form of targets and performance indicators is both necessary and welcome, following the failure of Conservative attempts to improve service quality through the market. Although she is critical of the continuing paucity of resources devoted to community care as well as the inequalities which persist both among disabled people themselves and between those with disabilities and the rest of society, Morris acknowledges that centrally imposed targets for the social services are important if local good practice is to be monitored effectively. In the same vein, it may be that New Labour should seek to increase central control in transport policy. Page describes how the government lacks the political will to pursue potentially unpopular policies in relation to road transport and car usage, particularly in the wake of the fuel protests of September 2000, with obvious knock-on effects for the environment. More recently, the effective abandonment of the promise to shift travellers from road to rail – and continuing chaos on the rail-ways – has resulted in an extraordinarily fragmented and inefficient transport system. To be sure, these issues are complex and intransigent, as Page makes clear, but New Labour's reluctance to take greater central direction of trans-port contrasts markedly with its apparent willingness to do so in other areas.

CHAPTER 6

Employment Policy

DAN FINN

The 'jewel in the crown' of New Labour's first term in government was the performance of the economy and an increase in employment. Between May 1997 and the 2001 general election, the number of people in work increased from just over 27 million to more than 28.3 million and the number out of work and claiming jobseeker's allowance (JSA) fell from over 1.5 million to less than a million. In a White Paper, just before the last general election, the Prime Minister suggested that 'employment opportunities for all are in our grasp' and committed the government to work towards 'full employment with social justice' over the next decade (DfEE, 2001b: v).

Much credit for the success of New Labour's strategy has been attributed to relative economic stability and adept macroeconomic management but the Prime Minister also emphasized the contribution made by welfare reform. Welfare-to-work programmes had helped to 'overcome unemployment and disadvantage'. Reforms to the tax and benefit system also helped to 'make work pay' for those with dependent children. There was, however, 'more to do' and the Prime Minister committed the government to a further extension of 'employment opportunities to all' through the creation of an 'employment first' welfare state. This would ensure that the 'fruits of prosperity' reached the areas and groups of people who were still without work (DfEE, 2001b: v).

After the 2001 election victory, the government expressed the scale of its ambition by setting a range of targets to increase employment rates (especially for lone parents and in the most disadvantaged areas), reduce child poverty and tackle social exclusion. Key policy developments include the extension of tax credits to more of the low paid and reform of benefit rules to ease the transition to work. All working-age claimants were to attend 'work focused interviews' and New Deal programmes were to be intensified to reach 'harder to help' groups. The new approach also was accompanied by major institutional change. A Department of Work and Pensions (DWP) was created and the Employment Service (ES) and Benefits Agency (BA) have

111

been replaced by a 'Jobcentre Plus' Executive Agency. The aim is that, by 2005, the new agency will have integrated job search support and benefit payments for over six million people.

This agenda is formidable. The aim is to transform the primarily 'passive' support offered by the post-war welfare state into a more 'active' combination of services and benefits thought relevant to the employment and social conditions of the new century. Jobcentre Plus will be at the forefront of this transformation and will 'enshrine the principle that everyone has an obligation to help themselves, through work wherever possible'. In return, government has 'an equal responsibility' to provide work-related assistance for those 'who can' as well as ensuring 'greater security for those who cannot' (HM Treasury, 2001b: iv).

This chapter explains the background to New Labour's commitment to create an 'employment first' welfare state. It describes the New Deals and the interview-based regime now extended to all working-age benefit claimants. It also assesses the evaluation evidence to establish 'what worked' in the first phase of implementing the government's 'flagship' programme, the New Deal for Young People (NDYP). Finally, it identifies some of the challenges that confront the government if the rhetoric of an 'employment first' welfare state is to be realized in practice.

New Labour's Legacy: Remaking the Link Between Job Search and Benefit Entitlement

During the 1980s, the administrative link between job search and benefit receipt in Britain weakened significantly (Price, 2000). Between 1982 and 1986, unemployed people had to 'sign on' for their benefit at an unemployment benefit office and were not required to register with their local jobcentre. Reductions in the number of civil servants reduced the administrative capacity and inclination to both encourage and monitor job search and deter fraud. Even when employment started to recover, the data showed that a significant number of people claiming unemployment benefits had become 'inactive' and had stopped looking for jobs. The average duration of unemployment increased (Wells, 2000).

The turning point came in 1986 with the introduction of the 'Restart' initiative which involved mandatory job search reviews for anyone out of work for over six months. In 1989 it was followed by legislation requiring the unemployed to actively seek work and restricting the grounds on which they could refuse vacancies. This new regime was linked with radical institutional change in the unemployment market. In 1987–88 the delivery of training programmes for the unemployed was transferred to private sector-led Training and Enterprise Councils (Local Enterprise Companies in Scotland) and a 'modern' Employment Service was created as a 'Next Steps' Executive Agency. The ES immediately integrated unemployment benefit offices and jobcentres, thus creating a national network of over 1,100 jobcentres with about 35,000 staff. The ES worked closely with the larger, public sector BA which was responsible for the assessment and delivery of most social assistance and insurance benefits. The BA, however, played no role in delivering direct employment assistance.

Between the late 1980s and mid-1990s, the role of the ES changed significantly. The first trend involved reinforcing work incentives and monitoring the job-seeking behaviour of the unemployed. This was underpinned by the 'stricter benefit regime'. The second trend involved a move from longer term, labour market programmes towards low-cost measures aimed at stimulating job search. Both trends were underpinned by a performance targets regime geared to immediate job entry and removing people from the benefit system. The ES also was under constant pressure to reduce its operating costs and obtain better value for money (King, 1995; Price, 2000).

Over this period, the ES also became centrally involved in promoting the take-up of in-work state benefits. These were introduced to encourage benefit recipients with children to take low-paid and/or part-time jobs. In addition to housing and council tax benefit (claimable by low-paid workers), family credit, which directly supplemented wages, was gradually extended. By 1996 the credit was being received by over 600,000 families (many headed by lone parents), and ES officials were encouraging take-up through the production of individual 'better off in work' calculations. An earnings credit, available to people who left disability benefit, attracted far fewer claimants.

In this context, Britain's unemployed were redefined as 'jobseekers' by the 1996 Jobseekers Act (HMSO, 1994). Eligibility for the new job-seeker's allowance (JSA) required that unemployed individuals enter a jobseeker's agreement specifying the steps they intended to take to look for work and the minimum wages they would accept. ES staff were given a new discretionary power enabling them to issue a 'jobseeker's direction', requiring an individual to look for work in a particular way, to take other steps to 'improve their employability' or participate in job search programmes or training schemes. It was accepted that most unemployed people looked for jobs but the JSA regime was designed to intensify their activity and pressure those who were not genuinely looking for work. Following its introduction, JSA was estimated to have reduced the claimant count by between 100,000 and 200,000. This was partly due to tighter eligibility rules but also because JSA flushed out 'significant numbers of employed and inactive claimants from the count' (Sweeney and McMahon, 1998: 201). Evidence subsequently accumulated that the new regime increased job search activity among the more recently unemployed but was less effective with the long-term unemployed (Trickey et al., 1998).

By 1996, the British ES was able to promote itself as a high performance and high achievement agency with a reputation for implementing new national initiatives to short timescales. It could demonstrate that it had been administratively effective and had made a contribution to reducing unemployment, especially long-term unemployment, by engineering a close link between job brokering and benefit administration (Employment Select Committee, 1999, vol. I: xi). There was, however, controversy about the destination of those assumed to have benefited from the reduction in long-term unemployment. Sanctions increased, some of the long-term unemployed were 'churned' through programmes, others were placed in short-term jobs and many of the older, long-term unemployed were transferred to other benefits (Finn et al., 1998).

These criticisms were articulated by New Labour as it started to develop a very different approach to unemployment and social exclusion. The leadership welcomed the fall in unemployment but stressed that this masked the emergence of deep-seated problems. In particular, intergenerational unemployment continued to blight many disadvantaged areas; and in one in five UK households nobody of working age had a job. Economic activity rates were static and had fallen for older men. By 1996, over a million lone parents, mainly women, were dependent on state benefits; and the number of men receiving incapacity or long-term sickness benefits had doubled in a decade to over 1.7 million. Unlike the unemployed, most of the individuals of working age receiving other benefits had little contact with services and were likely to remain dependent for long periods of time. There was also considerable dissatisfaction among front-line ES staff and widespread scepticism about government employment 'schemes' among the unemployed, employers and providers (see for example, Employment Policy Institute, 1998).

Workfare, Redefining Full Employment and Welfare-to-work

From the late 1980s, the British approach to welfare reform and employment programmes was influenced by two major developments. There was an emerging international consensus about the importance of modernizing benefit systems so that they promoted labour market attachment and activity instead of paying 'passive' benefits (OECD, 1994). British policy makers were also influenced by the US debate on welfare dependency and workfare (Dolowitz, 1998). In the USA, the central argument maintained that the welfare state had become lax and that by giving income benefits without stronger work obligations, the state had undermined work incentives and encouraged the emergence of a dependent underclass (Murray, 1990). One of the key propositions to emerge from the USA was that individuals should 'work off' their benefit entitlement and that 'welfare' should be replaced by 'workfare'. Initially this was rejected by the Conservative government who had prioritized 'activation' through the introduction of the stricter benefit regime and JSA. However, just before it lost office, it had moved towards something like workfare through a proposed large-scale extension of 'Project Work' (a programme requiring the very long-term unemployed to work part time in projects of community benefit).

New Labour opposed Project Work but, by the mid-1990s, it dropped its previous opposition to compulsory programmes and JSA. This change reflected a transformation in New Labour's macroeconomic assumptions and its definition of full employment. New Labour had turned to the work of economists who challenged the view that the non-accelerating inflation rate of unemployment (NAIRU) had to be as high as it was in the UK. The new approach suggested that supply-side measures such as investment in human capital and labour market programmes could significantly lower unemployment, reduce public expenditure and help to create a more effective labour market (Layard et al., 1991). By 1995, Gordon Brown, the then Shadow Chancellor of the Exchequer, argued that government could not simply create jobs. Its role was to promote macroeconomic stability and provide 'economic and employment opportunities for all', a slogan subsequently characterized as the 'modern definition of full employment for the twenty-first century' (see for example, HM Treasury, 2001b). The first priority was to extend opportunities for the long-term unemployed and, in 1995, he committed a future government to the introduction of a 'New Deal for Britain's Under-25s' (Labour Party, 1995).

This extension of 'opportunity' through employment programmes was the core of New Labour's approach to welfare state reform. In a major 1997 speech, Tony Blair, the future Prime Minister, condemned Conservative policies 'which encourage(d) dependency and trap(ped) people in unemployment'. The alternative, however, was not merely to increase welfare state expenditure. The 'old equation of more spending and less injustice' was fundamentally flawed. Britain now spent more on the welfare state yet 'poverty, insecurity and inequality have increased on an unprecedented scale' (Blair, 1997a). The New Labour approach to welfare state reform would focus on services, 'not just cash benefits', and would be designed to 'help people meet change' in an increasingly insecure world. New Labour would champion 'fair but flexible labour markets' and increase 'the employability of our people through education and skills and an active employment service'.

One month after winning power, Prime Minister Blair confirmed that the 'greatest challenge' to his 'Welfare to Work' government was 'to refashion our institutions to bring the new workless class back into society' (Blair, 1997b). This speech was swiftly followed by the 1997 welfare-to-work budget which raised over £5 billion through a windfall tax on the profits of the privatized utilities. This was the first New Labour example of a 'hypothecated tax', in that the proceeds could be used only to fund the New Deal.

The New Deals

In the election, New Labour had pledged that during its first term in office it would help to find jobs for 250,000 18–24-year-olds who had been out of work for over six months. Financial and administrative priority was given to developing the NDYP and less well-resourced New Deals were swiftly introduced for the long-term unemployed, lone parents and people on disability benefits. By 2001, programmes had also been added for those aged over 50 and the partners of the unemployed. The objectives of the New Deals were to:

- increase long-term employability and help young and long-term unemployed people, lone parents and disabled people into jobs

- improve their prospects of staying and progressing in employment.

Each of the New Deals targeted the particular problems of a specific client group but they were all based on the principles first implemented in the programme for young people – 'more help, more choices, and the support of a Personal Adviser ... matched by a greater responsibility on the part of individuals to help themselves' (DfEE, 2001b: para. 1.33). This focus on support tailored to the needs of each individual was the 'key feature' that distinguished the New Deal 'from previous initiatives' (Hasluck, 2001: 230).

Despite the common framework, however, there are still significant differences in the level of resources allocated to each programme. Table 6.1 shows that the better funded New Deals have been the *compulsory* programmes targeted at the registered (predominantly male) unemployed. Far fewer resources have been allocated to *voluntary* programmes aimed at lone parents and people receiving disability benefits.

Table 6.1 New Deal employment programmes

	Start date	Estimated cost (£m 1997–03)	Number of participants (to November 2001)	Number of job entrants (to November 2001)
New Deal for young people	April 1998	1,470	731,900	345,000
New Deal 25 plus	June 1998	640	353,300	62,410
New Deal for lone parents	October 1998	340	305,030 (joined case load)	127,920
New Deal for disabled people	April 1999	165	20,000 (to June 2001)	8,000
New Deal for partners of the unemployed	April 1999	65	n/a	n/a
New Deal for people aged 50 plus	April 2000	65	n/a	n/a

Sources: Figures taken from pre-budget report, 2001 and show planned windfall tax expenditure on the New Deal (HM Treasury, 2001b). Data on NDDP participants and job entrants from HM Treasury (2001b: 29). Source for participants and job entrants on other New Deals: unpublished performance papers given to the New Deal National Employers Panel Performance Sub-Group, February 2002

New Deal Participation and Work-focused Interviews

Participation in the New Deals for the registered unemployed commences with an advisory 'Gateway' process. A personal adviser helps tackle employment barriers and provides assistance with job search, careers advice and guidance. If an individual is unable to get an unsubsidized job then they are required to participate in an employment or training option, which in the NDYP consists of:

• the employment option which provides a subsidized, waged job for six months with an employer

• the environmental task force (ETF) or voluntary sector option which provides up to six months' employment in a job with a wage or a 'benefits plus £15' package

• the full-time education and training option (FTET) which can last for up to a year.

All the options involve vocational training and there is a follow through process of advice and support for those unemployed at the time they complete their option. By the end of 2001 more than three-quarters of a million unemployed young people had entered the programme. There were, however, only 80,500 active participants, of whom about 60 per cent were in the Gateway (regular New Deal operating data can be accessed through www.cesi.org.uk).

Young people aged under 25 are usually required to enter the New Deal after six months' unemployment. For those aged over 25, a minimal New Deal programme originally was targeted at those out of work for over two years. In April 2001 this was replaced by a more intensive New Deal and those out of work for over 18 months must now participate or be subject to the same benefit sanction regime applied to the younger age group. The only significant variation involves 15 Employment Zones (see below).

Significantly, New Deal programmes for working age people, previously regarded as 'economically inactive', are being implemented within a mandatory, 'rights and responsibilities', framework. The childless partners of unemployed claimants, who are aged between 18 and 24, now are required to register as unemployed and, when eligible, to enter the New Deal. This requirement gradually is being extended to the childless partners of older unemployed people and the partners of those receiving other working-age benefits.

Participation in the less resource-intensive New Deals for Lone Parents (NDLP) and for people with disabilities (NDDP) remains voluntary, but attendance at '*work-focused interviews*' (WFI) is now mandatory. Lone parents who claim income support have to attend an initial WFI, and another six months later. Thereafter they have to attend annually. Most other working-age claimants have to attend an initial WFI and are then required to attend when their circumstances change or at least once every three years. The government is testing a more intensive interview regime for new incapacity benefit recipients and this is likely to be extended (DWP, 2002). A small number of claimants are exempt from WFIs and a variety of 'good cause' clauses allow for their deferral. Crucially, apart from the JSA unemployed, other working-age claimants cannot be required to participate in a programme or take a job.

Lone parents participating in the NDLP are referred to a personal adviser who guides them about potential jobs or skill development opportunities and gives them advice about childcare support. There is no formal 'menu' of options but, as the programme has evolved, access to training has been extended for those unready for job entry (Millar, 2002). By March 2002, over half of those leaving NDLP had got jobs which took them off income support, and another one in ten had taken up education or training. There was evidence that mandatory interviews had increased participation, with one in five agreeing to join the NDLP caseload (compared with between five per cent and ten per cent in the voluntary phase) (TUC, 2002: 9). The programme has been supplemented by increased financial support for child-care (delivered through tax credits) alongside a national childcare strategy which, it is claimed, will deliver 'a childcare place for every lone parent entering employment in the most disadvantaged areas' by 2004 (HM Treasury, 2001b: 29). The employment rate for lone parents increased from 44 per cent to 51 per cent between 1997 and 2001, and the NDLP and these other measures are central to securing the government's target of increasing the employment rate to 70 per cent by the end of the decade (National Council for One Parent Families, 2001: 7).

The New Deal programme for people with disabilities has been developed as a series of pilots and, since June 2001, is delivered through a 'national network of Job Brokers'. These NDDP brokers have flexibility in how they provide assistance and are paid by results, including a bonus payment for those whose participants are still in work after six months. The NDDP is only a small part of the government's strategy. The most significant element has been the introduction of new rights at work through anti-discrimination legislation, which are intended to increase employment for people with disabilities. The government has also introduced many 'micro' changes to disability eligibility rules and it is are starting to develop a package of employment options and advice services designed to provide a more 'coherent' system aimed at encouraging people on disability benefits to take up job opportunities (DWP, 2002).

The national New Deal programmes have been supplemented by area-based employment initiatives aimed at reducing long-term unemployment and joblessness in particular localities. The Employment Zones (EZs) are testing the concept of 'personal job accounts' for JSA claimants aged over 25 who have been out of work for over 18 months (or 12 months in a few zones). If an individual is selected, then participation is mandatory. The EZs are delivered by private sector contractors who have flexibility in deciding the content of employment assistance and are paid through an output-related funding system. In effect, the EZs are testing an alternative, both in terms of content and delivery, to the national New Deal model.

In another 20 areas, broader 'Employment Action Teams' are also being tested. The teams work with all 'jobless' people to 'support radical, innovative ways' of tackling 'specific local problems and obstacles to jobmatching'. The effectiveness of these voluntary programmes will be assessed through their impact on local employment rates. These area-based initiatives are expected to build 'synergy' between their activities, the New Deals and the regeneration programmes being supported through other government interventions, such as the 'New Deal for Communities' and the single regeneration budget (Social Exclusion Unit, 2001: 34).

'Making Work Pay'

The New Deals have been introduced alongside major tax and benefit reforms which, in combination with new rights at work (including the introduction of the national minimum wage), are aimed at 'making work pay'. One of the government's major objectives has been to replace the inherited 'in-work benefit system', paid through the BA, with a tax-credit system paid through employers and the Inland Revenue. Working families' tax credit (WFTC) was designed to help low-paid families with children and replaced family credit in October 1999. At the same time, a disabled person's tax credit (DPTC) replaced the disability working allowance. A childcare tax credit also replaced the 'childcare disregard' which was a feature of the two earlier benefits.

The government has promoted 'credits' as a key element of its welfare-to-work strategy and the introduction of a more generous level of payment increased recipient levels. By the end of 2001, WFTC was being received by 1.25 million families, with 145,000 benefiting from the childcare tax credit (HM Treasury, 2001b: 30). Simultaneously, about 29,000 disabled workers were in receipt of DPTC. The budget for tax credits has been significant and in its forecast for 2001–02, the government estimated it would spend 'an extra £6,000m on increased benefits and tax credits aimed at low-income families'. By contrast New Deal expenditure was estimated at about £900 million (Robinson, 2000: 25).

One consequence of tax credits for domestic couples was that payment went to the earner rather than the primary carer. This shift from 'purse' to 'wallet' raised important issues about the uneven distribution and control of household income (Goode et al., 1998). Subsequently, the government decided to disentangle the work incentive and child support elements of tax credits and in 2003 introduced a separate employment credit for low-paid workers and an integrated child credit for carers. The employment credit is underpinned by the minimum wage and is now available for most low-paid workers, including single people and childless couples, although it will not initially be extended to single people aged under 25 (HM Treasury, 2001b).

There are methodological and technical complexities to be considered in assessing the income and work incentive effects of the new tax credits (see for example, Brewer et al., 2001). Tax credits and increased child benefit have played a key role in reducing child poverty, although the Prime Minister had to acknowledge that the number of children lifted out of relative poverty was closer to half a million rather than the one million they had previously claimed (Blair, 2002a). Tax credits have also eased the 'unemployment' and 'poverty traps', by their relative generosity, ensuring that an individual is entitled to more money from work than from benefits. Nevertheless, the policy approach has been criticized for extending 'dependency' into employment; extending 'means testing' up the salary scale; complex and confusing regulations for employers and applicants; and concern about the potential impact on work incentives and employer wage-setting behaviour (Green, 1999).

Delivering the 'Employment First Welfare State': The Employment Service and Jobcentre Plus

New Labour gave the ES responsibility for delivering its New Deals. This decision provided continuity and enabled the incoming government to build its programmes on the JSA benefit regime. It gave the senior managers of the ES an opportunity to 'reinvent' the organization and rebuild its credibility with the unemployed, employers and other agencies. This involved the creation of a national network of New Deal partnerships; the introduction of a new generation of front-line personal advisers; contracting with a broad range of public, voluntary and private sector organizations for the delivery of new services and employment and training options; and changes to ES performance targets to encourage inter-agency working. Another key dimension of the strategy involved a major national political effort to engage employers and other organizations in the delivery of the New Deals.

While the government gave the public sector responsibility for delivering the New Deals, it also expanded the role of the private sector. Private sector organizations, in varying combinations with the ES, have been given contracts for delivering a broad range of employment programmes. New Labour was, however, less committed to the private sector-led Training and Enterprise Councils created in 1988. The government abolished them in England and replaced them with broader partnerships, the Learning and Skills Councils (LSCs), which are firmly based in the public sector. LSCs are responsible for distributing and allocating funding for all post-compulsory school-age education and training (apart from universities). They have been given a remit that includes improving the employability of disadvantaged groups but this is only one among their many competing priorities.

The most significant development in welfare-to-work service delivery was announced by the Prime Minister at the Labour Party conference in 1998 where he indicated that the government would create a 'single work-focused gateway' to the benefit system. By the end of 1999, twelve of what were then called 'ONE' pilots had been established to test ways of delivering the new service.

Evaluation evidence from the ONE pilots quickly illustrated the challenges this reorganization would face. There was incompatibility between the information systems of the different organizations, pressure from high caseloads and cultural differences among groups of staff. Ironically, the economically inactive received (and appreciated) a much better benefits advice service, but less than a third of lone parents and about a fifth of disabled people reported that they had discussed finding work or training (albeit this was higher than in comparable control group areas). Most job search activity was targeted at the regular unemployed. The 'most striking finding', according to a parliamentary inquiry, was 'how little effect the ONE pilots ... had on labour market outcomes' in comparison with control areas. The economically inactive did 'not appear to be being reached by the new work-focused agenda' (Work and Pensions Select Committee, 2002: para. 5).

In March 2000, Prime Minister Blair announced the most radical step yet, the merging of the ES and BA into a unified Working Age Agency (with housing benefit still separately delivered by local authorities). The new 'Jobcentre Plus' Agency would 'embed a culture of rights and responsibilities in the welfare system' and 'personal advisers will steer clients towards work or training' (Hansard, 16 March 2000: col. 257W). The aim is that by 2005 the agency will have integrated the work of 90,000 staff in 1,500 local offices, and will have modernized service delivery, particularly through the use of computers, telephones and online technologies. Jobcentre Plus offices are designed to reinforce the culture change. Largely open plan, they aim to deliver a 'queueless' professional service in a modern environment. The agency will be expected to process and pay benefits accurately and promptly, but the expectation is that clients will experience an 'employment first' approach.

The Jobcentre Plus regime is designed to avoid the confusion of the ONE pilots by separating the benefit advice and employment assistance elements of the claiming process. After contacting a 'customer service representative' through a call centre, a prospective claimant is allocated an interview where they are first seen by a 'benefit financial assessor'. They then see a personal adviser whose task is to assess employability and provide employment assistance. The JSA unemployed will be required to actively seek work and enter a New Deal after a specific duration of unemployment. Other claimants will be encouraged 'to think about work, joining a New Deal, or to participate in a series of voluntary meetings with a Personal Adviser to start preparing for work' (Work and Pensions Select Committee, 2002: 6). Inactive claimants who choose not to participate will undergo the same process when they attend their next WFI.

Evaluation and the Employment Impact of the New Deals

The New Deals have been subject to an intense evaluation programme. In addition to publishing monthly monitoring data, the government released over 60 official evaluation reports by the end of 2001. These studies assessed various aspects of the delivery, performance and impact of the evolving New Deals, WFIs and One pilots. The studies utilized a variety of methodologies and the intention has been that this accumulating evidence base should inform the development of policy and front-line implementation (for synthesizing reviews, see for example, Hasluck, 2000; Millar, 2000). This section reviews the evidence on the employment impact of the New Deals, especially the NDYP, the 'flagship' New Deal of the Labour government's first term in office, while the following section explores what the accumulated evaluation evidence tells us about what worked and did not work in the New Deal process.

At the end of 2000, the Labour government announced that it had reached its target of assisting 250,000 young unemployed people to find work through NDYP (DfEE, 2000). By the end of 2001, it was suggested that well over half a million people had found jobs through the various New Deals (see Table 6.1), and that some 53 per cent of NDYP leavers were entering employment. Just under 80 per cent of the jobs were 'sustained' for over 13 weeks. There is little information available about the quality of jobs taken by NDYP leavers but a national survey found high levels of job satisfaction among those in work 18 months after starting the programme and it reported some evidence of wage progression among those in employment (Bonjour et al., 2001).

In combination with continuing employment growth, the New Deals have helped to produce significant reductions in JSA unemployment, especially among the younger, long-term unemployed (McDonagh and Asvesta, 2002: Table 2). Between April 1997 and April 2002, the number of 18–24-year-olds out of work and claiming JSA for over 26 weeks (the point at which they enter the New Deal but are still receiving JSA) fell sharply from 87,700 to 39,800, a fall of over 55 per cent. The most dramatic impact was on those registered as unemployed for over a year, where the number fell from 90,700 to 5,100, a fall of almost 95 per cent. The reduction in the shorter term unemployed was less marked, with the number of those out of work for less than 26 weeks falling some 16 per cent, from 243,200 in April 1997 to 204,300 in April 2002. There were some cyclical factors at work but this data raises a concern that the New Deal might be 'recycling' some of the unemployed, rather than moving them directly into jobs (see below).

Establishing the *net* additional employment impact of the New Deals, the measurable economic difference they have made, is more complex. The most authoritative econometric findings come from evaluations of the NDYP carried out by the National Institute for Economic and Social Research (NIESR) (Anderton et al., 2000; Riley and Young, 2000) and the Institute for Fiscal Studies (IFS). Both studies concluded that there was a positive impact, with the IFS finding an 'economically and statistically significant effect on the flow of young men from JSA to employment' (Blundell, 2001: 34). The NIESR findings were themselves independently scrutinized by the National Audit Office, which judged that it was 'reasonable' to conclude that in its first two years NDYP was cost-effective, had directly reduced levels of youth unemployment by between 25,000 and 45,000, and increased youth employment by between 8,000 and 20,000 (NAO, 2002c: Part 3). These findings were borne out by a subsequent evaluation from the Policy Studies Institute which arrived at its estimates in a different way but which also found that the NDYP had reduced long-term youth unemployment and had positive impacts on youth employment (White and Riley, 2002). Evaluations of the New Deal for the over 25s and the NDLP suggest these programmes are also making net (if modest) additional impacts on employment outcomes (Lissenburgh, 2001; Millar, 2002).

There have been other, less favourable, assessments of the employment impact of the New Deals. Apart from those who suggest that the reduction in unemployment has simply reflected the strength of the economy, others point out that despite the reduction in long-term youth unemployment, about a third of those who participated in NDYP returned to unemployment and about one in five of those who did obtain a job failed to retain it for 13 weeks. Some of these young people are now entering the programme for a second or third time. This problem is most acute for young people from ethnic minorities and for those in many inner urban and depressed industrial labour markets where, it is suggested, the concentrated geography of unemployment leads to the 'recycling and churning' of participants and that local 'jobs gaps' have undermined the programme (Turok and Webster, 1998; Martin et al., 2001). In response, government economists have argued that appropriate vacancies arise in most local labour markets and that participation has reduced the 'scarring' effect of long-term unemployment, with those re-entering the programme exiting at the same rate as the newly unemployed rather than becoming 'detached' and entering long-term unemployment. In its 'next phase' of the New Deal, the government has responded by increasing efforts to achieve 'parity' of employment outcomes for ethnic minorities, and by introducing 'Step Up', a temporary job creation programme targeted at high unemployment areas and aimed at those who fail to get unsubsidized jobs after participating in the New Deal (DWP, 2001).

The 'net' employment outcomes of the NDYP remain contested and evaluation results for the other evolving welfare-to-work programmes, especially for lone parents and the older unemployed, have been challenged too. Nevertheless, the balance of the evidence supports the conclusion that the approach accelerates the return to work, especially of the long-term unemployed, and that the programmes contribute at least to some small net increase in employment (Blundell, 2001). What is less clear is whether the positive impacts associated with the NDYP and other programmes will be sustained, as more people pass through the various New Deals and as front-line staff grapple with the administrative challenge of implementing an 'employment first' regime.

What Worked in the New Deal: Opening the 'Black Box'

The initial phase of employment assistance offered through the Gateway period has been successful. Early planning assumptions were that 40 per cent of entrants would leave the New Deal from the Gateway. In reality, two-thirds of participants have left before taking up an option. The evidence shows a 'carrot and stick' effect, with most young people intensifying job search as a result of increased motivation and new techniques, with others doing so to avoid joining an option or benefit sanctions.

The introduction of personal advisers (NDPAs) has been welcomed by most participants. The evidence consistently has identified the intensive, individualized help from the NDPA as the key element of success (Legard and Ritchie, 1999; Thomas and Griffiths, 2002). Young people and lone parents place great value on having someone with whom they can build a relationship. At their best, advisers provide a wide range of individualized services, such as identifying barriers to work, helping with applications, contacting employers and discussing and clarifying employment goals. Unfortunately, not all NDPAs live up to their image and there have been concerns voiced regarding work pressures created by rapid policy changes and caseloads, with a greater proportion of people with more significant employment barriers. There has been disquiet among NDPAs working with the JSA unemployed regarding the balance to be struck between individual support and immediate job placement. One of the things valued in the New Deal was the shift away from the immediate job entry targets that had characterized the previous regime. By 2001, however, many felt, both inside and outside the ES, that the original individual focus of the NDYP was in danger of being undermined by a preoccupation with immediate job entry targets (Finn and Blackmore, 2002).

The weakest part of the NDYP has been in the options and 'follow through' phase, especially for those young people with significant employment barriers. Option providers have struggled to place more than 30 per cent of their participants into jobs. This underperformance has been attributable partly to the reality of clients with the greatest barriers and least motivation but also has reflected the tension felt by many providers about the extent to which they should or could fully focus on employment outcomes. This weakness has been compounded by the limited impact of the follow through process. Research with young people found 'marked differences' in the levels of follow through activity which ranged from 'intensive support to no identifiable post option activity' (O'Connor et al., 2000). Nevertheless, around 40 per cent of those leaving the follow through move into employment. Unfortunately this also means that nearly half of those leaving follow through have returned to the normal JSA regime.

Another weakness of NDYP was the uncertainty about what happened to those going to an 'unknown destination'. This 'disappearing' effect had been a characteristic of all the mandatory employment programmes introduced since the 1980s, but for the first time two surveys were to discover what happened to the one in three NDYP participants with 'destination unknown'. The most extensive survey, with a response rate of just below 50 per cent, led the researcher to conclude that he could find no discernible evidence that the most disadvantaged were disproportionately represented among those who could not be contacted (O'Donnell, 2001). Of the sample contacted, 56 per cent had initially left the New Deal to enter employment and just over 5 per cent reported that they had not been entitled to claim due to sanctions. Some had continued to 'sign on', others had been ill, and some had entered education or otherwise left the labour market. At the time of the survey, the status of the young people had changed, with 43 per cent reporting they were in work and 30 per cent JSA unemployed. The researchers found, however, that just under a third of those experiencing at least one of the living conditions associated with disadvantage (been in custody; slept rough; lived in a hostel/foyer; been in care) reported that they had left NDYP to enter full-time employment.

A broad range of agencies working with the most disadvantaged have stressed that the young people they work with tend to move in and out of jobs quickly and engage only intermittently with the New Deal (NDTF, 1998). The agencies have had some success when lobbying for improvements in the design of the programme but many have continued to express their concern that the disciplinary regime of the New Deals could exacerbate rather than help tackle social exclusion.

Initially the NDYP was covered by the existing JSA sanctions regulations but, in March 2000, the regime was intensified and, following a first sanction of two weeks' benefit withdrawal and a second of four weeks, an individual who fails to participate in the programme now loses benefit for 26 weeks. This regime was then extended to cover unemployed people aged between 25 and 50 who participate in the New Deal and/or EZ.

It has been difficult to measure the extent to which young people have been sanctioned but one estimate suggests that some 9 per cent may have experienced a benefit reduction during the Gateway phase (Gray, 2001: 378). During the option phase, the evidence on sanctions is clearer and the rate at which sanctions have been imposed has increased, with over 2,000 cases a quarter reported by 2001 (Working Brief, 2002: 6). These sanctions are imposed for either failing to attend, or leaving options without good cause, and they are largely experienced by poorly educated and less motivated young men with regard to participation in the ETF (Bonjour et al., 2001: 112–15). Although the number who experience a third sanction is small, qualitative evaluation has shown that while some then obtain a job, a significant minority of vulnerable young people had lost their benefits for six months and lost contact with services which should have assisted them (Saunders et al., 2001).

Despite the impact on this small minority, young unemployed people themselves express mixed responses when asked about benefit sanctions. Local case studies have found that although some resent the 'threat' to benefit entitlement, most accept that sanctions are justified either to put pressure on those not genuinely seeking work and/or to maintain discipline while participating in the programme (see for example, Finn and Blackmore, 2001).

Conclusion

New Labour's strategy for creating an 'employment first' welfare state has been subjected to much criticism. In a succession of journal articles, academics and others have assessed the merits of the New Deals and found them wanting. Many authors have concluded that the NDYP in particular is part of a coercive regime designed to make access to benefits more difficult and to increase competition for jobs at the lowest end of the labour market (see for example, Jeffs and Spence, 2000; Greater Manchester Low Pay Unit, 1999). The evidence reviewed in this chapter suggests that the reality of the new welfare state is more complex. The new programmes are not monolithic instruments of social control but contain multiple, sometimes conflicting, objectives aimed at promoting labour market efficiency, controlling benefit payments and enhancing the welfare of individual unemployed people. There may be problems with the immediate employment focus of the New Deals and Jobcentre Plus, but there has been progress in improving the quality of service available to the long-term unemployed and other working-age claimants, and there is evidence that the approach accelerates their entry into work.

Further Reading

Lodemel, I. and Trickey, H. (eds) (2000) *'An Offer You Can't Refuse': Workfare in International Perspective*, Bristol: Policy Press.
Peck, J. (2001) *Workfare States*, New York: Guilford.

CHAPTER 7

Social Security Policy

ALAN DEACON

Social security benefits account for nearly one-third of all government spending in the UK. In 1999–2000, the total benefits bill was over £100 billion, equivalent to £1,700 for every man, woman and child in the country. Over 30 million people, more than half the total population, were receiving income from at least one social security benefit (Emmerson and Leicester, 2000: 3). The scale and cost of the social security system means that it has long been at the forefront of debates about the future direction of the welfare state. If anything, however, the attention paid to social security policy has increased still further since the election of the first New Labour government in May 1997. This reflects the importance that New Labour attaches to the reform of social security within its so-called 'third way' on welfare.

The purpose of this chapter is to provide a brief commentary upon social security policy under New Labour. It is not possible to cover all aspects of social security, and most attention is paid to pensions and the measures taken to reduce child poverty. The first step, however, is to locate social security within New Labour's broader strategy for welfare reform.

Introduction: A 'Third Way' on Social Security?

The notion of a 'third way' has been lauded and derided in equal measure, and this debate cannot be covered here (Powell, 1999; Driver and Martell, 2000). In broad terms, however, the 'third way' refers to the reappraisal of electoral strategy, philosophy and policies conducted by centre-Left parties in the US, UK and parts of Europe in the late 1980s and 1990s. Three elements of that reappraisal are relevant to a discussion of New Labour and social security.

The first is the emphasis in third way thinking on the need to adapt the values and institutions of social democracy to contemporary social and economic conditions. In 1998, for example, Tony Blair claimed that it was essential to adapt the welfare state to the 'big changes' that had occurred 'in the way we live'. The welfare state, he declared, was no more tailored to people's needs than a car or television set designed 50 years ago (1998a: 3).

The second is the belief that it is possible to adopt policies that were hitherto regarded as incompatible or which were previously associated with conflicting political ideologies. In the case of social security, for example, Tony Blair has spoken of the need both to reduce the 'gross inequalities that continue to be handed down from generation to generation' (1998b: 3), and 'to tackle the growing underclass' (1996b: 9). The third element is the consequent emphasis on the need to strike a new balance between the rights and the responsibilities of claimants. Anthony Giddens, for example, has suggested that 'a prime motto for the new politics' might be 'no rights without responsibilities' (1998: 65). Each of these third way themes can be identified within New Labour's policies on social security. Conversely, the success or otherwise of those policies may shed some light on whether the third way is a coherent and integrative philosophy as New Labour claims, or an unprincipled hotch-potch as the government's critics allege.

New Labour has repeatedly contrasted its third way on social security with the failings of the benefits system that it inherited from the Conservatives. Under the previous government, spending on benefits had nearly doubled in real terms, but, far from falling, the numbers in poverty had also nearly doubled. On the conventional measure, around 14 million people were living in relative poverty when New Labour took office (Howard et al., 2001: 42–3). In New Labour's analysis, the most fundamental problem was that the welfare system as a whole had become too passive. It provided financial support but it did not give people the help and encouragement they needed to make the most of their opportunities. This was particularly true of the 'benefits system', which had 'failed to adapt to changes in the labour market and society'. It had 'increasingly concentrated solely on paying benefits to people, rather than providing them with active help to get off benefits'. As a result, benefits had 'become part of the problem; not the solution' (DSS, 1999: 29).

In March 1998, the government's Green Paper on welfare reform argued that this was disastrous for individual claimants, who all too often were chained 'to passive dependency' rather than helped to 'realise their full potential' (DSS, 1998a: 9). New Labour had become convinced that the old approach was also self-defeating. Even a government that was committed to tackling poverty would find that it could not do so simply by raising benefits, at least in the case of people of working age who did not have a significant disability. The reason for this was that the more benefits approached an adequate level, the greater would be the concerns about their effects on incentives to work and save. New Labour was now persuaded that the only way out of this 'catch-22' was to redefine the role of benefits for people of working age. Rather than being a permanent source of income, they were to provide a period of temporary support, during which the claimant would acquire the skills and motivation she or he needed to secure paid employment. The government's aim, it said, was now 'to rebuild the welfare state around work' (DSS, 1998a: 23).

> Our ambition is nothing less than a change of culture among benefit claimants, employers and public servants – with rights and responsibilities on all sides. Those making the shift from welfare into work will be provided with positive assistance, not just a benefit payment. (DSS, 1998a: 24)

This determination to change the culture is exemplified most clearly in the various New Deals that are discussed in Chapter 6. Nevertheless, it also shapes social security policy in a number of ways. First, if paid employment is to be encouraged and even enforced, then it also has to be rewarded. In Tony Blair's words, 'work must be made to pay if welfare is to be made to work' (1997a: 6). This has led New Labour to boost the incomes of those in low-paid jobs through a series of tax credits. Second, New Labour's rhetoric about the respective rights and responsibilities of claimants and government is not confined to people of working age. This was made clear in the government's first report on its anti-poverty strategy:

> It is our role to help people who can work to do so, and it is the responsibility of all individuals to take up the opportunities which arise. Likewise, it is our duty to ensure there is a sound pensions infrastructure and it is the responsibility of those who can save for their retirement to do so. (DSS, 1999: 119)

Moreover, these rights and responsibilities are not simply a matter of a contract between individuals and government. For New Labour they are much broader and deeper than that. They touch upon people's responsibilities as parents, neighbours and tenants, and as members of a wider community. It is this belief that has led New Labour to increase the element of conditionality within the benefits system. The New Deals are now only one example of the way in which an individual's entitlement to benefit is conditional upon his or her behaviour (Dwyer, 1998; Dwyer and Heron, 1999; Heron, 2001). This trend is likely to continue during New Labour's second term. In a speech during the 2001 election, for example, Blair reaffirmed his conviction that 'active responsibility' must be at the heart of welfare reform (2001: 1), and in March 2002 he strongly defended the idea that child benefits be withheld from the parents of persistent truants (BBC, 2002).

Third, and most importantly, New Labour's rhetoric about paid work and rights and responsibilities is a means to an end. Its objective is to restore popular support for welfare and persuade the voters that it is in their own interests to fund the welfare state. New Labour believes that the electorate will not be won over unless it is convinced that benefit fraud is being tackled and that those who benefit most directly from benefits and services are also fulfilling their own obligations. 'Matching opportunity and responsibility', says Blair, 'is the only way in the modern world to obtain consent from the public to fund the welfare state' (1996b: 10).

This chapter looks briefly at the extent to which New Labour has achieved its objectives in the field of social security. Before doing so, however, it is necessary to provide a broad overview of the social security system and the major trends in expenditure immediately before and after 1997.

Social Security Spending: An Overview

Spending on social security has doubled in real terms since 1978/79. Within this overall increase, however, there have been significant changes in the relative importance of different benefits. These are indicated in Table 7.1, which shows total spending in constant (1998/99) prices, and the way in which that spending was divided between the major benefits. A more detailed analysis of spending trends can be found in DSS (2000), while Emmerson and Leicester (2000) provide a clear outline of the individual benefits.

The cost of the basic retirement pension is still higher than that of any other single benefit, although its share of total spending has fallen by a third since 1978/79 (line 1). This fall reflects the decision taken by the Thatcher government in 1980 to link the basic pension to prices rather than earnings. This policy has been broadly continued by New Labour, and it has been offset only partially by the increase in the share of spending going on the state earnings-related pension (SERPS). The decline in relative spending on pensions is in sharp contrast to the increase in the proportion going on housing benefits, which almost trebled under the Conservatives (line 18). The total budget doubled over the period, and so this reflects an almost six-fold increase in spending on housing benefits in real terms. This was due in part to an increase in the number of claimants, but even more to a very sharp rise in housing association and local authority rents.

The most significant shift indicated in Table 7.1, however, has been the near doubling of the proportion of spending that goes on means-tested benefits, and the decline in the proportion spent on contributory benefits (lines 22–23). By 2001/02, only 45 per cent of expenditure was on contributory

Table 7.1 Social security spending by principal benefits

		1978/79 %	1988/89 %	1992/93 %	1996/97 %	2001/02 %
I	Retirement pension – basic	47.5	39.5	33.7	31.7	31.6
2	Retirement pension – e/related	–	0.16	1.8	2.3	4.8
3	Retirement pension – total	47.5	39.66	35.5	35.0	36.4
4	UB & JSA contributory	4.0	2.3	2.4	1.0	0.5
5	JSA: means-tested	–	–	–	2.0	2.8
6	Sickness benefit/statutory sick pay	4.5	2.3	2.4	0.1	–
7	Invalidity benefit	5.3	7.1	8.3	–	–
8	Incapacity benefit	0	0	0	8.3	6.4
9	Attendance allowance	1.0	2.1	2.1	2.6	2.8
10	Invalid care allowance	–	0.35	0.5	0.8	0.8
11	Severe disablement allowance	0.5	0.66	0.8	1.0	0.9
12	Mobility allowance	0.3	1.4	–	–	–
13	Disability living allowance	–	–	2.6	4.9	5.7
14	Income support: pensioners	3.5	3.3	5.0	4.2	3.8
15	Income support: under-60s	6.3	12.1	14.7	11.5	8.2
16	Child benefit	11.2	9.5	7.5	7.2	8.0
17	Family credit/family income support	0.15	0.8	1.2	2.3	–
18	Housing benefit	4.5	8.0	10.5	12.3	11.5
19	Rate rebate/council tax benefit	2.4	2.9	2.2	2.5	2.8
20	Working families' tax credit	–	–	–	–	4.3
21	**TOTAL (£m)**	**50,986**	**69,931**	**87,770**	**97,182**	**102,792**
	of which:					
22	Contributory	66.0	55.0	49.5	45.7	45.1
23	Means-tested	17.0	27.7	33.6	34.8	33.5
24	Non-contributory/non-means-tested	17.0	17.3	16.9	19.5	21.4

Source: Calculated from Department of Social Security (2000)

benefits, and nearly all of this was accounted for by pensions and incapacity benefits. Outside these two, contributory benefits have all but disappeared.

Table 7.2 shows how total spending is divided among different groups in the population. In no case has the proportion remained anything like constant over the period. Most strikingly, the share going to the unemployed rose and then fell sharply in line with labour market conditions. At the same time, the proportion spent on people with a long-term illness or disability has

Table 7.2 Social security spending by claimant group

	1978/79 %	1988/89 %	1992/93 %	1996/97 %	2001/02 %
Pensioners	55.1	50.0	45.4	44.3	46.5
Unemployed people	8.7	11.4	12.4	8.3	5.1
Short-term illness and widows	8.9	5.4	5.3	5.0	4.1
Children	11.3	9.9	7.9	7.5	8.0
Long-term illness and disabilities	11.2	15.4	19.6	24.2	24.3
Families	4.8	7.9	9.4	10.7	12.0
TOTAL (£m)	**50,986**	**69,931**	**87,770**	**97,182**	**102,792**

Source: Calculated from Department of Social Security (2000)

more than doubled, while that spent on pensioners has fallen steadily. Again it is important to remember that the total budget has doubled, and so this means that spending on sickness and disability benefits has more than quadrupled in real terms. The most important shifts in spending since 1997 are examined in more detail in the following sections.

An End to Child Poverty?

The most significant single development in social security policy under New Labour has been Tony Blair's declaration that it was the 'historic aim' of his government 'for ours to be the first generation to end child poverty' (1999a: 17). This pledge has since been followed by a commitment to reduce child poverty by 25 per cent by 2004 and halve it by 2010.

In making these commitments, New Labour has adopted the conventional definition of poverty as living in a household whose income is less than 60 per cent of the median income for that size of household. The median income is not the average income but is the income of the household in the middle of, or 'halfway up', the income distribution. The adoption of this definition makes New Labour's target all the more challenging, since what will be important will be the relative change in the incomes of households at the bottom and middle of the income distribution. Even a substantial rise in the incomes of the poorest households will not reduce the numbers in poverty, if it is matched or exceeded by the rise in the incomes of middle-income households. In effect, New Labour is committing itself to a significant measure of redistribution within the bottom half of the income distribution. It has to narrow the gap between the poorest families with children and similar fami lies on middle incomes. As the director of the Child Poverty Action Group has recently acknowledged, this ambition contrasts sharply with that of the previous Conservative government. 'The political paradigm has more than shifted, it has been shattered' (Barnes, 2001: 10).

In truth, Blair's announcement also marked a shift in New Labour rhetoric. Both in opposition and in the early days in government, Blair and his senior colleagues had spoken little about poverty. Instead they had talked about what Peter Mandelson had called 'today's and tomorrow's underclass'. This, he said, consisted of 'people who had lost hope' and were 'trapped in fatalism', and it was not a problem that could be tackled by 'an extra pound a week on benefits' (Mandelson, 1997: 6–7).

There are, then, three questions that arise immediately: Why did New Labour make this commitment? How does it expect to fulfil it? What progress has it made to date?

Part of the answer to the first question lies in the timing of Blair's announcement. While in opposition, New Labour had given an undertaking that it would not exceed the spending plans of the previous Conservative government for the first two years it was in office. This period was just about to expire when Blair made his pledge. In large part, however, New Labour's commitment reflects a growing recognition of the extent to which the opportunities open to people during their lifetime are diminished by the experience of poverty in childhood. In March 1999 – eleven days after Blair's speech – the Treasury published what it described in a press release as 'shocking conclusions' about the 'passage of inequality from generation to generation' and about the 'persistent and scarring nature' of childhood poverty. These conclusions were based upon analyses of the life experiences of two cohorts, one of which consisted of all those born in one week in March 1958 and the other of all those born in one week in April 1970. The central message of these analyses was that 'people's life chances are determined by who their parents were rather than their own talents and efforts' (HM Treasury, 1999: 31).

Evidence of this kind strikes at the heart of the claims made for the third way. Advocates such as Anthony Giddens have argued that what distinguishes the third way from Thatcherism is its commitment to equality of opportunity (Giddens, 2000: 89). They have also recognized that it will not be possible to lessen the present inequalities of opportunity without tackling child poverty. As a government document put it in 1999:

The key to tackling disadvantage in the future is the eradication of child poverty ... We need to break the cycle of deprivation, to stop it being transmitted through generations. (DSS, 1999: 5)

Moreover, subsequent studies have suggested that these intergenerational inequalities are becoming more rather than less evident (HM Treasury, 2001a: 2).

This is not to suggest that the government's pledge to end child poverty was just a response to research findings, policy making is always much more complicated than that. Even so, as Brewer and Gregg have noted, this evidence was 'probably crucial in assembling the political will to address child poverty' (2001: 6). It has also been suggested that New Labour was – and still is – receptive to these arguments because the complexity of the factors involved in the 'cycle of deprivation' fits easily with the eclectic, integrative style of thinking that characterizes the third way (Deacon, 2002a; 2003).

Turning to the question of how New Labour expects to achieve its goal, the first and most important point to make is that its strategy rests on the premise that it is paid work that offers the quickest and surest route out of poverty. It follows that New Labour's objective is to reduce the number of children being brought up in workless households and ensure that those who do move from welfare to work are financially rewarded for having done so. The programmes by which the government is seeking to attain the first objective are discussed in Chapter 6. The second – that of making work pay – is to be achieved through the introduction of a minimum wage, reductions in the rate of income tax and insurance contributions levied on low-paid workers and a new system of tax credits.

The most important of these new tax credits is the working families' tax credit (WFTC). Despite its name, this is a means-tested benefit that supplements the take-home pay of low-paid workers with children. It takes the form of a guaranteed income, the level of which depends upon the number of children in the family. The credit is then withdrawn as the claimant's income rises above the guaranteed amount (an outline of WFTC can be found in Emmerson and Leicester, 2000). WFTC is markedly more generous than its predecessor family credit and it was being received by 1.3 million families by the end of 2001. As Table 7.1 shows, it accounted for 4.3 per cent of all social security spending in 2001, twice the proportion going on family credit in 1996/97.

During its first term, New Labour also increased the rates of child benefit paid in respect of all children, and the allowances for children within the principal means-tested benefits. In 2003, it will introduce two new tax credits. A working tax credit (WTC) will supplement the wages of single people and couples without children in low-paid jobs. Much more significant, however, will be the new child credit (CC). This will integrate the allowances for children within the major means-tested benefits. Henceforth there will be two sources of support for children; the universal child benefit and the means-tested CC. Like child benefit, the new CC will be paid to the main carer and the amount paid will be calculated in the same way, whether or not the head of the household is in paid work (Inland Revenue, 2001).

The new CC will be paid to a far larger number of families than the existing means-tested benefits, and the government hopes that this will lessen the stigma currently attached to means-tested support (HM Treasury 2001a: 18). These credits, however, are in the future. The more pressing question is what success – if any – has New Labour had to date?

There are two ways of assessing the impact of New Labour's measures to date. The first is to use computer modelling techniques to estimate the difference between the incomes of different households with and without the measures. On this basis, the effects are markedly redistributive. The Institute for Fiscal Studies (IFS) has calculated that between 1997 and 2002 the incomes of the poorest 10 per cent of households rose 18.5 per cent because of New Labour's measures. This compares with an increase of around 5 per cent in middle-income households and a slight fall for the richest 10 per cent of households. On the same basis, the net effect of New Labour's measures is to reduce the number of children living in low-income households by 1.2 million (Brewer et al., 2002: 29).

The second method is to look at the changes that have occurred in actual incomes, as measured by the Family Resources Survey. On this basis, New Labour's policies have had much less impact. As Table 7.3 indicates, the number of children in poverty has fallen by about 0.5 million and the total numbers in poverty by about 1 million.

There are three reasons for the discrepancy between the two sets of figures. The first is timing: not all of New Labour's initiatives were fully implemented

Table 7.3 People below 60 per cent of contemporary median income poverty line (after housing costs)

	1996/97	1997/98	1998/99	1999/00	2000/01
Total people – number	13.9m	13.6m	13.4m	13.3m	12.9m
Total people – proportion	24.6%	24.1%	23.7%	23.5%	22.6%
Of whom					
Children – number	4.4m	4.3m	4.3m	4.1m	3.9m
Children – proportion	34%	33.4%	33.2%	32.3%	30.5%
Pensioners – number	2.2m	2.3m	2.3m	2.4m	2.4m
Pensioners – proportion	26.6%	27.1%	27.1%	25.6%	24.6%

Source: Brewer et al. (2002: 33)

by 2000/01. The second is that the estimates assume that WFTC is received by all those who are eligible, whereas in reality take-up is only around 65 per cent. The third and most important reason for the difference is that the models estimate the impact of changes in benefits and taxes upon an otherwise static distribution of incomes. In the real world, of course, that distribution is not static. In reality, the underlying incomes of middle-income households grew at a faster rate than did the underlying incomes of the poorest households, and this offset the redistributive effects of New Labour's measures. This is crucial because it was explained earlier that what determines whether the numbers in poverty go up or down is the relative change in the incomes of poor and middle-income households. When the real wages, occupational pensions and other resources of middle or median households are rising faster than those of poor households, New Labour is aiming at a rising target. If, for example, the poverty line had been frozen in real terms between 1996/97 and 2000/01, the reduction in child poverty would have been of the order of 1.4 million and not 0.5 million (Brewer et al., 2002: 34).

An End to Pensioner Poverty?

New Labour's policies towards pensions have two central objectives. First, to reduce the incidence of poverty among those who have already retired. Second, to encourage those still in work to save more for their own retirement. The key question is whether the means by which New Labour is trying to achieve these twin objectives are compatible or contradictory.

The government's starting point is that there is now such a gulf between the circumstances of the better-off pensioners and the poorest pensioners that it would be wasteful to pay the same benefits to them all. It does not intend to halt the decline in the basic state pension, nor does it believe that people should look to the state for the additional pension which they will need if they are to avoid poverty in retirement. Policy thus rests on the assumption that pensions will continue to decline as a proportion of total social security spending and people will increasingly look to the private sector in retirement. At present, the state accounts for about 60 per cent of pensions income and the private sector for 40 per cent. The government expects that these proportions will be reversed by 2050 (DSS, 1998b).

At present around 25 per cent of pensioners are in relative poverty. This proportion is higher among older pensioners than among those who have recently retired, higher among women pensioners than men and higher among single pensioners than pensioner couples. At the other extreme, there is a growing number of pensioners in receipt of occupational or private pensions and with significant incomes from investments. New Labour's response to this growth in inequality within the pensioner population has been to channel help to the poorest through the means-tested minimum income guarantee (MIG). As its name suggests, this provides a minimum income below which no pensioner should fall, and the intention is to increase MIG in line with average earnings rather than prices.

The extent to which MIG will reduce pensioner poverty in the short run will depend critically on take-up. The middle estimate at present is that it is being claimed by some 1.6 million pensioner households, but that there are between 400 and 670 thousand pensioners who are eligible for MIG but do not claim it (Pensions Reform Group, 2001: 37).

The other objection to the MIG is that it that it penalizes those people who have made provision for their retirement and now find that others receive through the MIG an income comparable to that which they have earned through their savings and contributions. The extent to which this represents a disincentive to save is debated. As Stephen Driver (2002) has recently pointed out, if people are suspicious of governments then they are unlikely to feel sufficiently confident that MIG will be around when they retire to give up saving themselves. What is not in question, however, is that the situation created by MIG is unjust and is a source of great resentment. Moreover, the publicity given to this injustice can only reinforce the well-attested reluctance of many people to save more.

The government has tried to reduce the disincentives created by MIG by introducing from 2003 a new pensions credit (PC). This provides a guaranteed minimum income, plus a further 60 pence a week for every £1 of income for savings or private pensions. The PC thus provides some reward for small savings, although the problem reoccurs further up the income scale when PC itself tapers off. Moreover, the PC represents a further extension of means testing, and the government calculates that half of all pensioners will be receiving means-tested benefits when it is introduced in 2003 (Pensions Reform Group, 2001: 23). The PC is also extremely complex, particularly when it interacts with other means-tested benefits such as housing benefit. These problems led the Institute for Public Policy Research (IPPR), a think-tank normally sympathetic to New Labour, to urge the government to perform a 'pensions U-turn' and raise the basic state pension to the level of the MIG (IPPR, 2002).

The vehicle through which New Labour hopes to persuade people on modest incomes to provide for their own retirement is the stakeholder pension. These are private funded pensions that are subject to so-called CAT standards regarding cost, access and terms. All employers who have five or more employees and who do not offer an occupational pension were supposed to offer access to a stakeholder pension by October 2001. To date, however, stakeholder pensions have been very slow to take off, and the key issue in pensions policy during New Labour's second term will be whether the government should introduce some form of compulsion.

In 2001, for example, the Pensions Reform Group – chaired by the former Minister for Welfare Reform Frank Field – proposed that those in work be compelled to contribute to a universal protected pension (UPP). In return they would be given a guarantee that the UPP would be paid at a level above that of means-tested benefits, thereby safeguarding the value of any additional income from savings or other pensions (Field, 2002). Thus far, New Labour has strongly resisted further compulsion. It argues that this would be unfair on lower paid workers, and also on those who are able to provide for their retirement by building up a business (DSS, 1998b: 7). A far more powerful motive for avoiding compulsion, however, is the probable response of the electorate. The danger for the government is that higher rates of national insurance contributions would be viewed as a breach of the promise not to increase direct taxation.

The government's refusal to countenance compulsion runs two risks. The first is the so-called 'freeloader' problem; people will just not bother to save and will take their chances on the means-tested benefits that are available when they retire. The second risk is that left to themselves people will save but they will not save enough. By the summer of 2002, this particular chicken had come home to roost to spectacular political effect. A potent cocktail of falling stock markets, adverse tax changes in the financial services industry, lower interest rates, changing expectations of inflation and increased longevity was threatening to reduce considerably the value of private and some occupational pensions. These factors made it more expensive for employers to continue to offer so-called 'defined benefits schemes', in which the pension paid is a fixed proportion of the recipient's final salary. In response, many employers began to replace them with defined contribution schemes, in which the level of the pension paid depends on investment returns. Public concern at this trend was heightened by newspaper headlines that warned that some people may have to work beyond the current retirement age in order to secure a decent income in old age. To its evident consternation, New Labour found that pensions were now attracting a level of attention in the popular media and political debate that they had not received for decades.

Conclusion

This brief survey of social security policy under New Labour is necessarily incomplete. It is also potentially misleading in so far as some of the benefits that have not been discussed in detail are those which have remained untouched by New Labour's reforms. This is especially true of housing benefit and council tax benefit, which together account for over 14 per cent of total spending on social security and also generate a host of disincentives and anomalies. They are also extremely hard to reform unless the government is willing to either spend much more money or leave large numbers of claimants worse off (Kemp et al., 2002).

With that qualification, the obvious conclusion is that New Labour's third way is considerably clearer and less bumpy in respect of children and people of working age than it is in respect of pensions. The policy towards pensions remains a muddle. It is not clear how far the MIG and PC will alleviate the poverty of current pensioners. It is still less clear how far New Labour's exhortations will persuade those in work to save more for when they retire. In contrast, there is an underlying consistency of purpose and direction to the compulsion of the New Deals, the incentives in the new tax credits and the additional support to families through programmes such as Sure Start. In this respect, social security policy, and especially the strategy to tackle poverty, does support some of the claims made for the third way. New Labour has drawn upon and reached an accommodation between hitherto conflicting perspectives on welfare (Deacon, 2002b).

This is not to suggest that New Labour's policies in respect of children and people of working age are beyond criticism. The emphasis on paid employment, for example, is open to the objection that it undervalues other forms of work such as caring. Moreover, New Labour's approach is something of a gamble in two important respects. First, it is assuming that the labour market can absorb all the people that it hopes to move from welfare to work. This leaves it vulnerable to a downturn in the economy and consequent rise in unemployment. Second, New Labour is placing greater and greater reliance on means-tested benefits, which it prefers to call income-related benefits. The government believes that only by targeting benefits in this way can it tackle poverty and yet still release resources for education and health. This, however, rests on the assumption that these benefits will be claimed by all those who are eligible for them. Not only that, but while in opposition New Labour condemned means testing for creating disincentives to earn and save and penalizing the very qualities and attributes that welfare should foster – hard work, thrift and honesty. New Labour now has to trust that it can defy past evidence on the take-up of means-tested benefits, and confound its own predictions about the long-term effects of means testing on the behaviour and character of claimants.

Further Reading

For the latest statistics on poverty and inequality, see the website of the New Policy Institute, www.poverty.org.uk. The Institute for Fiscal Studies publishes regular commentaries and analyses of social security policies and income trends at www.ifs.org.uk.

Hewitt, M. (2002) 'New Labour and the Redefinition of Social Security' in M. Powell (ed.) *Evaluating New Labour's Welfare Reforms*, Bristol: Policy Press.
Deacon, A. (2002) *Perspectives on Welfare*, Buckingham: Open University Press.

CHAPTER 8

Housing Policy

JANET FORD

For a range of reasons, the 1997 incoming Labour government faced a housing system characterized by considerable problems. This chapter aims to consider a number of these problems and the development of housing policy from 1997 to mid-2002, in particular:

- the position the incoming Labour government faced with respect to housing

- the nature of its subsequent response

- the likely impact of its responses, and persistent outstanding matters.

The chapter takes as axiomatic that social, economic and political factors shape both the demand for, and the supply of, housing. They also influence the ways in which governments respond to housing need and housing aspirations. Within the UK, overall rising affluence has led to the demand for individualized housing solutions, while widening income inequality and the growth of poor households has highlighted questions about how good quality housing can be provided and paid for where income is limited. At the same time, global pressures tend to lead governments to curtail public expenditure and retreat from state involvement in the provision of services. The heightened level of risk in modern societies, for example labour market volatility and relationship dissolution, also contributes to debates about how housing can be sustained during periods of economic and personal dislocation. In considering social policies (including housing policy), all governments have the scope to respond in different ways to the problems they face and set distinct policy objectives. One important issue considered in this chapter is the extent to which the incoming Labour government in 1997 offered a distinct approach to housing or whether it sought continuity with the policies of previous Conservative administrations.

Housing in 1997

Although the backgrounds to the *specific* housing policy issues are discussed in detail as they arise, the chapter starts with an overview of major housing policy changes, and the key influences on policy development between 1979 and 1997. As implemented by successive Conservative governments, these policies resulted in some radical changes to the housing landscape which are summarized in Table 8.1. This table should be read carefully with respect to the source of the data – England, the United Kingdom or Great Britain, and its exact date.

Table 8.1 indicates, for example, the extent of tenure change over the period with owner occupation growing from 56 per cent of households to 67 per cent over 20 years. The extent to which this growth was supported by the policy of selling former council homes (the right to buy) is also clear. The dearth of new provision in the local authority sector is indicated, as is the poor condition of much of the stock that remained within the sector. Changes also

Table 8.1 Key changes in housing landscape, 1979–97

	1979	1990	1997
% owner-occupied properties (GB)	56%	–	67%
% local authority properties (GB)	30%	–	19%
Public sector housing* completions (UK)	88,590	17,877	1,474
Housing association completions (UK)	21,422	17,469	27,502
Sales of right-to-buy properties (England and Wales)	2,212	135,493	59,886
No. homelessness acceptance (England)	76,342	171,576	129,420
No. of unfit dwellings (England)	1,662,000 (1986)	1,498,000 (1991)	1,522,000 (1996)
No. in receipt of housing benefit (GB)	1,570,000	3,988,000	4,591,000
Average rents (England)			
Local authority*	£7.70	£23.74	£41.18
Housing association	£12.52**	£29.94	£51.35
Private sector (unfurnished market rents)	n/a	£44.80	£71.11
Unemployment of householders by tenure			
Mortgage buyer	3%	4%	1%
Local authority tenants	9%	11%	7%
Private sector tenants	4%	6%	5%

Data source: Wilcox (2001/2002, 2002/2003)
*   local authorities/new towns/govt. departments
** fair rent in 1979, assured rents thereafter

occurred in the socioeconomic composition of particular tenures, with a growing incidence of unemployment among social housing tenants. Homelessness also grew over the period, and despite a decline in the mid-1990s, at the point the Conservatives lost power, the number of households accepted as homeless was greater than in 1979. The number of households dependent on state support for housing costs (housing benefit) increased over the period, as did the (not unrelated) level of rents charged for social housing. Reference back to this table will be made at several points in the chapter.

The influences giving rise to the policies which brought about these changes are widely discussed in the literature (for example, Forrest et al., 1990; Cole and Furbey, 1994; Malpass and Murie, 1994) and need not be repeated in detail here. Fundamental influences were the ideological commitment to market-based provision (owner occupation) rather than collective provision (social housing), the belief that the power of local authorities should be curtailed and their role changed, and the assumption that the public sector could be made more efficient and accountable by being subjected to private sector management disciplines (the 'new' public management). Ideological preference was matched by electoral considerations. Homeownership was recognized as a widely held aspiration which, if facilitated, would bring votes, while the commitment to support private rather than public sector provision and, within the social/public sector, housing associations rather than local authorities was reinforced by the need and desire to limit public expenditure so as to meet the electoral commitment to lower personal taxation.

As a result of these policies, the incoming Labour government faced a series of problems. Its own analysis of the 'inherited' housing problem was set out by the minister for housing and local government. In Armstrong (1999) the following were noted:

- housing investment was at an all time low

- there was no strategy for dealing with the poor physical condition of the housing stock

- social housing was perceived as part of the problem (viewed as stigmatized and residualized) and not as part of the solution

- tenant involvement in decision making was minimal

- deregulation of the private rented sector had not led to any improvement in the physical conditions or management practices

- leasehold reform was muddled

- parts of the homeownership market were 'dysfunctional'

- any balanced housing strategy had been lost to the ideological goal of breaking up local authority housing.

There was some expectation that, having recognized the limitations and, indeed, damaging effects of policy over the past 20 years, the incoming government might adopt a different, more radical stance and seek to change the direction of policy in some fundamental ways. However, a number of early accounts of New Labour's housing policy reject this thesis (for example, Kemp, 1999; Cowan and Marsh, 2001). Rather, they argue that while Labour has given more prominence, and resources, to housing than the Conservatives did, issuing a housing Green Paper (DETR/DSS, 2000) in June 2000 and bringing forward a legislative programme, the approach and philosophy that now inform housing policy are a clear continuation of the principles and practice of previous Conservative governments. As will be shown below, market provision, market processes, the limitation of public sector housing provision and 'better' social sector management remain central objectives, albeit that more attention is being given to housing quality, tenant choice and tenant participation than was the case under the Conservatives.

Unsurprisingly, this continuity of approach was given a distinctive 'spin' in early pronouncements, but its essential elements were there for all to see. Initial indications came from the minister of housing and local government, who noted in a speech in 1997 that the 'cornerstones' of the approach to housing policy would be to ensure that housing markets worked well, there was value for money (efficiency) in the provision of public services, individuals were empowered and communities strengthened. These latter two concerns meshed with the wider objective of the incoming government to address social exclusion. A key aspect of doing this was the physical and social regeneration of currently marginalized communities. Here, the condition of housing was important but so too was addressing the large, single tenure, stigmatized enclaves of (primarily council) housing increasingly characterized by economic inactivity, due to the lack of skills among tenants, local economic decline or the 'address discrimination' claimed to be practised by employers which denied employment opportunities to those from stigmatized areas. This more explicit embedding of housing into wider agendas, alongside the growing reliance on market mechanisms and the rejection of local authority provision, led some to argue that we were seeing the end of housing policy per se. However, developments since 1997, as discussed below, suggest that distinct housing objectives remain and indeed may have more rather than less emphasis now than previously, while the significance of housing to a wide range of other policy areas (health, crime, education, social care and so on) has become more explicit.

One final issue must be mentioned in this introductory section. The 1997 Labour government came to power committed to establishing devolved government. With respect to housing, even prior to devolution in 2000, the Scottish Office had set key objectives for housing policy and housing was subject to the Scottish legal system. While the Scottish Executive has adopted many of the housing objectives seen in England, it also has a distinctive approach in some areas (for example with respect to the right to buy or the rights of homeless people). In Wales, however, where there had not been comparable autonomy, the Welsh assembly gained more control over the housing agenda, but within the continuing English legal framework (see Smith et al., 2000 for a discussion of policy issues and constitutional arrangements). There is a complex history of devolved government in Northern Ireland but under the 1998 Good Friday Agreement housing remains the responsibility of the Northern Ireland Housing Executive. A useful overview of current housing issues and policies is provided in Paris (2001), which concludes that devolution has not yet resulted in the emergence of any distinctive, new, locally determined agendas but instead more convergence with English policies. Thus, while the issues and responses discussed in this chapter typically have cross-country relevance, the exact extent to which this is the case may vary and has to be determined by further reading.

Setting the Agenda

The process of addressing the major 'deficiencies' identified by the incoming government has had at least two strands. First, and put rather simplistically, some immediate actions were taken in 1997 which released £800 million of the money which local authorities had received from the sales of council housing (but been constrained from using) to begin to address the widespread problems of poor housing conditions, a result of the low priority accorded to maintenance and improvement during the period of Conservative rule. There then followed a comprehensive spending review (CRS) in 1998, as a result of which some 'additional' money for housing became available over the period 1999–2002 (see Table 8.2), including a significant budget with which to address poor conditions and funding to support the policy of stock transfer (discussed later). In addition, those housing issues most visibly connected with social exclusion received some priority, in particular, homelessness (especially rough sleeping), with a commitment to reduce radically rough sleeping, overseen by a new Rough Sleepers Unit established within the (then) Department of the Environment, Transport and the Regions.

Table 8.2 Spending review 2000 – housing expenditure

	Plans agreed prior to review 2001/02	Total spending plans			
	2001/02 £ billion	2001/02 £ billion	2002/03 £ billion	2003/04 £ billion	Totals £ billion
Local authority capital	**2,305**	**2,305**	**2,465**	**2,545**	**7,316**
of which					
Housing-based credit approvals	2,305	705	793	842	2,341
Arm's-length management companies	0	0	160	300	460
Major repairs allowance	0	1,060	1,512	1,403	3,975
Housing corporation	**890**	**995**	**1,158**	**1,460**	**3,614**
Starter home initiative	0	50	100	100	250
Large-scale voluntary transfer pool	86	86	196	2,121	492
Supporting people	0	20	55	78	153
Safer communities supported housing fund	0	22	45	70	137
Disabled facilities grant	75	87	88	89	263
Home improvement agencies	7	9	9	9	26
Rough Sleepers Unit and homelessness	30	30	30	30	91
Lettings pilot schemes	0	6	4	1	11
Tenant participation grant	6	6	6	6	19
Neighbourhood wardens	0	2	3	5	10
Other housing expenditure	152	64	42	43	149
Total Housing (Departmental Expenditure Limit)	**3,552**	**3,682**	**4,201**	**4,647**	**12,530**

Source: Answer to Parliamentary Question, 25/7/2000

The longer term development of housing policy was set out in the housing Green Paper (DETR/DSS, 2000) entitled *Quality and Choice: A Decent Home for All.* The key principles were summarized by Cowan and Marsh (2001) and are set out below:

- Offering everyone opportunity, choice and a stake in their home, whether rented or owned

- Ensuring an adequate supply of decent housing to meet need

- Giving responsibility to individuals to provide for their own homes where they can, providing help for those who cannot

- Improving the quality and design of the housing stock, new housing and residential environment, helping to achieve an urban renaissance and protecting the countryside

- Delivering modern, efficient, secure, customer-focused public services and empowering individuals to influence them

- Reducing barriers to work, particularly in relation to benefit and rent policy

- Supporting vulnerable people and tackling all forms of social exclusion, including bad housing, homelessness, poverty, crime and poor health

- Promoting sustainable development that supports thriving, balanced communities and a high quality of life in urban and rural areas.

The principles above are a reworking of the earlier cornerstones (making markets work better, efficient public services, empowering individuals and strengthening communities) and, following a consultation exercise, led to a *Housing Policy Statement, The Way Forward for Housing* (DETR, 2000a), which set out a number of policy objectives. While there are themes relevant across tenures (for example choice, individual responsibility, market processes), the rest of this chapter picks up some key aspects of current housing policy by tenure.

Housing Policy: Towards Homeownership

The Conservative legacy

This chapter has already noted the growth in homeownership over the period 1979–97, and its basis in Conservative ideology and households' aspirations. To ensure this objective could be reached, Conservative policy had restricted local authority building, promoted the right to buy, and deregulated the financial services sector (ensuring an adequate supply of credit to those wishing to purchase a home). Widening access carried a potential need to support homeowners if their circumstances deteriorated. However, while the Conservatives had themselves inherited a state-provided safety net which paid the housing costs of those who lost their income (for an account of these policies, see Ford et al., 2001), from 1987 onwards, it was curtailed, reflecting rising cost, the belief that individuals should be responsible for sustaining their homeownership and an assumption that the insurance market could provide appropriate 'substitute' safety net products. As from October

1995, eligible borrowers (those in receipt of income support or jobseeker's allowance) have to wait up to nine months to receive help with mortgage interest payments (ISMI).

New Labour and homeownership

Current policy confirms owner occupation as the preferred and dominant tenure, reflecting both New Labour's adherence to the principles of market provision and individual responsibility, as well as households' continuing aspirations. Not surprisingly, there has been no rejection of the policy of right to buy (although there have been some changes designed to restrict this policy under certain circumstances in Scotland), and indeed New Labour has sought additional ways to ease the entry of low-income households.

There is an argument that a commitment to market provision, by definition, absolves government from any further policy intervention in that area. In practice, this is not the case, as market provision can under certain circumstances generate a set of problems that require a policy response; for example, with respect to homeownership, a lack of regulation may limit market effectiveness while external events such as an economic downturn may challenge the capacity of homeowners to meet their housing costs and remain in the market. Allowing too many to fail in this way is not only detrimental to the functioning of the market (and so to Labour housing policy), but failure incurs costs in the form of homelessness and demands for rehousing in the social sector. These developments are all the more likely as the policy of widening homeownership has resulted in a more diverse sector. Compared to 1979, a higher proportion of homeowners are non-white, semi-skilled or unskilled workers and self-employed but, critically for policy purposes, a higher proportion have low incomes, although overall the tenure remains an affluent tenure. Thus, widening access, along with the development of a more risk-laden society, potentially challenges the security of homeownership and households' ability to meet their housing costs. Given these developments, Labour policy towards homeownership is both to rely on the market and to develop policies to ensure *sustainable* homeownership.

Sustainable homeownership could be achieved by the state taking responsibility for the mortgage interest payments of homeowners who lost all income. However, as already noted, previous provision has been systematically curtailed and in any case it did not cover all eventualities or all groups of borrowers. The Labour government has chosen not to reinstate the safety net but rather has reinforced previous Conservative policy, whereby mortgagors are expected to take out private insurance to meet their mortgage payments for a period of up to 12 months in the event of a loss of income due to unemployment, accident or sickness. This reflects Labour's commitment to seeing individuals take greater responsibility for their housing. Following research, the government published a target for the take-up of mortgage payment protection insurance (MPPI) of 50 per cent by 2004. By mid-2002, take-up was 22.5 per cent, suggesting that the target is unlikely to be met. A key question underlying this policy objective is the extent to which events that challenge sustainable homeownership (unemployment, reduced wages and relationship breakdown) are 'insurable' events (Burchardt and Hills, 1997) and hence the extent to which it is appropriate to expect the market to provide. The 'effectiveness' of private insurance has also been raised, with research indicating that mortgage arrears are not always avoided and that disputes over claims can occur (Kempson et al., 1999). Critically, however, the policy of market reliance has never been tested under recessionary conditions which must be the litmus test of its effectiveness.

The government also argued that the market itself could increase the likelihood of sustainability through product innovation and especially the promotion of flexible mortgage products allowing overpayments in the good times which could be offset against under- or no payments when incomes were reduced or lost altogether. Such flexible mortgages are a rapidly growing sector of the mortgage market, and recent research has shown that overpayment is fairly widespread. While the research indicates that overpayment is not motivated by borrowers deliberately building a safety net against risks (rather borrowers are seeking to cut the overall interest costs payable on the mortgage and limit the period over which they are in debt), nevertheless, many borrowers will in practice have a cushion if risk materializes (Smith et al., 2002) and so such products currently can contribute to sustaining homeownership.

Quality and Choice in Public Housing

The Conservative legacy

By 1997, the social rented housing sector was associated with a wide range of problems. Housing policy in the preceding two decades had been directed towards minimizing the role of public housing in general, and local authority housing in particular (see Table 8.1 above). The right to buy had resulted in the loss of much of the better stock but, critically, the substantial cuts in public sector capital spending had limited new building to almost zero and prevented any significant repair and maintenance of the existing stock. By 1997, the backlog of repairs in local authority properties was valued at around £10 billion (later shown to be in excess of £19 billion), while local authorities could not easily borrow in the private market to fund improvements.

Housing need, however, had not diminished. The numbers living in crowded conditions had risen, there was a continuing shortfall between the number of households seeking housing and the number of sound dwellings, and the number of homeless households was greater in 1997 than was the case in 1979 (despite a considerable fall in the number of homeless households during the 1990s). Increasingly, local authorities could only house homeless households, creating problems for those seeking social housing via the waiting list and this situation had led to a downgrading of the priority accorded to homeless households in the 1996 Housing Bill.

One consequence of the processes outlined above was to increase the extent to which social housing housed marginalized, unemployed households, reinforcing its residualized nature (Forrest and Murie, 1988; Burrows, 1997b). Over the same period, the form of financial support provided to social housing tenants also changed, with a shift from subsidies to the buildings (bricks and mortar subsidies), which kept rents artificially low, to a personal subsidy in the form of a means-tested housing benefit. One impact of this change, coupled as it was with a policy to increase rents towards 'market' levels, raised housing benefit expenditure rapidly. These changes further reinforced the residualization process, as unemployed heads of households were increasingly located on the higher rent estates where the full costs of the rent were met through housing benefit.

Thus, policy towards public sector housing provision over the 1980s and 90s resulted in an inadequate supply of housing, the continuation of poor housing conditions and social and economic deprivation within the social sector. Crime, drug dealing and the withdrawal of retail, financial and leisure services characterized many estates and neighbourhoods, reinforcing the downward spiral of social housing. Towards the end of the Conservative period in government, growing dissatisfaction with social housing led to low demand in some areas (predominately, but not exclusively, in the north of the country and particularly where there was a plentiful supply of other forms of affordable housing) and some abandonment. Place-specific outcomes of the kinds discussed above contributed to a public perception that the sector as a whole was unpopular, inefficient and deteriorating, even though these views were sometimes challenged by local residents (Burrows and Rhodes, 1999).

Conservative housing policy had also been directed towards changing the organizational and administrative framework of social housing provision. This encapsulated the recognition that the state still had a duty to house those in need, but a rejection of the local authority as the main or even a significant provider. This rejection had both an ideological and financial basis (particularly the rules which prevented adequate borrowing by housing authorities to address the poor condition of the stock), reinforced by the belief that the housing management services provided were of a poor quality, inefficient and delivered in ways that were potentially disadvantageous to tenants. A White Paper (DoE, 1987) signalled the government's determination to curtail local authorities' activities by proposing mechanisms by which they could transfer responsibility for new and existing housing provision and management to other 'social' organizations (initially housing associations), alongside mechanisms of compulsory competitive tendering (CCT) for any services they retained designed to improve the efficiency and cost-effectiveness of the local authority sector. This 'transfer' policy carried with it the additional benefit that housing associations or similarly formed organizations could raise finance in the private market to fund repairs and so improve the stock, using the rental income stream to repay the loans. By 1997, 54 English local authorities had transferred part or all of their stock to housing associations (now called registered social landlords – RSLs). A fuller discussion of this early transfer process can be found in Mullins et al. (1993).

Conservative housing policy has also been characterized as 'unresponsive to consumer demand' (Somerville, 2001). As the stock shrank but housing need remained, the traditional emphasis on bureaucratic allocation persisted, further reinforcing the long-standing evidence of institutional discrimination (Henderson and Karn, 1987) and the limited emphasis given to tenant choice.

Labour and public housing; privatizing the stock?

Those hoping that the New Labour government of 1997 would confront and reverse the downgrading of local authorities as social housing providers will have been disappointed. Indeed, the signs that they *would* be disappointed were clear prior to the election, as during the 1990s Labour had come to see the benefits that the transfer policy in particular offered. Early initiatives to allow local authorities to use some of the capital receipts they had acquired through right-to-buy sales to address the backlog of repairs could not solve the more fundamental financial issues that both central and local government faced and this, with other considerations, fuelled the need for more radical solutions. Thus, landlords in tightly constrained financial circumstances saw that transfer offered them a way out of their dilemmas. Further, a more limited local authority sector 'chimed' with Labour's preference for more market-oriented provision.

The 2000 Green Paper (DETR/DSS, 2000) made explicit the extent to which the transfer process was seen as the way forward with respect to local authority housing. Three forms of potential transfer were outlined: a continuation of the existing transfer process to RSLs; the development of specific private finance initiatives (PFIs); and the establishment of local housing companies (LHCs). These latter provided for the local authority to retain ownership of the stock but required the establishment of an 'arm's length' management company able to provide a high quality service to tenants. Via these different means, the Green Paper noted a likely increase in the scale of transfer. In contrast with the 400,000 plus homes that had been transferred over the previous 12 years, the Green Paper indicated government support for up to 200,000 transfers *per year*, holding out the prospect that:

> If local authorities submit transfer proposals at that level, and if tenants support them, registered social landlords will become the majority providers of social housing from 2004 onwards. (DETR/DSS, 2000)

Thus, Labour's housing policy objective towards the public sector can be read as a policy to bring about the demise of a local authority provided and managed housing stock; a privatization process that, if achieved, would exceed the outcomes of the right to buy.

While reshaping ownership in the social sector, Labour housing policy is also directed towards modernizing management practices as a whole, providing a stronger focus on effective service delivery. Prior to its election, Labour had promised the abolition of CCT, but its embracing of managerialism saw CCT replaced with a regime entitled Best Value (the application of a series of inspection, audit and, where appropriate, 'kite-marked' processes now applied to public services).

Since the publication of the Green Paper, transfer proposals have accelerated and the sector is gradually being reshaped. However, some proposals have been rejected by tenants, including the proposed transfer of 70,000 homes in Birmingham. These rejections are an indication that the assumption that tenants are *necessarily* dissatisfied with local authority housing may be flawed. An early discussion of the potential limitations or flaws in a more extensive transfer policy is provided by Murie and Nevin (2001) and Perry (2000). In both discussions, the issues range from the essentially parochial (the significance of an effective local authority communications strategy; are there enough tenants willing to engage as elected participants in the new organizations and so on) to more complex issues of whether longer term benefits for tenants can be sustained along with the reshaping of the social housing sector. These writers draw attention to the potentially critical impact on a reshaped sector of the decline and regeneration of cities, where areas of housing against which debt is secured may become obsolescent, the ongoing relationship between local authorities and RSLs and whether subsequent tenants are likely to reap the same benefits (for example ongoing maintenance) as available to transferred tenants.

Extending tenants' voice and choice

The Green Paper (DETR/DSS, 2000) also sought to address some long-standing concerns around the unresponsiveness of public housing to the preferences of tenants, in particular in relation to the allocation of housing and other managerial practices. This lack of consideration, embodied in a highly bureaucratic form of housing allocation, was associated with institutional discrimination and concentrations of disadvantage. The following housing policy statement noted the housing policy objectives of widening social housing access and extending tenant choice. The wider social agenda of the Labour government designed to address social exclusion was clearly an influence on these developments, but the need to 'market' social housing in areas of low demand was a further, arguably the most significant, impetus to placing greater weight on tenant preferences (Pawson, 2000). There is also an explicit assumption underpinning these objectives that providing choice will alter behaviour and give rise to community and neighbourhood benefits.

> Applicants for social housing who are more involved in decisions about their new homes are more likely to have a longer term commitment to the locality. This will promote more sustainable communities ... it will increase personal well-being and help to reduce anti-social behaviour, crime, stress and educational under-achievement. (Pawson, 2000: para. 9.7)

The Labour government has therefore proposed a series of measures to respond to preferences and thus potentially widen access. It proposed, for example, that local authorities should be prohibited from 'blanket' exclusions (for example with respect to young people aged 16 or 17 and those with an institutionalized background), while tenants are to be allowed to reject accommodation that does not suit them, without immediate penalty, and allocation might be framed so as to respond to time on the waiting list rather than the traditional allocative mechanism of a points-based system. This latter development would enable those with the capacity to wait for the 'right' accommodation to do so without penalty. The Green Paper also endorses processes that seek to 'market' social housing vacancies, with prospective tenants potentially responding to advertisements (sometimes referred to as the 'Delft' model), integrate the waiting lists of local providers (common waiting lists) and support 'community' lettings, whereby a local authority might be enabled to shape the social mix of an estate or prioritize housing for certain groups of key (public sector) workers.

Equally, however, the concern with rights *and* responsibilities (or, expressed differently, with deserving and undeserving cases), which is a feature of much

Labour policy, results in a concern to identify the circumstances under which housing can be denied. Clearly, while wishing to widen access and choice, public housing is still directed towards meeting need and hence those not in need, or whose need is 'intentional', may be excluded. Other exclusions are in response to antisocial behaviour; neighbour nuisance, rent arrears and so on.

Taken together, New Labour is proposing a series of changes that look to introduce some market processes to social housing, while at the same time seeking to enhance social inclusion and set clear limits to the claims of irresponsible households. The working out of the relationships and tensions between individual, community and managerial goals remains one of the most fundamental questions raised by current policy and writers have begun to identify the potential fault lines. It is likely that choice will be hard to deliver in areas of high demand and that the more extreme the housing need, the less likely that choice can be exercised, particularly if it is based on an ability to wait for the preferred property.

Rents and housing assistance for social housing tenants

Successive post-war governments have been concerned about the basis on which rents should be calculated (determining the rent charged) and how to meet the rental costs of those tenants who are unable to pay. These two issues are intertwined and, *in principle*, addressing one involves addressing the other. The overall objectives towards rents pursued by the Conservative governments in the 1980s and 90s were in line with their general principles, as outlined above, in that they sought to bring some market discipline to the huge range of rents which characterized the social sector, not least by ensuring that the rents charged by both local authorities and housing associations gradually moved *towards* market rents (that is, those charged in the private sector). This was a centralizing tendency as, historically, social landlords had set the rents they saw fit, given the financial framework within which they operated.

As a result of the changes to rent policy, local authority rents in particular rose significantly during the 1990s (from a very low base) and, as they rose, so too did public expenditure on housing benefit (see Table 8.1). The tension between these policies was such that, by 1995, the Conservative government brought to a halt any further shifts towards market rents. (For a fuller discussion of the policy towards rents and housing support costs during the 1980s and 90s, see Malpass, 1990 and Cowan and Marsh, 2001).

The incoming Labour government inherited the situation described above. In addition, there were also a number of other implications of the then current rent policy which were problematic, not least in terms of the incoming government's commitment to increasing choice for tenants, and its wider policies of regenerating communities and ensuring social inclusion. For example, although rents were converging somewhat, the principles on which they were calculated differed between local authorities and housing associations. Similar (even adjacent) properties, but offered by different social housing landlords, could therefore have different rents. This was not only inequitable but also detrimental to attempts to create more market-like conditions. Further, there was growing concern that rising rents could result in the concentration of poor tenants on high rent estates (where housing benefit paid the rent) and/or reinforce the 'unemployment trap', whereby poor tenants were reluctant to take employment that led to their losing a disproportionate amount of housing benefit and being no better off in work than unemployed (Ford and Wilcox, 1994).

New Labour has embarked on the reform of social sector rents to make them 'fairer, more coherent and affordable' (DTLGR, 2000). Rents across the social sector will be set to a common template reflecting property value and regional earnings. As with the previous Conservative reform of rent setting, Labour's proposals are centralizing ones, limiting the autonomy of local landlords. However, they may be seen as proposals likely to widen the choices available to tenants, while at the same time producing an efficient, market-based allocation of property appropriate to tenants' household circumstances. The formula is likely to lead to substantial increases in rent in some places and in order to not overburden tenants (or housing benefit expenditure) increases are to be capped at no more than £2 a week (above an annual inflation adjustment) with rent restructuring being completed over a ten-year period.

Despite the fact that rent policy and policy towards the provision of assistance with housing costs are intimately related, only much later, in late 2002, did the government set in train any reform of the housing benefit system, and then only with respect to the private rented sector. Low-income homeowners buying their property with a mortgage and social tenants are not yet affected by reform. Both the principles of, and the flaws in, the current housing benefit system are well documented in existing texts (Malpass and Murie, 1999; Gibb, 2001) and were also outlined in the Green Paper and range through:

- slow and unresponsive administration (contributing to rent arrears and evictions)

- fraudulent claims

- an apparent disincentive to recipients to seek employment (work disincentive effects)

- the possibility, already noted, that, in combination with rent policy, housing benefit increases the spatial concentration of disadvantaged households.

The reforms put forward for the private rented sector, which will be piloted in a number of 'pathfinder' areas, include the payment of a 'standard' rent (rather than actual rents) based on a local reference, with the assumption that tenants will seek to find appropriate property or choose to top up their rent payments. Further, the administrative complexity of *reapplication* for housing benefit every time a tenant's circumstances change is to be replaced with a more streamlined system in order to limit the work disincentive effect. There will be a continued emphasis on addressing fraud and providing a better administrative service. While these reforms have generally been welcomed, nevertheless commentators are generally of the view that the whole process of reform is still slow.

Equally important in the debate about the need to reform housing benefit is the recognition that current policy is not 'tenure neutral'. As discussed earlier, homeowners only receive housing benefit (referred to as ISMI) if they have lost all income. Despite the Green Paper commitment to 'sustainable' homeownership, currently there is no *in-work* assistance with housing costs available to them. Leaving aside equity issues, as the number of low-income homeowners continues to grow, the consequences of the failure to provide in-work assistance with housing costs is likely to become more apparent, particularly in periods of interest rate increases, as mortgage arrears and homelessness increase. The failure to address this as a *housing* policy issue remains one of the outstanding issues for the current government and some of the reasons for this situation are discussed in Kemp (2000). At the same time, it has to be recognized that other policies, specifically the development of working families' tax credits, have increased the income available to poorer homeowners and hence provide assistance through a different route.

Conclusion

Labour has some clear housing policy objectives and is seeking to address a number of issues from the Conservative legacy. These include improvements in house conditions, more efficient and effective housing management, greater choice for tenants, reform of rent setting policy, support for homeless households and sustainable homeownership. A further concern is the connection made between housing and other policy areas, seen most clearly through the concern with neighbourhood regeneration. Some of these objectives and policies are 'new' and 'distinct' (for example in respect of rent restructuring) but some are essentially similar to those of the previous Conservative administrations, if slightly recast. Here examples are the continuation of stock transfer and sustainable homeownership. The extent of reform in other areas, for example with respect to the housing benefit system, has only recently been announced and has yet to be fully implemented and evaluated. Thus, continuity and change sum up the current housing policy objectives.

However, *in general*, the approach adopted to policy implementation is highly consonant with that adopted by the previous Conservative administrations, irrespective of whether the policy goals are the same or dissimilar:

- a growing reliance on the market
- the continuation of the introduction of marketization into social housing
- a reduced role for the local authorities as providers and managers of housing
- a greater centralization of policy prescriptions
- a greater reliance on private finance.

The discussion of housing policy since 1997 offered above has not dealt with all aspects of policy. Important omissions relate to the private rented sector (where key objectives are to improve management practices and address the worst conditions), to homeless households where there have been important changes with regard to local authority responsibilities (including the need to develop homelessness strategies) as a result of the 2002 Homelessness Act and the policy objectives with respect to the housing-related services of those in receipt of care, part of the policy known as 'supporting people'. The emerging issues associated with the local variation in housing markets have also not been considered (with the exception of the brief comments on low demand) but supply, demand and costs are increasingly geographically distinct, whether the focus is market or social housing, and the need for policies to address market variation and change is an emerging issue. Nevertheless, had space allowed for all these issues to be discussed, the conclusions drawn above would also have applied to varying degrees. However, the government announced in the Queen's Speech (13 November 2002) that there will be a new Housing Bill in 2003. Whether this opportunity is used to shift the pace of change in key areas of housing policy or reinforce key continuities remains to be seen.

Further Reading

Cowen, D. and Marsh, A. (eds) (2001) *Two Steps Forward: Housing Policy into the New Millennium*, Bristol: Policy Press.

Wilcox, S. (ed.) *Housing Finance Review*, York: Joseph Rowntree Foundation, Chartered Institute of Housing and the Council of Mortgage Lenders, 2000/2001, 2001/2002, 2002/2003. These volumes provide a series of articles on a range of contemporary housing policy issues and ready access to a wide range of statistical information on the housing market.

CHAPTER 9

Urban Policy

ROB ATKINSON

Since 1945 all governments have developed policies to address the problems facing Britain's urban areas. Until the late 1960s/early 1970s, these policies were largely concerned with the physical reconstruction of cities, mainly by replacing slum areas with new housing, in tandem with policies that sought to create new modern city centres and road networks. In both cases this involved demolition and rebuilding and represented a 'physical approach' to the problems of Britain's cities (see Atkinson and Moon, 1994a: Ch. 2). From the late 1960s onwards, government gradually developed an approach to urban areas which sought to tackle social and economic problems. By 1977 this had developed into a full-blown policy which sought to tackle urban economic and social decline and regenerate Britain's cities (see Atkinson and Moon, 1994a: Chs 3 and 4). Since 1977, all British governments have had an urban policy of some description, however, each has developed its own particular approach, reflecting the way(s) in which it conceptualized the causes of urban problems and the political priority it gave to addressing those problems (see Atkinson, 1995, 2000a).

In this chapter, we discuss the urban policy developed by the Labour government since its election in 1997, focusing on the priorities it attached to developing a 'joined-up' approach to urban problems, encouraging community participation and tackling social exclusion. However, to place this in context, first of all the chapter outlines New Labour's policy inheritance, before going on to discuss the post-1997 period.

Urban Policy pre-1997

In 1977 the then Labour government published Britain's first White Paper on urban policy – *Policy for the Inner Cities* (DoE, 1977). In essence, this document recognized that the causes of urban decline were complex and encompassed economic, social and physical causes. The government sought to develop an approach that tackled these problems by using partnerships to combine the actions of different parts of the public sector. In essence, it emphasized the need to ensure that the actions of government, at central and local levels, were coordinated in such a way that they complemented and reinforced one another (see Atkinson and Moon, 1994a: Ch. 4).

In 1979 the newly elected Conservative government, while accepting its predecessor's view that economic decline lay at the heart of the problem, began to develop a rather different policy. It believed that a key cause of urban decline was state intervention in the economy which prevented the market from functioning, stifled entrepreneurial activity and led the private sector to withdraw from urban areas. Moreover, it was thought that the welfare state was too expensive, deprived the private sector of resources and created a dependency culture among those reliant upon it for the provision of services. Part of the solution was, so far as it was politically feasible, to withdraw the state from both the economy and the provision of welfare services, thereby encouraging individual initiative and self-help. However, many of the programmes which had been running prior to the 1979 election continued throughout the 1980s, although they were gradually restructured to bring them more into line with Conservative thinking (see Atkinson and Moon, 1994a: Ch. 6).

During the 1980s, the dominant view was that urban areas had been left behind by a rising tide of the British economy – that they were islands of decline in a sea of prosperity. The distinctive policy element of this period was an experiment – that of encouraging the private sector to operate within specific run-down urban areas to redevelop them. This approach was under-written by grants, subsidies, tax relief, relaxation of planning controls and so on, designed to attract wealth creators back to the cities. It was believed that by allowing investors to make profits, they would then rebuild cities and create jobs which would 'trickle down' to those in need.

In terms of action, local government was increasingly marginalized and the property development industry took on a key role in an approach that became known as 'property-led urban regeneration' (see Turok, 1992; Imrie and Thomas, 1993; Atkinson and Moon, 1994a: Ch. 7). The best examples of this new area approach to urban revitalization were Urban Development Corporations and Enterprise Zones. Unfortunately, little thought was given to how the large number of projects related to one another, thus projects often ran side by side in a largely uncoordinated fashion.

As a result of sustained criticism, and the failure of 1980s' urban policy to achieve its aims, the period between 1990 and 1994 saw a gradual reorientation of policy. Local government was brought back in, although on terms largely dictated by the centre, and attempts were made to ensure that the needs of those who experienced the worst effects of urban decline were integrated into urban initiatives. City challenge, although a rather short-lived initiative, was the first example of this (see De Groot, 1992; Atkinson and Moon, 1994b). As well as giving a central role to local government and local communities, it was also notable for introducing the idea of competition as a method of allocating urban resources. Government portrayed competition as the most efficient method of allocating resources and developing innovative regeneration schemes and the best way to harness local talent and initiative.

By 1993 government had decided to initiate a major review of urban policy, the outcome was the single regeneration budget (SRB). The SRB began in April 1994 (DoE, 1993). While largely adhering to Conservative orthodoxy on the causes of urban decline, the SRB acknowledged, at least tacitly, the need for greater coordination in the regeneration process. Its objectives explicitly stated that local people should be engaged in and benefit from regeneration (DoE, 1993). The initiative brought together 20 programmes from five central government departments under the overall coordination of the DoE to ensure greater organizational coordination between departments whose programmes had an impact on urban areas. This central restructuring was complemented by the creation of Government Offices of the Regions (GORs) – composed of the regional offices of the Departments of Trade and Industry, Employment, the Environment and Transport, plus a senior representative from the Home Office – in each of the English regions. Regeneration partnerships at local level were the main means by which the SRB was implemented at local level. They were to be multisectoral partnerships involving the public, private, voluntary and community sectors. The creation of such partnerships was a condition for receipt of funding, which was allocated on a competitive basis.

While many commentators gave the SRB a guarded welcome, concerns emerged over its effectiveness and ability to achieve its objectives (see Oatley, 1998; Imrie and Thomas, 1999). In essence, these criticisms boiled down to three issues.

1. There was little evidence, despite the organizational changes introduced, that coordination had actually increased. Policy at and between levels remained fragmented.

2. Community participation was largely illusory and there was still very little evidence that deprived communities were benefiting from regeneration (see Atkinson and Cope, 1997).

3. Finances available for urban regeneration were actually being reduced (see Atkinson, 1999a: 77 8).

Urban Policy post-1997

Prior to its election in 1997, New Labour had signalled its intention to address urban problems in a more coherent manner and ensure that combating social exclusion would be a key part of both urban policy and its wider policy agenda. In opposition, Labour had broadly welcomed the SRB and had indicated that it would be retained, should Labour win the 1997 election. Indeed, the new government appeared to accept the general diagnosis of urban problems offered by previous Conservative governments, when it stated that areas of multiple deprivation in cities had been 'largely by-passed by national economic success' (DETR, 1997a: s. 2.2). This comment implied that the causes of urban decline lay in the areas themselves rather than in the wider societal context. What was new in terms of the urban policy agenda was the emphasis on social exclusion and a renewed, almost evangelical, belief in the effectiveness of joined-up policy and action. In particular, the latter point was reflected in an obsessive belief that more could be extracted from the same, or fewer, resources.

In the summer of 1997, the Department of Environment, Transport and the Regions (DETR)[1] issued supplementary guidance for round 4 of the SRB (DETR, 1997b). The guidance informed partnerships that their bids should reflect the government's manifesto commitments and take account of proposed programmes (such as welfare-to-work and action on drugs). It also emphasized the need for 'a concerted attack against the multiple causes of social and economic decline'(DETR, 1997b: 1) which tackled 'the needs of communities in the most deprived areas' (DETR, 1997b: 2). Moreover, GORs simultaneously issued 'Regional Regeneration Frameworks', which encouraged bidders to ensure that all partners were actively involved in the development of partnerships and bids. A consultation paper on the future of regeneration policy (DETR, 1997a) was also published, which reflected these new priorities and discussed new ways to develop urban regeneration. Perhaps the most important aspect of this paper related to the method by which SRB challenge funds would be distributed in future. The paper opted for a continuation of competition in the allocation of funds, although the term 'controlled competition' would perhaps be a more accurate description. Also it stated that there would be 'clear regional criteria and frameworks ... ensuring the bulk of resources go to the areas of greatest need' (DETR, 1997a: 10).

While welcoming the holistic approach of city challenge and the SRB, the paper (DETR, 1997a: s. 4.7) argued that:

> policies have generally had a more limited (or at least less measurable) impact on tackling social exclusion and empowering local communities. Overall progress has

been slowest in the most deprived areas. In some cases, where deprivation is entrenched, regeneration action can do no more than mitigate problems or prevent their further development. This process can take a considerable time; often longer than the lifetime of individual projects or even programmes.

The significance of this quote is that it signals the importance of addressing social exclusion in urban areas, the recognition that regeneration in some areas will require sustained long-term action and identifies key themes that are reflected in later policy developments. In particular, social exclusion was almost immediately given a high priority on the urban policy agenda as well as on the government's wider policy agenda by the setting up of the Social Exclusion Unit (SEU)[2] shortly after the 1997 election.

Subsequently, in 1998, the SEU published a consultation paper on urban regeneration (or neighbourhood renewal as it was to be increasingly described) – *Bringing Britain Together: A National Strategy for Neighbourhood Renewal* (SEU, 1998). This paper represented an attempt by government to develop a new approach to urban regeneration, building upon the SRB. In many ways, the document contains a remarkably frank recognition of past failures, including:

> the absence of effective national policies to deal with the structural causes of decline; a tendency to parachute solutions in from outside, rather than engaging local communities; and too much emphasis on physical renewal instead of better opportunities for local people. Above all, a joined up problem has never been addressed in a joined up way. Problems have fallen through the cracks between Whitehall departments, or between central and local government. And at the neighbourhood level, there has been no one in charge of pulling together all the things that need to go right at the same time. (SEU, 1998: 9)

The aim was to create a holistic and strategic national approach within which area-based initiatives (ABIs), such as the SRB, would play a key role and communities would be key stakeholders. To further this objective, in 1999 Regional Development Agencies (RDAs) were established for the eight English regions, with the objective of developing a regional strategy to address the problems, including those of urban areas, in each region.

In 1999 the report of the Urban Task Force *Towards an Urban Renaissance* (1999) highlighted similar issues, although it placed much greater emphasis on the need for regeneration to be design-led. The report stressed the importance of high quality urban design in making cities attractive places in which to live and work and the need to use 'public finances and incentives to steer the market towards opportunities for lasting regeneration' (Lord

Rogers, Introduction, Urban Task Force, 1999: 8; see also Rogers and Power, 2000). Despite being criticized for its excessive focus on the role of design to the detriment of economic and social factors, the Urban Task Force report was an important document[3] that stimulated discussion and helped to create the context for the subsequent urban policy White Paper.

In policy terms, the first fruit of this new approach was the New Deal for Communities (NDC), with 17 areas being designated in 2000 and a further 22 in 2001. NDCs are in many ways the first test-bed of Labour's idea that urban areas which have suffered the most extensive decline require long-term programmes. They will run for ten years, with each area receiving between £40 million and £50 million over its lifetime. From the outset, each NDC is required to think about forward strategies that will continue the project, or key elements of it, after funding has terminated. They are also intended to provide a test-bed for the development of a new integrated approach that can then be assessed and the lessons generalized. The lessons learnt from NDC about 'what works?' and how best to deliver services are intended to be mainstreamed by other public service providers, thus they represent, in theory at least, part of a wider attempt to shake up the whole public sector and how it operates.

A less adventurous and less generously funded source of regeneration funding was also created by the 2000 Comprehensive Spending Review – the Neighbourhood Renewal Fund (NRF). The NRF began in 2001 and is directed at the 88 most deprived local authorities – the aim being to improve public services in these areas. Initially it was set up to operate for three years, with total funding of around £900 million. The 2002 Comprehensive Spending Review extended its life for a further three years and allocated an additional £975 million for the final two years. However, many of those working locally in regeneration have criticized the relatively short life of this programme when compared to the seven-year SRB (discontinued in 2000) projects and ten-year NDCs.

The clear intention of *Bringing Britain Together* (SEU, 1998) and all subsequent urban reports and initiatives is to create a comprehensive and coordinated approach in which all the pieces of the urban regeneration jigsaw will actually fit together. Moreover, according to Tony Blair, this requires 'a ten to twenty year plan to turn round poor neighbourhoods' (SEU, 1998: 8).

In November 2000 the long-awaited urban White Paper was finally published – *Our Towns and Cities: The Future. Delivering an Urban Renaissance* (DETR, 2000d). To be somewhat brutal, the White Paper contained very little that was new: all the themes outlined above were reiterated. In the foreword, John Prescott, the Deputy Prime Minister and then Secretary of State at the DETR, stated:

Our guiding principle is that people must come first. Our policies, programmes and structures of governance are based on engaging local people in partnerships for change with strong local leadership. (DETR, 2000d: 5)

The White Paper attempted to do two things: first, to create a *vision* of urban living; and, second, to create a *framework* in which all the various initiatives and themes previously announced can be brought together and operate in a holistic and coherent manner. The *vision* 'is of towns, cities and suburbs which offer a high quality of life and opportunity for all, not just the few' (DETR, 2000d: 7). The *framework* is one that aims to facilitate coordination, collaboration and partnership; these are the means by which effective policies and programmes will be delivered and resources directed at problems. Thus, it should come as no surprise to hear that joined-up strategies and joined-up working are the watchwords. To this end, government agencies at national, regional and local levels are exhorted to work together.

A Cabinet Committee on Urban Affairs was set up to coordinate overall policy at central government level:

- the Neighbourhood Renewal Unit (NRU) was created in the DETR to carry forward the national strategy for neighbourhood renewal

- a Regional Co-ordination Unit (RCU) to ensure that any central policies with a subnational impact complement one another and that RDAs and GORs work together

- local strategic partnerships (LSPs) to ensure strategic and joined-up working at the local level.

All these initiatives are designed either to reduce the number of existing central government initiatives with an impact on urban areas, or to ensure their actions complement and reinforce one another. In part, this is an attempt to rationalize and streamline the increasingly complex nature of urban governance that many have come to perceive as an obstacle to urban regeneration. The White Paper also signalled the end of the SRB, although nothing has been put its place, leaving something of a void. Thus, the period since 1998 has seen an endless series of reports and official publications (most notably the SEU, 1998; Urban Task Force, 1999; DETR, 2000c, 2000d; SEU, 2001) and initiatives (such as LSPs,[4] the RCU, the NRU in the DETR, neighbourhood management, the neighbourhood renewal fund; community strategies).[5] All have sought to create a holistic and integrated approach to urban regeneration.

   This is the overall context in which urban policy has developed over the past decade. There have been successive attempts to construct a policy framework and organizational structures that tackle 'joined-up problems in a joined-up way'. More generally, since 1997, there has been a strong emphasis on countering social exclusion, facilitating social inclusion/integration and ensuring that communities both participate in and benefit from the regeneration process.

Key Challenges

Readers should bear in mind that New Labour has increasingly argued that its policies in general are determined not by politics or ideology, but on 'what works?' (see Davies et al., 2000). In terms of the development and provision of public services it is determined to develop an extensive evidence base in order to identify what works and what does not. This stance has strongly influenced ideas about urban policy, although to date the evidence base remains rather meagre, and initiatives such as NDC are seen as playing a key role in rectifying this situation.

   The development of urban policy since 1997 has thrown up a number of challenges that the government needs to address if its urban policy is to have any realistic opportunity of achieving its aims. These are:

● a joined-up approach to urban problems

● encouraging community participation

● tackling (urban) social exclusion.

Developing a joined-up approach

As noted, the aspiration to ensure that all parts of the urban regeneration jigsaw fit together is by no means new. As far back as 1977, government was aware of the problems created by the lack of coordination between the actions of different government departments and also the unintended impacts of 'non-urban' policies on urban areas. The SRB was also intended to create a framework within which all the parts would fit together into a coherent whole. While it is clear that this has been an aspiration of governments for over 25 years, there is no doubt that New Labour is more committed to achieving this goal than any of its predecessors.

Yet despite this commitment to a joined-up approach, all the evidence suggests that action has been anything but joined-up. If we look at the example of the various ABIs (such as Education Action Zones, Employment Zones, Health Action Zones) launched since 1997 that have impacted on urban areas, it is clear that each has tended to reflect the priorities and targets of its own parent department in Whitehall. Moreover, there has been little, if any, coordination at central, regional or local levels among the initiatives. A number of recent reports (DETR, 2000b, 2000c; PIU, 2000; NRU, 2002) have highlighted this lack of coordination and the problems caused by the avalanche of urban-related ABIs launched since May 1997.

It should be recognized that this is not a problem specific to urban initiatives but applies more generally across government (PIU, 2000). Moreover, the PIU (2000: Ch. 2) argues that, at local level, this excess of initiatives is leading to 'partnership fatigue' that exhausts the local capacity of individuals and organizations actually to participate effectively and thereby undermines the general thrust of policy.

Significantly for urban policy, a recent report by the Treasury – *Government Interventions in Deprived Areas* (HM Treasury, 2000) – has argued that the primary responsibility for tackling (urban) deprivation should lie with the main programmes and that this requires a refocusing of those programmes. The report argues that:

> Targeted initiatives, including holistic regeneration programmes, have a role to play. But they should be part of a clear framework for tackling deprivation, rather than the main tool for doing so. (HM Treasury, 2000: 2)

At one level this perspective supports the importance of a 'joined-up' approach to urban problems, but it also recognizes the need for mainstream policies (such as social security, health, education, employment and economic policy) to play the major role. The implications of this recognition are far-reaching and imply the need for all policies to be assessed in terms of their direct and indirect impact on urban areas. However, it is highly unlikely that central government departments will assess policies in this way, let alone change them to ensure that they contribute actively to tackling urban problems, or at least to not making them worse. Furthermore, this approach implies the need for policies directed at both people and places that work together to tackle social exclusion in all its forms and wherever it exists.

Perhaps because of this preference for 'joined-upness', the government has tended to focus on the need to change the ways in which policies are delivered. This is part of the agenda for modernizing local government and operates through initiatives such as Best Value and local public service agreements and is viewed as increasingly central to addressing urban problems. Yet, with regard to deprived areas, there is little real evidence that any significant changes have taken place to date. Most service providers at local level have proved reluctant, or unable, to significantly change the ways in which they deliver services to these areas. The health service still tends to operate separately from the local authority, and even within local authorities there is little real evidence to support joined-up working to address urban problems (see Alcock et al., 1998).

Multi-sectoral regeneration partnerships have continued to be the main vehicle for the development and delivery of urban policy at the local level. However, the multiplication of such partnerships has actually created an increasingly complex system of governance at local level that few, if any, understand. Moreover, it places enormous strains on the relatively small number of people who participate in them. LSPs are intended to rationalize and simplify these local systems, providing them with greater coherence and allowing for easier collaborative working. However, LSPs have few real powers and even fewer resources to carry out these tasks and it is uncertain whether they will be able to bring the fragments that currently constitute urban policy together in a coherent manner at local level.

At a more specifically urban policy level, the NDC is intended to develop new ways of addressing problems in the worst areas and ensure that the lessons learnt are mainstreamed by service providers at the local level. Although this is a relatively new initiative, the evidence so far is that many mainstream service providers have tended to view NDCs as just another ABI, and few seem to understand how government intends NDC to impact on their activities. There is little evidence of links being built between mainstream service providers and NDCs and even less that the former are learning lessons about 'what works?' from the latter.

At a regional level, the picture is no better: RDAs and GORs are the key regional bodies. RDAs are charged with developing regional economic strategies which address a region's problems, including the urban ones. They also are still responsible for the SRB (although now terminated, the final round projects will run until 2007) and many are developing some form of regional urban strategy of their own. However, RDAs have shown little interest in the social regeneration of urban areas and their focus has increasingly been on economic issues and 'bricks and mortar' regeneration. Nor do RDAs appear to be internally coherent. There is a general view that they are still coming to grips with their role and have yet to really develop a regional perspective or the means to implement one when it is developed. GORs, on the other hand, are responsible for the social side of regeneration. Among their responsibilities are social exclusion/inclusion, local authorities, LSPs and NDCs. While GORs have sought to actively and enthusiastically involve themselves in these areas, many of them still retain an internal structure that reflects the regional elements of the departments, and their priorities, which were brought together in 1994. Thus, internally, they often do not reflect 'joined-up working'. Perhaps more worryingly, and this is despite the creation of the RCU, GORs and RDAs do not have a particularly good track record of working together. Too often they appear unaware of what each is doing and there is little evidence that the 'social' and 'economic' sides of regeneration have been brought together at the regional level to create a framework which will facilitate and support local-level regeneration. The creation of two separate regional bodies, with different operating priorities and cultures, was never likely to succeed and it increasingly looks to have been a mistake. This regional division has arguably increased fragmentation and made life more difficult for local regeneration projects. It is to be hoped that in the forthcoming reform of regional governance this is rectified.

Encouraging community participation

As already pointed out, since the early 1990s, community participation has been allocated a key role in urban regeneration at a local level. Successive initiatives have sought to secure a central role for communities in urban regeneration partnerships. The NDC represents the most recent, and arguably thoroughgoing, attempt to create 'community-led' regeneration partnerships which place the needs of local people at the centre of developments.

The problems associated with community participation are well documented (see Atkinson and Cope, 1997; Atkinson, 1998, 1999b). Many excluded communities lack the capacity to effectively participate in partnerships where other players in the 'regeneration game', who have superior resources and knowledge, frequently set the agenda. Indeed, even where local communities do have the capacity to engage effectively in partnerships, they often find themselves disadvantaged by the need to 'learn a new language', which frequently makes it difficult for them to effectively express their own interests in partnerships (see Atkinson, 1999c). Moreover, it should not be assumed that communities are coherent, identifiable bodies with a single set of interests. Conflicts of interest frequently exist within communities and make it difficult to articulate a coherent series of proposals which partnerships can address. Furthermore, only a small number of people from local communities will be actively engaged in these activities, leading to the possibility that they will succumb to 'participation fatigue' as the constant launching of initiatives makes more and more demands on their limited time.[6]

Another unresolved issue is who exactly is it that community representatives represent? Community representatives on partnership boards may find themselves in a potentially contradictory situation. On the one hand, they have been chosen (whether by elections or other means) to represent the community, but, on the other hand, they are part of a corporate body composed of other partners which has the responsibility for regenerating an area in whatever way it thinks best. The point is that community representatives may find themselves in a minority on the partnership board over particular decisions, but will be expected to act in a manner consistent with collective responsibility. This involves determining what are the 'best interests of the partnership'; these will not necessarily coincide with the community's interests. For one thing, if community representatives challenge the dominant notion of 'best interests' within the partnership, they are likely to be labelled as 'troublemakers'; for another, if they are seen not to be representing the legitimate interests of the community, there is a risk of opening up a gap between represented and representers.

The introduction of the 'community' – however constituted – into regeneration partnerships offers both opportunities and threats to governance. For instance, it can lead to a better use and targeting of resources, a smoother development process and the development of significant community capacities for self-help, empowerment and democratic participation. However, it can also produce resistance to particular forms of development (for example flagship projects), calls for more social expenditure that cannot be met from meagre budgets, demands for more democratic control of projects and disruption in state–private sector relationships. Moreover, communities, particularly deprived ones, do not necessarily have an existing capacity to organize themselves or the resources which would allow them to participate in partnerships as equal partners. To achieve this level of organization requires the investment of significant resources over a considerable period of time and the willingness of other partners to support this process, both financially and in terms of the development of community infrastructure (for example knowledge, confidence, self-organizing abilities). Too often, local government, partly as a result of the timetables imposed to submit bids to central government, has conceived and developed projects with minimal levels of community input. While there are examples of regeneration projects in which communities have played a crucial role, and hopefully the NDC will provide more examples of this, at best community involvement has rarely risen above the level of consultation.

Tackling (urban) social exclusion

Prior to the election of New Labour, social exclusion did not figure in the official discourse of the British government, although programmes such as City Challenge and the SRB arguably represented a de facto attempt to address it. Social exclusion, as both a concept and a policy, is thus relatively new to Britain, having its origins in France and the activities of the European Commission (see Atkinson, 2000b; Atkinson and Davoudi, 2000; MacGregor in this volume). Nor is there any general agreement on the meaning of the term or its implications for policy in general and urban policy in particular. While the government has developed a range of policies to tackle social exclusion, the main emphasis has been on reintegrating the long-term unemployed into the labour market (through welfare-to-work policies and the tax system). Social exclusion and poverty have often been used as if they were interchangeable, reflecting the descriptive nature of the concept as it currently exists. Moreover, given the long-term dominance of a neoliberal policy agenda in the UK, there has been an unwillingness to tackle deeper issues of inequality or provide more generous welfare benefits to those living in poverty and dependent upon the welfare system for their income.

New Labour has emphasized the complex and multidimensional nature of exclusion and has deliberately adopted a flexible definition as:

> a shorthand term for what can happen when people or areas suffer from a combination of linked problems such as unemployment, poor skills, low incomes, poor housing, high crime, bad health and family breakdown. (SEU, 2001: 10)

Reflecting the dominance of the economic/work agenda, urban policy initiatives have placed considerable emphasis on addressing the issues of local economic decline and unemployment (or 'worklessnness' as it has increasingly become known) in problem neighbourhoods or 'excluded spaces'. The reintegration of these areas and those living in them is to be achieved primarily through bringing them back into the mainstream economy. However, there is little evidence to suggest that ABIs such as City Challenge, the SRB and the NDC have, or will, succeed in creating viable local economies in these areas or of creating decent and sustainable forms of employment for those who live there. In part, government has sought to address this latter problem through a growing emphasis on education in order to ensure that children from these neighbourhoods are able to compete in the wider job market. However, once again, there is little evidence to suggest that these policies have been successful, although the NDC will provide a test-bed for such beliefs.

One notion that been seen as central to tackling social exclusion in excluded spaces is social capital. People and groups living in these areas are thought to be 'poor' in terms of the social capital that would enable them to participate in the wider economy or urban regeneration partnerships. In some cases, it has been argued that the forms of social capital present may actually serve to isolate communities from mainstream society (that is, they become inward-looking and have a very clear sense of 'them' and 'us'). Clearly, there are major difficulties in deciding exactly what forms of social capital are present and how relevant they are to facilitating engagement in the wider society and community participation (see Forrest and Kearns, 1999: Ch. 2). Moreover, it should not be assumed that the necessary forms of social capital can easily be developed. The work of Robert Putnam (1993) implies that the forms of social capital (such as trust, shared norms and cooperative horizontal networks) considered necessary for effective democracy and to 'compete' in the contemporary world are not easily developed and must be deeply embedded in the social, cultural and economic relations of an area.

Nor are all excluded spaces the same. Some areas are largely made up of people who are there as a result of powerlessness rather than choice, and this is often the only relationship they have in common with one another. These spaces, which are often areas of unpopular social housing, experience high levels of population turnover and thus lack 'stability'; in such areas, the task of community capacity building is particularly difficult as few residents identify with the area. On the other hand, some excluded spaces (such as more traditional working-class areas with high rates of long-term unemployment) contain relatively stable populations who have a distinct sense of community but also a very sharp awareness of their separation from society. While both types of areas are excluded, very different capacity building strategies are required in each. Involving local people in regeneration partnerships also represents an attempt to build social capital and reintegrate people from these neighbourhoods into the wider political structures of society. But, as we have noted, community participation has been problematic and to date only small numbers of local people have been involved. Once again, the NDC is a crucial test-bed.

Overall, while tackling social exclusion is a key objective of urban policy, its relative newness makes it difficult to come to any firm conclusions. However, we would suggest that the strong emphasis on the economic and employment aspects of current regeneration initiatives runs the risk of ignoring many people and groups who are unlikely ever to enter (or re-enter) the formal economy.

Conclusion

What, then, can be said about New Labour's urban policy after six years in government? Consistent with its supposedly pragmatic and non-ideological third way, New Labour has retained elements of the preceding Conservative government's agenda while attempting to develop initiatives of its own. Broadly speaking, New Labour has tacitly acknowledged that the causes of urban problems do not simply lie within the areas concerned, but has proved reluctant to address wider structural causes. The government's adherence to the belief that globalization is a fact of life to which nations and govern-ments must accommodate themselves means that it has been unwilling to turn to demand-side policies and a more redistributive welfare system. Instead, it has turned flexible labour markets and fiscal rectitude into an act of faith. One result has been a tendency to assume that discovering the 'right' organizational configuration will somehow allow more to be extracted from the same, or fewer, resources – hence the emphasis on joined-up working. Parallel to this is a view that excluded spaces, and those living in them, are the product of a mixture of state intervention and the feckless behaviour of those living in them. Thus, the need to modernize public services and change the behaviour of the socially excluded through a mixture of moral exhortation, financial incentives and stronger forms of social control. Communities are invited to participate but this participation has to conform to government timetables, meet departmental targets and deliver measurable outcomes.

Somewhat ironically, government has proved unable to reform itself to create joined-up government, although New Labour would no doubt blame those working in the public sector rather than accept that what they are searching for is an ideal that is unlikely ever to be achieved. I would suggest that this notion of joined-up working is something of a chimera because it assumes that there is one best organizational form in which to develop and deliver services. It also draws attention away from the fact that there are genuine differences over the causes of urban problems and how to address them. New Labour strives to portray its approach as being pragmatic, sensible and non-ideological, yet this conceals the very fact that it has key tenets upon which it is not prepared to compromise and with which others disagree (see Atkinson, 2000a).

While some progress has undoubtedly been made in addressing urban problems, it is difficult to say that Labour has performed noticeably better than its immediate Conservative predecessor. Although, to be fair, many of the things it is trying to do are likely to take ten, or more, years to come to fruition. The problem is that people will continue to live in run-down urban neighbourhoods and many of them are likely to view New Labour's many initiatives as yet more in a long line of promises which have failed to change their lives or the areas they live in.

Further Reading

Imrie, R. and Thomas, H. (eds) (1999) *British Urban Policy, An Evaluation of the Urban Development Corporations,* London: Sage.
Oatley, N. (ed.) (1998) *Cities, Economic Competition and Urban Policy,* London: Paul Chapman.

Notes

1 After the 1997 election, the DoE was merged with the Department of Transport to create the DETR. After the 2001 election, the department lost the environment portfolio and was renamed the Department of Transport, Local Government and the Regions (DTLR). In the early summer of 2002, the DTLR was broken up with a separate Department of Transport once again created. The vast majority of the DTLR's functions have gone to the Office of the Deputy Prime Minister (ODPM) under John Prescott. The ODPM is responsible for urban policy, addressing social exclusion, regional and local government, the cross-cutting agenda on social exclusion/inclusion and neighbourhood renewal. Readers should bear in mind that Scotland, Wales and Northern Ireland have somewhat different institutional arrangements to those in England, but the general thrust of urban policy is almost identical in each country.
2 The SEU's role is a wide one: to stimulate new thinking and ways of tackling social exclusion as part of the process of drawing up a national strategy; and to draw attention to the complex and multidimensional nature of social exclusion and highlight the need for 'joined-up' action at and between national, regional and local levels.
3 Lack of space prevents any detailed discussion of this report, readers interested in reading more about the report should turn to *Town and Country Planning,* September 1999, pp. 258–81.
4 According to the Guidance on LSPs:

> The aspiration behind local strategic partnerships is that *all* local service providers should work with each other, the private sector and the broader local community to agree a holistic approach to solving problems with a common vision, agreed objectives, pooled expertise and agreed priorities for the allocation of resources. (DETR, 2000b: 3)

The Guidance goes on to state that LSPs will 'provide a single overarching co-ordination framework within which other, more specific local partnerships can operate' (DETR, 2000e: 6).
5 Under Part I of the Local Government Act, 2000, local authorities have a duty to prepare community strategies, with LSPs playing a key role in drawing up these documents. The DETR's guidance (DETR, 2000f, para. 39) states:

> The aim of community strategies is to allow local communities to articulate their needs and priorities. However, action at the local level will inevitably take place against a backdrop of priorities established at national and regional level.

It goes on to state:

> It is important in seeking the views of communities, that councils and their partners do not inadvertently raise expectations that they cannot meet. Clear parameters need to be established and communities must be given to understand the context and constraints within which public service providers operate (such as central government expectations and targets, resource levels and statutory limitations). (DETR, 2000f: para. 56)

6   In response to these problems, and as part of a more general attempt to develop, support and sustain community participation, a Community Empowerment Fund, worth £35m over three years, will be available to the 88 most deprived areas that qualify for the Neighbourhood Renewal Fund. A further £50m will provide small grants to support social entrepreneurs and community organizations over a three-year period in disadvantaged areas (SEU, 2001: 28).

CHAPTER 10

Education Policy

KEVIN J. BREHONY AND ROSEMARY DEEM

For most of the 20th century, after it had overtaken the Liberals as the main party of opposition, Labour was *the* party of education. Fighting first for secondary education for all then, after the Second World War, for comprehensive secondary schooling, Labour saw state-provided education principally in terms of its capacity to reduce social class inequality. In the 1970s, Labour's commitment to the social democratic settlement began to waver. From then onwards, a critique of comprehensive schooling, school curricula and teachers started to emerge, bringing Labour closer to the critique of comprehensive schools and school standards initiated by the New Right from the late 1960s.

By the time Labour returned to power in 1997, the policy landscape in education had been radically changed by years of neoliberal experimentation, coupled with authoritarian populism, marked principally by Thatcherite policies in successive Tory governments from 1979 onwards. Those years produced legislative change comparable with the landmark legislation of 1902 (the introduction of local education authorities) and 1944 (universal secondary education). The dramatic changes to education were found particularly in the 1988 Education Reform Act and its subsequent establishment of a national curriculum and national testing of pupils' educational standards for England, Wales and Northern Ireland. This legislation also laid the foundations for local management of schools and made provision for state schools to leave the control of local education authorities under the grant maintained schools initiative, both of which facilitated a gradual erosion of the basis of local government's provision of publicly funded education.

A key issue facing New Labour when it came to power was the extent to which it should pursue social democratic policies. Like other analysts of New Labour's policies in education (Docking, 2000; Tomlinson, 2001), we are concerned with whether New Labour's approach did depart significantly from that of previous Conservative governments. This chapter also examines whether New Labour's policies are best characterized as neoliberal, social democratic or something else, such as the third way, an approach much vaunted in New Labour's first term (Giddens, 1998, 2000).

Third way policies purport to move away from both neoliberalism, with its emphasis on the primacy of markets, and social democracy, which focuses on the use of the state to reduce social inequalities, to produce policy initiatives that blend public and private alternatives differently in different policy areas – the core focus being on 'what works?'.

New Labour's Public Policies: Continuities and Similarities

There are a number of features of New Labour policy, such as 'modernization', that reappear frequently in different forms of public policy (Newman, 2001). The most significant continuity is New Labour's insistence on its election in 1997 that it would stick to the public expenditure limits set by the previous Conservative administration. This only changed during its second term of office after June 2001.

From a high of 6.5 per cent of GDP in 1975/76, public spending on education, declined to 4.7 per cent in 1988/89. It rose to 5.2 per cent in 1994/95, but by Labour's election in May 1997, education had fallen to 4.5 per cent of GDP in 1998/99 and 1999/2000. Expenditure rose in 2001 to 5.0 per cent and Treasury estimates suggest that it will be 5.3 per cent of GDP by 2003/04 (Glennerster, 2001b). Contrary to some New Labour claims, the proportion of GDP devoted to public spending on education is not in line with other advanced economies. In 1998, for example, it was higher than Germany and Italy but lower than France and Belgium. In traditionally social democratic countries, such as Sweden and Denmark, spending on education stands at 8.0 per cent or more (OECD, 2001). This is the economic context in which Tony Blair's, 'education, education, education' sound bite to the 1996 Labour Party conference should be placed. The insistence on not raising taxes in the first New Labour administration meant that there was restricted room for manoeuvre in most areas of public policy.

There are also many other continuities across different New Labour social and public policies. These include the focus on public–private partnerships, the ebbing away of trust in bureau-professionals (Mintzberg, 1983) and an emphasis on what is sometimes called the 'new managerialism' (including target setting and performance management) as a means of managing public service organizations on the same basis as private sector enterprises (Clarke and Newman, 1997; Exworthy and Halford, 1999a). Implicit in this approach, of course, is the privileging of the private over the public and particularly the embrace of business management techniques as the model of efficiency to be followed by the public services – a stance that has been labelled 'corporate populism' (Barnett, 2000; Jesson, 2002). In addition, other shared features include the strengthening of an audit culture for all public service organizations and their staff (Power, 1997), selective use of academic research and academic expertise (particularly when findings 'fit' policies already initiated) and a plethora of 'something for something' initiatives, where service providers have to bid for resources while core funding is simultaneously reduced.

Another important characteristic of New Labour's policies is the promotion of diversity and flexibility, which has much in common with what has been referred to as post-Fordism (Rustin, 1994; Menter et al., 1997). In addition to flexibility, writers on post-Fordism often make much of the impact of new technologies, especially information and communication technologies (ICT). Advocacy of ICT is a feature of New Labour's policies but some observers believe that it is often closer to fetishism than any rational policy based on its likely uses (Marshall, 2001; see also Burrows in this volume).

Another significant aspect of New Labour education policy is devolution. Since devolution and the introduction of the Scottish parliament, the Welsh assembly and the Northern Ireland assembly, the education systems of Northern Ireland, Scotland and Wales have increasingly begun to exhibit evermore marked differences from the education system in England. Historically, of course, there have always been some differences, notably in Scotland. Scotland has no national curriculum, admits higher education students to four-year degrees (with an ordinary degree awarded after three years, honours after four) at 17 years of age rather than 18 as in the rest of the UK, has a long-standing General Teachers Council (rather than a very recent one created in England) and a fully comprehensive system of secondary education, with no specialist schools as developed in England. Centripetal tendencies in education policy have accelerated since devolution, not only in Scotland but also in Wales and Northern Ireland. For instance, Scotland and Wales have abolished undergraduate tuition fees while England retains them, and Northern Ireland has ceased to publish league tables of exam performances in schools. However, at the time of writing the government has dissolved the Northern Ireland assembly as a result of a continuing dispute between Sinn Fein and the Ulster Unionists around disarmament, and control of education has been taken back by Westminster. The effect of this on Northern Ireland's education policies in the medium term is currently unclear.

Finally, as suggested in the Introduction to this volume, the need to satisfy the interests of the middle class appears as a prime determinant of New Labour's education policies and a strand running through them all. This is not simply a case of reading off from the fact that New Labour's electoral success was achieved by capturing a substantial proportion of middle-class votes (Roberts, 2001). For some New Labour strategists, the alternative to retaining the middle-class use of state schools was their migration to private schooling (Barber, 2002). If this were to occur, the argument runs, social cohesion would be threatened. Retention of middle-class votes is thus an important consideration, and may explain why middle England has benefited substantially from New Labour's education policies of diversity and choice (Gewirtz, 2001).

From Social Class to Social Exclusion

Social class was very much part of old Labour, a social democratic legacy that New Labour jettisoned in favour of the concept of social exclusion. Views of educational outcomes that linked them to social class origin were dismissed by New Labour as sociological determinism. They preferred a version of voluntarism in which, ostensibly, anything could be achieved regardless of circumstance. Poverty was not to be used as an excuse for low educational attainment (Barber and Sebba, 1999). In place of education as a means for reducing class inequality was placed a supply-side vision of education as integral to human capital formation and economic efficiency. There is still a meritocratic vision, for example, in the White Paper, *Schools Achieving Success* (DfEE, 2001), but the role of 'opportunity' is subordinated to, or at least restrained by, the need to compete in the global economy. Even before coming to power, it was being pointed out that the Labour Party's reconciliation of economic efficiency with social justice was contradictory (Thompson, 1996) and so it has proved to be (Whitty, 2001).

   Other forms of social inequality that significantly shape educational attainments have been considered to a greater extent, for instance gender and ethnicity (Tomlinson, 2001). However, gender has been taken into account only sporadically, with attention focusing largely on boys' achievements (or their absence), despite continued evidence of the lower level of women's wages in employment and their major role in child, dependent and household care (Equal Opportunities Commission, 2002). On a more positive note, the Special Educational Needs and Disability Act 2001 applies to all educational institutions from 2002 onwards, with responsibility on those institutions to make reasonable provision for study by students with disabilities. Furthermore, the Race Relations (Amendment) Act 2000 has given all public bodies a duty not only to avoid unlawful discrimination but also a duty to promote racial equality. Schools, HE and FE institutions are now required to prepare and publish a race equality policy.

Such attention is sorely needed in education. A recent review of research on educational inequality concluded that the achievement gap between 16-year-old white pupils and their Pakistani and African-Caribbean classmates had almost doubled since the late 1980s (Mirza and Gillborn, 2000). New Labour replaced the Section 11 funding which provided support for the education of pupils from ethnic minorities via local education authorities with the ethnic minority achievement grant. This money is devolved to schools and intended to provide equality of opportunity for all ethnic minority groups, black or white.

All in all, however, New Labour's record on equality issues in education is thin. Despite the fact that the government argues that it has made social exclusion a central concern, recent ministerial comments appear to 'blame' those in poverty for a range of behaviours, including their failure to find work, and certain kinds of lifestyle, which are considered to be at odds with New Labour's conception of social obligation and duty – rather than focusing on the massive and increasing inequalities in the distribution of income (Levitas, 1998). Indeed, it has been suggested that social exclusion as a concept underlying social policy has little to do with fundamental income inequalities such as low pay and inadequate household incomes, and can produce no practical means of tackling the latter at all (Hills et al., 2002). We now turn to a more detailed look at some of Labour's individual policies on schools and post-compulsory education.

School Standards

One of the most frequently used terms in New Labour's discourse on education is 'standards'. The Department for Education and Employment (DfEE) was set up in 1995 when the Department for Education merged with the Department of Employment. The new title signalled the end of any lingering attachment to liberal humanist conceptions of education for its own sake and emphasized the role of education in employment. Following the general election in June 2001, a new Department for Education and Skills (DfES) was established. Earlier, in 1997, a School Standards and Effectiveness Unit, headed by Professor Michael Barber, had also been established. This unit came out of the 1987–92 shadow education secretary's advisory group, which had a particular interest in school effectiveness research. 'Standards' was a term long fallen into disrepute in education in the UK, along with the 19th-century system of payment by results, although it became popular with New Right critics of progressive education in the 1970s. The term re-entered the mainstream vocabulary of English education when Her Majesty's Inspectorate (HMI) was restructured in 1992 and became the Office for Standards in Education (OFSTED). This renewed emphasis on standards was also linked to the standards-based school reform movement in the United States. The approach is focused on content and teaching rather than learning and learners, arguing that attainment will rise if clear standards are provided defining what pupils and students should know and be able to do. A further claimed benefit is that teachers can understand what they need to teach and need to know, the implication being that teachers did not previously know what was required of them.

The standards approach is bound up with the concept of continuous improvement as discussed by Michael Barber (2002). This concept in turn is associated with the total quality management movement and the work of the American management theorist, W. Edwards Deming (2000). Other fashionable management concepts which appear in Barber's writing are those of the 'learning organization' and 'business process re-engineering' (Barber, 1996). Taken together, these notions amount to a managerialist ideology. However, it is difficult to determine whether New Labour's education policies are derived from this or whether it merely provides a legitimation for continuous assaults on bureau-professionals and the subsumption of the processes of education under a crude business calculus of inputs and outputs which may, at worst, exacerbate social inequalities and, at best, leave them undisturbed.

Much of this ideological discourse emanates from North America. Policy borrowing from the USA (Halpin and Troyna, 1995) is an evident characteristic of New Labour, also found in Thatcherism. What is also evident is New Labour's enthusiasm for the goal of a 'world-class education', a concept that had been discussed in the USA in the early 1990s (Haynes and Chalker, 1997), together with 'world-class standards'. Both terms were a response to the apparent failure of US pupils to perform well in international comparisons of educational attainment such as the Third International Mathematics and Science Study (TIMSS) tests (Atkin and Black, 1997) and the questionable assumption that economic success was dependent on improved results in such tests. On the day he became Prime Minister, Tony Blair declared New Labour's intention to create a world-class education service. Ball, observing this, raises the question of whether or not New Labour's education policies are simply, 'local manifestations of global policy paradigms' (Ball, 1999). But Ball may have underestimated the extent to which New Labour is at the centre of the production of this discourse. It is noticeable, for example, that New Labour's education policy is framed within the general theme of the international struggle for economic survival. What is innovative is the constant representation of the global economic system as overdetermining, with no alternative but to adapt to it. This inevitability is illustrated by an excerpt from a speech by Tony Blair to head teachers in 1999:

> The rise of the global economy, with fewer and fewer barriers to mobility, has changed the whole basis on which nations secure their prosperity. Sector by sector, countries compete on the quality and flexibility of their skill base. By flexibility, I mean the capacity of people to acquire new skills, fast, throughout their careers, building on a high level of general education acquired at school. (Blair, 1999b)

When New Labour came to power, it inherited the national curriculum, which does very much what the advocates of standards-based reform promoted, setting out what is expected of pupils and teachers. Instead of reversing the centralizing measures that had led to the prescription of curricula and assessment, New Labour embarked on some further centralization of its own in the form of a national literacy hour, emanating from the School Standards and Effectiveness Unit, introduced in primary schools in 1998. This measure was soon followed by a national numeracy hour. This was a set of policies that New Labour took over from the previous Conservative government, partly from the national literacy project set up by the DfEE in 1996. Extra resources and specialist training for teachers supported these initiatives but they represented a massive intervention into what had previously been the domain of professional discretion. Micro-management on this scale signalled a decline in the trust accorded to teachers and an impatience with previous policy implementation.

New Labour's motive for this heavy emphasis on raising standards was revealed in the new government's first White Paper, *Excellence in Schools*. The White Paper identified new challenges, some of which arose from international competition (DfEE, 1997) and also discussed the national targets in literacy and numeracy. Speaking in 1998, the then schools minister, Stephen Byers, declared that 80 per cent of all 11-year-olds should meet the standards set for their age in literacy and 75 per cent in numeracy by 2002. The question of how these standards are arrived at or what they actually stand for is one that has largely been avoided by New Labour. In 2001, the proportion of pupils reaching the expected level in literacy stalled at 75 per cent and in numeracy the proportion fell one per cent below the previous year. The government missed its ambitious key stage 2 targets again in 2002 (Ward, 2002). How much this slowdown in the pace of improvement is due to the natural weakening of the initial impetus created by a new innovatory environment is difficult to judge, although it is relevant to note that critics have pointed to the distorting effects on the rest of the curriculum caused by the increasing concentration on literacy, numeracy and the accompanying test regime (Wiliam, 2001). Even if the targets are met, however, the fact remains that between 20 per cent and 25 per cent of 11-year-olds are still failing in school. Although the social effects of academic failure and segregation have been well known since at least the 1960s, this knowledge has apparently not dented enthusiasm for streaming and setting in schools, with official encouragement coming from the 1997 White Paper (DfEE, 1997).

Selection and Differentiation

Nowhere in education policy is New Labour's break with its social democratic past more visible than its approach to secondary schooling. Selection is now to be encouraged and not opposed as in the past. Public schools have been left alone and the 164 grammar schools can only be abolished if a majority of parents in their feeder schools want them to be. In an apparently left-leaning move, the 1,155 grant maintained schools (GM) set up by the last Thatcher government, all with the capacity to control their admissions, were abolished, although most took the option of transforming themselves into 'foundation schools'. Like GM schools, these also had control over their admissions but with a reduced percentage of pupils they were permitted to select. As their funding is lower than it was under GM status, some institutions have introduced parental cash contributions.

In spite of the considerable diversity among comprehensive schools brought about by size and geographic and social location, New Labour's White Paper argued that:

> The demands for equality and increased opportunity in the 1950s and 1960s led to the introduction of comprehensive schools. All-in secondary schooling rightly became the normal pattern, but the search for equality of opportunity in some cases became a tendency to uniformity. (DfEE, 1997: 11)

Before the 2001 general election, a considerable controversy was engendered by the Prime Minister's chief press secretary, Alistair Campbell, when he referred to 'bog standard comprehensives'. What Campbell's remark clearly signalled was opposition to the idea of the 'common school', the ideal of egalitarian supporters of comprehensive schooling for many decades.

The theme of opposition to uniformity is a constant one in New Labour's education discourse, notwithstanding the contradiction it presents in the light of the government's continuation of Conservative policy of the centralization of the curriculum and pedagogy. Where once variety was a codeword for class distinctions in education, 'diversity' now serves a similar function. Evidence of increasing diversity in schooling is provided by the specialist schools. These began as technology colleges under the Tories. Currently there are 685 of these schools, although the government intends that one in four secondary schools will have 'specialist' status by 2003.

There are currently eight different types of specialist college: the original specialisms of technology and language plus sport and arts in 1997 and now four new specialisms: business and enterprise, engineering, science and mathematics and computing. In order to qualify for designation as specialist schools, which brings increased funding, schools have to produce a four-year school and community development plan complete with targets and performance indicators. Continued designation depends upon satisfactory performance. A school must also raise at least £50,000 in sponsorship in order to be considered. Specialist schools can select up to 10 per cent of their pupils by aptitude in the specialism but according to OFSTED, 'one in five schools have not made the best of the opportunity' (OFSTED, 2001).

Like all selective schools, pupils attain higher results at GCSE than in non-selective schools. Preliminary research on non-selective specialist schools shows that they obtain better results than other non-selective schools (Jesson, 2002). Other research shows that specialist schools produce more polarization and social segregation as they admit proportionately fewer pupils from poorer backgrounds (Gorard and Taylor, 2001). In so far as there is evidence of value-added in specialist schools, the question is raised about whether this is due at least in part to the additional funding received.

Even more diversity in the range of schools is envisaged. The White Paper *Schools Achieving Success* announced plans for new specialisms and a large increase in the number of specialist schools (DfES, 2001a). More controversially, it also advocated an expansion in the number of faith schools. These will take the form of city academies which are designed to replace existing poorly performing schools. Similar in many respects to the Tory's city technology colleges, they are to be owned and run by sponsors, thereby conforming to New Labour's policy of public/private partnerships. Sponsors may be businesses, individuals, churches and other faith groups, voluntary bodies who will provide 20 per cent of the capital costs. Flexibility will be a distinguishing characteristic and they may be permitted, for example, to disregard parts of the national curriculum. Consistent with New Labour's enthusiasm for ICTs, they will use the new technologies to support all aspects of learning, as the specialist schools and the city learning centres are already doing.

Excellence in Cities

The 'excellence in cities' programme was introduced in 1999. The education of disadvantaged and disaffected pupils in inner city areas has been the target of a host of initiatives aimed at tackling underachievement. Some, like the Education Action Zones, have been relatively unsuccessful in attracting the business sponsorship once seen as integral but, rather than being killed off entirely, such policies get transformed into something else. Other policies such as learning mentors, learning support units and excellence challenge are part of a bewildering stream of policy initiatives aimed at inner-city pupils.

City learning centres (CLCs) exemplify New Labour's infatuation with ICT, as they are intended to provide ICT-based learning opportunities for pupils at the host school, pupils at a network of surrounding schools and the wider community. It is intended that by March 2004, there will be over 100 CLCs operating in excellence in cities areas across the country. Another element of the excellence in cities initiative is the selective emphasis of the 'gifted and talented' programme aimed at 'disadvantaged able children', defined in ways reminiscent of the genetically inherited notion of intelligence as a group of gifted and talented pupils, including 2–10 per cent of pupils in each year group. The intention behind this initiative is not only to raise standards but to help 'recapture parental support for inner city schools'.

One outcome of New Labour's pursuit of diversity is that there are now at least 13 different kinds of schooling arranged in a hierarchy headed by private schools. Funded in different ways, the history of differentiated provision is one in which hierarchies develop among schools and there is no 'parity of esteem' (Banks, 1955) granted to them. It was the lack of parity of esteem between grammar and secondary modern schools that was a principal criticism of the old selective system. Among the new types of school are beacon schools, numbering 1,000 in 2001. The principal idea behind these schools is that they should share good practice with other schools.

All these new types of school, which also have new kinds of governance and admissions policies, weaken the local education authority (LEA), once seen by Labour as providing a counter to centralization and an arena for the practice of representative democracy. Having decided, as did the national efficiency movement at the beginning of the 20th century, that efficiency is more important than democracy, New Labour has intensified the Tory policy of attacking LEAs. In addition to creating new categories of school outside the control of the LEAs, they have been undermined further by inspection by OFSTED and privatization of some 'failing' authorities.

Privatization

In 2001, 8 per cent of pupils were attending private (public/independent) schools. This figure shows some growth since 1979–80 when 5.8 per cent of pupils attended private schools. The high proportion of private school pupils gaining places at Oxbridge threatens New Labour's meritocratic vision but there appears little inclination to disrupt the means by which the ruling classes are culturally reproduced. Private schools, after all, are quantitatively insignificant, although *qualitatively* highly important: to increase their number to any great extent would undermine their main attraction, which is exclusivity, and the social distinction that accompanies it.

Privatization for New Labour takes a number of forms other than making all schools directly fee-paying. Under the 1999 School Standards and Framework Act, for instance, the government assumed the power to intervene where an LEA is declared by OFSTED to be failing to carry out its duties. In such circumstances, the secretary of state is granted the power to 'outsource' the services previously provided by the LEA to private organizations recognised by the DfEE. One of these, NordAnglia, a stock exchange-quoted company with a variety of interests in education, saw its turnover grow from £40 million in 1997 to £66 million in 2001, a substantial share of this figure being derived from outsourcing. Among LEAs that have experienced some measure of privatization are the London boroughs of Hackney, Islington, Southwark and Haringey, as well as Liverpool, Walsall, Bristol, Leicester, Sandwell, Doncaster, Sheffield, Rotherham and Leeds. Significantly, in the light of the charges of the failure of local democracy, many of these areas are those where working-class populations experience multiple disadvantages.

Post-compulsory Education – New Labour and the New Labour Market

Post-compulsory education is becoming increasingly important in relation to social inequality, since more and more young people are now continuing their education past the school-leaving age of 16. The participation rates of 16–18-year-olds in education and training have continued to grow, so that by the end of 2000, only 24 per cent of this group were not in education or training and just 9 per cent were not in education, training or employment (DfES, 2001b).

The majority of New Labour's policies in the post-compulsory field have been concerned with human capital and the requirements of the labour market. There is little sign in most of the policies emanating from New Labour of any concern for human development, the advancement of human knowledge or the contribution that education can make to the quality of life. Rather, despite a developing rhetoric about lifelong learning, the main focus of attention in the post-school field has been on people aged 16–30 and their participation in further and/or higher education and work-based learning. Not every policy has been successfully implemented; there are always unintended consequences, sometimes arising from the lack of so-called joined-up thinking across different policies.

Individual learning accounts

Individual learning accounts (ILAs) were a major feature of the 1997 election manifesto. Learning accounts for adult learners, which involved a small level of government subsidy for course fees, were under discussion from before the first term of office of New Labour. They appear in the Dearing Report on Higher Education and the Kennedy Report, *Learning Works*, on widening participation in further education (Kennedy, 1997; National Committee of Inquiry into Higher Education, 1997). The ILA scheme was aimed at encouraging adults not currently in formal education to return to learning through courses in work-related skills such as information technology (although little attention was paid to the gender inequalities in access to post-school education and training highlighted in *Learning Works*).

At first all those who opened an ILA got £150 towards training; later this was replaced by means-tested discounts worth up to £200. The target of one million adults with ILAs was reached in March 2001, a year earlier than anticipated, albeit with some £60 million more spent than the anticipated £200 million in the first two years of the scheme. However, by autumn 2001, there were many rumours of fraud and misselling of ILAs to people not eligible to hold them. The scheme was closed to new entrants in November 2001 when it was revealed that bogus 'trainers' and 'trainees' had managed to siphon away many of the ILA subsidies. The private company Capita (a specialist in facilities management rather than education), which was awarded a £55 million contract to run the scheme's computers and call centres, failed to provide an early alert to the DfES of growing problems with the scheme. It was further suggested by the House of Commons All-Party Education Committee in a report on the ILA fiasco that in awarding the contract to Capita, the DfES had confused quality assurance with registration, a problem previously encountered by government departments in awarding computer contracts (All-Party Committee on Education, 2002).

ILAs could certainly be described as having elements of both neoliberalism (vouchers being a principal mechanism for using in quasi-markets) and social democratic approaches (since trying to encourage and assist all adults to participate in some form of learning and training is an egalitarian move). In the end, ironically, the former defeated the latter, although at the time of writing the scheme is about to be relaunched.

Learning to succeed: a divided post-compulsory education

A government White Paper published in 1999, *Learning to Succeed*, set out New Labour's plans for post-16 education and its organization. Post-16 education is a key arena in which to address the life chances of those social groups (working-class women and men, members of black ethnic minority groups, people with disabilities) without significant access to or funding for higher education or training. In theory, access to post-16 education and training should represent a continuation of the principles of the comprehensive school in the post-compulsory arena, while not privileging academic study over other forms of study such as vocational training, which has so often been the case in past UK education policy (Unwin, 2002). However, as Parry (2001) notes, despite the emphasis on lifelong learning, the separation between further and higher education has been maintained. Following the White Paper, a new parent body, the Learning and Skills Council (LSC), replaced both the Training and Enterprise Council and the Further Education Funding Council. However, the separate funding body for higher education was left alone, allegedly for two reasons. First, universities are national and international, not just regional, in their contribution. Second, including the additional complexities of the university sector would make it even more difficult to bring order to the already complicated world of post-school education and training. However, as Parry notes, at that time about one in nine HE students in England was already studying in an FE rather than HE environment, with a smaller proportion of this group studying an FE course franchised by an HE institution (Parry, 2001).

The consequence of maintaining the distinction between further and higher education is that while both appear to be underfunded for the work they are expected to undertake, the conditions for students studying HE courses in FE colleges usually include less favourable staff–student ratios and less well-qualified staff than in the universities. Since the FE sector is where New Labour is now expecting much of the expansion of working-class participation in HE to be located, the consequences of a divided post-compulsory education system for issues of equity are evident. New Labour's policies on post-compulsory education appear to be driven less by social democratic principles than by neoliberalism. Agencies such as the LSC are a means of bringing in both the private sector (heavily represented on national and local LSCs) and the market to post-school education. It is to New Labour's policy on widening participation in higher education that we now turn – a policy that, at first sight, appears to have remained faithful to its traditional social democratic principles.

Widening Participation in Higher Education: Who, What and Why?

There has been a plethora of initiatives on widening participation to higher education under New Labour (Watson and Bourne, 2001). These include special initiative funding for taking students from disadvantaged backgrounds and students with disabilities, funding for building FE and HE partnerships and improving the quality of provision for students with disabilities, a postcode premium for recruiting disadvantaged students, extra money for HE summer schools to encourage entrants from disadvantaged backgrounds and for recruiting more state school students, and setting up a national mentoring pilot project for students from disadvantaged backgrounds. There have also been various financial support initiatives for those who do get accepted onto higher education courses, although these do not seem sufficient in the face of the rising debt levels of most HE students. In summer 2002, a House of Commons committee also suggested allowing educational maintenance agreements to be extended from further education or school study to the first year of university study, although this has yet to be agreed.

The main target groups for widening participation seem to be potential students from social class V (the lowest) and students with disabilities. Women and ethnic minority groups have high representation in higher education (Comptroller and Auditor General, 2002a), although social class and membership of particular ethnic groups need to be taken into account here. Young women from social class V and both women and men from African-Caribbean groups remain underrepresented. Although the social class V participation rate has more than doubled since 1991/92, increases in the participation rate of all students have left the proportion of class V relative to other social class groups and especially class I, much the same as a decade ago.

Disability remains another barrier to HE entry. Eighteen-year-olds with a disability are only 40 per cent as likely as those without a disability to enter higher education. While the proportion of HE students reporting a disability went up by 50 per cent in the five years up to 2001, the most common disability reported was dyslexia. In an attempt to deal with these issues, the Special Needs and Disability Discrimination Act 2001 applies to higher education from 2002 onwards, and will require institutions not to discriminate against qualified applicants with disabilities and make reasonable provision for supporting their learning.

In the 2001 election manifesto, New Labour set a target for the year 2010 of 50 per cent of those aged between 18 and 30 having the opportunity to benefit from higher education (currently it hovers around 40 per cent). The primary motive for the 50 per cent target seems to be an economic one. Estelle Morris, secretary of state for education at the beginning of New Labour's second term, declared that:

> eight of ten new jobs created over this decade will require skills and qualifications of a higher education level. A 1 percentage point increase in the number of workers with higher education qualifications raises GDP by 0.5 per cent ... £4bn. Our competitors have higher rates of university participation. (Morris, 2002)

The possibility that there is no simple relation between GDP and educational achievement, that competitors with higher participation rates might also devote a greater part of GDP to higher education and that a good proportion of these new jobs are in highly specific fields does not appear to be considered. Like its Conservative predecessors, New Labour seems unaware of research which shows that as increasing numbers of people acquire a degree, the value of that degree in the labour market (in terms of both economic and cultural rewards) is reduced (Brown and Scase, 1994, 1997). Somewhat ironically, Estelle Morris resigned as secretary of state for education in autumn 2002, following a double-headed furore, first over alleged government, Qualifications and Curriculum Authority and exam board interference to lower AS and A2 level grades, and, second, over missed education targets (including the politically sensitive target of infant class sizes).

A report by the National Audit Office in 2002 noted HE providers' complaint that the extra money available to them for widening participation does not cover the cost of supporting students from disadvantaged backgrounds (Comptroller and Auditor General, 2002a). The report also noted that 20,000 part-time entrants each year who attracted the widening participation premium already had a degree or higher qualification. It observed that constant bidding for funds makes long-term planning difficult, there is inadequate support for students studying part time and some of the funding for students from state schools goes to those institutions whose record on increasing admissions from this sector is poor. If this catalogue of problems is added to the existing funding problems of universities (UK public spending on higher education is a smaller proportion of GDP than many other EU countries and about a third of that spent in the USA), then the New Labour dream of world-class universities seems destined to remain just that – a dream.

A White Paper was expected in the autumn of 2002 discussing the way forward for higher education funding in England and Northern Ireland – this was eventually published in January 2003, having been delayed by the resignation of the secretary of state, Estelle Morris, and her replacement by Charles Clark. By November 2002 there was considerable speculation that top-up fees would be introduced. This was fuelled by a speech by the minister for higher education (England), Margaret Hodge, to university vice chancellors in which she admitted that UK higher education was in financial crisis, and by meetings of some elite universities to discuss alternative means of funding higher education. The 2003 White Paper suggested that top-up fees be replaced by a Graduate Contribution of up to £3,000 per student per annum repayable on an income-contingent basis after graduation. Means-tested maintenance grants of £1,000 per annum are to be reintroduced to encourage young people from the poorer sections of the community to go into higher education. But neither of these measures will be sufficient to avoid considerable levels of debt on graduation for the majority of students. The White Paper also suggested that the main expansion in higher education provision for underrepresented groups will be through two-year foundation degrees, to be offered by teaching-intensive universities (the rules which currently tie university status to research and research degree awarding powers are to be changed) and further education colleges. Thus, disadvantaged students will probably find themselves taking a different type of degree in an institution which has little or no involvement in research. Although the White Paper also suggests more rigorous teaching standards for universities and annual student satisfaction surveys to be overseen by the National Union of Students, whether this approach will convince potential applicants to apply for university places and risk debt in the process remains to be seen. Meanwhile in Scotland there are still no plans for fees of any kind and Wales would like to follow this road if it is allowed to do so (the Welsh assembly has fewer powers than the Scottish parliament). Thus, students from England are likely to be attracted to Scottish universities which, paradoxically, could face an exodus of academic staff unless alternative means of funding pay increases and infrastructure development are identified.

In relation to widening participation then, an apparently social democratic policy has many neoliberal elements and has so far failed to achieve its objectives, partly because there are so many, often contradictory, initiatives in existence. Finally, it is worth pointing out that the government has paid little attention to the 50 per cent of young people who will not enter higher education and what they are to be offered as part of the lifelong learning agenda.

Conclusion

After examining the context of New Labour's education policies and the emphasis on social exclusion, a number of different strands of New Labour's education policies in relation to schools and post-compulsory education have been reviewed. Although many of these policies have an apparent element of concern for social justice and social democracy within them, in many instances this concern is more apparent than real. Five characteristics stand out:

1. The shift to the concept of social exclusion from Old Labour's concern about material social class inequalities.

2. A move away from comprehensive education at secondary level.

3. New Labour's focus on constantly shifting policy parameters and initiatives which make longitudinal evaluation of policy outcomes extremely difficult.

4. The government's interest in the market and the private sector as a way of revitalizing public policy and its related invoking of new managerialism techniques as a means of regulating and controlling the public services.

5. Its obsession with pleasing middle-class voters, particularly where low rates of income tax are concerned.

New Labour has shown no more interest in redistributing income between rich and poor than its Conservative predecessors and, in general, its education policies reflect a greater concern with 'differentiation' than equality, and with economic competitiveness rather than social justice.

Further Reading

Docking, J.W. (ed.) (2000) *New Labour's Policies for School: Raising the Standard?*, London: David Fulton.
Tomlinson, S. (2002) *Education in a Post-welfare Society*, Buckingham: Open University Press.

CHAPTER 11

Health Policies

CAROLINE GLENDINNING

The National Health Service (NHS) occupies centre stage in the Labour government's drive to modernize public sector services. Indeed, the NHS has become the focus of both very considerable levels of new investment and exceptionally high political stakes, so much so that, in 2002, the Prime Minister invited the public to base its judegment of the government's performance at the next election on its success (or otherwise) in improving the NHS. Over the preceding 20 years, the annual real terms[1] growth in NHS expenditure remained at around 3 per cent. Between 1997 and 2001, annual real terms growth doubled, to 6.1 per cent (Jones, 2001). Further increases in funding for the NHS were announced in the 2001 and the 2002 budgets, taking annual real terms growth up to 7.4 per cent for the years 2002/03 to 2007/08. This level of real terms growth in NHS funding is almost three times higher than for the public sector as a whole, and has been committed for a much longer period (other public sector real terms growth remains at 2.5 per cent for only the two years 2004/05 and 2005/06) (HM Treasury, 2002). In cash terms, the additional investment announced in the 2002 budget increased total spending on the NHS across the United Kingdom from £65.4 billion in 2002/03 to a projected £105.6 billion in 2007/08. Calculated as average spending per household, this represents a 48 per cent increase, from £2,370 annually per household in 2001/02 to £4,060 per household in 2007/08 (HM Treasury, 2002).

Whether this increased investment is a response to evidence of the widening gap between UK health spending and performance and the average for other European Union countries (Wanless, 2001), or simply reflects electoral expediency is not clear. Nevertheless, the level of additional investment in the NHS by the self-proclaimed New Labour government bears a remarkable resemblance to Old Labour expenditure patterns, which privileged state over other forms of welfare – although, as this chapter will argue, the conditions attached to these new resources and the ways in which they are to be spent reflect definitively New Labour modes of governance.

Although the current government has claimed the term 'modernization' as its own – and increasingly uses it in a confrontational and divisive way to dismiss critics of its methods – many longer term continuities can nevertheless be discerned. Newman (2001: Ch. 3) argues that current modernization strategies originated in the early 1990s and describes them as characterized by a belief in rational, scientific management, the application of business ideas to promote efficiency and, increasingly, an emphasis on consumerism and responsiveness to users. Distinctive New Labour nuances to the modernization project include a softening of market mechanisms, a new emphasis on collaboration and partnership, both within and between sectors, and greater inclusivity in the policy-making process. Labour's modernization is also:

> more strongly oriented towards the delivery of new policy agendas in health, education and social welfare, areas in which the delivery of policy outcomes [is] critical to Labour's continued political success. (Newman, 2001: 52)

In addition, within the context of the NHS, modernization carries strong overtones of a challenge to traditional bastions of autonomy and power on the part of professional elites and trade unions, if these impede efforts to improve efficiency and responsiveness.

This chapter will outline the challenges facing the incoming 1997 Labour government in relation to the NHS, describe its policies for tackling these challenges and critically evaluate the prospects for the success of these policies. The empirical evidence on which the chapter draws focuses on developments in primary and community health services – those services provided by general practitioners (GPs), their practice-based staff and community-based nursing and other related health practitioners. Improvements in the equity and ease of access to these services, their flexibility and responsiveness to patients, the quality and consistency of services and their collaborative capacity are all key elements of the government's modernization agenda. It is therefore in relation to these sectors that some of the most dramatic and far-reaching changes have been introduced since May 1997. Moreover, changes in primary and community health services will at least partly determine the overall performance of the NHS in relation to the highest profile political indicators concerning waiting times, admissions to and discharge from the acute hospital sector. Lastly, developments in primary care illustrate well the wider tensions endemic to New Labour's transformation of welfare governance (Exworthy, 2001) – the relationships between central policies and their local implementation and management and the organizational and professional factors which are likely to exert a profound influence on the success (or otherwise) of the government's aspirations.

1997: The Challenges

Many of the difficulties faced by the incoming Labour government in May 1997 had already been fully acknowledged by the previous Major government. Indeed, three White Papers published during 1996 (DH, 1996a, 1996b, 1996c) had drawn attention to the fragmentation, inflexibility and highly variable quality of primary health services delivered by self-employed, independent contractor, small business GPs. Arguably, the fragmentation and variable quality of primary health services had been increased by the experience of GP fundholding, where some GPs (or groups of GPs) held budgets with which to purchase hospital and community health services for their patients. While evidence of improvements in the costs and quality of hospital services purchased by fundholders was equivocal, some of the clearest benefits were discernible in the new services which GPs were able to purchase or provide within their practices (Glendinning, 1998) – gains which were not enjoyed by the patients of non-fundholding GPs.

The 1996 White Papers also highlighted the lack of coordination between the services provided by GPs from their practices and the community nursing and other services delivered by NHS Trusts; the inflexibility of traditional methods of funding general practice and the consequent inability to respond to local variations in health needs; and the constraints imposed by traditional career structures, divisions of skills and expertise between doctors, nurses and other health professionals (Glendinning, 1998). These problems – and some of the solutions to them as well, which had been rushed through parliament just before the 1997 election – were inherited by the incoming government.

Some of these inherited problems dated back to the inception of the NHS in 1948. Over the subsequent half-century, GP and other family practitioner services (dentists, opticians, pharmacists) had remained funded and administered separately from hospital and community health services. In particular, GPs had vigorously defended their position as independent, self-employed contractors to the NHS. GP services had also remained largely demand-led, with expenditure levels determined by a combination of demand from patients and GPs' own patterns of professional behaviour (for example in relation to drug prescribing or requests for laboratory investigations). This, combined with GPs' role as gatekeepers to more costly hospital services, had exposed them to growing scrutiny and prompted renewed searches for ways of imposing cash limits and managerial discipline (Elston, 1991). Consequently, throughout the early years of the 1990s, health policies in Britain had espoused the centrality of primary care and policy documents contained increasing references to a 'primary care-led NHS' (NHSE, 1994). This phrase denoted both a shift in resources and activity away from the secondary, hospital sector to primary and community health services, and the development of a major role for GPs and other primary care professionals in shaping and managing the NHS as a whole (Petchey, 1996).

Other challenges faced by the incoming government were less long-standing and reflected the neoliberal, market-oriented approach which had dominated welfare policy in the more immediate past. One such challenge was the evidence of widening socioeconomic inequalities and their consequences for the increasingly unequal incidence of ill health, morbidity and mortality. An independent inquiry into inequalities in health, commissioned soon after Labour took power in 1997, showed that although death rates among both women and men across all social groups had fallen, differences in life expectancy between those at the top and bottom of the social scale had widened markedly:

> These growing differences across the social spectrum were apparent for many of the major causes of death, including coronary heart disease, stroke, lung cancer and suicides among men, and respiratory disease and lung cancer among women. (Acheson, 1998: 13)

Widening social class differences were also clearly apparent in the incidence of morbidity and other risk factors such as high blood pressure, accidents and obesity.

A further challenge for the incoming government arose from the politics of the NHS during the Thatcher and Major governments and, in particular, the impact of GP fundholding. The internal market reforms were highly controversial, nowhere less so than in relation to the gradual expansion of opportunities for GPs to hold budgets with which they could purchase or commission hospital and community health services for their patients. Although GP fundholding was not originally a major component of the internal market reforms (Glennerster et al., 1994), it became the central element of the policy of promoting a primary care-led NHS, 'in which decisions about the purchasing and provision of health care are taken as close to patients as possible' (NHSE, 1994: para. 1). By 1997, just over 50 per cent of all GPs were fundholders or members of fundholding groups (European Observatory on Health Care Systems, quoted in Exworthy, 2001).

The internal market of the early 1990s and GP fundholding in particular were intended to reshape hospital and community health services, employing market mechanisms to tackle problems of access, quality and costs. Overall, the evidence suggests that marginal improvements in these areas did result, particularly in relation to high profile, consumer-sensitive issues, such as waiting times for hospital admission (Glennerster et al., 1994; Le Grand et al.,

1998). Much more significant, however, were the changes which many fund-holding GPs made in the range of services provided within their practices for their patients. Counsellors were employed in GP practices to deal with common psychological problems; chiropody and alternative therapies were purchased; diagnostic testing and minor surgical procedures could be carried out in the surgery; and specialist outpatient clinics were arranged in local GP surgeries to enhance their accessibility to patients (Roland and Shapiro, 1998).

Developments such as these of course depended on the voluntarism of individual GPs to become fundholders and their imagination and enthusiasm for initiating change (Ennew et al., 1998). GP fundholding was very unevenly spread; patients in more affluent, suburban areas were much more likely to experience improvements in both their local primary care services and their access to hospital services than people living in poorer, inner-city areas. In contrast, deprived areas with very high levels of health and social care needs still tended to employ higher proportions of single-handed GPs who practised without additional ancillary staff or services (Leese and Bosan-quet, 1995; Lunt et al., 1997).

However, experiences during the 1990s had also shown how difficult it could be to change the behaviour of GPs, whose professional leaders had resolutely resisted any compulsory change to their status as independent contractors to the NHS. Although a new GP contract in 1990 had imposed new requirements on the profession (such as the obligation to offer annual health checks to all patients aged 75-plus) and introduced new financial incentives to provide services, these were not effective levers for changing professional practice. Moreover, the imposition of the 1990 GP contract had created considerable difficulties between the government and the medical profession and incoming Labour ministers were reluctant to introduce further compulsory changes which risked a high profile row with the profession. Furthermore, although a new GP contract might have enabled additional, universal service and quality standards to be introduced, it would still have failed to tackle the fragmentation between GP, community health and other NHS services. The family services health authorities, which administered GPs' contracts from 1990, remained separate from the health authorities that were responsible for mainstream hospital and community health services. There were no mechanisms by which loosely connected (and sometimes competing) networks of primary and community health service professionals and practices could be transformed into a consistent, integrated service. Moreover, apart from the 'capping' of GP fundholders' prescribing budgets, expenditure on primary care services remained demand-led and therefore also inequitably distributed.

It should come as no surprise that increasing inequalities in the levels and quality of services should result from the NHS quasi-market, with its implicit assumption that excellence would emerge naturally from the free play of market forces. Nevertheless, the inequalities and variations *within* primary care which the incoming government inherited were as much of a political problem as the 'two-tier' system of access to hospital care which had resulted from GP fundholding (Le Grand et al., 1998). The abolition of fundholding had been a major electoral pledge while the Labour Party was in opposition, bolstered by its appeal to its historical credentials as the original architects of a universal, taxation-funded NHS in 1948. Within seven months, a White Paper was published (Secretary of State for Health, 1997), which proposed major changes in the structure, organization and funding of the NHS.

Responses: Labour's Reforms

From GP fundholding to primary care groups and Trusts

The White Paper *The New NHS: Modern, Dependable* proposed 'nothing less than a major culture shift' (Hunter, 1999: 19) for English primary care. At its core was the replacement of the jigsaw of GP fundholding, multi-funds, total purchasing and locality commissioning groups, with a single type of organization, primary care groups (PCGs). PCGs were to cover *all* the GPs in a locality, typically around 50 GPs and 100,000 patients. PCGs have responsibility for:

- promoting the health of the local population

- commissioning community health and hospital services from NHS Trusts

- developing primary care services by working across GP practices

- integrating primary and community health services

- collaborating with local authority social services on both planning and service delivery.

These functions were to be carried out within the framework of an overarching health improvement plan (HImP), which sets out the local strategy for delivering health improvement targets. Depending on their expertise and organizational capacity, PCGs were to operate at one of four levels of independence and autonomy from their local health authorities, eventually becoming freestanding primary care Trusts (PCTs), accountable to mainstream NHS management structures and responsible for both commissioning hospital services *and* providing community health services.

PCGs/Ts have responsibility for a unified budget, made up from three formerly separate funding streams: the budget for hospital and community health services (82 per cent); for GP prescribing (15 per cent); and for the costs of GP practice infrastructure (for example diagnostic and computer equipment and ancillary staff – 3 per cent) (HFMA/NHSE, 2001). The size of this budget is determined by a new funding formula which reflected the sociodemographic characteristics of the locality rather than historical patterns of spending, and was capped (for further details, see Wilkin and Glendinning, 2002). In turn, and reflecting the role of primary care as the gatekeeper to more expensive services, PCGs/Ts are expected to set, and manage, indicative[2] budgets for their constituent GP practices' expenditure on drug prescribing and hospital and community health services.

In April 1999, 481 PCGs, covering the whole of England, went 'live'. By April 2001, 260 of these, covering 47.7 per cent of the population of England, had developed sufficient organizational capacity to become autonomous PCTs. However, a number of PCGs had already merged with each other, so the total number of organizations immediately shrank to 424. The remaining PCGs became Trusts in 2002. Mergers between PCGs/Ts have had a dramatic impact on the size of the populations covered by these new organizations; if all planned mergers proceed, the average population covered by a PCG/T will rise from 105,000 in 1999 to 193,000, with the populations of those new PCGs/Ts created through mergers averaging 224,000 (Bojke et al., 2001).

Subsequent policy statements (DH, 2000, 2001a) have developed the government's expectations for PCTs. These are expected to 'become the lead NHS organization in assessing need, planning and securing all health services and improving health' (DH, 2001a: 5):

> Devolving power and responsibility to PCTs lies at the heart of our proposals. PCTs will be the cornerstone of the local NHS ... PCTs will also be expected to ensure that more power is available for frontline staff. (DH, 2001a: 13)

The devolution of budgets and local strategic responsibility to PCTs was complemented by the abolition in April 2002 of local health authorities, which had hitherto held and distributed local budgets and taken a major role in local health services planning and commissioning. Local health authorities are replaced by a smaller number of strategic health authorities, covering populations of around 1.5 million people and responsible for:

- providing 'strategic leadership'

- ensuring 'strong and coherent professional leadership'

- managing the performance of local NHS Trusts and PCTs

- supporting programmes to 'improve the quality and consistency of care … through the development of clinical networks across organizations' (DH, 2001a: 6–17).

As a result, PCTs

> will take responsibility for securing the provision of the full range of services for their local populations … [and] … have a clear lead in developing local services and will be able to tailor services to local needs. (DH, 2001a: 14)

Although the implications of these structural changes will be discussed in the next section of this chapter, two points need to be highlighted here. First, the 'professional leadership' exercised by PCTs is heavily dominated by GPs. Studies of the governance of PCTs demonstrate how, reflecting their majority position on PCT boards, GPs have by far the greatest influence over decision making than does any other professional or managerial group (Glendinning et al., 2001; North and Peckham, 2001; Dowswell et al., 2002). This professional hegemony brings with it some potential constraints on the development of corporate responsibilities and strategic perspectives commensurate with the substantial responsibilities of PCTs. For example, it may be difficult to reconcile the individualistic medical model of general practice with a wider concern about public health (Hunter, 1999). Conflicts between GPs' roles as patient advocates and their involvement in allocating budgets (with related responsibilities for rationing resources) may generate resistance among at least some professionals (Marks and Hunter, 1998). Moreover, GPs' professional perspectives and culture may diverge from those of other professional groups such as nurses and social services managers, who are also represented on PCT boards and who have much greater familiarity with the corporate environments, dynamic budgets and strategic decision making expected of PCTs:

> What the GPs on the Board are concerned about is what happens to their individual patients. I don't think they've quite evolved to the stage where they're thinking strategically yet.

> [I'm] used to talking to the health authority on the same level in terms of 'Let's talk strategic … high level plans.' At the PCG Board … I have been the one that's banging on the table saying 'It is your responsibility. When you're at the Board

you're still a GP but you're taking the wider management role and accountability.'
(Social services representatives on PCT/G boards, quoted in Glendinning and
Rummery, forthcoming)

The other feature of these new primary care organizations warranting early
comment is the growing gulf between their substantial corporate responsibilities and the management and infrastructure resources which are available
to support them in discharging these responsibilities (Wilkin et al., 2001;
Tobin, 2002). Using the redistributed savings from the abolition of GP fundholding, PCGs/Ts' management budgets were set at £3 per person. In
contrast, evidence from evaluations of total purchasing (an extended form of
GP fundholding) estimated their management costs to be £17–£18 per
person (Mays et al., 1998) and a detailed projection of the management costs
of one PCT has estimated them to be £11 per person (Place and
Newbronner, 1999). This is one reason for the mergers between PCGs/Ts,
as they have allowed scarce management resources to be pooled – albeit with
the added consequence of increasing the scale of demands on the newly
enlarged managerial infrastructure.

Equity, clinical quality and consistency

The 1997 White Paper resonated with references to equity, fairness and
universality. It contained several proposals which reflected the desire of the
Labour government to reconstruct a 'national' health service which could
guarantee consistent treatments and standards of service:

> based on need and need alone – not on your ability to pay or on who your GP
> happens to be or on where you live ... a one-nation health service offering fairness
> and consistency to the population as a whole. (Secretary of State for Health, 1997:
> 5 and 55)

In one respect, these measures represent a political response to the diversity
that had emerged in the course of the internal market in general, and as a
consequence of GP fundholding in particular. However, they have also been
increasingly closely linked to the modernization enterprise, as they represent
the potential means of raising the quality of health services to a consistently
high standard across the country as a whole.

First, the National Institute for Clinical Excellence (NICE) was established
to identify and promote appropriate (that is, effective and cost-effective) forms
of treatment and ways of delivering that treatment. As well as making recom-

mendations to government on the cost-effectiveness and affordability of specific treatments, it also approves evidence-based clinical guidelines for managing medical conditions. Second, National Service Frameworks (NSFs) establish performance benchmarks and targets in relation to specific clusters of services. By the end of 2001, NSFs had been published covering cancer, heart disease, paediatric intensive care, diabetes, mental health services and services for older people. Third, another new organization, the Commission for Health Improvement (CHI), is responsible for monitoring and judging performance in NHS Trusts and other organizations, including PCTs. 'Performance' includes the extent to which NICE guidelines and NSFs are being met. CHI is expected to report every four years on the performance of every NHS organization in ensuring fair access to services, cost-effectiveness, appropriate outcomes of care and responsiveness to patients. The 'rewards' for good performance are organizational autonomy and guaranteed access to extra funding. The 'penalty' for persistent failure is takeover by external managers sent in by government.

These measures have profound consequences for the principle of professional autonomy – 'the legitimated control that an occupation exercises over the organization and terms of its work' (Elston, 1991: 61) – and particularly their clinical autonomy:

> The creation of NICE and CHI can be interpreted as the most recent and aggressive expression of a managerial take-over of the NHS … In the old NHS, authority was assumed to lie with the clinical professionals by virtue of their skills, traditions and patient contact. (Charlton, 2000: 18)

The activities of NICE and CHI and the introduction of NSFs affect all health professionals – doctors and nurses, whether working in hospitals or the community – but the impact on GPs, with their history of independence from mainstream NHS management, is particularly profound. The means by which this cultural sea change is effected is that of 'clinical governance'. Clinical governance 'brings clinical decision-making into a management and organizational framework' (Donaldson and Muir Gray, 1998: S38) – specifically the organizational framework of PCTs. It extends earlier approaches to quality improvement, embracing clinical decision making as well as the process of care; and places responsibility for the quality and consistency of clinical decisions (adherence to NICE guidelines and NSFs, for example) firmly in the hands of NHS organizations and professionals themselves:

> clinical governance … is not simply about improving the quality of care offered, but is also about corralling professionals so that they become rather more corporate players in the NHS 'family'. (Hunter, 1999: 11)

By locating responsibilities for clinical governance within PCTs and other NHS organizations, the focus of professional regulation is firmly shifted from external mechanisms (government regulation, accreditation by professional bodies and so on) to 'self-managing organizational systems, procedures, guidelines and protocols' (Newman, 2001: 90).

The strategies being used by PCTs to fulfil their new clinical governance responsibilities include:

- development plans for GP practices

- personal learning plans for GPs

- educational events for GPs and their practice staff

- cross-practice audits

- the development of local guidelines, for example on appropriate treatments for coronary heart disease.

PCTs are beginning to employ financial incentive schemes to reward participation in audit activities or meeting targets; and setting contracts which include specific quality measures. PCTs are also responsible for dealing with poor performance on the part of their constituent health professionals and GP practices. Strategies used here include informal discussions, offering training and allocating extra resources to poorly performing practices. Clinical audit and sharing information on comparative performance are additional methods employed by PCTs for engaging poorly performing practices in the quality improvement strategies being used by their peers. More punitive measures – withholding resources from poorly performing practices and conducting formal disciplinary proceedings – have so far rarely been used (Campbell et al., 2001).

While the impact of these measures on the actual quality of services received by patients has yet to be established, they signify a major cultural change in the traditional independence of GPs and their practices. Systems have now been established to facilitate communication between GPs and other practice staff and – a particularly sensitive development – to make comparative information about the quality of their clinical treatments and other services available across the PCT. In many instances, this information is no longer anonymized, so that individual GP practices can be identified, at least by members of the PCT board. A few PCTs are even contemplating making such information available to the public (Campbell et al., 2001).

Improving health and reducing health inequalities

Concern over the evidence of growing health inequalities, and therefore the extent to which morbidity and mortality might be prevented, also featured in the 1997 White Paper. Health authorities were given responsibility for assessing the health needs of the local population and drawing up a strategy for meeting those needs, in collaboration with PCGs/Ts, local authorities and other local interests (Secretary of State for Health, 1997: Ch. 4). The NSFs also include measures for preventing ill health. In turn, these responsibilities are also shared by PCTs.

However, here the high profile of GPs in the governance of PCTs may act as a hindrance, at least in the short term. GPs have jealously guarded their roles as autonomous professionals with an ethical duty to act as advocates for individual patients: 'the roles of patient's advocate and population planner may overlap and conflict with one another' (Gillam et al., 2001: 90). PCGs' responsibility for improving health may also be confounded by a lack of consensus on the meaning of the phrase and its operational application. Among PCT key personnel, interpretations of 'health improvement' range from core NHS activities of providing good quality health services (particularly in the areas of coronary heart disease and mental health, where service interventions and targets are clearly prescribed by NSFs), to encompass broader and less easily specified objectives, such as tackling the socioeconomic and environmental causes of ill health and enhancing well-being (Abbott et al., 2000).

Consequently, some PCGs/Ts have been focusing their health improvement interventions on developing relevant primary care services – introducing guidelines, setting up registers of patients with long-term health conditions, assessing health needs and establishing or extending services. Other PCGs/Ts have been engaging in more proactive health promotion initiatives, such as sexual advice services for young people, support for young parents, exercise on prescription, preventing falls and accidents and offering welfare benefits advice in primary care settings. A third cluster of activities focuses on community development and related community initiatives, including employing community workers (Florin et al., 2002). Indeed, a majority of PCGs/Ts have established relationships with other statutory services and initiatives (urban regeneration, leisure and education) whose activities impact on health, and most are making financial contributions to initiatives intended to improve health – again, community development projects, leisure, exercise or recreation programmes, support for carers, welfare benefits advice and accident prevention programmes are among the most common (Gillam et al., 2001). Although the sums of money involved may represent only a tiny fraction of PCGs/Ts' overall budgets, they have considerable symbolic significance within an NHS which has traditionally been preoccupied with treating, rather than preventing, illness.

Active collaboration with other organizations is at the heart of PCGs/Ts' strategies to improve health and reflects the acknowledgement in the Acheson Report and subsequent Green Paper (Acheson, 1998; Secretary of State for Health, 1998) of the social, economic and environmental causes of illness, which disproportionately affect poorer individuals and communities:

> The NHS will have a major role – in identifying the things that make people ill – promoting public health and reducing the present gross inequalities in health. But we have got to use the whole machinery of Government to tackle things that make people ill. (DH, 1997)

A separate initiative, the establishment of Health Action Zones (HAZs), explicitly addressed the importance of collaboration. Twenty-six HAZs were set up across England in two waves during 1998 and 1999. They cover 34 health authorities, 73 local authorities and a total population of 13 million in areas of high deprivation. A sum of £290 million was made available for the three years from 1999/2000, with the expectation of a further three years' funding from 2002/03. Most HAZs have worked within the framework of their local HImPs, but have 'trailblazed' innovative ways of delivering HImP objectives. High on the list of these innovations is the importance of engaging and involving the widest possible range of local stakeholders – statutory organizations, voluntary agencies and local communities:

> By bringing professionals, communities and organizations together, it was envisaged that HAZs would create a capacity for change throughout the health system, reducing red tape, transforming service design and delivery, fostering innovation, disseminating good practice and 'joining-up' other existing initiatives. ... Partnership in this context meant creating conditions for change through developing sustainable cross-sector relationships. (Barnes and Sullivan, 2002: 82)

It is intended that these innovations should become absorbed into mainstream ways of working.

However, both the health improvement responsibilities of PCGs/Ts and the development of HAZs have subsequently been shaped and focused by central government activities – in particular, the increasingly heavy emphasis on very specific, short-term and easily measurable targets for improving health and reducing disease. For example, HAZs covering Lambeth, Southwark and Lewisham and Manchester, Salford and Trafford both decided to focus on improving the health and well-being of children and young people in their respective localities. Within their first year, however, they were informed by central government that their focus was too narrow; they and the other 24 HAZs are now required to focus instead on the national priorities of cancer, coronary heart disease and mental health (Barnes and Sullivan, 2002).

Similarly, PCGs/Ts have also reported how their priorities for health improvement are determined by NSF priorities such as reducing coronary heart disease and improving mental health (Gillam et al., 2001):

> It doesn't necessarily feel like there's a particularly good balance between the county-wide HImP which ... is all national priorities ... and what we've actually been able to feed in locally. (PCG Chief Officer, quoted in Abbott et al., 2000: 16)

The more immediate demands of establishing and rapidly developing new organizations have also taken their toll on wider health improvement activities; preparation for moving from PCG to Trust status is a large organizational burden which tends to overshadow all other activities. In the context of this heavy organizational development agenda, PCGs/Ts have inevitably given lower priority to activities which are not compulsory or do not have urgent deadlines (Abbott et al., 2000).

The Challenges of Implementation

Some of the changes described in this chapter constitute intensifications of previous policy trends, others represent major structural and cultural transformations in key sectors of the NHS. The biggest change is undoubtedly in the position of GPs who, despite retaining their independent contractual status, are now incorporated into, and members of, organizations that exert control over both the levels of resources available for their practices and their clinical decisions and behaviour. Moreover, through these organizations, GPs have become directly accountable to mainstream NHS management systems. Consequently, transformations may be anticipated in the traditional culture of general practice, from an emphasis on professional autonomy and patient advocacy, towards a culture that gives greater priority to corporate and collective responsibilities for the equitable distribution of resources and quality of services provided across the locality as a whole. The devolution of resources – eventually up to 75 per cent of the total NHS budget – to organizations in which GPs play a major role, completes the process begun in the early 1990s of transferring strategic decision making and resource allocation to front-line health professionals. Indeed, this control is considerably extended, because PCTs have responsibility for all the hospital and community health services, prescribing and GP practice infrastructure resources for their areas, compared to GP fundholders who commanded the resources for a limited range of services to be enjoyed by only their patients.

This transformation can be characterized as the final triumph of management over professional autonomy. Drawing on Alford's (1975) theory of structural interests, North and Peckham (2001) analyse the position of GPs and other professionals within PCGs/Ts and conclude that their status as 'professional monopolizers' has been seriously challenged by 'state corporate rationalizers'. However, this is not simply a straightforward realignment of power relationships and dominant regimes. Clarke and Newman (1997: 76) for example, describe the strategy of cooption, which 'refers to managerial attempts to colonize the terrain of professional discourse, constructing articulations between professional concerns and languages and those of management'. Devolution, delegation and a concern with quality and the standards of services are commonly employed strategies for engaging professional interests and involving them in corporate cultures and visions. Similarly, North and Peckham (2001: 431–2) point out that the establishment of PCGs/Ts seeks to:

> organize the work of professional monopolizers in primary care through the agency of some who become corporate rationalizers from within ... in time the culture is likely to be assimilated throughout general practice.

The twin responsibilities of PCTs, for allocating resources (including the imposition of financial incentives and penalties) and being accountable for the clinical quality of services provided by professionals within the PCG/T, are profoundly important elements in this process of cultural transformation whose significance cannot be underestimated.

Nor should it be assumed that the 'corporate rationalizers' embody a simple, undifferentiated managerialism. Walby and Greenwell (1994) identify two contrasting styles of management in the NHS. Taylorism (or 'scientific management') involves centralization, detailed supervision, efficiency improvements and the identification of tasks which can be delegated to less skilled (and less expensive) workers. Financial incentives and surveillance play a big part in the implementation and enforcement of Taylorist managerial regimes. 'New wave management' in contrast, involves delegation and devolution, seeking to both involve and build on front-line workers' expertise and self-discipline. Both styles of management are apparent in the NHS reforms described in this chapter. On the one hand, the devolution, accompanied by considerable rhetoric, of budgetary responsibility down to 'front-line' NHS professionals is redolent of new wave management. On the other hand, the infrastructure of clinical governance – the promulgation of clinical guidelines and 'evidence-based' medicine, and the potential rewards and penalties for those who do and do not adhere to them – has echoes of an earlier, 'scientific' managerial style.

In another respect too, the reforms have strong echoes of Taylorism. The rhetoric of devolved responsibility has been accompanied by a very marked strengthening of the control by central government over the performance of primary care professionals and organizations at local levels. Targets, audit systems and performance management regimes are all part of a burgeoning audit culture which, as Clarke and Newman (1997: 80) point out, represents a strategic response from central government to the threat of localization and dispersal of the welfare state.

The strengthening of central control under a cloak of devolutionary rhetoric is a central feature of New Labour's approach to the welfare state and public policy more generally, which is also apparent in many other sectors (see Glendinning et al., 2002). However, in a number of respects this strengthening of centralized control and accountability also threatens the success of the government's attempts to reform the NHS through the transformation of primary care. First, it is already clear that some important elements of the government's reform package – particularly the concerns with health inequalities and health improvement – risk being eclipsed by more urgent tasks. This is not simply a question of priorities – it is also a question of the more-easily-measured taking precedence over the more-difficult-to-measure. Some professional and organizational activities are easier to measure and then convert into targets, indicators and league tables. Improving health and demonstrating beneficial health outcomes are among the more difficult and are certainly considerably harder to operationalize and count than, for example, waiting times for GP appointments or compliance with approved prescribing strategies for specific conditions. As Hunter (2001: 58) points out, the consistently high emphasis on making structural changes and improving the performance of specific services 'overshadows the government's health strategy and rather marginalizes it in the process'.

Second, there may be a limit to how far GPs and other primary health professionals are willing to be incorporated into the management enterprise if their 'freedom to manage' becomes little more than the routine implementation of central guidelines and performance indicators. Third, there are simply problems of capacity, in a sector of the NHS which has been experiencing repeated organizational change since the early 1990s and which is seriously short of management resources. The massive structural and cultural changes required to 'shift the balance' and devolve responsibilities to PCTs risk creating serious tensions within local organizations which are already occu-pied with changing front-line services (DH 2001g: Appendix A) – on which, of course, their performance will also be closely scrutinized. As Hunter (2001: 60) concludes, the government's reform agenda 'remains locked into an outmoded management style borne of inexperience and ignorance of the complex management task confronting public services like the NHS'.

Further Reading

Dowling, B. and Glendinning, C. (2003) *The New NHS: Modern, Dependable, Successful?* Buckingham: Open University Press.
Wilkin, D. and Glendinning, C. (2002) 'Modernizing Primary Health Care in England; the Role of Primary Care Groups and Trusts', in R. Sykes, C. Bochel and N. Ellison (eds), *Social Policy Review 14*, Bristol: Policy Press.

Notes

1   'Real terms' growth is the extra money available, relative to the expansion of the economy, with pay and prices held broadly constant.
2   'Indicative' budgets are notional – they indicate what a practice is *expected* to spend and carry no rewards or penalties for under- or overspending. As in the case of the prescribing budgets allo-cated to GP fundholders, they may be used for a few years to prepare a practice for the devolu-tion of an actual budget.

CHAPTER 12

Community Care or Independent Living?

JENNY MORRIS

A possibly apocryphal, but entirely believable, story: when the Department for Health and Social Security was split into the Department of Health and the Department for Social Security in the 1980s, a journalist noticed that there was no mention in the accompanying press release of which central government department would have responsibility for social services. Telephoning the government's press office to find out who would cover social care, he was told that 'social security' (that is, the benefits system) of course came under the department so named, thus compounding an impression held by many that the services which provide support to children and families, mentally ill, disabled and older people are to a large extent invisible in the context of national policy debates.

Support services for older and disabled people are especially invisible. Children's and mental health services hit the headlines when a death provokes a search for someone to blame. The NHS occupies a particular place in the electorate's and therefore politicians' hearts. In contrast, unless delivery of support services to disabled and older people affects the NHS – as it does in the context of 'bed blocking' – the British media, and therefore politicians, exhibit little interest. When journalists Polly Toynbee and David Walker evaluated New Labour's first term of office in their book *Did Things Get Better?*, community care did not even get a mention (Toynbee and Walker, 2001).

Yet the years 1997–2002 have seen a mass of policy initiatives in the social care field, all dominated by New Labour's primary concerns of identifying 'what works?' and putting in place a funding and policy framework that determines the way in which local government operates. To a large extent unimpeded by ideological baggage, New Labour has responded almost entirely pragmatically to the tensions and opportunities of the community care system it inherited in 1997.

211

What Did Labour Inherit?

There were four distinct aspects of policy relating to community care and disabled and older people which New Labour inherited from the Conservatives in 1997.

Residential care versus domiciliary services

When New Labour came to office in 1997, it inherited a system of meeting the needs of older and disabled people laid down by the NHS and Community Care Act, passed by the previous Conservative government in 1990. This legislation had primarily been fuelled by the desire to halt increasing expenditure on residential care. Prior to 1990, those whose income fell below a certain level were entitled to the payment of residential and nursing home fees through the social security system. In contrast, it was much harder to get personal care services to enable someone to remain living at home, particularly as domiciliary services provided by local authorities tended to be confined to help with housework and shopping.

The 1990 Act placed responsibility onto social services authorities for assessing a person's needs and purchasing residential care where this was deemed necessary. It was thought that this would halt the increasing expenditure on residential care – a budget (borne by the Department for Social Security) which had grown hundredfold between 1979 and 1989 – and instead encourage local authorities to support people to remain in their own homes. Indeed, social services authorities rapidly shifted into providing (or purchasing from the independent sector) personal care to the most frail and disabled people in their own homes, and away from providing help only with housework and shopping. Over the period 1992 to 1997, the numbers of people receiving two hours or less domiciliary care per week decreased while those receiving five hours or more per week increased (DH, 1998a: 14).

Nonetheless, these developments did not halt the increase in the numbers entering residential or nursing care, partly because it was not always cheaper to provide intensive care at home. Social services authorities tended to set a financial ceiling on the amount of money they would spend to enable someone to remain living at home. It also became increasingly clear that cutting the provision of low levels of domiciliary care was uneconomic, as this precluded the preventive or rehabilitative assistance which could help someone to avoid admittance to, or remaining in, hospital or long-term care.

'Service user involvement' and direct payments

The Conservative government had shown some commitment to the rights of individuals to have more say in how their needs were met. For example, the policy guidance which accompanied the 1990 Act encouraged the involvement of older and disabled people themselves in decisions about how support was delivered. It was this commitment to individual rights (which found a more natural home within Conservative libertarian philosophy than within traditional Labour collectivism) which finally led the Conservative government to pass the Community Care (Direct Payments) Act in 1996. This piece of legislation, long campaigned for by the disability movement, enabled social services authorities to make cash payments to disabled people to enable them to purchase their own support services.

Although it had been illegal for social services authorities to make cash payments in lieu of services prior to the 1996 Act, another system of making cash payments to pay for support had in fact been set up in 1986. This came about as a concession to the opposition to changes in the social security system, which had abolished a little used domiciliary care allowance for disabled people who needed assistance with personal care. The Independent Living Fund (ILF), set up with a budget of £5 million for a five-year period, made regular monthly payments to what it was assumed would be a few hundred 'severely disabled' people. By 1992, its annual budget was £97 million and over 18,000 people were receiving ILF grants.

By 1997, therefore, the campaign by the disability movement and the operation of the ILF had provided a new model for the meeting of personal care needs. The Conservative government had resisted extending either the ILF or direct payments to older people but it was clear from younger people's experiences that this system could deliver the choice and control which both Labour and Tories said should be aimed for.

The health and social care divide

New Labour inherited two systems of meeting older and disabled people's needs, which operated under different legislative, funding, organizational and professional frameworks. It had long been recognized that health and social services operated as if there was a 'Berlin Wall' between them but previous initiatives to address this inefficient and inflexible division had been fairly superficial. Social services has always been the less powerful (in political terms) side of this divide. This is partly because it is less visible in terms of public interest. The NHS is a universal service and political parties vie for the role of its champion; social services is mainly seen as for troubled children and 'problem families' – a minority rather than a majority interest.

The separate funding and statutory frameworks within which health and social services operated required a distinction to be made between 'health care' and 'social care'. New Labour was faced with increasing evidence that while this separation was easy and sensible in the context of acute hospital services, it was much less so when someone needed support in order to live in their own home.

The role of 'informal carers'

The final 'plank' of community care which New Labour inherited from the Conservative government was a recognition of, and from the Tories, an ideological support for, the role of 'carers'. Over the previous 20 years, the word 'carer' came to be used to describe someone who provides unpaid support – friends, relatives and neighbours whose support made it possible for many older and disabled people to remain living in their own homes. Previous critics of community care policy had argued that 'care *in* the community' was actually 'care *by* the community' (Bayley, 1973). They pointed out that the unpaid work of carers (predominantly women) was in fact a crucial part of previous (Labour and Conservative) governments' commitment to alternatives to institutional care (Finch and Groves, 1983). The Conservative government had positively embraced this role for carers, linking it to their ideological support for 'the family' and denial of the concept of 'society' and collective obligations. The fact that it had been calculated that it would cost between £15 billion and £24 billion per year to replace this unpaid work undoubtedly added to this philosophy (DH, 1991: 13).

Setting New Labour's Policy Agenda: The *Modernising Social Services* White Paper[1]

This White Paper, published in the first year of New Labour's first term of office, argued that social services was failing older and disabled people in a number of ways (DH, 1998a: 6–7):

- 'vulnerable adults' were not being adequately protected from abuse and neglect

- poor coordination between different agencies meant people's needs often remained unmet and, for example, older people often remained in hospital for longer than necessary

- inflexibility in the way services were delivered meant people tended to be fitted into services rather than services tailored to meet people's needs, in many instances increasing 'dependency and exclusion'

- there was a lack of clarity about standards and what people should be able to expect from services

- there was a lack of consistency between and within local areas about who received services and in levels of charging for services

- evidence of differences in the unit costs of services indicated that some authorities were inefficient in their use of resources.

The White Paper announced the government's intention of undertaking a 'series of reforms that will lead to a radical improvement of social services' (DH, 1998a: 7).

Tackling the Health and Social Care Divide

The Health Act 1999 made it possible for local health and social services to work together in three different ways (all of which had previously been hampered by existing legislative and regulatory frameworks):

1. Pooled budgets, where health and social services pool local budgets to meet needs

2. Lead commissioning, where one organization delegates its responsibilities and funding to another organization to meet needs

3. Integrated provision, where two organizations jointly provide a service.

Subsequent legislation (the Health and Social Care Act 2001) set up primary care Trusts (PCTs) to commission local health services and increased the opportunities for joint funding and joint working.

The government's primary aim was to prevent unnecessary admissions to hospital and the long-term care system. Two influential reports had drawn attention to a 'vicious circle' of reliance on institutional care for older people. The Audit Commission's *The Coming of Age*, published in 1997, was a timely focus on the way that, while the NHS spent less and less on long-term nursing care, local authorities were funding ever-increasing numbers of older people in independent sector residential and nursing care. *Investing in Rehabilitation*, published in 1998 jointly by the King's Fund and the Audit Commission, emphasized the potential for enabling older people to regain independence and avoid unnecessary stays in hospital or admission to long-term care.

There have been three main criticisms of these reforms, from the point of view of their implications for community care. Groups representing older and disabled people have expressed their concern that health issues may come to dominate the provision of services, with less recognition of people's support needs. This has particular implications for younger disabled people who may need support in order to look after children, or take on paid employment. Social services authorities have pointed out that they are accountable to their local population in a way which PCTs are not. And finally, there is evidence that PCTs are 'desperately short of capacity to develop partnerships with social services' (King's Fund, 2002: 10).

Who Pays for Community Care?

The one issue which has captured the public's interest in the field of community care policy has been the question of who pays for long-term residential and nursing care. A Royal Commission was set up in 1997 and was intended to address how long-term care for older and disabled people, both in their own homes and other settings, should be funded. This issue had caused some political discomfort to the previous Conservative government, with newspaper stories of older people having to sell their homes in order to pay for residential care. Articles about people who had paid tax and national insurance all their lives and worked hard to buy their own homes, yet who were prevented from passing this asset on to their children, made uncomfortable reading for a government committed to encouraging homeownership and family self-sufficiency.

New Labour was not so burdened with this particular contradiction between political aims and the consequences of social policy, but was still faced with a general concern that an increasing older population, coinciding with fewer women taking on the role of 'informal carer' for older relatives, would lead to an unsustainable demand for public resources to be spent on residential care. In fact, the Royal Commission concluded that the United Kingdom had already experienced whatever 'demographic timebomb' was going to occur (Royal Commission on Long Term Care, 1999: 13–14) and that the availability of 'informal care' would remain fairly constant for the foreseeable future (Royal Commission on Long Term Care, 1999: 17–18).

However, the Royal Commission's recommendations made less comfortable reading for a government which seemed to have severed its links to a political tradition which had espoused universalism and condemned means testing. The

Commission proposed that, while living and housing costs should still be subject to a means test, assistance with personal care (as well as nursing care), whether received in the home or a residential setting, should be free at the point of delivery based on assessment of need. Two members of the Royal Commission dissented and their recommendation that only nursing care should be free at the point of delivery was more to the government's liking. It is likely that, but for the concept of nursing care being inherently tied up with the Holy Grail of 'health care free at the point of delivery', the government would have been tempted to go along the road of charging for nursing care delivered outside a hospital setting (that is, in a nursing home or at home).

After a long delay, therefore, the government decided that only nursing care delivered by a qualified nurse (in the home or a residential setting) should not be subject to a means test. In Scotland, however, the Royal Commission's recommendations were accepted by the newly devolved Scottish Executive. Arguments still continue about whether free personal care is affordable, with New Labour placing more emphasis than the Royal Commission did on the cost implications of evidence that there will be a significant increase in the number of over 85-year-olds over the next 30 years.

In the meantime, there has been a gradual increase in the number of local authorities charging those who use domiciliary services. In recognition of varying practices throughout the country, the Department of Health issued statutory guidance, with the intention of creating consistency between one authority and another (DH, 2001e), but with the consequence that local authorities are now effectively applying a means test when assessing whether someone should pay for support services and how much. Disabled people's organizations were successful in arguing that disability-related expenditure should be allowed for and the Department of Health has therefore had to issue quite complex practice guidance on this matter (DH, 2002a). Disability organizations were also successful in arguing that income from paid employment should not be counted in a charging assessment. The government agreed to this on the grounds that disabled people would otherwise experience disincentives to paid employment.

Older People and Community Care

Just over a million older people receive some form of support from their local social services authority. Half of these are supported in their own home, the remainder in residential or nursing homes. Most are over 80 years of age. As discussed below, the main source of support remains that provided by family, friends and neighbours.

The numbers of residential and nursing home placements funded by local authorities more than doubled during the latter part of the 1990s, as local authority funding took over from funding through the social security system. However, 2001 saw the first decrease in the numbers of people funded in residential care by local authorities (DH, 2001b). The changing pattern of domiciliary care continued throughout the 1990s: between 1992 and 2000, the number of hours provided per service user increased by 65 per cent but the numbers receiving a service decreased by a quarter; the average number of hours provided to service users more than doubled (from 3.2 hours per week to 7 hours per week), with about half of households receiving six or more visits per week in 2000, compared with only 16 per cent in 1992. In addition, the proportion of hours provided by the independent sector increased from 2 per cent in 1992 to 56 per cent in 2000 (DH, 2001c).

New Labour's main policy initiative concerning older people has been the National Service Framework for Older People. National Service Frameworks (NSFs) were introduced in the NHS Plan (DH, 2000) which emphasized their importance for driving through change. By 2001, five NSFs had been published, three more were in development and the government intends that in future there will be one NSF published each year. The role of the NSFs is to:

- set national standards and define service models for a defined service or care group
- put in place strategies to support implementation
- establish performance milestones against which progress within an agreed timescale will be measured.

Each NSF is developed with the assistance of an external reference group which brings together health professionals, service users and carers, health service managers, partner agencies and other advocates. NSFs are thus a mechanism for pursuing New Labour's desire to set targets and monitor performance, but are also an opportunity to promote the involvement of service users in policy development.

The NSF for Older People is mainly concerned with greater efficiency in the delivery of health care services but the first standard addresses age discrimination in terms of access to health and social care, something which had been ignored by the Conservative government. The standards also attempt to address the continuing problem, recognized under the previous government, of older people remaining in hospital for longer than necessary because of lack of rehabilitation or support services in the community.

Resources were allocated (£750 million over three years) to address this issue. The Department of Health also put out new statutory guidance, the single assessment process, in order to bring together health and social services when carrying out assessments and putting in place care plans.

People with Learning Disabilities and Community Care

It is estimated that there are 1.2 million children and adults in England with a mild-to-moderate learning disability and 210,000 with 'severe and profound learning disabilities'. Services to people with learning disabilities have always been an important part of community care policy. Indeed community care policy has its origins in the movement of people out of the old mental handicap hospitals, from the Mental Deficiency Act of 1913 and culminating in the commitments to community services set out in the 1971 White Paper, *Better Service for the Mentally Handicapped* (Fairleigh Committee, 1971). However, by the time New Labour took office in 1997, it was widely recognized that while the majority of people with learning disabilities now lived in the community, they were still living very limited lives (DH, 1998b; Ryan, 1998).

Following wide consultation, including with people with learning disabilities themselves, the government published a White Paper setting out a new strategy for learning disability services (DH, 2001f). Underpinning the strategy was a recognition that people with learning disabilities 'should have the same opportunities as other people to lead full and active lives and should receive the support needed to make this possible' (DH, 2001f: 17). The objectives adopted by the strategy included enabling people to have more choice and control in their lives, living in 'ordinary housing', participating in family and community life, and in employment. The strategy set out a number of initiatives:

- new national objectives to be set for local services, with new targets and performance indicators. A national Learning Disability Task Force (including people with learning difficulties and parents) will advise the government on implementation.

- the setting up of local Learning Disability Partnership Boards (including people with learning difficulties) which will have responsibility for planning services, using Health Act flexibilities to draw up Joint Investment Plans and local action plans.

- ring-fenced capital and revenue funding (£50 million, plus an Implementation Support Fund of £2.3m per year over three years), which will be allocated for identified priorities, including developing community services for the people remaining in long-stay hospitals, developing integrated services for children and adults with high levels of needs, advocacy services (£1.3 million a year for three years), and a national information centre and help line.

• new guidance on person-centred planning (DH, 2002b).

The White Paper was widely welcomed. Concerns remain, however, about provision for children and adults with high levels of support needs (J. Morris, 1999, 2001). This relatively small group are increasing in number, partly as a result of higher survival rates of premature babies, those with congenital conditions and people who sustain brain injuries. The increasing numbers of children and adults with autistic spectrum disorder are also inadequately catered for and there is particular concern about the failure of health and social services to work effectively together with education services at both a national and local level to meet the needs of this group of children (Abbott et al., 2001; Loynes, 2001).

Disabled People and Community Care

Although the majority of disabled people are in fact over retirement age, and the largest group under retirement age are those with learning disabilities, the term – in the policy context – is generally used to apply to people of working age with physical and/or sensory impairments. In fact, community care policy has seen no major initiatives in respect of people with physical and/or sensory impairments in the way that there has been for older people and people with learning disabilities. Indeed, the restructuring of responsibilities within the Department of Health in 2001 left responsibility for this group somewhat incongruously allocated to the section headed by the chief nursing officer, prompting concern that in the drive to bring health and social care together, this particular group would be forgotten.

Yet, more generally, New Labour's policies concerning disabled people are the most radical. Community care policy cannot be discussed in terms of how it applies to disabled people without also discussing New Labour's policy agenda on work, benefits and anti-discrimination legislation. Over the past 20 years or so, disabled people have increasingly been recognized as individuals who have been discriminated against in all areas of their lives (education, employment, housing, access to goods and services) and who are, to use the disability movement's phrase, not in need of 'care' but in need of their human and civil rights. The incoming Labour government kept its commitment to set up a Disability Rights Commission, to implement the Disability Discrimination Act passed by the Conservative government in 1995. This anti-discrimination legislation has also been further extended to education and to cover smaller as well as large employers. Most significantly, New Labour's emphasis on paid work as the way out of social exclusion, and the desire to cut the ever-increasing amount of money spent on incapacity benefit, fuelled policy developments such as the New Deal for Disabled People, and joint investment plans. The underlying philosophy was 'work for those who can, support for those who cannot'.

Disability organizations have generally taken a broader, less employment-focused view of social exclusion, arguing, for instance, that the delivery of community care services should take into account people's support needs relating to parenting, lifelong learning and participation in the community generally, as well as removing the barriers to employment. A key mechanism for delivering support in a way which enables disabled people to do the things that non-disabled people take for granted has been the development of direct payments, as discussed above, a policy initiated by the previous Conservative government in response to many years of campaigning by disabled people and their organizations.

It is difficult to overestimate the radical nature of direct payments (and the cash grants made by the ILF). Giving disabled people themselves the cash to enable them to purchase the assistance they need undermines the role of the family and informal carers in providing care. It also undermines professional expertise because self-assessment of need is an integral part of the system of direct payments, as is the rejection of the idea that personal assistance can be divided into 'nursing care', 'personal care' and 'housework', and that each type of task will need to be done by a different person. The system has also boosted local self-help groups. When direct payments were first introduced, the government recognized that individuals would need the support of personal assistance support schemes, pioneered by Centres of Independent Living run by disabled people themselves. It was made clear that local authorities would be expected to resource such schemes, although there has been concern, expressed by the disability movement, that charitable organizations run by non-disabled people are winning contracts to provide this support (Carr, 2000).

It was probably inevitable that New Labour would eventually admit that means testing direct payments and ILF grants (or indeed support services provided by local authorities) would create a disincentive to paid work, if people's income was assumed to be available to pay for personal assistance. In spite of a general retreat from universalist principles in the field of community care, the government finally agreed, in November 2001, that earned income should not be counted when assessing what contribution a disabled person should make towards the cost of personal assistance. This concession was rapidly followed by a similar concession by the ILF. This, of course, opens up a glaring anomaly in the way that older people's pension income is treated and will inevitably lead to further pressure on the government to abolish means testing in the provision of community care services.

The government was also responsive to pressure from disabled parents to recognize support needs relating to parenting tasks. The Health and Social Care Act 2001 and subsequent guidance (DH, 2002c) made it clear that social services departments should respond to the support that disabled parents needed to look after their children, rather than, as had happened too often in the past, assuming they were incapable of parenting and taking their children into care. Direct payments were also extended to 16- and 17-year-olds by the Carers and Disabled Children Act 2000, in recognition of the fact that many young disabled people want to take more control over the support they require. In particular, it is hoped this initiative will enable young disabled people to participate in social and leisure activities without having to rely on their parents for assistance.

National Strategy for Carers

New Labour, like the Conservatives, recognized the importance of the unpaid work of families, friends and neighbours for any community care policy. The *General Household Survey* (ONS, 2002) found that there were 6 million people – one in eight of the population – providing some kind of support to older and disabled people and about 850,000 provided more than 50 hours help per week.

The national strategy for carers, launched in 1999, announced a new ring-fenced grant to local authorities of £140 million over three years to provide services for carers. New legislation (Carers and Disabled Children Act 2000) gave carers the right to have their needs assessed and local authorities the power to provide services directly to carers. Carers could also elect to have direct payments in order to make their own arrangements to meet their needs. In recognition of the financial disadvantages experienced by some carers, the government's new pension system (the 'second state pension') enables time spent caring to be counted towards the state pension.

Although carers' groups have welcomed New Labour's initiatives, there is still criticism of the failure to provide carers with an entitlement to support from their local social services department.

Monitoring Performance

New Labour has been criticized for overwhelming health and social services with a bewildering mass of performance targets. These are certainly large in number, and not always well coordinated, but, to be fair, the importance of monitoring performance is directly related to the replacement of market forces as a mechanism for bringing about improvements in quality and efficiency of services.

New Labour has not placed the emphasis that the previous Tory government did on the power of the market to respond efficiently and effectively to demand. The Conservatives created a so-called internal market in the NHS and imposed compulsory competitive tendering (CCT) on local council services. These mechanisms were intended to open up public monopolies to the 'discipline' of competition and thereby, it was argued, create better value for money and more flexible services. The incoming Labour government formally abolished both the internal market and CCT. Nevertheless, the in-principle separation of purchasers and providers remained in both health and social services, with PCTs being set up as purchasers of health care, and local authorities increasingly using private and voluntary providers of residential and home care rather than in-house services.

However, instead of improvements in quality and value for money being left to market forces, New Labour introduced a steadily increasing number of targets and performance indicators against which health and social services were to be measured. The two main mechanisms were the national priorities guidance and the performance assessment framework. A National Care Standards Commission was also set up and issued national minimum standards against which services are to be measured.

The various systems for monitoring the performance of social services and promoting good practice have proved fertile ground for a continuing commitment to service user involvement. Consultation with service users, and their satisfaction with services, was placed at the heart of Best Value reviews – a system for evaluating local authority services which replaced CCT. The social services inspectorate (SSI) has increasingly involved service users and carers as lay assessors when carrying out inspections of local authority services. The government also showed its commitment to service user involvement by appointing Jane Campbell, a disabled person and long-time disability activist, to be the chair of the new Social Care Institute for Excellence.

Unresolved Issues

Resources

Critics of New Labour identify that, while steps have been taken to modernize social care and there have been increases in funding, the community care system is still chronically underfunded. The three years from 2001 to 2004 will see an average real increase in funding to social services departments of 3.5 per cent per year (DH, 2001d). However, there is evidence that the costs of providing support services and residential care are rising more quickly than allowed for in the government's standard spending assessment. Moreover, there are increasing numbers of people aged over 80 (those most likely to need help from social services) and this increase is projected to continue over the next 30 years (Personal Social Services Research Unit, 2001).

The consequences of historical and continuing underfunding of community care are evident in the fact that social services departments spent on average 8.9 per cent above their standard spending assessment in 2000/2001 and this is set to rise to 9.7 per cent in 2001/2002. In addition, many social services departments are overspending on their locally set budgets. About a fifth of total overspending is accounted for by services to older people (Help the Aged, 2002).

The squeeze on local authority budgets has had an impact on the residential and nursing home market. While fees for residential and nursing homes have increased in recent years above the general rate of inflation, the level of fees paid by local authorities has not always kept pace. This has meant that charities or self-funded residents' fees subsidize the places of those funded by local authorities. The number of residential and nursing home places has declined – 50,000 places were lost between 1996 and 2001. Fears that many more homes would be forced out of operation as a result of new national minimum standards prompted a government 'climb down' in the summer of 2002. Nevertheless, a number of homes had already been forced to close and the continuing squeeze on the level of fees which local authorities are prepared to pay remains of concern to the sector.

The chronic underfunding of community care has also impacted on the way support is provided within people's own homes. As we have seen, home care services are now supporting fewer people but those people have higher levels of needs. While the community care reforms of the 1990s encouraged social services departments to carry out needs-led rather than service-led or resource-led assessments, in practice, shortage of resources made this very difficult. Assessments, particularly of older people's needs, were often mainly concerned with measuring dependency levels and using this information to decide whether an individual qualified for a service.

The pressure on resources encouraged the practice of translating 'care needs' into time-limited care tasks. Contracts with private sector agencies were often based on tight specifications of the time allocated to certain tasks. The quality of services was also undermined by recruitment and retention problems. These were created, it was argued, by the limited job satisfaction experienced by care workers, who are graded as manual workers, 'treated as if they were part of a production line', and whose pay rates, in many areas, are less than that paid by local supermarkets (Lewis and Sawyer, 2001).

The pressure on resources has also resulted in continuing age discrimination in terms of whether people are supported to live in their own homes. This is in spite of the intention, enshrined in the NSF for Older People, to outlaw age discrimination in the delivery of health and social services. Local authorities – required by the government to use their resources in the most cost-effective way – set cost ceilings on care packages to support people in their own homes and these limits are set in relation to the relative costs of residential care. In 2001, the average gross weekly expenditure in England on residential or nursing care was £342 for an older person, £669 for a younger adult with a learning disability, £423 for a young adult with mental illness and £512 for a younger adult with a physical and/or sensory impairment (Help the Aged, 2002). Social service departments therefore will commonly spend less on supporting an older person at home than they will supporting a younger disabled person, and this means that older people are forced into residential care at lower levels of support needs.

Moreover, even though it is now more possible for disabled people to live independently in their own homes, with support purchased either by their local social services department or by themselves (using direct payments and ILF grants), those with the highest levels of needs still face the risk of having to go into residential care. There are wide variations in the experiences of people with high levels of support needs, depending on how much their local social services is prepared to pay and to what extent disabled people manage to access direct payments and ILF grants. Some people are forced into residential care as a direct result of the cost ceilings imposed by the ILF and social services departments (Kestenbaum, 1999).

Institutionalization or 'a full life in the community'?

Community care was criticized in the 1990s for providing no more than 'institutionalization within the community' (Morris, 1993). New Labour's rhetoric may talk about delivering choice and control and enabling people to 'lead full lives in the community', but the constraints created by a shortage of resources are compounded by negative social attitudes towards those who need support in order to go about their daily lives (Disability Rights Task Force, 1999; Knight and Brent, 1999).

Of those receiving home care services, 83 per cent are aged 65 and over, 63 per cent are aged 75 and over and 31 per cent aged 85 and over. Community care policy and practice is therefore inevitably dominated by the needs and circumstances of older and very old people, and profoundly influenced by how our society sees old age. Older people are generally seen as unproductive, dependent and as having very little to offer (Age Concern, 1999).

Dependency on others for the physical tasks of daily living is viewed particularly negatively in our society. To counter this, the disability movement has argued for a redefining of 'independence' to mean, not doing things for oneself, but having choice and control over the support required to go about one's daily life – thus the importance of direct payments and the ILF, which enables people to employ their own personal assistants.

When the SSI produced its guide for local authorities on developing assessment procedures in 1991, the first two principles concerned enabling people to 'live a full life in the community' and to 'be in charge of their own lives and make their own decisions including decisions to take risks' (SSI, 1991: 6). Although current guidance uses some of the same rhetoric, the emphasis is much more on the role of professional assessment in determining level and type of need and whether this fits into eligibility criteria laid down by central government (DH, 2002c). Social services departments are supporting higher numbers of very frail older people living in their own homes, and it is perhaps inevitable that, for example, the emphasis is increasingly on how to manage risk from the professional and service provider perspective rather than upholding the right of people to take risks in their daily lives. Negative attitudes towards people with high levels of support needs – those with significant communication and cognitive impairments and people with dementia – also influence the way services are provided, and these groups are increasing in numbers.

The bridging of the health and social care divide may be intended to bring the benefits of multidisciplinary assessments and 'seamless service', but health is the stronger partner in this relationship and this brings its own disadvantages. Age Concern, for example, argued that government guidance on establishing a single assessment process focuses too much on physical and health needs and not enough on social, cultural and emotional needs (Age Concern, 2001: 4). People who need support in order to be parents, to work and be active in their local communities continue to find that support is either not available (Fraser and Glick, 2000) or is provided in ways which do not facilitate 'ordinary life' (Cunningham, 2000).

While the White Paper *Modernising Social Services* announced the government's intention of tackling abuse against 'vulnerable people', evidence remains of very poor standards of care experienced by many people living in residential homes and, in particular, high levels of medication often being used inappropriately (Stokoe, 2001). Evidence is also emerging of the largely hidden abuse experienced by older people (women *and* men) at the hands of their family and/or domiciliary workers (Pritchard, 2002).

Conclusion

In the face of the obstacles of negative attitudes towards older and disabled people and a chronic shortage of resources, there has been progress towards the goal of according people their human and civil rights. Work with people with dementia, for example, has illustrated how high quality care can be delivered (Heiser, 2002) and how they can be consulted and involved in decisions about their care (Allan, 2001). The government has extended direct payments to older people and has encouraged the take-up of direct payments by people with learning disabilities, including those with significant cognitive impairments. Moreover, although the numbers using direct payments remain small, the Department of Health continues its support of the policy, and also continues to fund the National Centre for Independent Living, run by the British Council of Disabled People. The exemption of earned income from the charging system relating to community services, direct payments and the ILF is an important step towards the disability movement's goal of creating a 'level playing field' for disabled people.

Attitudes towards older and disabled people are improving, and this is reflected in both the rhetoric and aims of government initiatives. The biggest stumbling block to protecting and promoting older and disabled people's human rights remains the level of resources available for the support they require. To address this issue, the government will need to move beyond the inevitably limited focus on the NHS and address the issue of whether society as a whole is prepared to put more resources into enabling people, of whatever age, who need support with daily living activities to 'lead a full life in the community'.

Further Reading

Henderson, J. and Atkinson, D. (2003) *Managing Care in Context*, London: Routledge.

Malin, N., Wilmott, S. and Manthorpe, J. (2003) *Key Concepts and Debates in Health and Social Policy*, Buckingham: Open University Press.

Williams, F. (2003) *Social Policy*, Cambridge: Polity Press.

Note

1   Another White Paper, *Modernising Mental Health Services* (DH, 1998c), set out new initiatives for mental health services, an important part of community care but this policy is not covered in this chapter.

CHAPTER 13

Criminal Justice Policy

TIM NEWBURN

> I have always believed that politics is first and foremost about ideas. Furthermore, ideas need labels ... The 'third way' is to my mind the best label for the new politics which the progressive centre-left is forging in Britain and beyond. (Tony Blair, 1998a)

On both sides of the Atlantic during the final decade of the last century, so-called Centre-Left political parties sought to revitalize their electoral appeal through a broad process of policy reformulation and image redesign. The process by which the Democrats and Labour became 'New Democrats' and 'New Labour' has been broadly characterized as one of 'modernization' (see Newman, 2001). In policy terms, modernization, according to advocates, meant an attempt to find a 'third way' – a means of transcending old dichotomies and, in particular, that of old-style social democracy on the one hand and neoliberalism on the other. In crime control terms, this was presented as recognizing the links between social exclusion and crime, while also acknowledging personal responsibility for crime and disorder or, to put it in better-known terms, to be 'tough on crime and tough on the causes of crime'.

How has this played out in practice? Have successive New Labour administrations led to a fundamental shift in the governance of Britain in this area or have we merely witnessed the reworking of the neoliberal agenda characteristic of the Thatcher and Major governments? More particularly, what was the reality of the third way in criminal justice? Can we see the staking out of new institutions, approaches and discourses, or has New Labour simply continued with the punitive rhetoric and practice established under Michael Howard from the early 1990s on?

Predictably, this is a difficult landscape to describe briefly and characterize easily. First of all, it has been a site of enormous activity. There have been two home secretaries since May 1997. First, Jack Straw for the whole of the first term, followed by David Blunkett after the 2001 general election. Both are comfortably New Labour in outlook; both fairly populist, or at least ambitious enough to keep an extremely keen eye on the headlines in the tabloids. Each has ensured, in his own way, that the Home Office has been at, or close to, the forefront of government activity in the past five years. Without wishing to reduce penal politics to the actions of one office holder, it is nonetheless the case that understanding the home secretary is central to understanding the Home Office. This has long been the case and, although the terms and conditions of the office have changed in many important respects, Sir Edward Troup's observation in the 1920s that 'the terms "Home Office" and "Home Secretary" are almost interchangeable' continues to contain more than a grain of truth (Troup, 1925: 3).

There is not the space here to discuss the full range of criminal justice and penal policy under New Labour. My approach will be to focus on those areas that seem most important to, or most emblematic of, the New Labour penal project. In doing this, I want to use the lens of modernization as a means of framing some reflections on how crime control policy has developed since 1997 in the UK. There are a number of ways of characterizing modernization in this area (see, for example, Raine, 2001; Richards and Raine, 2001). I want to use the White Paper on *Modernising Government* (Cabinet Office, 1999) in which it set out the following three aims:

- Ensuring that policy making is more joined up and strategic

- Making sure that public service users, not providers, are the focus, by matching services more closely to people's lives

- Delivering public services that are high quality and efficient.

Writing in the late 1970s, Michael Moriarty (1977: 132–3) then Assistant Under-Secretary of State in the Home Office, observed that:

> it is unusual for an incoming government to bring with it anything approaching a detailed blueprint of penal policy. This is not really surprising. Although the maintenance of law and order remains a basic task of any government, the methods of performing it are simply not of great importance in comparison with the major economic and social issues of the day which rightly preoccupy the political parties and other organs of society.

He was writing, of course, at a time when there remained considerable bipartisan agreement over so-called law and order issues. As we know, this situation changed relatively quickly in the years following to a position now where crime and related policy are continuously towards the top of the public and political agendas. Partly as a result of this, and the remarkable period of time the Labour Party had been in opposition, Jack Straw arrived in the Home Office in 1997 with something that very closely resembled a blueprint for penal policy. Indeed, many of the details of what he wanted to achieve had already been published in remarkable detail (Labour Party, 1996). At the forefront of his blueprint was reform of the youth justice system.

Managerialism and Youth Justice Reform

At the heart of much of the reform of the process of governing in the past five years has been a shift away from simple concern with policy outputs and a move towards concern with, wherever possible, measurable outcomes. Thus, crime recording procedures have been reformed, virtually all criminal justice agencies are now performance monitored and the reformed youth justice system, at the heart of New Labour's criminal justice project, for the first time has an overarching aim and a body, the Youth Justice Board (YJB), responsible for overseeing its performance. The majority of these policies were developed by Labour while in opposition, initially when Tony Blair was the shadow home secretary, then more fully under Jack Straw, supported by Alun Michael and Norman Warner. The proposals for root and branch reform of the youth justice system were influenced very significantly by the Audit Commission.

Established to promote economy, efficiency and effectiveness in public services, the Audit Commission became increasingly influential in criminal justice during the course of the 1990s. Although its initial focus was on policing (Morgan and Newburn, 1997), by the middle of the decade it had turned its attention to the youth justice system and added its voice to the growing roll-call of commentators calling for increased emphasis on 'criminality prevention' and, in particular, support for those interventions early in life which, research suggests, hold out the best hope for reducing youth crime (see for example, Farrington, 1996; Faulkner, 1996). At the same time that the Labour Opposition home affairs team were preparing their proposals for youth justice reform, the Audit Commission was engaged in its first major inquiry into young people and crime. The parallels between the Labour Party's pre-election consultation document, *Tackling Youth Crime and Reforming Youth Justice* (Labour Party, 1996), and the Audit Commission's hugely influential report, *Misspent Youth* (Audit Commission, 1996), are striking – both in terms of the issues covered and the proposals each contained (Newburn, 1998).

The Audit Commission's critique was biting. It described the youth justice system in England and Wales as uneconomic, inefficient and ineffective. It was highly critical of the existing cautioning system and, in particular, the use of repeat cautioning. Far too little in the way of resources was being committed, it felt, to actively engaging with and challenging young people, and far too much on simply 'processing' them. The agencies with responsibility for young people did not possess a common mission and coordination between them was poor. The problem, according to the Audit Commission, was that:

> the agencies dealing with young offenders have different views about what they are trying to achieve ... these different approaches need to be reconciled if agencies are to work together and fulfil their different responsibilities.

According to the Audit Commission, it was not just the approach of youth justice teams that was problematic. The whole court system, it suggested, was becoming less and less efficient. In its most damning indictment, it suggested that:

> overall, less is done now than a decade ago to address offending by young people. Fewer young people are now convicted by the courts, even allowing for the fall in the number of people aged 10–17 years, and an increasing proportion of those who are found guilty are discharged.

The system, it argued, needed to be streamlined and speeded up. Its proposals were taken up in the Labour government's immediate post-election White Paper, *No More Excuses* (Home Office, 1997b), in which it said that there was:

> Confusion about the purpose of the youth justice system and the principles that should govern the way in which young people are dealt with by youth justice agencies. Concerns about the welfare of young people have too often been seen as in conflict with the aims of protecting the public, punishing offences and preventing offending.

The 1998 Crime and Disorder Act brought in a raft of changes, three of which are central to New Labour's focus upon 'outcomes'. First, in an attempt to ameliorate the confusion identified initially by the Audit Commission, an overarching mission for the whole youth justice system – 'to prevent offending by children and young persons' – was created for the first time. The second was the establishment of the YJB. With an enormous legislative programme envisaged, the new home secretary established a Youth Justice Task Force in June 1997. The chair of the task force was Norman Warner, who had been adviser to Jack Straw in opposition, and its secretary was one of the authors of the Audit Commission report. When, as a result of section 41 of the Crime and Disorder Act, the YJB became a non-departmental public body sponsored by the Home Office, Warner became its chairman and the Audit Commission author its first chief executive. The YJB's principal function was to monitor the operation of the youth justice system and the provision of youth justice services, together with monitoring national standards and establishing appropriate performance measures. The 1998 Act also allowed the home secretary to expand the YJB's role and, from April 2000, the YJB also became the commissioning body for all placements of under-18s in secure establishments on remand or sentence from a criminal court. As a result of the comprehensive spending review, the YJB's role was later expanded to include commissioning places from prison service Young Offender Institutions (YOIs), local authority secure units and Secure Training Centres (STCs). In this connection, the Board advises the home secretary, is responsible for planning and setting standards and accredits establishments that operate according to those standards.

The final significant change in this area was the creation of Youth Offending Teams (YOTs). Prior to the 1998 Act, youth justice teams, composed mainly of social workers, had had primary responsibility for working with young offenders subject to non-custodial penalties, and for liaising with other criminal justice and treatment agencies in connection with that work. Stimulated by a concern with efficiency and consistency on the one hand, and by a pragmatic belief in multi-agency working on the other, New Labour's new model YOTs had to include a probation officer, a local authority social worker, a police officer, a representative of the local health authority and someone nominated by the chief education officer. YOTs have been in operation in all 154 local authority areas since April 2000. Social services remain the major player in local youth justice, contributing 55 per cent of the YOTs' resources. They are followed by the police (13 per cent), probation (10 per cent), local authority chief executives (9 per cent), education (7 per cent) and health (6 per cent) (Renshaw and Powell, 2001).

It would be a most incomplete picture to leave youth justice reform here however. For, in addition to a very significant overhaul of the system, the Crime and Disorder Act 1998 and the Youth Justice and Criminal Evidence Act 1999 both introduced major changes in the sanctions available to the youth court. The initial legislation included a raft of new orders including: detention and training orders, action-plan orders, parenting orders, reparation orders, antisocial behaviour orders and curfew orders. As the title of the Act implied, influenced by Wilson and Kelling's (1982) 'Broken Windows' thesis, it was not just crime but *disorder* that was to be targeted. The orders promised both earlier and more targeted and intensive interventions with young people. Both the child safety order and the curfew order applied to children under 10. The principle of *doli incapax* was abolished, removing the extant presumption, rebuttable in court, that a child under the age of 14 is incapable of committing a criminal offence. The cautioning system was overhauled, removing the option of multiple cautions, and replacing it with reprimands and final warnings. Simultaneously, via the action-plan order, the reparation order and the reformed cautioning system, significantly increased emphasis was placed by government on the idea of reparation and the potential involvement of victims in the criminal justice process. This was reinforced by the introduction of the referral order in the Youth Justice and Criminal Evidence Act 1999. In effect a mandatory sentence, the referral order applies to all young offenders pleading guilty for the first time to an offence in the youth court. They are then referred to a Youth Offender Panel, consisting of two local community members and one member of the local YOT who, with the offender, their parent(s) and possibly the victim, jointly devise a programme of activities for the young person designed both to challenge their behaviour and to make reparation. Although the changes brought about by the two Acts may well not 'amount to a "restorative justice revolution"' (Dignan, 1999: 58), they nonetheless represent a serious attempt to incorporate elements of restorative justice within a system that had been becoming increasingly, and rather uniformly, punitive.

The Crime and Disorder Act 1998 and Partnership Working

The second feature of the New Labour modernization project, and central to the delivery of its criminal justice policies, has been partnership working. One of the Labour government's major concerns – illustrated in the discussion of youth justice above – was that the major agencies which made up the criminal justice system failed in practice to work together to common aims and objectives. In that instance, its response was the creation of multi-agency YOTs. In many cases, not only did criminal justice agencies have very different agendas, at a simple geographical level they didn't even work within contiguous boundaries. In response, New Labour has sought to realign delivery: the police, crime and disorder partnerships, the prison service and the national probation service now all share common boundaries. In addition, it established crime and disorder partnerships as a key mechanism for planning, managing and auditing delivery.

The degree of difference between the outgoing Conservative government and the new Labour administration was well illustrated in the opening paragraphs of the latter's consultation document, *Getting to Grips with Crime* (Home Office, 1997a: 3–5), which said:

> Even though the previous administration chose not to implement the Report, many of Morgan's key findings have in fact been taken on board spontaneously by partnerships all over the country, to their benefit – and more importantly – that of local communities ... The years that have elapsed since Morgan have seen a complete acceptance of the partnership concept at all levels of the police service. The service now explicitly recognizes that it cannot cope with crime and disorder issues on its own ... The Government accepts the principle set out in Morgan that the extent, effectiveness and focus of existing local activity would be greatly improved by clear statements in law as to where responsibility for this work lies.

Sections 5 and 6 of the Crime and Disorder Act 1998 placed a statutory duty on chief police officers and local authorities, in cooperation with police authorities, probation committees and health authorities, to formulate and implement a strategy for the reduction of crime and disorder in the area. In this manner, the Act sought to stimulate considerable changes in the working practices of the main organizations responsible for crime control and the administration of crime prevention. Since the implementation of the Act, these crime and disorder partnerships (over 370 of them) have the responsibility for carrying out audits of local crime and disorder issues, to consult widely with the community on the basis of these audits, publish a local crime and disorder strategy based on the audit and consultation, identify local performance targets and report annually on progress in relation to the targets.

Under New Labour, partnerships have become the primary political means provided by the state for delivering crime prevention (Hope, 2001). Crime and disorder partnerships are but one of many, joining YOTs, Drug Action Teams, drug reference groups, and a proliferation of community-wide interventions with their own multi-agency committees such as Sure Start, New Deal and the Home Office-funded pathfinder projects, in a territory that, as Crawford (2001) notes, is supposed to be 'joined up' but remains, in reality, fragmented.

There are major tensions here, for this shift, as many commentators have noted, has required a reinvigoration of local mechanisms and capabilities simultaneously as government managerialism has led to increased centralization. Some critics have suggested that 'there is the clear danger that what can be reduced in crime and disorder is largely synonymous with what can be counted, audited and easily targeted (McLaughlin et al., 2001: 311). Indeed, McLaughlin and colleagues go on to argue that behind the apparently neutral language of 'evidence' and 'auditing', there is a centrally driven process taking place in which the 'script of governance' is being rewritten.

Within youth justice, for example, New Labour has been responsible for both the creation of local delivery mechanisms in the form of YOTs and a highly managerialist central function in the shape of the YJB. New Labour has sought to reinvigorate and redirect local agencies, but has rarely displayed much trust that such agencies will perform adequately unless they are closely and regularly monitored. The supervisory state relies increasingly, and unsatisfactorily, on the use of audit as the primary means of governing performance (Power, 1997).

The Probation Service and 'What Works?'

At the heart of the modernization agenda has been an emphasis on 'what works?' and 'cost-effectiveness'. The what works? paradigm has led to an apparent government desire to prioritize evidence-based policy and practice, invest massively in research and evaluation and promote accreditation programmes. Not only is there an inherent centralizing momentum in the what works? paradigm, however, but there is also a tension between what one might characterize as *effective* interventions ('what works?') and *efficient* justice (what it costs and how long it takes). Across government the Treasury has become increasingly important. Just as the comprehensive spending review gave impetus to the adoption of the what works? paradigm so, via the Treasury-led emphasis on cost-effectiveness, the linking of costs to outcomes and the measurement of the financial impact of interventions have determined much of the shape of the government's crime control agenda. Nowhere has this been more visible than in relation to the community penalties and the probation service.

Part of the attraction of the third way in criminal justice was the promise it held in steering a course between Old Labour welfarism and New Labour punitiveness. At the heart of this programme was the explicit distancing of government from old-fashioned 'nothing works' pessimism and the rise of the 'what works?' agenda. This has had its most profound effect on the probation service and the system of community penalties in England and Wales. Influenced in particular by cognitive-behavioural approaches developed in Canada and by research, especially meta-analytical research (Andrews et al., 1990; Lipsey, 1992), which claimed to show significant impacts with some offenders under some circumstances, the 'what works?' agenda revived, albeit in a more limited fashion, faith in the idea of rehabilitation (Raynor and Vanstone, 2002).

In a classic piece of New Labour managerialism, an entirely new vehicle was created for the implementation of a what works?-led agenda in relation to non-custodial penalties. With relatively little public discussion, and no visible professional dissent, after almost a century, the 54 local probation services in England and Wales were disbanded and replaced by the national probation service for England and Wales in April 2001. The aim was that this new service would be more effectively controlled from the centre and that the raft of new programmes, influenced by the what works? agenda, could be rolled out quickly and as uniformly as possible. In fact, it had originally been mooted that the prison and probation services be merged into a single corrections service (Home Office, 1998). In the event, this didn't take place, although it remains very much on the New Labour agenda at the time of writing.

In 1999, a Joint Prisons and Probation Accreditation Panel (JPPAP) was established. Like the YJB, the JPPAP is a non-departmental public body. Chaired by Sir Duncan Nichol, and comprising a range of academics and criminal justice professionals, the panel's central function is to accredit programmes that, on the basis of rigorous research, are believed to reduce re-offending. According to the panel (JPPAP, 2001), the principles associated with effective interventions include:

- Effective risk management

- Targeting offending behaviour

- Addressing the specific factors linked with offenders' offending

- Relevance to offenders' learning style

- Promoting community reintegration

- Maintaining quality and integrity of programme delivery.

Progress has been significant, according to Raynor (2002: 1189–90), himself a member of the panel:

> From being unable in 1997 to point to more than a handful of evaluated effective initiatives, the Probation Service had been transformed within a few years into an organization able to offer quality-controlled programmes throughout England and Wales, in what is believed to be the largest initiative in evidence-based corrections to be undertaken anywhere in the world.

The 'what works?' approach has been by no means without its critics. Indeed, Raynor and Vanstone have noted more recently that while,

> it is true that the evidence base in Britain is still fairly small, and although existing research projects will enable it to grow rapidly, not all of it will necessarily support

the management decisions which have already been taken. Some of these may have to be changed if the commitment to evidence-based policy is to be maintained. (2002: 105)

The probation service, in the form of its main union NAPO, has been critical of the impact of the approach on the ability of its members to use their own skills and judgement when working with offenders. Others have been sceptical about the research evidence itself, querying whether the evidence for some programmes was as firm as it was presented as being (Merrington and Stanley, 2000) or questioning the apparent adherence to a narrow cognitive-behavioural-dominated model of working with offenders (Mair, 2000).

The what works? agenda has, of course, affected more than just the probation and prison services. 'Evidence-based policy' has become the mantra for both the Home Office itself and for the major criminal justice and crime prevention agencies. The strategies published by crime and disorder partnerships are intended to be based on evidence drawn from local crime audits. Future performance is then measured against indicators based on the strategy. Although its impact has been less, for there has been much greater resistance, there have also been attempts to inculcate similar ideas within the police service.

Better Late than Never? Police Reform

Jack Straw's tenure as home secretary was marked by one important, and brave, political act in the area of policing: the establishment of the Macpherson Inquiry into the murder of Stephen Lawrence. On 22 April 1993, Stephen Lawrence was standing at a bus stop with a friend, Duwayne Brooks, when they were approached by a small group of clearly hostile and abusive white youths. Although Brooks was able to escape and call for help, Stephen Lawrence was stabbed twice and died within a short period of time. The subsequent inquest in 1997 resulted in a unanimous verdict of unlawful killing 'in a completely unprovoked racist attack by five white youths' (Macpherson, 1999). To date no one has been successfully charged with Stephen Lawrence's murder.

The previous home secretary had refused to countenance a public inquiry. However, Straw met with Mr and Mrs Lawrence within two months of taking office and afterwards said that:

it is not an option to let this matter rest. I recognize that a strong case has been made by Mrs Lawrence for some form of inquiry and I am actively considering what she put to me. (Macpherson, 1991: Appendix 1)

The decision to establish an inquiry, chaired by Sir William Macpherson of Cluny (formerly a high court judge) was announced on 31 July, the terms of reference of which were to be:

> To inquire into the matters arising from the death of Stephen Lawrence on 22 April 1993 to date, in order particularly to identify the lessons to be learned for the investigation and prosecution of racially motivated crimes.

The inquiry reported in February 1999, made over 70 recommendations and memorably described the Metropolitan Police as 'institutionally racist'. Policing post-Macpherson has been the subject of considerable scrutiny and inquiry. How much has really changed in the attitudes and behaviour of the police is, however, questionable (see, for example, the research reported in FitzGerald et al., 2002).

One of the most significant changes within criminal justice in the past 20 years has been the transformation of the police service generally, and the Association of Chief Police Officers (ACPO) in particular, into a formidable pressure group (Jones and Newburn, 1997; Savage et al., 2000). Numerous home secretaries have fought shy of taking on the police service; only Ken Clarke of all the Tory home secretaries who served under Thatcher and Major seemed willing to enter the fray. When Jack Straw took office in 1997, it was an open secret in the Home Office that the new home secretary viewed the police as the last great unreformed public service and was keen to do something about it. With the conspicuous exception of the establishment of the Lawrence Inquiry, he set in train very little that might be described as especially challenging to the police service. Reform appeared to be back on the agenda in the weeks leading up to the 2001 general election, but again there seemed to be little enthusiasm for anything radical. The arrival of David Blunkett led to immediate change – both in tenor and practice.

It might not be his first choice for comparison, but Blunkett bore more of a resemblance to Ken Clarke than to Jack Straw. A conviction politician, and one apparently not in the slightest afraid of a dust-up, Blunkett's very first (official) announcement as home secretary was the setting up of a Standards Unit for the police, very much along the lines he had established for schools when in charge of the DfES. The core objective of the unit was said to be to identify and disseminate best practice in the prevention, detection and apprehension of crime in all forces in order to reduce crime and disorder as well as the fear of crime. The home secretary summarized the purpose of the unit as being to:

> Identify where good practice is working and work out where and how standards can be raised by spreading best practice. The heart of its task will be to identify and

remove the barriers to success, identify solutions and help forces cut down on bureaucracy. It is not about publishing league tables or 'naming and shaming'. It is about providing real, practical help based on what works, through tailored and targeted operational training.

In addition to the Standards Unit, he let it be known that a White Paper containing proposals for reform of various aspects of the police service would also shortly be published. Released in early December 2001, the White Paper, *Policing a New Century: A Blueprint for Reform* (Home Office, 2001b) focused on police performance, police numbers, bureaucracy and red tape, pay and conditions, occupational health and the possible introduction of community support officers and accredited organizations to undertake patrol activities and tackle low-level crime. The proposals for reformed pay and conditions stimulated the main police unions into action and even brought an apology from the home secretary at a Police Federation conference.

It was the introduction of community support officers that was the most radical of the proposals, however. Almost a decade earlier, a committee established by the Police Foundation and the Policy Studies Institute had recommended experimentation with alternative forms of police patrol (Police Foundation/PSI, 1994; see also Morgan and Newburn, 1997), only to be roundly criticized by ACPO and New Labour in opposition for recommending 'policing on the cheap'. By 2002, however, the fiscal realities were such that it was difficult for any politician to avoid the conclusion that the level of policing seemingly demanded by the public could not easily be provided from within the public purse. A form of public–private partnership was proposed – not that such language was used. Using the more mellifluous idea of 'an extended police family', and underpinned by the 'Broken Windows' philosophy, the White Paper proposed, and the Police Reform Act 2002 incorporated, proposals that agents and agencies such as neighbourhood and street wardens, security guards in shopping centres, park keepers and 'other authority figures' (Home Office, 2001b: para. 2.31) could be accredited by, and work alongside, the police in a formal capacity. More controversially, the government proposed a power to enable chief constables to appoint support staff to provide a visible presence (that is, to patrol) in the community. These 'community support officers' would be under the control of the chief constable and would have limited powers to detain suspects, stop vehicles and issue fixed-penalty notices.

The Home Office was primarily responding to the problem of limited resources in making such a proposal. While much of the police service appeared sceptical at best, and somewhat hostile in many cases, the Metropolitan Police – also subject to considerable resource pressures – was at the forefront of taking the idea of community support officers forward, with the first of the new officers patrolling London in late 2002. Directly and indirectly, through a number of its measures, New Labour has stimulated further moves in the direction of a more complex and fragmented policing division of labour. The Police Reform Act 2002, via the creation of community support officers and the accreditation of extended police family members, is the most visible of the measures. Arguably, however, the Crime and Disorder Act 1998, in conjunction with Best Value and the increasing emphasis placed upon consumer demand, will prove to be just as important in the process of extending and formalizing the mixed economy of policing (Newburn, 2001).

Modernization, the Courts and Sentencing

Large-scale sentencing reform has been on most home secretaries' agendas since the early 1990s. Kenneth Clarke led the assault on the 1991 Criminal Justice Act and its 'just deserts' philosophy. Howard carried on where Clarke left off, adding his own brand of American-inspired populism in the form of 'three strikes' mandatory minimums in the Crime (Sentences) Act 1997. Jack Straw, although no fan of mandatory minimums in opposition, activated not only the drugs and violent crime mandatories soon after becoming home secretary, but also the much more controversial, and probably more damaging, burglary provision a year later. Straw was operating within difficult territory. The modernizing agenda led in the direction of significant reform of both the organization of the courts and the framework of sentencing. Populist pressures meant that any reform would have to be located, at least in part, within a punitive rhetoric. However, both because of the crippling costs and a continuing, if usually hidden, scepticism about the extent to which prison really did work, both Straw and Blunkett were loathe to continue to drive up the prison population.[1] In order to stimulate fresh thinking, and possibly to distance himself from politically difficult ideas, Straw set up two reviews: the Review of Criminal Courts in England and Wales under Lord Justice Auld (Auld, 2001); and the Review of the Sentencing Framework under John Halliday (Home Office, 2001a).

In the view of one of its members, Michael Tonry, the Halliday Review was misconceived (Tonry and Rex, 2002: 2), being insufficiently independent from Home Office politics:

> In particular, the need to accommodate Jack Straw's policy preferences for 'seamless sentencing', close community supervision, 'custody plus' sentences and punishment increments for successive offences, and to avoid Straw's forbidden ground of

the reconsideration of mandatory minimum penalties, distorted the proposals that were made. (Tonry and Rex, 2002: 2–3)

The eventual outcome of both reviews was a White Paper, *Justice For All* (Home Office, 2002), which recommended a broad range of reform measures, again using the language of modernization. Most notably, these included the scrapping of the double jeopardy rule (recommended by Macpherson), unifying the administration of the magistrates' and crown courts, increasing magistrates' sentencing powers from 6 to 12 months, creating 'intermittent' prison sentences, 'custody plus' (in which offenders serve a short prison sentence of between two weeks and three months followed by at least six months' community work) and 'custody minus' (a new suspended sentence). Extra expenditure is to be provided to modernize prisons and improve information technology, all aimed at joining up the criminal justice system, together with the creation of a national Criminal Justice Board and a new cabinet committee to oversee reform. The overall aim of the reform process is to 'rebalance' the criminal justice system in favour of victims and witnesses at the expense of defendants. Its approach, thereafter, is pragmatic rather than philosophical, attempting to reduce delays and increase detection and conviction rates. With its emphasis on systems, efficiency and the greater involvement of victims and witnesses, the White Paper is a quintessentially New Labour modernizing document.

Crime, Government and Image Management

No discussion of New Labour would be complete without some reference to issues of image and news management. In the criminal justice arena, politicians' concern about how they are likely to be perceived has had a profound effect on policy making in recent years. The past two decades have seen a progressively intensifying battle by the two main political parties to be seen as the party of law and order. This struggle was at its clearest in the five years after Labour's 1992 election defeat. In this period, as the Democratic Party in the US had done before it (Baer, 2000), Labour sought to reinvent itself and, particularly, to relocate itself as a party more in tune with what were perceived to be middle England's concerns about crime. The most visible sign of change was Blair's famous sound bite, 'tough on crime and tough on the causes of crime'. It was important not simply because it signalled a third way in law and order, but because it allowed the then shadow home secretary to utter a New Labour 'keyword' (Fairclough, 2000) – tough – twice in the space of ten words.

A preoccupation with language – particularly the language of toughness and punitiveness – has frequently distracted attention (often by design) from, and sometimes seemingly undermined, some of New Labour's more thoughtful and more constructive approaches to crime and punishment. In the lead-up to the 1997 general election, this manifested itself in a wholesale importation of American crime control rhetoric, including both the idea of 'zero-tolerance' (Newburn, 2002) and the manifesto proposal, later acted upon, to create a 'drugs tsar' (Quayle, 1998). This concern with image is the source of much of the ambiguity and tension in the New Labour project. As two influential New Labour architects put it in the early 1990s:

> the lessons which the British left can learn [from the US] are not so much about *content* – although there is valuable intellectual exchange already underway – as about *process*. (Hewitt and Gould, 1993: 48)

It is here that the tensions between short-termism and the longer term modernization project have perhaps been clearest. Thus, against a background of progressive and sometimes impressive reforms in the first three years of the first term, with a huge parliamentary majority and continuing falls in recorded crime, the Labour government rarely looked like it was confident in the face of even relatively minor 'bad news' stories. As one example, not long after the case of the Norfolk farmer, Tony Martin, the Prime Minister still felt compelled to write a memo to his director of communications in which he sought to regain the apparently lost ground. In the memo, dated 29 April 2000 but leaked in July, Blair said:

> On crime, we need to highlight the *tough* measures: compulsory tests for drugs before bail ... the extra number of burglars jailed under 'three strikes and you're out'. Above all, we must deal *now* with street crime, especially in London. When the figures are published for the six months to April, they will show a small – 4 per cent – rise in crime. But this will almost entirely be due to the rise in levels of street crime – mobile phones, bags being snatched. This will be worst in London. The Met Police are putting in place measures to deal with it; but as ever, we lack a tough *public* message along with the strategy. We should think now of an initiative, eg locking up street muggers. Something tough, with immediate bite that sends a message through the system. Maybe, the driving licence penalty for young offenders. But this should be done soon and I, personally, should be associated with it. (*Sun*, 17 July 2000)

There are numerous other examples from the past five years. The timing of the activation of the third of the 'three strikes' provisions in the Crime (Sentences) Act 1997 was dictated not by criminal justice concerns but by the desire to bury a particularly bad news story. There followed the Prime Minister's speech in Germany, to a bemused audience, in which he outlined, apparently to the surprise of the Home Office, plans to introduce fixed penalties and raised the spectre of police officers marching young offenders to cashpoint machines on a rowdy Saturday night to pay their on-the-spot fines. The more recent, again Prime Ministerial, announcement that the new coordinated street crime initiative would crack the problem by September 2002 (Prime Time, *Police Review*, 26 July 2002) distracted attention almost entirely from the proposed White Paper and led to widespread concern within the police service about the possibility of operational control of policing from Whitehall. Although the Prime Minister may be the main culprit in this regard, New Labour home secretaries have been far from immune. David Blunkett, in particular, has at various points issued statements which appear highly critical of the 'prison works' approach adopted by Michael Howard and then made highly punitive public speeches within days of each other.[2] Neither Straw nor Blunkett has appeared unequivocal on what he feels should be happening to the prison population. Both have seemed uncomfortable with continuing rises in the numbers incarcerated, but neither has acted in a way that might have significantly altered the situation (with the rather limited exception of the home detention curfew).[3]

Conclusion

Although there are clear continuities between New Labour and previous administrations (Smith, 2000), not least in some of their punitive rhetoric, there are also clear differences. Indeed, even in that regard, there have been changes, for some of the populist punitiveness of the pre-1997 period has been toned down or jettisoned altogether. Similarly, the corporatist modernizing agenda, although clearly a descendant of the 1980s' version, is also radically different from it. In particular, the rise to prominence of the 'what works?' paradigm, and the centralizing managerialist initiatives under New Labour, signal a major departure from previous arrangements. Criminologists have been somewhat reluctant to acknowledge the positive elements in such developments. It is undoubtedly right to be concerned about the likely impact of increasing managerialism; the pitfalls are well known and the dangers are real. However, it is important not to lose sight of the fact that New Labour's 'systemic managerialism' (Bottoms, 1995), particularly in youth justice and social crime prevention, has led to the development of an organizationally more creative and coherent environment. Both the 'new youth justice' and local crime and disorder prevention arrangements are significantly better funded and therefore *potentially* better placed to deliver necessary services, than the systems they superseded.

Nonetheless, given the circumstances outlined above, it should be no surprise that New Labour's record, like its public pronouncements, is a mixed one. The modernization project has diverse tributaries in which, at heart, the desire to produce technically competent, well-resourced and publicly responsive local systems of delivery has continually been in tension with a strong desire to manage and control from the centre. An uneasy mixture is the consequence. The radical reform of youth justice, which contained a genuine attempt to empower local youth justice practitioners, was accompanied by the establishment of a powerful and controlling bureaucracy in the centre in the form of the YJB. The rationalization of the geographical boundaries of local criminal justice agencies, and the creation of potentially powerful new local partnerships and responsibilities, was accompanied by the release of increasing numbers of central directives and performance measures. To date, New Labour appears to be an administration that believes in the importance of local services and local delivery, but does not yet quite trust those responsible to provide such services in a consistent or effective manner.

In parallel, and perhaps equally importantly, the modernization project, which included a full-scale overhaul of the Labour Party itself and its communications strategies (Gould, 1998), has been characterized by a *confidence deficit*. Successive New Labour administrations, underpinned by overwhelming parliamentary majorities, and faced by a disorganized and toothless opposition, have rarely looked like having the confidence to take advantage of this unparalleled position of power. Electoral success in recent times has undoubtedly been partly contingent on the ability of politicians to persuade voters that they will be 'tough' on crime (Downes and Morgan, 2002). Once elected in 1997, and established in an impregnable position in parliament, it should have been possible for the 'tough on the causes of crime' element of New Labour's message to be as visible as its more punitive counterpart. This has rarely been the case, however. In practice, the undoubted achievements of New Labour in the arena of home affairs – the reform of the youth justice system, the gradual embracing of restorative justice ideas, the establishment of crime and disorder partnerships, changes in the treatment of cannabis possession and elements of police reform – have tended to be masked by, and occasionally undermined by, knee-jerk policy making and populist, short-term rhetoric. Quite apart from the erosion of civil liberties and the continued increasing use of incarceration and other forms of punishment that parts of the New Labour project have entailed, the danger is that the opportunity to break out of the punitive policy-making cycle of the last decade will be lost.

Further Reading

See chapters by David Downes and Rod Morgan in consecutive editions of
    Maguire, M., Morgan, R. and Reiner, R. (eds) (1994, 1997, 2002), *Oxford
    Handbook of Criminology*, Oxford: Clarendon Press.
Home Office (1997) *No More Excuses*, London: Home Office (summarizes New
    Labour's approach in its first term of office).
The Home Office website (www.homeoffice.gov.uk) is enormously useful.
Regularly updated prison population statistics can be found at: www.hmprison-
service.gov.uk/statistics. Up-to-date information can also be found at the
NACRO website (www.nacro.org.uk) and that of the Howard League for Penal
Reform (www.howardleague.org).

Notes

1   In a speech on 19 June 2002 at a conference on modernizing criminal justice, for example, Blun-
    kett said: 'In the past eight years the prison population has risen from just over 40,000 to just over
    70,000 and a fat lot of good it's done us in crime control terms.' See also Blunkett's speech to the
    National Association of Probation Officers on 5 July 2001, at: www.society.guardian.co.uk/
    crimeandpunishment/story/0,8150,517211,00.html.
2   For example, in a speech to the Prison Service on 4 February 2002, David Blunkett said: 'Prison is
    an expensive way of denying people liberty. A new intermediate option could reduce costs dramati-
    cally, giving us more money to spend on crime reduction.' Then, on 20 March 2002, in a speech on
    street crime, he said: 'What we need is practical action on the streets at local level to tackle the thugs
    that are striking fear into our communities. What I want to do is to put the fear back where it
    belongs, with those that seek to break the law and terrorise others.' Both speeches are available at:
    www.nds.coi.gov.uk/coi/coipress.nsf/GHO?openview&start=3.1&count=92&expand=3&quarter=
    1&year=2002.
3   At the time of writing, the prison population has reached 72,867. When Labour came to power
    in 1997 the figure was just over 61,000.

CHAPTER 14

Transport and Social Policy

MATTHEW PAGE

This chapter explores New Labour's record in an often underregarded area of public policy. It is an area where New Labour hoped to make a real difference, following the emergence of new ideas about transport policy during the previous Conservative administration. A new secretary of state with the ear of the Prime Minister, in charge of a new 'superministry' and with a real interest in transport matters, promised great things but was overoptimistic about what could actually be achieved in the government's first term. A wide range of constraints also made themselves felt and John Prescott was also guilty of underestimating the strength of existing trends and the difficulty of significantly changing behaviour in the short term. In the end, transport became a highly contentious issue and the 'radical change in transport policy' which was promised in the 1998 White Paper (DETR, 1998a) was tempered by the electoral imperative of avoiding the label 'anti-motorist'.

Nevertheless, progress was made, but it was mostly confined to the less obvious areas of the strategic and legislative framework within which transport operates. It remains to be seen whether progress can be made on the more intractable transport issues, as this will inevitably involve offending one powerful group or another and constraining lifestyles which have evolved over many years to become increasingly dependent on relatively cheap and plentiful road transport.

Transport – A Social Policy?

Traditionally, transport has not been viewed in the same way as other areas of social policy, for example health or education. It is difficult to imagine a politician suggesting that their priority was transport without acquiring a reputation as something of an eccentric. To some extent, transport has been seen as a technical issue – just a question of letting the engineers and the economists get on with it. Given sufficient resources, the argument goes, transport will be able to deliver the level of accessibility required. Two reasons for this view are that the social implications of transport policy have only emerged slowly and relatively recently and the transport profession has traditionally been dominated by people whose expertise lies in the construction or operation of transport infrastructure or systems. Hillman (1986) suggests that this has come about partly as a result of historical circumstances and characterizes this development as:

- *Early years* – an abundance of road space for the traffic being carried, therefore less competition for road space, so transport planning was largely the responsibility of the highway engineer, who was concerned with simply providing for the traffic.

- *Traffic management* – as traffic increased, more techniques were used to manage traffic (parking controls, one-way systems) and model and predict flows, and technical innovations (computerized traffic signal control) were developed.

- *Social problems* – transport policy has to be seen as part of wider social policy and includes considerations such as adjudication of conflict, judgement of environmental conflict and solution of social problems.

Hillman suggests that transport planners are ill-equipped to deal with the most recent (the last) of these developments and therefore a lot of the underlying considerations which are important to contemporary transport planning.

The thrust of research into transport issues has also been on the technical side, with little emphasis on the political realities of delivery or the social consequences. The dominant paradigm has been that if sufficiently accurate models can be developed linking measures to outcomes and if the decision makers and/or users can be persuaded to quantify their relative valuations of, say, environmental impacts, the value of time, the value of accidents, and so on, it is just a question of pulling the lever and an 'optimum' transport policy will emerge.

On the other hand, transport choices involve the allocation of finite resources to different interest groups, the most obvious being space and time to move about. Transport constrains where we live, where we work, where we take our leisure and our social networks. How we choose to fund, organize and regulate transport has major implications for public health and wider social inequalities (BMA, 1997). Transport can (or should) act as a constraint on other policies, for instance choice in education, or efficiency in health service provision. Transport is also one of the areas of serious public concern over policy. People are more likely to mention transport when asked about local issues that any other topic. According to the Commission for Integrated Transport (CfIT), people are concerned about the costs of owning a car, congestion and the effects of pollution on health and global warming (CfIT, 2001). A substantial majority expect transport problems to get worse over the next decade. Transport is also one of the most ubiquitous of social services, virtually everyone, every day, uses a publicly funded transport facility (the road).

However, transport is often seen as slightly apart from the normal political discourse. When developing the Leeds transport strategy at the end of the 1980s (Leeds City Council and West Yorkshire Passenger Transport Authority, 1991), Leeds city council built a political consensus around a package of measures. This was partly because it was felt that transport was 'too important to be left to the politicians', but it was also because there was a pragmatic realization that, in a situation where delivery was likely to be a long-term process, the only way forward was to gain cross-party agreement to the entire package. This approach recognizes that the 'solutions' to transport problems are not obvious and perhaps do not even exist in the way that improvements in other areas of social policy can be easily identified. Addressing transport problems involves difficult trade-offs because of the simple physical impossibility of providing enough access for everyone in the way they would prefer. Providing accessibility is always going to be a balancing act, characterized by Engwicht (1993) as the balance between movement space and exchange space, that is, space to get to places and space to actually do things.

Another reason that transport issues have not been treated in the same way as other areas of social policy is that the conflicts are not along the traditional party political lines. While Labour has been seen as favouring public transport and the Conservatives as championing the private motorist, this has by no means been a consistent dichotomy. Labour has encouraged wider car ownership and use (Adams, 1990), while the Conservatives have sought to improve public transport and reduce reliance on the private car (DoT, 1996). In recent years, the differences between the parties have been even less clear-cut, with both seeking favour with the electorate by jostling for position to be seen as 'the motorists' friend', partly because car ownership and use are now so widespread across society. It is now clear that the interest groups concerned with transport are not easily identified as 'Labour' or 'Conservative', if they ever were.

Transport Policy to 1997

The dominant themes of post-war transport are the continuing growth in road traffic and the widening of car ownership so that about two-thirds of households now have access to a car (Figures 14.1 and 14.2). The most obvious reason for these trends is that living standards have increased while the costs of owning and running a car have not increased as much (Figure 14.3). Over the years, the number of trips made has not gone up as fast as the number of vehicle kilometres, indicating that as people have acquired cars, they have chosen to use them to travel longer distances, rather than making more trips. People have used ready access to the car to relax constraints in other parts of their lives, for example where they live, shop and work. As car users have increasingly chosen to travel longer distances, local facilities have become uneconomic or the opportunity has been taken to centralize services or employment, further fuelling traffic growth and disadvantaging those without cars.

As it became clear that traffic was having a major impact on urban areas, the government commissioned the influential Buchanan Report (Ministry of Transport, 1963). This recommended, very much in the spirit of the time, wholesale redevelopment of urban areas to cope with rising traffic levels, but also found that even with this level of redevelopment, some form of traffic restraint was likely to be necessary to safeguard the urban environment. The report was enthusiastically welcomed at the time by both political parties. As governments of both political persuasions funded the motorway building programme, there was some redevelopment of urban areas, but not on the scale that Buchanan deemed necessary. The financial and social difficulties of

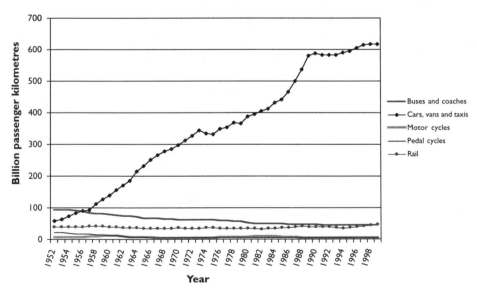

Figure 14.1 Traffic by mode, 1952–99

Source: DfT (2002; Table 9.1)

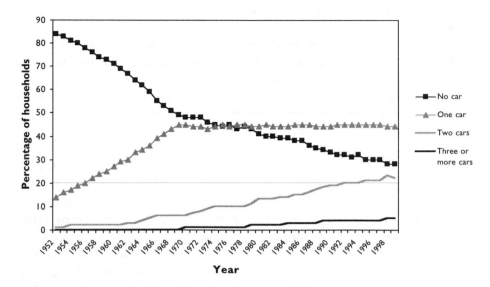

Figure 14.2 Car ownership, 1952–99

Source: DfT (2002: Table 9.4)

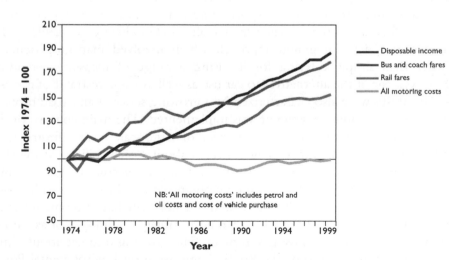

Figure 14.3 Costs of running a car compared to disposable income and alternative forms of transport

Source: DETR (2000g: Chart 3c)

adapting urban areas to the car were becoming evident, but traffic restraint was never seriously considered, as envisaged by Buchanan.

In the 1980s, the increase in the use of the private car fitted with Thatcher's political philosophy of self-improvement. To try to stem increasing levels of subsidy and introduce the discipline of the market, bus services outside London were privatized and deregulated. This put most of the system outside public control, apart from the subsidy of some socially necessary services. There were significant increases in traffic in the 1980s associated with growth in the economy and this led to a revised *National Road Traffic Forecasts* (DoT, 1989a), which projected a rise in traffic over the years 1988 to 2025 of between 83 per cent and 142 per cent. The publication of the forecasts was accompanied by the announcement of an ambitious plan for road building (DoT, 1989b), called *Roads to Prosperity*, clearly aimed at providing for the rises in traffic.

However, as the figures presented in the *National Road Traffic Forecasts* were studied, it became clear that there fundamental problems with the long-term direction that transport policy was taking. The existing policy was characterized as 'predict and provide', but it was becoming abundantly clear that it was simply impossible to provide for the levels of traffic that were being predicted. The problem was most acute in urban areas, where the scope for increases in capacity was smallest, but it was difficult to see how inter-urban traffic could be accommodated, even with the ambitious road building plans in *Roads to Prosperity* (Adams, 1990). As a result of this concern over the long-term implications of transport policy, new ideas emerged and were brought forward as the so-called 'new realism' (Goodwin et al., 1991). This suggested a new integrated approach which involved managing demand rather than simply catering for it, using a range of measures including improvement of the alternatives to car use as well as some restraint of car use.

The 1990s were also characterized by a growing series of anti-road protests as the road building programme was implemented. The main concern of the protestors was the environmental impact of large-scale road infrastructure, which sat uneasily with increasing concerns about sustainability and the shift in other areas of government policy towards a greater concern for the environment. These protests became highly organized and involved a wide cross-section of people, many of whom would not normally have become involved in direct action and some of whom would normally be thought of as natural supporters of a Conservative government. The growing disquiet about transport policy was added to by the Royal Commission on Environmental Pollution's report *Transport and the Environment* (1994) which was critical of transport trends and policy. Partly as a result of the growing concerns, the government made adjustments to the roads programme, although a more pressing and immediate reason was probably a shortage of finance. The government also pressed ahead with the politically motivated privatization of the rail industry, splitting it up into hundreds of different companies. The running of the services was franchised out to 25 different train operating companies running under different subsidy regimes, but they owned neither the infrastructure, nor even the trains they used. Some control was retained, mostly through the award of train-operating franchises, but even this was at arm's length from the government.

In response to the uncertainty surrounding transport policy and the concerns about the long-term implications of continued traffic growth, the transport secretary, Brian Mawhinney, organized a 'great transport debate' to discuss the balance between economic growth, protection of the environment and support for personal choice. This debate resulted in a Green Paper *Transport: The Way Forward* (DoT, 1996). This publication did indicate a change in emphasis, with a recognition that improvements to public transport were needed to help to reduce dependence on the car. In the dying days of the administration, the government allowed the passage of the Road Traffic Reduction Act 1997 which put a responsibility on local government to produce a report on existing and forecast levels of traffic in their area, with targets, although the original requirement actually to reduce traffic was not included in the Act. Soon after the Act was passed, the Conservative government was defeated in the 1997 general election.

New Labour – New Transport Policy?

One of the first moves of the incoming Labour administration was to create a new superministry; the Departments of the Environment and Transport were combined to produce the new Department of the Environment, Transport and the Regions (DETR). The logic was to integrate two policy areas with clear links which had seemed to be drifting apart under the Conservatives, but the move created a large, unwieldy department. John Prescott was appointed secretary of state for the environment, transport and the regions and also deputy Prime Minister. This immediately gave transport an importance it had not enjoyed for many years. John Prescott was a transport enthusiast who had shadowed the position for many years and, more importantly, had significant influence within the government.

Prescott was committed to changing travel behaviour and even promised soon after the election that 'I will have failed if in five years time there are not many more people using public transport and far fewer journeys by car' (*Guardian*, 6 June 1997). This was a bold statement, particularly the assertion that he could reduce car usage. Figure 14.4 shows the relationship between passenger kilometres, tonne kilometres and GDP, so Prescott was setting himself against a well-established trend, beneath which lay a host of personal aspirations towards car ownership and use at many levels in society. While the public mood may have been for a radical change in transport policy, the underlying drivers of traffic growth were still robust and likely to remain so. This was clear from the publication of the 1997 *National Road Traffic Forecasts* (DETR, 1997c), which indicated a lower level of growth than the 1989 forecasts, but only because the predictions of economic growth were lower.

Soon after the start of the new administration, the DETR started a round of consultation with the publication of a consultation document on the development of an integrated transport policy (DETR, 1997d). This activity mirrored the previous Conservative administration's 'great transport debate' but the consultation paper set a more radical tone, stating that 'the forecast growth in road traffic is clearly unacceptable', but also reminded consultees that there were 'tight constraints on public funding'. It was clear that the new emphasis was to be on integration and here the Labour administration hoped to distinguish itself from the previous government which had avoided use of the term. It had already integrated central government consideration of the environment, transport and land use policy by creating the DETR, however, it was not clear what integration might mean in practice and whether it was possible to achieve. Integration could be considered at a number of different levels, for example the integration of land use and transport policies, integ-

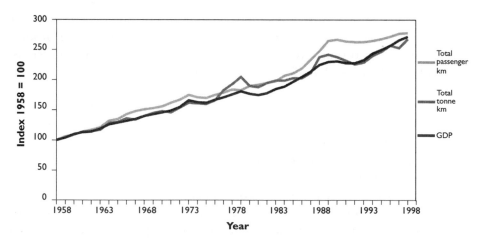

Figure 14.4 Passenger kilometres, tonne kilometres and GDP

Source: DETR (2000g: Chart 3a)

ration between different levels of government, integration between widely different policy areas (for example consideration of the transport effects of health, education or wealth-creation policies) or simply integration between different modes of transport. To achieve much of this integration, extensive cooperation between different bodies would be required. In the practical area of transport, many of the organizations responsible for delivery had been privatized and therefore put outside the immediate control of the government.

The government passed the 1998 Road Traffic Reduction Act which imposed a similar responsibility to the 1997 Act on central government to produce a report on existing and forecast traffic levels at a national level.

The Transport White Paper and Transport Act 2000

Following on from the extensive consultation, the long-awaited transport White Paper *A New Deal for Transport: Better for Everyone* was published in July 1998 (DETR, 1998a). The White Paper was welcomed on all sides of the debate, although the overall tone was not significantly different from the Conservative's *Transport: The Way Forward* (DoT, 1996). The document actually contained only a few firm proposals of any significance and its popularity was due partly to the fact that it managed to offend no one, by offering improvements in public transport while recognizing the importance of the car and promising better maintenance and management of the existing roads. These potential improvements were described in the White Paper's own foreword as arising out of a 'consensus for radical change in transport policy', but by attempting to make things 'better for everyone', the document implied that the emphasis was to be on improvements to public transport, rather than measures to restrict car ownership or use.

The White Paper did make a number of changes to the strategic and administrative framework for transport, although these were not immediately obvious to the travelling public. Five-year Local Transport Plans (LTPs) were proposed to replace the annual round of local government bids for transport funding. These plans would give local authorities a more long-term expectation of funding in order to deliver integrated transport at the local level and also allow them much more freedom in how they allocated funding for local transport improvements. Extensive guidance on the preparation of LTPs was provided and the first (provisional) LTPs were submitted in July 1999, with full LTPs submitted a year later.

The White Paper also set up the Strategic Rail Authority (SRA), although this existed only in shadow form until the passage of the Transport Act in 2000. The SRA was to take responsibility for providing a 'clear, coherent and strategic programme for the development of our railways', a lack of which was widely seen as a weakness in the structure of the privatized railway. It also created the Commission for Integrated Transport (CfIT) to provide independent advice to government on the implementation of integrated transport policy, and was led by Professor David Begg who had personal experience of implementing transport policy at a local level. Over the next few years, the Commission published a series of reports on transport policy and the government's plans.

One important development in the White Paper was the promise to introduce legislation to allow local authorities to use road user charging and workplace parking levies to reduce congestion. The legislation was to be framed so as ring-fence (hypothecate) the proceeds from such schemes to pay for improvements to local transport – this was widely recognized as being crucial in getting such a policy accepted. At this stage, the DETR was keen to encourage local authorities to use the powers (after they had been legislated), but it was left up to local authorities to take the initiative.

The government also announced a 'new approach to appraisal' (NATA) to be applied to trunk road investment proposals. The dominance of simple cost–benefit calculations over other considerations such as environmental impacts had been seen as a problem for some time. The NATA used an appraisal summary table to convey the impacts of the proposals under five different criteria: the environment, safety, the economy (which included cost–benefit analysis calculations), accessibility (especially for those without a car) and integration. At the same time as the White Paper was published, a revised roads programme was outlined (DETR, 1998b) which applied NATA to the schemes currently on the DETR's books. As a result, a number of road schemes were abandoned or shelved. Interestingly, the summary tables used to decide on the schemes were published, making the decision-making process transparent, indeed it was possible to analyse the decisions and confirm that there was a logic to them (Nellthorp and Mackie, 2000).

Over the next year or so, the government published a series of White Paper 'daughter' documents, enlarging on its proposals and inviting comments on particular aspects. These included the proposals for road user charging and workplace parking levies (DETR, 1998b) and improvements in bus-based public transport (DETR, 1998a), which the DETR regarded as an important mode for improving mobility for those without a car. For some time, local authorities had been entering into 'quality partnerships' with local bus operators. These were agreements that transport providers would improve their service in response to local authority investment in infrastructure, but these were difficult to enforce because they had no legal standing. With open competition on the street, there was no way of barring the infrastructure improvements to anyone who wanted to run a bus, whether or not they had improved their service. The government proposed to allow 'quality contracts' with a legal basis, to get round the legislation on free and fair competition in the provision of public transport.

Crucially, the promised legislation which backed up the proposals in the White Paper was delayed and the Transport Act 2000 did not become law until more than two years after the publication of the White Paper. In the meantime, momentum was lost. Local authorities got used to the new LTP system, but the government did not significantly increase funding on local transport because of the restrictive departmental spending plans it had committed itself to in its manifesto. Government funding of the railway industry actually fell because of the reductions in subsidy that were built in to the franchising agreements made at the time of railway privatization. There were also signs that the government's commitment to the new agenda was wavering in the face of media criticism of its perceived 'anti-motorist' stance. There seemed to be a feeling that Prescott's attempts to achieve a 'modal shift' risked alienating large numbers of car-owning voters. A 'Motorists Forum' was established as a part of the CfIT and Gus McDonald, widely perceived as more 'motorist-friendly', was appointed to a ministerial position to work closely with Prescott on the development of firm transport proposals. In November 1999, after intense lobbying from motorists' organizations and road hauliers, the chancellor announced his intention to abandon the fuel duty escalator originally established by the Conservatives to increase fuel prices by greater than the rate of inflation on environmental grounds. In January 2000, the government's first report under the Road Traffic Reduction (National Targets) Act 1998 (DETR, 2000g) adopted the position that tackling congestion and pollution should be the government's priority, rather than traffic reductions per se.

In the light of limited funding, a number of councils did develop proposals for road user and workplace parking charging schemes, with the aim of using them to help to pay for badly needed local transport improvements.

When it came, the legislation did give the SRA legal standing and legalized road user and workplace parking levies. Prescott was able to convince the Treasury that these funds should be hypothecated to local transport improvements for the first ten years of their operation. This was an important and unprecedented step, but local authorities were still suspicious that if large amounts were raised by such measures, central government might use this as an excuse to choose not to allocate government money. Also included in the legislation were powers to draw up quality contracts for bus operations, but the procedures that needed to be followed were difficult.

The Ten-year Plan for Transport

Before the Transport Act actually became law, the government put forward its plan to 'deliver the scale of resources required to put integrated transport into practice' (DETR, 2000g). *Transport 2010 – The 10 Year Plan* outlined a huge programme of investment in public transport and road improvements over the next ten years, a longer planning period than had been contemplated before. The headline figure for total expenditure was £180 billion and while there was some argument over whether this figure was accurate and whether all of it would materialize, this was nevertheless an enormous injection of funds.

This largesse was possible because of relaxations on government spending limits, but also because there was a feeling that something had to be delivered by the government on transport. However, it was clear that there would be very few changes visible before the election so, on transport at least, Labour would have to rely on the promise of things to come. The plan itself was a balance of public transport and road improvements. The government seemed to have decided that improvements to the road network, especially bypasses and other improvements to inter-urban roads, were necessary, on the other hand, funds were promised for major public transport schemes as well. Anticipated spending was actually about equally split between roads, railways and other transport spending, most of which was to go towards local transport. There was a clear imbalance, however, in the source of the funds; for road improvements, most of the money was to come from the public purse, whereas it was anticipated that the lion's share of rail investment would come from the private sector. The high level of spending on the railways was also of interest, given the government's commitment to reducing social exclusion. Expenditure on the railways tends to benefit the rich rather than the poor because the poor travel less by rail.

One drawback of the suddenness and size of the increase in funding became apparent after the announcement of the significant increase in funding for local transport at the end of 2000 (for 2001–02) (see Figure 14.5). Spending on this scale certainly hit the headlines, but local authorities found it difficult to respond – they had survived on modest levels of funding since the mid-1990s and simply did not have the staff to develop the schemes to spend the money on. A severe skills shortage developed since it was impossible to train up the skilled staff necessary in the short term.

A number of urban light-rail schemes were also given funding through local transport spending, sometimes where the councils concerned must have almost given up hope of getting their projects off the ground after the government had earlier publicly supported bus-based public transport over expensive, though high-quality, light-rail schemes (DETR, 1999). The sudden availability

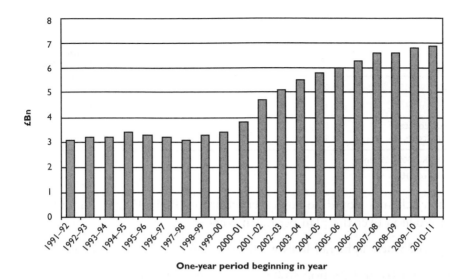

Figure 14.5 Public and private investment in local transport
Source: DETR (2000g: Table A3)

of funds on this scale meant that one of the major motivations for local authorities to consider road user charging or workplace parking levies was simply removed. One can only speculate how different things might have been if the government had extracted a promise from interested local authorities to put in place such charging schemes as a condition for receiving some or all of the funding for their flagship public transport improvements or road schemes.

Behind the ten-year plan lay the development of a 'national transport model' which was used to calculate the effects of the plan. This analysed the measures in the plan and used a series of assumptions to calculate such outputs as the impact of the plan upon congestion, traffic and emissions of carbon dioxide. The impacts of the plan are shown in Table 14.1, with the figures taken from the plan itself and the background analysis (DETR, 2000g, 2000h). The plan assumed that motoring costs per kilometre would decline by 20 per cent in real terms by 2010. The table shows what was thought was likely to happen without the plan, the likely effects of the plan itself and what the effects of the plan were likely to be if motoring costs stayed constant in real terms. As well as an assumption of declining motoring costs, a number of other assumptions were made when developing the plan, which included:

- Eight large towns and cities as well as London would bring in congestion charging schemes and a further 12 would levy workplace parking charges.

Table 14.1 Traffic, congestion and CO_2 emissions in 2010

	Traffic on all roads (percentage change from 2000)	Congestion on all roads (percentage change from 2000)	CO_2 emissions from transport (change from 2000)
Baseline	22	15	+0.7 MtC
Plan	17	−6	−0.9 MtC
Plan plus constant motoring costs	13	−12	−1.7 MtC

Source: DETR (2000g, 2000h)

MtC − tons of carbon

These schemes would be implemented from 2004/05 and would bring in £2.7 billion over the plan period in total

- Up to 25 new light-rail lines would be implemented by local authorities

- A sustainable distribution strategy would be put in place

- Restrictive land use policies would be adopted to improve the attractiveness of walking, cycling and public transport.

The plan included an impressive array of targets to be achieved between 2000 and 2010:

- An increase in rail use of 50 per cent

- An increase in bus use of 10 per cent

- A doubling of light-rail use

- A 40 per cent reduction in those killed and seriously injured in road accidents

- An 80 per cent increase in rail freight's share of the market

- A trebling of the number of trips by bicycle.

The plan was widely welcomed, partly because it represented a step change in the level of funding for transport and partly because it took a more long-term view of the investment necessary in transport infrastructure than had previously been the case. There were a few complaints that the government had prioritized large-scale infrastructure investment in its enthusiasm to convince the electorate that something was being done and overlooked the contribution that could be made by smaller scale changes aimed at improving things at the very local level for walking and cycling.

Further criticism of the plan was delayed as transport hit the headlines for various different reasons in the autumn of 2000.

The Fuel Crisis

The government had inherited the fuel duty escalator from the Conservative administration which had introduced it in 1993 as an environmental measure. It was a commitment to raise duty on road transport fuels by 5 per cent more than the rate of inflation every year. The incoming Labour administration had continued with the policy and enthusiastically increased the annual rise to 6 per cent. At this time the fuel duty escalator was seen as an important element of the integrated transport policy and the UK's efforts to cut its emissions of greenhouse gases in line with international agreements. Perhaps sensing growing unease over fuel prices, the chancellor discontinued the measure in the 2000 budget, when fuel duty was raised only in line with inflation. Past rises in duty had not been particularly noticed by the public because reductions in the other components of the pump price of fuel had meant that prices had not significantly increased. However, since Labour had come to power, the price of crude oil had tripled and, by the summer of 2000, there were increasing protests at the high price of fuel and the high proportion of it that was accounted for by duty and VAT.

After oil refinery blockades in France had forced the French government to address high fuel prices, groups of local farmers and hauliers in the UK decided to protest at fuel prices by stopping tankers leaving their local oil refineries. The protest quickly spread and while the protests were mainly peaceful, tanker drivers were not prepared to pass through them. Very quickly, fuel supplies were restricted up and down the country and over just a few days, aided by panic buying, the fuel situation became critical. The government was slow to respond to the gravity of the situation and the protestors maintained a high level of public support with opinion polls suggesting that large numbers of people were unhappy about fuel prices. The protestors called the protest off after just a week, before any serious damage was done, but the government and its standing in the opinion polls were badly shaken by the experience. Interestingly, many of the short-term effects of the crisis were in line with the objectives of the integrated transport policy, such as greater use of public transport, lower levels of congestion, more walking and cycling and so on. It was clear that adjustments could be made by the motoring public, but only as a result of unusual conditions.

In response to the protests and conscious of the high level of public support they had received, the government announced that changes in fuel duty equivalent to about a 6 per cent reduction in the pump price of fuel would be made (Glaister, 2001). The most obvious lessons to be learnt from the protests were the level of public support for reductions in fuel duty and the lack of awareness on the part of the government (and many others) of the intensity of these feelings. The government had also appeared unprepared and did not put forward a robust defence of its policy of high fuel taxes. Interestingly, its main argument seemed to be that this level of tax was necessary to pay for public services, rather than the environmental case, which was the original justification for the policy. There is solid evidence that fuel prices do restrain traffic and therefore help to reduce emissions of greenhouse gases. Table 14.2 summarizes the results from two reviews of the published literature (Goodwin, 1992; Glaister and Graham, 2000) which show remarkable agreement. The long-term effects are greater, because many of the decisions people make which have the greatest effects on fuel use are long-term ones. When using fuel prices to restrain fuel use, it is therefore important to give consistent signals about fuel prices in order to influence decisions such as which car to buy, where to live, whether to take a particular job and so on. The government's defence of high fuel taxes on the basis that the money had to be raised somewhere was also revealing. Fuel duty had become a major source of revenue for the Treasury, which made people suspicious about the motives of the government in having it at such a high level.

The protests also revealed uncomfortable truths about the level of car dependency and, perhaps more surprisingly, the level of reliance on road freight. 'Just-in-time' production techniques had meant that industry had come to rely on reliable, cheap and timely road transport for many interrelated processes. Once road transport was interrupted, the system started to unravel very quickly and seemingly unrelated problems started to multiply down the supply chain.

Perhaps the most important long-term effect of the protest was the constraining effect it is likely to have on future transport policy. Government badly misjudged the mood of the motoring public and does not want to risk anything which might cause a repeat of the experience. The government is likely to be even more sensitive to claims of being 'anti-motorist' and therefore the incident is likely to have a fundamental influence on future transport policy. Most obviously, the government will not feel able to use fuel duty as a traffic or fuel use restraint measure for some time.

Table 14.2 The long- and short-term effects of a 10 per cent rise in fuel prices

	Short term	Long term
Effect on traffic	−1.5% (1) to −1.6% (2)	−3% (1 and 2)
Effect on fuel consumption	−2.7% (2) to −3% (1)	−7% (1) to −7.7% (2)

Source: summarized from Glaister and Graham (2000) and Goodwin (1992)

(1) = figure from Glaister and Graham (2000)
(2) = figure from Goodwin (1992)

Trouble on the Trains

About a month after the fuel tax protests, on 17 October 2000, the 12.10 London to Leeds express derailed near Hatfield, killing four people. While in some ways not a major incident in itself, this accident occurred in the near aftermath of two earlier disasters at Southall and Paddington – both more costly in terms of human life – the three accidents together appearing to indicate serious deficiencies in the rail network. Importantly, the reason for the Hatfield crash had major implications for the rail industry: it was caused by a damaged rail, unrepaired because of administrative complications and mistakes which went to the heart of the privatized railway. Railtrack's response was extreme. The company imposed widespread speed restrictions and brought the railway system to its knees because of its concern that a similar accident could happen elsewhere.

Labour had inherited a privatized and fragmented railway industry with separate companies in charge of the infrastructure (Railtrack), operations (the train-operating companies) and the rolling stock (the rolling stock companies), all linked by complicated contractual obligations. Conscious of the costs involved, Labour had given no commitment in its 1997 manifesto to renationalize and it left the structure largely as it found it, with the exception of the creation of the SRA to take over some of the regulatory functions and help to develop the system. The railways were experiencing strong and unexpected growth in patronage, which was probably largely due to wider economic growth rather than the efforts of the industry itself but which fitted with Labour's integrated transport policy.

The immediate effects of Hatfield were a severe drop in patronage and a jolt to the public's confidence in the industry. Railtrack suffered significant financial damage as the train operators used penalty clauses to claw back revenue losses. More fundamentally, the incident made the shortcomings in the structure and administration of the rail industry apparent, with Railtrack's confusion over the state of its network and the failures of the complicated contractual systems necessary for even maintaining the system.

The incident also showed how little control the government actually had, and it was difficult to see how the commercial imperatives of the privatized industry could be made to deliver what the government wanted. The immediate concern post-Hatfield was safety, but according to the ten-year plan, rail also has to play its part in (for instance) reducing congestion on the roads. The train operators, quite understandably, are focused on their own profitability and have no direct interest in wider transport objectives. Improving peak time services – the most obvious way of attracting people out of their cars at the most congested times of day – is expensive as it involves acquiring extra rolling stock and extra train paths. The train operators would far rather fill up off-peak trains which they are obliged to run anyway because of the passenger service requirement agreed to as part of the franchise.

Despite the public's obvious concern with transport, it did not feature to any great extent in the general election campaign in 2001, perhaps because neither party felt it had anything to gain from raising it. After the election, there was a departmental reorganization and many of the environmental responsibilities of the DETR were moved over to a new Department of the Environment, Food and Rural Affairs (DEFRA). Transport was included in the remit of the Department of Transport, Local Government and the Regions (DTLR). Prescott was moved, although he retained an interest in regional policy and Stephen Byers took over at the DTLR.

During Byers' tenure, the financial position of Railtrack deteriorated in the summer of 2001 and the minister, reluctant to pump yet more public money into the company, effectively forced it into administration. This move was widely welcomed within the Labour Party and among the travelling public, but it put into question the government's ambitious plans for attracting private finance into the industry. In the event, in the wake of Byers' resignation in October 2002, a separate Department of Transport was created (responsibility for local and regional government going to the office of the deputy Prime Minister). The new department, under Alistair Darling, has presided over the creation of Network Rail, a not-for-dividend commercial company charged with the task of operating, maintaining and renewing Britain's railways. Network Rail's acquisition of Railtrack was completed in October 2002, Railtrack now existing as an operating company of Network Rail. Whether this reorganization will succeed in reducing current levels of rail chaos remains to be seen – as of December 2002 the signs are not good.

How Has New Labour Fared?

Even before the White Paper was published, there was scepticism about whether radical change could actually be delivered (Tight et al., 2000 collected data over this period). This centred around whether the political will was there to carry through the unpopular measures which were widely felt within the profession to be the only ones which might be effective in reducing traffic. On the other hand, there was a surprisingly swift backlash against even the relatively gentle measures proposed in the White Paper, despite the widespread support it at first commanded. The general public still seemed concerned about congestion, pollution and the other adverse impacts of road transport, but the all-important motorists' lobby had less of an appetite for the more radical measures to tackle them. The public also wanted to see some 'progress' on transport issues, whatever that meant.

The government's response was the ten-year plan, with the emphasis on delivery, but this was not enough to prevent widespread dissatisfaction on transport issues from adding to the support given to the fuel protests. Glaister (2001) suggests that this represented the emergence of a new force, the 'motoring majority', given that two-thirds of households have at least one car and three-quarters of adults live in households with a car.

More recently, there has been criticism of the ten-year plan itself. At first this centred on whether the promised benefits would materialize. Goodwin (2001) analysed the report's predictions of congestion reduction and found that the actual benefits were so small that they were unlikely to be noticed. There has also been more fundamental criticism of the ten-year plan and the general direction of transport policy. The Transport, Local Government and the Regions Select Committee (2002: para 138), while welcoming the plan, felt that it failed to provide 'a vision for a more equitable, safer and more efficient transport system'. Its detailed comments included the failure to address the imbalance between public transport and the car by its reluctance to actively restrain car use or address the growing cost imbalance between public transport and car use. The committee felt that the government had failed to provide a lead in the difficult area of how to cope with future traffic demand and that the way we pay for road use should be re-examined. CfIT's report on the ten-year plan (CfIT, 2002) also called for the government to take a lead on road user charging to restrain traffic and argued that this might command majority support if it was linked to improvements in public transport. More surprisingly, the Royal Automobile Club (RAC, 2002) also advocated road user charging, with the condition that it should be fair and transparent and linked to improved transport infrastructure.

The Social Exclusion Unit (SEU) also issued its interim findings on transport and social exclusion at about the same time (SEU, 2002) and found that transport policy favoured the well-off over society's disadvantaged. The emphasis in the ten-year plan on spending on the railways and reducing congestion on the roads was bound to favour those who travel most, while rising bus fares had adversely affected non-car owners. The report concentrated on what it saw as the two main problems – how to improve access for the socially excluded and reduce the disproportionate adverse impacts of traffic on the same people, but also calculated that the plan would have regressive effects, distributing benefits towards those on higher incomes.

Where Next?

The fundamental problems of transport remain similar to those explored by Buchanan 40 years ago – an imbalance of demand and supply. It is inconceivable that enough infrastructure can ever be provided to allow everyone to experience the levels of mobility currently enjoyed by the most affluent in our society.

However, the fundamental drivers of demand still exist. These include growing affluence and the fact that owning and running a car is becoming more affordable, widely held aspirations of car ownership, expectations of use into the future which influence location decisions, the growth in the number of households and the increase in the number of active, driving licence holding older people. It is difficult to see how these can be significantly affected, never mind reversed. In a democratic society, how can the 'motoring majority' be convinced that it is in their interests to accept some restrictions on their mobility? As the fuel crisis showed, the car has become embedded in our way of life and car dependency is ingrained in our culture. The car is widely recognized as a flexible, convenient way of enjoying independent mobility, but it has also allowed people to take up opportunities which they would not otherwise have been able to enjoy and relax constraints on their lives, be they temporal or geographical. These are benefits which it is easy to take up, but far more difficult to give up willingly.

In the transport area, there is a tendency to look to technical solutions such as improvements in vehicle technology, which have delivered significantly reduced vehicle emissions, and more sophisticated traffic signal control systems, which have successfully managed some of the traffic growth in urban areas. However, it is unlikely that technical fixes will be able to cope with the rises in traffic which are anticipated. In the absence of any other policy, this means traffic restraint by queuing or, put simply, more and more congestion. The widely advocated policy of road pricing has its own problems as well. While it may be effective at restraining demand, how equitable is it that those least able to afford the benefits of car use might be priced off the roads so that the rich can enjoy less congestion (at a price). While no one likes congestion, there is a degree of equity in the queue.

New Labour has favoured a policy of improving the alternatives to car use so as to tempt people out of their cars, but this approach has two problems. As the CfIT made clear (CfIT, 2002: 2), 'good public transport, while an essential prerequisite, is not enough'. The other problem is that, as the SEU observed (SEU, 2002), adopting this policy risks allocating public resources towards those who are better off already, whether it is by improving train services, investing in high-quality public transport such as tram systems or providing benefits to car drivers such as park-and ride-schemes. In the effort to shift people from cars to public transport, the needs of those who have no choice tend to get overlooked.

It is difficult to see how New Labour has actually made progress on these fundamental issues. Where New Labour has started to make a difference is in the consideration of the extra dimension of social exclusion and transport. Glaister (2001: 19) suggests that car ownership and use is now so widespread that 'it may well be the case that if governments wish to help the poor then it is more effective to find a way of helping the lower income motorist than the generality of rail users'. Helping low-income motorists does nothing for many of the most socially deprived who do not, and never will, have the use of their own car, because they are too young, too old, too poor or simply medically unfit to drive.

Aside from the changes in the strategic and legislative framework within which transport operates, which may yet prove to be important, perhaps New Labour's lasting legacy is to show the contradictions inherent in Thatcher's 'great car economy', although what policy should replace it is still very much in doubt.

Further Reading

DETR (1998) *A New Deal for Transport: Better for Everyone*, Cm 3950, London: Stationery Office.
CfIT (2002) *CfIT's Initial Assessment of the Ten Year Transport Plan*, London: CfIT.

Part III

NEW CHALLENGES: SOCIAL POLICY IN A NEW CENTURY

Introduction

As suggested in the Introduction to this volume, the study of social policy is more than the study of developments in established areas of welfare. Contributions to Part III look beyond 'policy', narrowly conceived, to issues which either persistently challenge governments and policy makers, or involve 'emergent' difficulties that might influence assumptions about the role and nature of social policy. Part III begins with Regan's chapter on 'Paying for Welfare'. Regan considers different methods for funding welfare spending, taking two big spenders – health and pensions – to illustrate the range of mechanisms available. Clearly preferring direct taxation as the most 'honest' method of funding public services, she nevertheless acknowledges the principal dilemma confronting chancellors who choose this route – balancing improved service provision against the potential electoral damage caused by tax rises.

The European Union is also a well-known source of dilemmas for British governments. In his chapter, Geyer considers the nature of the social policy interaction between the EU and the UK, arguing that, in true third way fashion, New Labour has abandoned Conservative obstructionism in favour of a more pragmatic approach to Europe. This strategy has given the UK greater influence in EU social policy, although, conversely, Geyer suggests that the EU can be regarded as a positive influence on British social policy, through the creation of basic social standards such as the EU fundamental rights charter, and the European emphasis on the importance of local and regional actors in the social policy process.

The final three chapters in the volume involve a certain leap of imagination because the focus is on *potential* implications for welfare. Turning to ICTs first, Burrows discusses both the developing e-government agenda 'from above' and the role of ICTs in restructuring social relations 'from below'. In his view, government efforts to 'informatize' welfare lag behind concurrent developments in civil society. The growing potential of virtual self-help networks could have substantial consequences for social policy as information-rich welfare consumers challenge the received opinions of putative experts, thus undermining traditional sources of, for example, medical or educational authority. These emergent processes may also prove deleterious for the information-poor, although Burrows rightly cautions against making simplistic assumptions about the nature and existence of a 'digital divide'.

Turning to environmental issues, Fitzpatrick points out that although academic discussion about social policy and the environment has increased enormously in recent years, environmentalism has hardly penetrated the consciousness of elected politicians. His chapter first examines the environmentalist critique of welfare and New Labour's – largely inadequate – response to what is increasingly perceived as a growing ecological crisis, before considering the kind of measures required for a thorough 'greening' of social policy.

Finally, working right at the frontier of contemporary developments, Shakespeare considers the impact of genetics on prevailing assumptions about welfare. Although the effects are frequently overdramatized by the media, he nevertheless acknowledges that new genetic technologies could influence attitudes to health care in particular, creating new classes of patient, as well as posing awkward ethical dilemmas about the use and potential abuse of genetic screening. As Shakespeare notes, issues of this kind risk the reassertion of eugenicist beliefs about 'population selection', the anxiety being that people with disabilities, and others, may experience a reversal of the gains made towards human and social rights for marginal groups in recent years.

CHAPTER 15

Paying for Welfare in the 21st Century

SUE REGAN

Labour came to power in 1997 claiming it had shed its image of 'tax and spend'. It had stood on a platform of no tax rises and a promise to keep within the previous Conservative government's spending plans for its first two years in office. This stance revealed the Labour Party's determination to distance itself from previous Labour governments. By the 2002 budget, a very different picture had emerged. The government had committed itself to step changes in spending on key public services as well as an increase in direct taxation through raising national insurance (NI) by an additional one per cent. This remarkable shift should not be underestimated. It revealed a recognition of political and public realities on how to achieve decent public services and a well-functioning welfare state, and crucially the need to pay for them. The Labour government in 2002 was indeed committed to 'tax and spend'.

Welfare provision, whether it is retirement pensions or health services, can be financed out of public or private funds or a mixture of the two. General taxation is the main source of public funds in this country and remains the primary means of paying for our largely universal public services and our welfare benefits. This chapter explores political, media and public attitudes towards the role of taxation in paying for welfare. The chapter then turns to public–private partnerships and questions their relevance in debates over funding and/or provision of public services. Using health and pensions as examples, other funding mechanisms are then explored. The chapter concludes by suggesting what the key political challenges will be if the government is to deliver on its reform agenda.

The Importance of Taxation

Debates over taxation are always highly contentious. It is a highly emotive issue for individuals and is fuelled by the popular press. Sensible and non-sensationalist debates about taxation are rare, with politicians frequently making claims that do not stand up to scrutiny. The Tories positioned themselves as the tax-cutting party throughout the 1980s, and although they did cut income tax rates, the total share of taxes in national income only fell in the 1990s, and was accompanied by rising budget deficits (Table 15.1). Labour spent much of its first term failing to acknowledge that it had raised

Table 15.1 Tax and spend

Year	General government net borrowing (% of GDP)	Public sector current receipts (% of GDP)	Total managed expenditure (% of GDP)
1979–80	3.0	40.7	44.8
1980–81	3.8	42.4	47.3
1981–82	3.3	45.8	48.1
1982–83	3.1	45.5	48.5
1983–84	3.8	44.5	48.3
1984–85	3.3	44.4	48.1
1985–86	2.6	43.1	45.5
1986–87	2.3	42.0	44.1
1987–88	1.3	41.1	42.1
1988–89	−0.9	40.7	39.4
1989–90	0.3	39.9	39.7
1990–91	1.4	39.0	40.0
1991–92	3.7	38.6	42.3
1992–93	7.4	36.6	44.2
1993–94	7.8	35.8	43.6
1994–95	6.5	36.9	43.2
1995–96	5.0	37.8	42.6
1996–97	3.9	37.4	41.0
1997–98	0.8	38.5	39.2
1998–99	−0.6	39.0	38.4
1999–00	−1.7	39.4	37.6
2000–01	−1.7	40.1	38.2

Source: HM Treasury (Budget, 2002)

taxes. The overall tax burden under Labour rose significantly in the years after the 1997 general election.

Conventional wisdom would have one believe that all individuals want is lower taxes, and will only vote for parties that promise them. Research into public attitudes does show a complex and somewhat contradictory set of beliefs. But a consistent finding is that if people could be confident that paying higher taxes would mean better public services, then they would be willing to pay. The annual *British Social Attitudes* survey consistently reveals that a large majority of people support increased spending on 'health, education and social benefits', even if this means higher taxes. Nearly two-thirds of respondents continued to choose the 'increased tax and spending' option in 1998 during Labour's first two years of spending restraint (Hills and Lelkes, 1999).

However, a key finding of recent public attitudes to work (Commission on Taxation and Citizenship, 2000) is the sense of 'disconnection' people felt between the taxes they pay and the public services which the taxes pay for. People did not know where their money was going and were not convinced that the government spent the money wisely. There was a widespread perception that public money was often wasted. This is an unhealthy state for both bringing about the necessary reform in public services but also for the state of democracy. Taxation pays for government and is therefore a crucial element in the democratic process. As Henry Neuburger has put it:

we have to promote the idea of tax as a contribution to the maintenance of the welfare state and not as a deadweight burden ... A modern democratic state requires adequate levels of taxation. The most consistent poll finding we have about tax is that a large majority of people agree with this analysis ... They believe in the productive enabling state and the means to finance it. (quoted in Hills, 2000: 4)

It is, therefore, important to shift the debate on taxation. Taxes are a crucial part of achieving a workable society whereby public services and government can exist. The Fabian Society's Commission on Taxation and Citizenship (2000: 55) saw the 'reconnection' of individuals to the taxes they pay as a priority for reform. 'The tax and public spending system should seek to "connect" the public better to the taxes they pay and to the public services which they finance.' A framework is needed which helps individuals to understand what taxes they pay, what the money is spent on and what difference it makes. A more open and honest approach is needed. Only then might individuals have greater confidence in government performance and accountability.

The Commission on Taxation and Citizenship made two broad recommendations for how this might be achieved: better information and hypothecation. Faith will not be restored in the tax system without people knowing where taxes are spent. A 'citizen's leaflet' sent to every citizen explaining in simple terms how the tax system works, and how tax revenue is spent, would be one means. Wider information sources such as the media, the Internet and libraries is another.

Hypothecation or earmarking of taxes has both its advocates and critics. The Commission on Taxation and Citizenship recommended earmarking for time-limited taxes for special capital expenditures, for example investment in public transport infrastructure projects, with such taxes abolished once the funds have been raised. It also supported (with a minority of commissioners opposed) the introduction of a fully hypothecated NHS tax. The use of 'tax and public service pledges' when governments seek to raise the rates of principal taxes is a highly diluted notion of earmarking but still tries to make this link in the public perception.

This thinking was what Gordon Brown was appealing to in his 2002 budget. Although he did not adopt any actual hypothecation or earmarking of the revenue to be raised from increased NI contributions, he did explicitly state that the money was to pay for the increases in spending on the NHS. He made a direct link between extra spending on health and the proposed increase in national insurance contributions (NICs). (This perhaps further confuses the purpose of our NI system. NI, being a form of social insurance, is supposed to be hypothecated for social security benefits but this connection has been eroded over the years. This issue is discussed further below.)

Shifting the Debate on Tax and Spend

The 2002 budget does mark a turning point in the Labour government's approach to tax. Until this point, there had been extreme reticence in admitting the need to raise taxes in order to afford public service reform. The government sets policy to meet two firm fiscal rules. The 'golden rule' states that over the economic cycle, the government will borrow only to invest and not to fund current spending. The 'sustainable investment rule' requires public sector net debt as a proportion of GDP to be held over the economic cycle 'at a stable and prudent level. Other things being equal, net debt will be maintained below 40 per cent of GDP over the economic cycle' (HM Treasury, 2002: 4). In order to ensure sound public finances in the medium term and keep within these fiscal rules, the chancellor announced that from April 2003, there would be an additional one per cent NIC by employers, employees and the self-employed on all earnings above the NIC's threshold. He chose NI rather than income tax to soften the blow in people's perceptions, but it will make little difference to most people's pockets. Many on the left were Left surprised and delighted at the chancellor's bold move.

As mentioned earlier, the tax burden had already been rising since the 1997 election. The significance of the 2002 budget move was that the government was prepared to raise a direct tax rate on households and, as a direct tax, it would have been very difficult to conceal it. In this sense, it was an open and honest tax rise.

If a more honest debate about taxation is welcome and necessary, then it is also needed in relation to the 'spend' side of the equation. The Labour government met some criticism in its early years, not for its attempts to alleviate poverty, but for the manner in which it was embarking on this agenda, namely by stealth (Lister, 2001). A whole range of policies and significant public funds have been devoted to pursuing the government's 'opportunity' agenda. Among these are the tax and benefit reforms to make work pay, the Sure Start programme, the Children's Fund and the range of New Deals. More remarkable are the government's pledges to eradicate child and pensioner poverty and monitor these through an annual audit which will monitor progress in tackling poverty and social exclusion. From the start, the chancellor's budgets have been notably progressive. Those at the bottom of the income scale have made significant gains while those at the top have made small losses. And yet, the chancellor and his colleagues have consistently denied this is redistribution. The 'r' word was banished from the Labour lexicon.

But does it really matter what language the government chooses to describe its agenda? Many would-be supporters are perhaps ambivalent because they do not realize how much the government has done. As Ruth Lister (2001: 66) points out 'doing good by stealth has the disadvantage of not being seen to be doing good'. Moreover, it does not help to move the debate forward in the direction of more honesty about taxing and spending – a debate which ultimately must be had if we are to have a fairer society and world-class public services. Redistribution by stealth is not healthy for democracy or for helping to bring about the public support necessary for tax and spending priorities. It has failed to inspire Labour's core supporters with a vision for a more just society, and it has failed to inspire the general public about the need for more taxes to pay for a fairer society. Doing good by stealth may be a good short-term political strategy but it can only take you so far.

In a recent speech in the London borough of Hackney, the Prime Minister reaffirmed the government's commitment to tackle poverty and social exclusion. He also crucially resurrected the 'r' word. 'It must be a Britain in which we contribute to re-distribute power, wealth and opportunity' (Blair, 2002a).

Table 15.2 Relative winners and losers under New Labour

	Spending as % of GDP				
	1989–90	1993–94	1996–97	2000–01	2005–06
Education	4.6	5.1	4.7	4.6	5.6
Health (net)	4.7	5.5	5.3	5.6	7.1
Law/order/protective services	1.9	2.3	2.1	2.2	n.a.
Transport	1.5	1.8	1.3	1.0	1.3

Source: Robinson (2001)

Interestingly, although it was a passing reference in Blair's speech, No. 10 chose to spin the redistribution theme to the media – a clear appeal to the left of the party. The *Daily Mail*'s response was a classic example of the tabloid media's relationship with the politics of tax. In bold, three-inch letters was the headline 'New Tax Blow for Middle Classes', despite there being no mention of tax increases in the speech. The spectre of 'redistribution' was enough.

Whether the general public have the appetite for 'taxing to redistribute' is highly questionable, but they do seem to have some appetite for 'taxing to spend on public services'. Thinking back to the debate in the run-up to the 1997 general election, it would seem the debate has moved and moved in the right direction. While the notion of taxing and spending does seem to have undergone a partial rehabilitation, the priority must be to raise the quality of public services – to 'tax, spend and improve' (Commission on Taxation and Citizenship, 2000). (For recent changes in the allocation of public resources, see Table 15.2.)

The Irrelevance of Public–Private Partnerships

There has been much confusion in debates about renewing our public services in relation to the use of *public–private partnerships* (PPPs)and in particular the private finance initiative (PFI). This confusion finds its roots in a fundamental misunderstanding about the distinction between the funding and provision of public services. It is often assumed that if a service such as education is provided by a public agency, then it must also be funded out of public funds and if a service is provided by a private agency, then it must be funded privately (Glennerster, 1997). These examples are just two on a wide spectrum of options.

This confusion spills over into debate into PPPs. An assumption is often made that PPPs are a threat to publicly funded universal services – 'privatiz- ation by the backdoor'. The Institute for Public Policy Research's Commis- sion on PPPs (IPPR, 2001) set out to challenge misconceptions about PPPs and outline a clear rationale for what and when they can contribute. The IPPR Commission (IPPR, 2001:1) distanced itself from two intransigent positions on public–private relations:

> we reject a privatisers' vision of public services; their aim is always and everywhere to increase the role of the private sector in the provision and funding of public services. Their desired outcome is smaller government and residualised public services. On the other, we distance ourselves from a public monopoly perspective which holds that as a matter of principle public services should always and every- where be provided by the public sector.

In terms of 'what additional contribution can PPPs make to *paying* for public services?' the answer is 'none'. It is a misunderstanding that PPPs bring extra funding to the public services. As the IPPR Commission concluded, interest in PPPs should sit on a reassertion of the case for publicly funded universal services. Where PPPs can contribute is in improving the quality and responsiveness of publicly funded services, and potentially deliv- ering better value for money.

Confusion over PPPs' role is nowhere more acute than in relation to the PFI. A spurious argument is often made that using private finance to pay for capital investment allows government to undertake more projects than other- wise would have been the case. All PFI projects are publicly funded and incur future liabilities for the exchequer. It is also important to remember to keep a sense of perspective in general in relation to PPPs:

> The overall picture is one of continuing dominance of services that are publicly funded and publicly provided. The Private Finance Initiative still plays a fairly modest role in relation to overall levels of investment, accounting for nine per cent of total publicly sponsored gross capital spending between 1997 and 2000. (IPPR, 2001: 73)

Where PPPs can add value is in promoting greater diversity in the way in which public services are provided and projects are procured. There has been far too great a reliance on a limited range of providers, thereby missing out on the experience and skills which exist in voluntary and private organiz- ations. It also means that public agencies have had less choice in securing services, and this has meant less innovation and cross-sector learning than might be the case under a more diverse collection of providers.

Paying for Health

'The NHS is the public service most valued by the British people.' So began the NHS Plan (DH, 2000: 2) and it is reiterated at the beginning of Wanless' first report (Wanless, 2001) on the future resourcing of the NHS. It is no surprise that the profile of the government's 'education, education, education' agenda was soon complemented and then surpassed by a concern with reforming the health service. The health service is important not only to the overall health and quality of life of the nation – a not insignificant responsibility – but it is also important, as the country's largest employer and is highly valued by individuals. Eighty per cent of people think that the NHS is critical to British society and must be maintained, and 75 per cent want to retain a universal service and oppose a two-tier health service (Wanless, 2001).

It is now acknowledged that underspending over the past 30 years, together with outdated organization and delivery mechanisms, has led the NHS to fall behind people's expectations and what can be received in many other countries. To tackle these problems, the chancellor has announced a substantial increase in spending on health care. Health spending will rise by more than a third in real terms over a five-year period.

In many areas, the government has committed itself to ambitious spending targets; its most ambitious goal being to raise total UK spending on health care to the EU average by the end of the current parliament. It became clear in the aftermath of the 2001 general election that realizing such objectives would require an increase in taxes – hence the NI rises announced in the 2002 budget.

A key measure of the Labour government's success will be whether the electorate perceives public services as having improved. This means building the capacity of public services to deliver and narrowing the gap between expectations and reality. Funding mechanisms could be important here. For example, it is often argued that insurance systems make clear the cost of health care treatment to the individual and this can lead to more responsible patient behaviour and a better understanding of resource constraints.

The Wanless review was established in 2001 to estimate the resources required to run the health service in 20 years' time. The terms of reference specify that it should examine the resources required for a publicly funded health care service. The review took the view, however, that the method of funding the health service was itself a factor determining the resources which will be needed and so discussed the merits of different funding mechanisms, comparing general taxation, social insurance, so called 'out-of-pocket' payments and private insurance. Health is a useful example to compare these different funding arrangements. While general taxation is the predominant method of funding public services, this is not the case in other countries and need not be the case in the UK in the future.

Funding approaches can be classified into four categories. In relation to health care, no country relies solely on one method of funding, but countries do have very different balances between the various methods:

- General taxation

- Social insurance

- Direct payments by service users (or out-of-pocket payments)

- Private insurance.

In the UK, NI represents the remains of our social insurance system. It is often thought of as general taxation because the relationship between contributions and benefits has been eroded over the years. There have been numerous welfare and public pension reforms which have broken this link, most notably the reductions in the relative value of the basic state pension and the state earnings-related pension during the 1980s. National insurance looks less like a separate social insurance system, whereby people expect there to be clearly defined entitlements honoured by government, and more akin to general taxation.

General taxation

General taxation is widely regarded as efficient from both a macro- and microeconomic perspective. Under tax financing, the government has both a strong incentive and capacity to control costs. The Wanless Report claims, as have others, that we may have gone too far in controlling costs in the UK, leading to considerable underspending in the UK health service compared to other countries. General taxation also involves low administration costs. But where general taxation perhaps steals the show, particularly from a Centre-Left perspective, is that it ensures universal access irrespective of ability to pay. It entirely separates individuals' financial contributions and their use of health services. This ability to separate the rate of contribution and service take-up does not occur in other funding mechanisms.

Social insurance

In social insurance systems, earnings-related contributions by employers and/or employees are made into a social insurance fund. It is the predominant form of funding in many other European countries, including France, Germany, the Netherlands and Belgium (Table 15.3). Like private insurance, social insurance establishes a contract between the insured individual and the provider. It therefore only makes sense to consider social insurance for public services which cover particular risks. These would include ill health, unemployment and old age. It does not make sense to fund public goods such as the national defence and transport infrastructure via an insurance mechanism.

Social insurance contributions are raised from a narrower base than general taxation, from employers and employees rather than a wider group of taxpayers. As with tax finance systems, access can be universal and not based on ability to pay. However, it is worth remembering the origins of the term 'social exclusion', first used in France. The French used the term to describe

Table 15.3 Primary funding mechanism and expenditure on health systems in the EU 15

	Primary method of funding	*Expenditure as a % of GDP*		
		Public	*Private*	*Total*
Germany	Social insurance	8.1	2.4	10.5
France	Social insurance	7.7	2.1	9.8
Netherlands	Social insurance	6.4	2.1	8.5
Sweden	Tax	7.1	1.4	8.5
Portugal	Tax	4.9	3.3	8.2
Austria	Social insurance	5.7	2.2	7.9
Denmark	Tax	5.7	2.0	7.7
Belgium	Social insurance	6.7	0.9	7.6
Italy	Tax	5.3	2.3	7.6
Spain	Tax	5.8	1.6	7.4
Finland	Tax	5.6	1.7	7.3
Greece	Tax	5.3	1.8	7.1
Ireland	Tax	5.3	1.8	7.1
Luxembourg	Social insurance	6.5	0.6	7.1
UK	Tax	5.7	1.0	6.7

Source: European Parliament (1998)

those people who were excluded from the benefits of the social insurance system and for whom other provision consequently had to be made.

It is also important to remember that social insurance schemes differ widely. Some approximate private insurance, while others look very similar to tax-based systems. However, the extent to which contributions reflect ability to pay does differ significantly between countries. Social insurance can be made progressive or regressive through different contribution rates.

Social health insurance schemes in the EU are associated with higher than average levels of health care spending, in particular with higher *public* spending. But why this is the case is not clear (Wanless, 2001). EU social insurance systems are weakly associated with higher levels of public satisfaction. This might be because the insurance mechanism provides a clearer link between contribution and entitlement. A social insurance arrangement could specify more precisely the extent of cover and match expectations with reality. But this is problematic. For many services, it is difficult to specify which risks are covered and with medical advances these change over time. Moreover, there are many unknown risks, such as the impact of increased life expectancy on the need for health care. For these reasons, social insurance systems tend to devolve decisions over entitlement to medical professionals in a similar way to tax-funded systems.

Direct payments by individuals

Patients are sometimes responsible for their own costs as they are incurred. Elements of many UK public services operate on this basis, such as prescription charges, dental and eye treatment. Individuals are also increasingly choosing to pay privately for specific interventions as and when they need them, partly to avoid long waiting times. Charges can help to limit the amount of health expenditure that the government has to fund publicly and help to encourage responsible use of resources by limiting unnecessary treatment. However, there is evidence that charges have led to less use of preventive care and can discourage people seeking treatment at all. The costs of these behavioural effects clearly feed in over the longer term.

While certain vulnerable and low-income groups are exempted from out-of-pocket payments in the UK, direct payments are unrelated to income and are therefore regressive in their impact on people who do have to pay. And charges are much more likely to discourage the less well-off than those who can easily afford payments.

Private insurance

Reliance on private insurance tends to create health systems which are largely demand led and exhibit poor cost control. The nature and coverage of private insurance differ significantly across countries. In some, it is relied on by the majority, for example the US. In others, it is largely taken out by higher income groups such as in Germany and indeed the UK.

Where private insurance covers the majority of the population as the sole means of cover, access to health services is dependent upon the level of insurance cover which individuals can afford and contributions are based on an individual's health and risk rating by the insurer. The poorer, older and less healthy thereby end up with the highest premiums. This is clearly highly regressive and inequitable.

Shifting the funding base for health services in the UK?

The current government is committed to maintaining general taxation as the main funding mechanism for the health service. In relation to health, debate on these alternative funding mechanisms is likely to increase. The Conservative Party, while naturally inclined to greater private funding, has also expressed an interest in exploring social insurance. So far, the Conservatives have failed to challenge the basic model of universal provision funded by general taxation. But this may change. Alternative funding mechanisms offer them the opportunity to reduce state involvement in the core public services, thereby transferring power to individuals and the private sector. They might then be able to 'generate a distinctive promise of reduced taxation, increased personal choice and more competition' (Brooks, 2001). And this may appear attractive if the Labour government fails to deliver on the health service in the eyes of the electorate.

Paying for Pensions

The funding of pensions is as controversial an issue as they come. It has been very difficult for the Labour government to win public support for its complex mix of pensions policies, despite significant recent increases in public spending on pensioners (Brooks et al., 2002). Again, there are a number of ways in which to pay for pensions. The state can pay and, to do so, raises revenues through taxes or NICs, the costs of which are borne by the individual. Alternatively, employers can pay, as they do now through

NICs or employer contributions to occupational schemes. In modestly efficient labour markets, such payments will be factored into the gross wages received by individuals. Finally, individuals can pay directly by purchases of private pensions products and their own savings. It is often forgotten that provision for retirement, as with all public services, is in the end funded by individuals. The balance to be struck is among individuals paying for their own pensions directly, individuals paying indirectly through employer contributions and individuals paying collectively for the provision of tax and NI-funded pensions.

Since 1988 and the introduction of personal pensions, the UK has arguably been moving towards a greater emphasis on direct individual responsibility in pension provision. This move is exacerbated by the shift in employer pension provision from 'defined benefit' schemes, where the risk of varying rates of return to assets in adverse market conditions is borne by employers and/or the state, to 'defined contribution' schemes, where the burden of risk is transferred to the individual by virtue of the strengthened link between individual contributions and final levels of provision. In such an environment, two factors increase in importance: first, it is vital that individuals understand the risks that they face and are able to plan accordingly. Second, if individuals do face increasing risks, it becomes more important that the state provides an acceptable basic minimum.

There is a pressing need for clarity over the rights and responsibilities, as well as the risks and rewards, implied by individual, employer and public/collective funding of pensions. Each must be clear about the roles of the others. Without this, planning becomes impossible. While this is a common issue in public policy, it is particularly severe in the realm of retirement issues because of the timescales involved. At present, individuals and companies – and many would include the government – are frequently confused about the present arrangements and unconvinced that they are robust to future policy change.

A key issue of debate is the balance between 'fully funded' and 'pay-as-you-go' pensions. Sometimes a simple story is told that because funded pensions involve saving now, this will result in an increase in national savings, which will result in an increase in productive investment, which will lead, in turn, to a higher national output, so allowing more generous pensions to be paid. However, this story can break down at any point. If saving into pensions is encouraged, there may be substitution away from other forms of saving and total national saving may not go up. A lot also depends on how the government responds in terms of its own contribution to national savings, that is, whether it continues to run a budget surplus (which adds to national saving) or a budget deficit (which subtracts from national saving).

There is no automatic way that extra savings can be translated into extra productive investment and higher national output. Funding is not inherently superior to pay-as-you-go (Barr, 2001).

Public pension provision has become less generous and more complicated over the past 20 years. Many older people feel that successive governments have broken an implicit contract between the individual and the state, in which a decent standard of support was the quid pro quo of paying NICs. The challenge for government is to establish a new contract for retirement with the public, a settlement which is robust to changes of government because it is workable, sustainable and publicly supported.

Paying for Welfare: What Next?

There are difficult challenges ahead for the government. It is likely that the Conservative Party will continue to explore different methods of funding. There will be further debate on the merits of social insurance and greater private funding, and the government will need to make its case again for universal public services funded through general taxation. Funding aside, there is a fundamental question about whether the extra money going into our public services will make a difference. Will extra spending on the health service produce better outcomes? If this question is to be answered in the affirmative, it is likely to require the NHS to work in a very different way as it spends its extra money. Moreover, if the health service does produce better outcomes, will this lead to greater public satisfaction? The pattern of spending required for meeting certain targets related to promoting social equity may not be the pattern needed to satisfy wider public expectations for the public services. For example, tackling health inequalities may not require reduced waiting times. In fact, better health outcomes may well be achieved not through the health budget but through improved housing and benefits (Robinson, 2001).

We should not be too optimistic that the public, the media or politicians have stopped deluding themselves that improved public services and adequate welfare provision can be paid for out of thin air. We will not know whether the chancellor's gamble in increasing NI for the health service will pay off for a while. April 2003 is when people will feel the increase in their reduced pay packets. The next general election will ultimately be the point when we can judge whether the public is willing to pay the price. Of course, we cannot be sure that the tax rises will be sufficient to meet Labour's ambitious social and economic targets; Gordon Brown's pre-budget report in November 2002 admitted that Treasury growth forecasts for 2003/04 had been overoptimistic, with the consequence that the government would have to borrow in order to meet its stated commitment to improve public services. In such a fiscal climate, taxes may have to rise again. The difficulty is that, while public attitudes surveys do show that people are content with *more* tax and spend, this does not mean they want *much* more (Hills, 2000). Will the public have the appetite for further tax increases?

Further Reading

Commission on Taxation and Citizenship (2000) *Paying for Progress: a New Politics of Tax for Public Spending*, London: Fabian Society.
Robinson, P. (2001) *Time to Choose Justice*, London: IPPR.

CHAPTER 16

The European Union and British Social Policy

ROBERT GEYER

For much of the 1990s, the central question for European social policy and welfare state research was whether European social policy regimes could survive in a context of increasing Europeanization and globalization. A major branch of this debate was the role of EU social policy. Could it support and protect the European social policy regimes, counterbalancing the increasing market orientation of the EU and lead to some form of European-wide welfare state? Or was it merely a meaningless talking shop that would passively, or even actively, undermine existing social regimes?

As the 1990s progressed, the answers to these questions became increasingly clear, but the core question began to change. Despite a multitude of reforms, European social regimes were proving to be remarkably resilient and adaptive to the twin challenges of Europeanization and globalization (Geyer, 1998; Swank, 1998; Hirst and Thompson, 1999; Ferrera and Rhodes, 2000; Geyer et al., 2000; Taylor-Gooby, 2001). Likewise, EU social policy did develop a wide range of policies and became increasingly influential in certain policy areas and some social policy regimes. However, the creation of some form of unified European social regime/welfare state seems as distant as ever (Sykes and Alcock, 1998; Bonoli et al., 2000; Geyer, 2000a; Kleinman, 2002). In this context, the central question for EU social policy shifted from whether it could save/replace/undermine the distinctive national regimes to how does it interact with those regimes?

This chapter will not attempt to answer this question conclusively. As will be argued later, this is the job of future research programmes and institutes. However, this chapter will outline a general approach to this new central question in four steps. It will provide a brief 'map' of the development and policy contours of EU social policy. Then, it will explore the complex, variable and subtle ways in which EU social policy interacts with British social policy and examine whether New Labour significantly altered the EU–UK social policy interaction. Next, it will briefly discuss two main theories for describing EU–UK social policy interaction and suggest a theoretical 'complexity' framework for understanding this interaction. Finally, it will briefly speculate on whether EU social policy helps or hinders British social policy.

What Does EU Social Policy Look Like?

Coming to grips with EU social policy is a particularly difficult task since it is so different from the typical welfare state model. Most fundamentally, it has minimal funding. Even if one includes all the various structural funds as a very general type of social policy, the total is only about €40 billion/£24 billion annually, about a third of the EU budget, less than half of one per cent of EU GDP, or about €100/£60 annually per capita. By comparison, total spending on broadly defined welfare aspects in the UK currently accounts for around 60 per cent of general government expenditure and around 25 per cent of UK GDP, about €7,500/£4,500 per capita (Cochrane et al., 2001: 77). The total EU social budget is about half the annual budget of the NHS. This financial weakness is amplified by a noticeably fragmented and distant policy-making process and relatively weak social actors and supporters within EU institutions.

Historically, EU social policy grew out of the political/military bargains embedded in the European Coal and Steel Community (ECSC) and European Economic Community (EEC), the 20th-century's development of Western European social policy, the 'embedded liberalism' (Ruggie, 1982) of Western European capitalism, and the need to assuage the fears of sceptical workers and trade unions (Leibfried and Pierson, 1995; Falkner, 1998; Hantrais, 2000). Its secondary position was clearly indicated by its weak foundations in the Treaties of Paris and Rome. These treaties emphasized the need to protect and improve living and working conditions, promote early forms of Euro-corporatism and, as stated in art. 118 of the Treaty of Rome, promote policy development in

> employment; labour law and working conditions; basic and advanced vocational training; social security; prevention of occupational accidents and diseases; occupational hygiene; (and) the right of association, and collective bargaining between employers and workers. (European Union On-line http://european.eu.int)

Article 119 stated that 'men and women should receive equal pay for equal work'. Finally, arts. 123–8 dealt with the creation and operation of the European Social Fund.

Due to the general stagnation of the EEC in the 1960s, it was not until the early 1970s that significant social policy progress was again made. The 1969 Hague Summit brought social policy back onto the EC agenda by arguing that it was a necessary complement to the economic integration envisioned by European Monetary Union (EMU). As the final communiqué of the 1972 Paris Summit stated:

> [the member states] attached as much importance to vigorous action in the social field as to achievement of economic union ... [and considered] it essential to ensure the increasing involvement of labour and management in the economic and social decisions of the Community. (Brewster and Teague, 1989: 66)

Linked to this strategy was the 1974–76 Social Action Programme (SAP) which laid down three broad areas for policy action: 'the attainment of full and better employment', 'improvement of living and working conditions' and 'increased involvement of management and labour' and specified 35 proposals for action.

As it happened, just as this radical plan for the expansion of EC social policy was created, the EC lapsed into another period of stagnation and uncertainty. Following the oil shocks and massive currency fluctuations of the early 1970s, the attempts to create EMU and a coordinated European response to the crisis were abandoned. Moreover, the 1970s and early 1980s saw a number of membership changes and quarrels that crippled further EC developments.

In all three areas of the SAP, developments were limited not only by the international situation, but also by the internal structure and dynamics of the EC itself. The general strategy of policy 'harmonization' undercut the ability of the Community to reach any agreements on social policy issues. The institutional weakness of the European Parliament (not even directly elected until 1979) and the Economic and Social Committee meant that social actors, such as the ETUC and European socialists, were less capable of promoting social policies within the EC. The power of the Council and the demands of unanimous voting on all major social policy questions clearly limited their development. Finally, with the rise of Margaret Thatcher in Britain in 1979, all EC social policy initiatives had to pass the barrier of militant, free-market ideology.

With the prevailing philosophy of revived free-market liberalism, weakness of EC social policy supporters and militant opposition of the British government, social policy in the 1985 White Paper and 1986 SEA (Single European Act) was kept to a minimum. Only art. 118a established qualified majority voting (QMV) procedures in the Council: 'to encourage improvements, especially in the working environment, as regards the health and safety of workers'.

Despite these limitations, the SEA did lay the foundation for the late 1980s' 'Social Dimension'. Comprising the Social Charter (a listing of 12 areas of fundamental social rights) and the subsequent SAP, the Social Dimension performed a delicate balancing act between general support for the internal market project and specific proposals for curbing the excesses of the common market. The Social Charter was approved as a 'solemn declaration' (opposed by the UK) and the battle over social policy shifted to the particular elements of the 1989 SAP. A key Commission strategy at the time was to try to use the QMV status of health and safety issues under art. 118a as a Trojan Horse for a wide array of other policies. During this period, social policy made significant gains due to the efforts of the activist Delors Commission, the growth of European-level interest group activity, and the final acceptance of European integration by the Western European Left.

Despite grand plans and substantial effort, the late 1980s and early 1990s produced rather limited results in EU social policy. Most of the legislative elements of the Social Dimension were rejected, put on hold or watered down. However, with the creation of the 1991 Maastricht Treaty and revival of European Monetary Union (EMU), Jacques Delors brought social and regional policy back onto the agenda. Regional policy was expanded and social policy was given a fresh impetus through a number of institutional changes (the expansion of EU Parliament powers, creation of QMV in new areas of social policy, promotion of the 'social dialogue' between capital and labour, creating a new form of social policy initiative by agreement between EU capital and EU labour) and the creation of the Social Protocol. This seemingly clear advance for EU social policy was complicated by the unique procedural device of the British 'opt-out' clause. Using this device, Britain was allowed to opt out of future qualified majority-approved social policies, which removed a major source (British opposition) of EU Council resistance to many EU social policies, but also greatly complicated both the legal foundation and implementation of EU social policies, since they could not legally or financially affect the UK.

During the mid-1990s, social policy progress remained slow, but support for it continued to build. The Maastricht Treaty, after various delays, was finally ratified in 1993. In 1994, three wealthy pro-social policy states, Austria, Finland and Sweden, voted to join the EU. Social policy NGOs continued to develop at the European level. Most importantly, in May 1997, the British Conservative Party, the arch opponent of EU social policy, was decisively defeated in the general election by the Labour Party, who immediately promised to end the British social policy opt-out clause.

During the debates preceding the 1997 Amsterdam Treaty revisions, social policy was completely overshadowed by concerns with EMU, integrating new

Eastern European members, and the new section in the treaty dealing with employment policy. With the defeat of the British Conservative government in May 1997, the Social Protocol was quickly integrated into the basic text of the Amsterdam Treaty. The treaty gave a clear commitment to the EU to address a variety of forms of discrimination in art. 13. However, the treaty refrained from making substantial spending commitments to new social policy areas and dropped measures for improving the position of the elderly and disabled from art. 137 (Duff, 1997: 73).

The subsequent Commission of the European Communities' (CEC) publication on social policy, *Social Action Programme 1998–2000* (CEC, 1998), clearly reflected this consolidating approach. The document focused on just three main areas: jobs, skills and mobility; the changing world of work; and an inclusive society. It contained the usual array of social policy proposals, but framed many of them in the new light of employment policy. With the integration of the employment section into the Amsterdam Treaty and the subsequent creation of the employment policy guidelines, the Commission clearly saw an opportunity for justifying and expanding social policies through their linkage to employment creation.

The current state of EU social policy is summarized in Table 16.1.

Table 16.1 EU social policy

Policy area	Original base in the treaties	Selected current base in consolidated treaties	Attained QMV status under ...
Free movement	EEC (arts. 3c, 7, 48–51)	Arts. 3, 14, 39–42, 61–9	SEA (arts. 49, 54)
Health and safety	ECSC (arts. 3, 35), EEC (arts. 117, 118)	Arts. 3, 136, 137, 140	SEA (art. 118a)
Employment rights	No direct reference until Maastricht	Art. 137	Unanimous voting
Working conditions	ECSC (art. 3), EEC (arts. 117, 118)	Art. 137	SEA (art. 118a)
Worker participation	No direct reference until Maastricht	Art. 137	Maastricht Social Protocol (art. 2)
Social dialogue	ECSC (arts. 46, 48), EEC (arts. 193–8 creating ESC)	Arts. 136, 139	Maastricht Social Protocol (art. 4)
Gender	EEC (art. 119)	Arts. 13, 137, 141	Maastricht Social Protocol (art. 2)
Anti-poverty/exclusion	EEC (arts. 2, 3)	Arts. 136, 137	Maastricht Social Protocol (art. 2)
Anti-discrimination against racism	No direct reference until Amsterdam	Art. 13	Unanimous voting

cont'd

Table 16.1 *continued*

	Original base in the treaties	Selected current base in consolidated treaties	Attained QMV status under ...
Public health	No direct reference until SEA (arts. 100a, 130r)	Arts. 3, 152	Maastricht (art. 129)
Elderly	No direct reference until Amsterdam	Art. 13	Unanimous voting
Disability	No direct reference until Amsterdam	Art. 13 and Declaration at end of Amsterdam	Unanimous voting
Youth/training	EEC (arts. 50, 118, 125)	Arts. 149, 150	Maastricht (arts. 126, 127)

Source: Geyer (2000a: 204)

Current Developments

Since the end of the 1990s, three main developments have dominated the European social agenda: the European Employment Strategy; the 2001–06 European Social Agenda; and the growth of new policy methods.[1] The European Employment Strategy, which emerged out of the 1997 Amsterdam Treaty (Title VIII, arts. 125–30), was a spillover from the success of EMU. It was an attempt by pro-employment actors and key member states to raise the profile of employment issues through the development of a coordinated employment strategy. This strategy had four main priorities: improving employability; development of entrepreneurship; encouraging adaptability; and reinforcing equal opportunities. It was based on indirect cooperation and the open method of coordination as laid out in the Luxembourg Process (CEC, 2001: 6). Subsequent Council meetings clarified and promoted the strategy, particularly the 2000 Lisbon meeting.

The *Social Policy Agenda* was the first major document of the new employment and social affairs commissioner, Anna Diamantopoulou. In line with the emphasis on employment and the economic importance of social issues, it stressed that the 'guiding principle of the new Social Policy Agenda will be to strengthen the role of *social policy as a productive factor*' (CEC, 2000c: 7). It went on to outline 34 new proposals under the headings of job creation, working environment, promoting a knowledge-based economy, free movement, social protection, combating poverty and exclusion, gender equality, fundamental rights, combating discrimination, promoting quality in industrial relations and dealing with enlargement issues. The document promoted the adoption of 20 pieces of pending legislation, but did not specify any radically new proposals for particular legislation.

Equally important, both the Employment Strategy and Social Policy Agenda recognized and encouraged the development of two new and related means of social policy development: *mainstreaming and the open method of coordination*. In the European context, mainstreaming emerged out of the activities of gender activists who were attempting to surmount the limitations of EU social policy by bringing gender issues into the mainstream of general EU policy making (Geyer, 2000b, 2001). As defined in 1998 by the Council of Europe, gender mainstreaming was:

> The (re)organization, improvement, development and evaluation of policy processes, so that a gender equality perspective is incorporated in all policies at all levels and at all stages, by the actors normally involved in policy-making. (Council of Europe, 1998: 15)

In a context of few new legislative developments and constrained budgets, mainstreaming offered gender activists a number of opportunities for expanding gender policy making, strengthening gender NGOs, influencing the agenda-setting process and raising awareness of gender issues. By the end of the 1990s, mainstreaming EU gender policy had become a successful strategy and brought gender issues increasingly into the core of EU policy making. This success encouraged other social policy actors to duplicate this strategy. By 1998, most major EU social policy NGOs had mainstreaming strategies and in the Social Policy Agenda, the Commission stated that 'the use of mainstreaming as a tool will be strengthened and further developed' (CEC, 2000c: 15).

The open method of coordination (OMC) grew out of the development of the Employment Guidelines process created at the Luxembourg Summit (De La Porte et al., 2001: 296; Hodson and Maher, 2001). As summarized in De La Porte et al., (2001), OMC in EU social policy developed:

> primarily because – against the background of the integration of monetary policy and the close coordination of macro-economic policy, along with a general commitment to promoting supply-side policies for flexibility and employability – national and EU authorities have recognized the need to work together on policies for social cohesion. (p. 296)

The OMC involved a number of policy strategies, the most important of which was benchmarking (although mainstreaming is often included as an OMC strategy) Benchmarking involved a move away from strategies of harmonization and central decision making and towards a 'post-regulatory' approach to governance, in which there is a preference for procedures or general standards with wide margins for variation, rather than detailed and non-flexible (legally binding) rules (De La Porte et al., 2001: 302).

Both mainstreaming and OMC gave EU social policy supporters new tactics for promoting and developing EU social policy and for strengthening European social policy actors and supporters.

Overall, one is still struck by the relative weakness of EU social policy. It has seen significant developments and is pursuing a number of innovative policy strategies. However, the impact of the EU in many of these new policy areas is noticeably limited – a few members of staff, a couple of proposals and an action plan or two. Moreover, EU social policy actors have been innovative, because they were in such a weak position that they had no other choice. They had to link into health and safety policy in the late 1980s and employment policy in the late 1990s and create new policy strategies because their own power base and traditional strategies were so limited.

How Does EU Social Policy Interact with UK Social Policy?

The quick and easy answer to this question is that EU social policy has not radically restructured the UK social policy regime. As Hine and Kassim argued, 'Member states remain the primary institution of European social policy, and have in general resisted EU action in this domain, but important inroads have been made nevertheless' (Kassim and Hine, 1998: 212). However, it does interact with UK social policy in a variety of ways depending on which level, policy area, time frame and institution one is observing. Moreover, this interaction may have a significant impact.

The difficulty is that EU social policy is so variable and interwoven with the UK social policy regime that it is extremely difficult to disentangle causal relationships and gauge its true impact. For example, it is easy to point out that EU social policy has affected the development of certain sub-fields of social policy, particularly labour and gender policy, and has had virtually no effect on other sub-fields. Moreover, few would dispute that new types of EU social policy strategies (OMC, mainstreaming and so on) are having a noticeable impact on UK institutional and elite policy learning and adaptation or that EU social law is playing a growing role in a number of UK social policy areas. Similarly, there is general agreement that EU social policy has created new opportunities for greater input from some UK social policy actors in both the European and national policy process, or that certain regions have benefited significantly from the social aspects of the EU structural funds.

In more subtle ways, EU social policy has been, at times, a major area of policy debate between the Labour and Conservative Parties. During the 1970s and early 1980s, neither party paid much attention to EU social policy. With the revival of the EU in the mid- to late 1980s and the development of the EU's Social Dimension and Social Charter, EU social policy became a major issue separating the Conservative and Labour Parties. The Major government continued this separation until its demise in 1997. Since the rise of New Labour, with its more pragmatic approach to the EU and European social policy, this political division has noticeably lessened. Likewise, at an internal party level, EU social and labour policy was used by Labour Party elites to modernize the party and distance it from the trade unions (Shaw, 1994; Geyer, 1998). For Labour in the late 1980s and early 1990s, the Trades Union Congress (TUC) had become an increasing electoral burden. Labour needed to distance itself from the TUC in order to show its strength and independence as well as its willingness to accept a more market-oriented industrial relations order. As the EU developed, particularly its social dimension and specific proposals such as the European Works Councils Directive, Labour could argue that the EU was the appropriate level for industrial relations regulations while passively agreeing to increased marketization within the UK.

Overall, what this confirms is that EU–UK interaction is variable, complex and subtle. The obvious challenges of attempting to trace the detailed causal relationships of these various aspects are clearly beyond the limits of this chapter, but do raise the next question: how can we understand EU–UK social policy interaction? But first, we must ask whether New Labour has significantly altered it.

Has New Labour Significantly Altered EU–UK Social Policy Interaction?

In a fundamental sense, the answer, as yet, is no. The basic parameters of the UK welfare state and social policy regime have been remarkably stable over the past 20 years. Of course, there has been significant change in certain policy arenas, housing in particular. Nevertheless, the areas of tension and agreement between the EU and the UK have remained noticeably stable. For example, due to the voluntaristic nature of UK industrial relations, it has always been difficult integrating the more corporatistic aspects of EU policy, such as works councils and capital–labour dialogue, into the UK. On the other hand, due to the relatively well-developed nature of UK disability rights, the EU is often trailing the UK policy regime and hence has little impact in the UK.

However, at an administrative and policy level, New Labour has significantly altered the EU–UK social policy relationship by abandoning the determined obstructionist policies of the former Conservative government and adopting a more pragmatic approach. As a number of UK governmental elites in various departments explained in interviews during 2000–01,[2] EU social policy was easy under the Conservatives. All officials just said 'no'. If interaction or learning occurred, it had to be hidden so as not to embarrass the Conservative government. Many officials expressed relief at the election of the Labour government, if only to give themselves more freedom to interact with EU policy developments.

This more pragmatic approach fits in well with the new, more integrative and inclusive approach to social policy legislation which has been emerging from the EU in the 1990s. The success of the Employment Guidelines, the mainstreaming of gender policies, the development of social inclusion, pensions and health guidelines and action programmes and the development of the open method of coordination have all suited the emergence of the pragmatic New Labour approach to social policy development. This has been particularly important in the area of labour policy, where the EU has adopted a much more market-sensitive strategy for employment creation and development, training and labour market regulations. In essence, by adopting a pragmatic position on EU social policy, New Labour has created a much more influential role for the UK in EU social policy development and taken EU social policy out of the media headlines and depoliticized it.

Is There a Theoretical Framework for Understanding This Interaction?

First, it is important to note that although there has been a good deal of work on the relationship between the EU and UK and some work on the relationship between certain policy areas (monetary policy in particular), there has been very little work on the EU–UK social policy relationship. Hence, there is no well-developed theoretical framework. Nevertheless, there are a variety of theoretical strategies for approaching EU–UK social policy interaction. I will briefly mention and explore two of the most recent: multi-level governance and policy transfer theory and argue that they lead the researcher towards traditional comparative social policy and/or complexity theory.

Multi-level governance (MLG) emerged out of a mixture of international relations and European integration theory debates in the mid- to late 1990s (Putnam, 1988; Smith and Ray, 1993; Marks et al., 1996a, 1996c; Hooghe and Marks, 2001). MLG theorists tried to move away from unitary and historically static interpretations of EU policy dynamics and argue that the EU was not dominated by intergovernmental or supranational dynamics, but exhibited aspects of each in varying degrees at different times and policy arenas. For MLG theorists, the EU is composed of 'overlapping competencies among multiple levels of governments and the interaction of political actors across those levels' (Marks et al., 1996b: 41). In essence, for MLG theory, each policy area and member state has its own distinctive and interactive relationship to the EU and this relationship varies over time and by policy area. As Cowles and Risse (2001: 236) concluded in their recent study of Europeanization:

> Europeanization does not result in the homogenization of domestic structures. Member states face varying degrees of adaptational pressures to the 'regulatory patchwork' of EU rules and regulations. Different factors restrain or facilitate their adaptation to these Europeanization pressures. Yet, the transformation of domestic structures takes place all the same, oftentimes in rather fundamental ways.

Similarly, policy transfer (PT) theory emerged in the mid-1990s particularly in relation to the study of policy transfer between the USA and the UK (Rose, 1993; Dolowitz and Marsh, 1996; Bennett, 1997; Stone, 1999). PT theorists concentrated on examining the processes through which policies were transferred and/or learned from one policy, institutional, political arena to another. In general, these works concentrated on the policy transfer as a voluntary 'learning' process between independent states. However, PT theory could be applied to learning between different levels of government and in coercive situations as well. PT theorists argued that policy transfer could lead to policy convergence, but that the transfer of policies was not a simple linear process and that it often led to unintended results and consequences due to the different nature of the national policy arenas.

Interestingly, despite its obvious implications, PT theorists only recently (with the early exception of Rose, 1993) began using their concepts to describe EU policy dynamics (Bomberg and Peterson, 2000; Radaelli, 2000). For these theorists, recent development of EU policy transfers has been driven by:

> exchanges between national authorities who share a common concern to solve policy problems, as well as causal understandings and technical expertise. In essence

EU policy transfer is a pro-active – and only rarely coercive – approach to the Europeanization of public policy. (Bomberg and Peterson, 2000: 7)

From this perspective, PT strategies have evolved because member states have become increasingly dissatisfied with traditional EU policy methods. The growth of open methods of coordination, mainstreaming and so on is a clear indicator of the success of this new approach, which provides a range of substantial political and policy benefits. It may also promote convergence. However, PT theorists are quick to emphasize that the growth of EU policy transfer does not imply convergence. As mentioned above, learning can have both convergent and divergent outcomes. Moreover, policy transfer does not replace all policy dynamics. It is a growing area, but one which interacts with rather than dominates traditional policy methods.

In general, these two new theories of policy action and development are not dissimilar from the general theoretical concepts of Anthony Giddens' (1998, 2000) 'third way', particularly in terms of their emphasis on the complexity and openness of the evolution of policies. Moreover, they are good descriptions of the EU policy process. However, are they really scientific theories in the traditional sense? They are not very parsimonious, admitting as they do that many other factors are at play in EU policy development. They do not explain causality very well, seeing multiple influences on particular outcomes. They are not predictive, emphasizing historical openness. Moreover, they do not lead to universal rules, each case has its own dynamics.

If MLG and PT theory are good descriptions, but poor theories in a traditional sense, what should the student/researcher/policy actor do to begin to recognize and understand the open, multi-level and complex nature of the EU member state policy process?

There are two linked answers to this question: a continual process of description-oriented comparative policy research and complexity theory. Due to the complexity and evolving nature of the EU–UK social policy relationship, a continuous effort will need to be made to explore the particular aspects of the interaction of international, national and sub-national dynamics. This work is currently being done in a variety of research settings and is the 'bread and butter' of a number of universities, governmental departments and independent research organizations. However, the trick is to try to bring together as many descriptive strands as possible. In the case of EU–UK social policy interaction, researchers should try to interweave the processes of policy transfer at the EU level with increasing influence of sub-national actors in the national arena, while at the same time keeping an eye on the dynamics of other policy arenas and social policy dynamics in other member states. This is a very difficult job, but provides academics and policy actors with the 'real-life' descriptive research upon which to base their teaching and actions.

On the other hand, researchers must confront the problem of complexity. Complexity theory (Eve et al., 1997; Kiel and Elliot, 1997; Byrne, 1998; Cilliers, 1998; Geyer, 2003; Rihani, 2002), which emerged out of the physical sciences in the mid-20th century and has increasingly spilled over into the social sciences at the beginning of the 21st century, offers a new paradigmatic framework for confronting complexity. Traditional social science was based strongly on an orderly and linear Newtonian vision of the world. Universities legitimated and solidified this orderly orientation by dividing the various sciences into distinctive vertical 'fields'. Much of the work of 20th-century social scientists was driven by the desire to either ignore or eliminate physical and human complexity. Examples include the self-interested and rational 'economic man' in neoclassical economics and rational actor in voting behaviour.

From a complexity perspective, the physical and human worlds contain phenomena which are orderly, complex and disorderly and all three of these types of phenomena exist and interact with each other. Moreover, within these ranges of phenomena exist complex systems which have numerous interacting units, generally rely on simple rules yet can evolve in multiple directions. Hence, from a traditional linear perspective, the EU and its policy process is an annoyingly incoherent and chaotic structure that must be ordered if it is ever going to be effective and legitimate. On the other hand, from a complexity perspective, if the EU is seen as a complex system rather than an inherently orderly one, then the open, evolving and uncertain nature of EU–UK social policy interaction may be an indication of its healthy and 'normal' development.

Does the EU Help or Hinder UK Social Policy?

This is the really difficult question. The quick answer is: it depends on where you look and where you are coming from. For UK trade union activists, the EU has provided a legal floor and policy initiatives that a Conservative or Labour government would almost never have promoted. For UK gender policy promoters, the EU has provided a number of policy developments and legal opportunities for equal opportunity development. For elderly and disability policy activists, the EU has developed a few initiatives, but very little to pay much attention to. On the other hand, for UK employers, EU social policy has often been seen as a disruptive and annoying burden. At a governmental level, some policy elites praise EU social policy for its learning opportunities. Others use it to put pressure on other departments. At a regional/local level, it is often praised for its financial benefits and its emphasis on including local and regional actors. However, one will never know what policies would have emerged if the UK had not been a member of the EU. Hence, can there be a general answer to the question?

Using a traditional scientific approach, no, using a complexity approach, yes. The detailed outcome of EU–UK social policy interaction is obviously impossible to predict in the long run. However, I would argue that whatever the particular outcomes, EU social policy will enhance UK social policy in three main ways:

1. It will continue to strengthen the fundamental political and institutional base of the UK social policy regime through its creation of fundamental EU social standards. The current struggle over the creation of an EU fundamental rights charter is only the most recent example of this tendency.

2. It will continue to enhance the role and input of local and regional actors in the UK social policy process. Due to the dominance of London and Whitehall, UK social policy has historically been dominated by central organizations (Ashford, 1982). With its regionally based funding and focus on integration of local and regional actors, the EU has significantly encouraged the role and opportunities of local/regional actors, significantly increasing the complexity of UK social policy.

3. It will continue to significantly open the UK system to new social policy methods and strategies. As demonstrated by the PT literature, the UK has historically focused on policy models from the USA. However, with the growth of institutionalized EU elite interaction, adaptation and learning, as demonstrated by the Employment Guidelines process, UK social policy elites will increasingly interact with and learn from the various European models, rather than just the American.

The particular outcomes of these three factors in any given area of UK social policy are nearly impossible to predict. However, their general influence, strengthening a fundamental framework for social policy development, increasing local/regional input and interaction and increasing the learning and interaction of policy elites, should lead to a healthy and continually evolving UK social policy regime which will be capable of adapting to the challenges of globalization, Europeanization or whatever new 'ization' emerges in forthcoming years.

Further Reading

Bonoli, G., George, V. and Taylor-Gooby, P. (2000) *European Welfare Futures: Towards a Theory of Retrenchment*, Cambridge: Polity Press.

Byrne, D. (1998) *Complexity Theory and the Social Sciences: An Introduction*, London: Routledge.

Cilliers, P. (1998) *Complexity and Postmodernism: Understanding Complex Systems*, London: Routledge.

Cowles, M.G.J., Caporaso, J. and Risse, T. (eds) (2001) *Transforming Europe: Europeanization and Domestic Change*, Ithaca: Cornell University Press.

Geyer, R. (2000) *Exploring European Social Policy*, Cambridge: Polity Press.

Notes

1 A fourth development, the integration of EU social policy into the new Eastern European member states is also a major challenge. However, due to obvious space constraints and the limited impact on the UK regime, this factor is not discussed.

2 Funded by a grant from the Nuffield Foundation to explore the Europeanization of British social policy I was able to perform nearly 70 semi-structured interviews with UK and EU civil servants and policy actors.

CHAPTER 17

Information and Communication Technologies and Social Policy

ROGER BURROWS

The convergence of new media such as the Internet, digital television, cell phones and other information and communication technologies (ICTs) has been highlighted as significant in any number of recent accounts of economic (Castells, 1996), social (Webster, 2002) and cultural change (Lash, 2002). This chapter considers how such ICTs are beginning to impinge upon contemporary developments in UK social policy. The chapter begins, by way of context, by briefly examining some of the ways in which ICTs are implicated in the broad social transformations that are generating new challenges for contemporary social policy. It then considers how some of the traditional institutions of the welfare state are themselves responding to the opportunities and challenges that ICTs provide by reviewing some of the main issues involved in the implementation of *e-government* and electronic service delivery (ESD). This discussion of what might be seen as the deployment of ICTs in relation to social policy from the 'top down', is followed by a brief consideration of how the use of ICTs from the 'bottom up' might influence our broader understanding of the possible trajectory of the future of welfare. The chapter concludes with a brief consideration of some of the theoretical assumptions which underpin current debates about ICTs and social policy.

Social Policy in a World of Networks and Flows

Social policy needs to engage with debates about the social functioning of ICTs because of their role in facilitating a set of social transformations that are restructuring both the social distribution and nature of social problems. Urry (2000a, 2000b) for instance, argues that the very notion of the 'social' to which social policy has traditionally been orientated is becoming defunct. He argues that 'mobilities' of various sorts are transforming the historic subject matter of the social sciences, which have tended to focus upon individual societies and their generic structural characteristics. He argues that various 'global "networks and flows" undermine endogenous social structures that possess the powers to reproduce themselves' (Urry, 2000b: 186). This is leading, he argues, to the powers of national societies – and thus the powers of national social policies – to decline (Jessop, 2000). What are these diverse 'mobilities' that constitute this supposed new world of networks and flows which are so undermining of 'societies' as traditionally understood? For Urry they are made up of 'peoples, objects, images, information, and wastes; and ... the complex interdependencies between [them]' (Urry, 2000b: 185).

Perhaps the most influential analysis of the role of ICTs in such processes is that offered by Castells (1996, 1997, 1998) in his monumental deciphering of what he terms the *information age*. Castells' main point is that the growth and application of ICTs of various sorts has been the main facilitator of shifts towards, what he views as, an increasingly integrated global *network society*. By this he means that the global economy is characterized by the almost instantaneous flow and exchange of information, capital and cultural communication and that these flows now order and condition both consumption and production in quite profound ways. Social policy thus confronts a new world order in which work, leisure, travel and all the other basic categories of social and economic life are subject to changes in which ICTs are deeply implicated. Consider, for instance, some of the consequences of this conditioning for one of the central issues which social policy confronts – that of social inequality.

For Lash (2002: 4), one of the most influential theorists of the emergence of the information age, the sorts of processes that Castells describes lead to a situation in which 'the paradigm for inequality in the industrial order' is fundamentally altered. For Lash, social inequality in the information age is 'less and less defined by relations of production' and regarded more and more as the outcome of processes of social exclusion where 'exclusion is first and foremost something that is defined in conjunction with information and communication flows'. Such processes manifest themselves in a range of institutions and practices, but a good illustration of how they work can be seen at the level of urban geography in, what Graham and Marvin (2001) have recently termed, processes of *splintering urbanism*.

This notion refers to the reconfiguration of urban space that occurs when previously undifferentiated access to networked urban infrastructures – electricity, gas, water, sewerage, transport systems, telecommunications and so on – are 'unbundled' by processes of privatization, liberalization and the application of new technologies (Graham and Marvin, 2001: 138–77) This unbundling results in highly differentiated access to an increasing range of goods and services in what may be called *premium networked spaces*. In global cities such as London – but, in less pronounced forms in all large cities – premium networked spaces are splintering away from their proximate urban landscapes as they simultaneously connect with international circuits of economic, social and cultural exchange (in the manner described by Castells). Such premium networked spaces tend to overlay neighbourhoods that are already subject to various forms of advantageous socio-spatial *partitioning* (for example 'good' school catchment areas) and zoning (for example conservation areas). This, of course, does not happen by chance. Such localities are targeted by companies utilizing a range of geodemographic marketing strategies (Graham, 1997, 2000) to attract 'suitable' consumers to their developing premium networked services. Likely to be of particular importance in the future are patterns of access to broadband digital services and how these mesh with other types of urban infrastructural networks and correlative patterns of spatial partitioning.

From this perspective, it is clear that processes of social exclusion are as much a product of the actions of global producer interests and the manner in which locally advantaged consumers respond to them as they are to do with the attributes and actions of the populations being excluded. As Graham and Marvin (2001: 382) express it:

> Certain powerful users are starting to look beyond the taken-for-granted point of consumption – the phone or Internet terminal, the electricity socket, the car ignition key, the water tap, the street – at the configuration of the whole technical and mobility system that supports their transport, street, communication, power and water needs ... In the process the relative infrastructural connections of less powerful users, and the spaces in which they live, seem to become more and more fragile and problematic.

Not only do ICTs underpin such processes of unbundling and partitioning but they also provide the means by which more advantaged groups negotiate the social spaces created by such processes. The 'informatization' of neighbourhood consumption that geodemographic websites such as www.upmystreet.co.uk, www.homecheck.co.uk and www.homestore.com represent provide the informational resources by which strategically inclined social groups are able to find 'their' place within complex and dynamic urban spaces. At the same time, other technologies such as algorithmic surveillance systems (Norris et al., 1998) provide the means by which the social control and coordination of populations perceived as problematic in the new information order are themselves digitized (Burrows, 1997a).

The work of Castells, Urry, Lash, Graham, Marvin and others clearly provides insights into a range of social problems that social policy increasingly confronts which are strongly mediated by the introduction of ICTs of various sorts on a global scale. But, of course, social policy and the institutions of the welfare state are themselves not immune from the transformative qualities of new technologies (Burrows and Loader, 1994). As societies change, institutions of welfare change. These changes are many and varied and they are not uniform across all welfare sectors (Hudson, 1999). In recent years such changes have come to be described in terms of the emergence of *e-government*. In the next section we review this e-government agenda.

ICTs and the Institutions of the Welfare State

E-government has been defined as:

> providing public access via the Internet to information about all the services offered by central government departments and their agencies; and enabling the public to conduct and conclude transactions for those services. (NAO, 2002a: 1)

As such, e-government is a general policy aspiration, 'a strategic direction for the way in which the public sector will transform itself by implementing business models which exploit the possibilities of new technology' (Cabinet Office, 2000: 5).

According to Pleace and Quilgars (2002), the origins of this strategy are easy to identify. Throughout the 1990s, whole tiers of administration in large private sector companies were replaced by computer networks. Computerized systems, such as call centres, computerized telephone call handling systems and websites, began to provide 24-hour access for customers and greatly reduced overheads. Computer networks were used across many aspects of business, replacing large numbers of administrative staff, reducing costs and, of course, putting significant numbers of people out of work. Such systems of ESD originated in the USA and the Federal government was quick to see what was happening in the private sector and saw a way to reduce the costs of public administration (Dawes et al., 1999). The idea of e-government, which was also being heavily, strategically promoted by a number North American hardware and software companies, soon took hold across the rest of the advanced economies. Beside England, national strategies are in place in Scotland (Digital Scotland) and Wales (Wales Information Society Initiative) and in Australia (Johnson, 1999), Singapore, Canada, Germany, France and throughout the EU (Chatrie and Wright, 2000).

In the UK, political interest in the e-government agenda began under the Conservatives with the 1996 Green Paper *government.direct* (Cabinet Office). However, this was quickly superseded by a far more radical New Labour agenda. New Labour has come to view ESD as central to its policies (for a fuller analysis see Hudson (2002) and NAO (2002b)). At the beginning of 2000, the Office of the E-Envoy, which reports directly to the Prime Minister, (www.e-envoy.gov.uk/), was established to oversee and drive forward e-government. In the *Modernising Government* White Paper (Cabinet Office, 1999) the government set a target that all services, with exceptions for operational and policy reasons, should be 'available electronically' by 2008. The Prime Minister then announced in March 2000 that this date should be brought forward to 2005.

Progress with the implementation of e-government has recently been the subject of detailed reports by the National Audit Office (NAO, 2002a, 2002b). These suggest that by the end of 2001, just over 50 per cent (274 services) of all government services were online in one way or another and that by the end of 2002, 75 per cent (386 services) will be. The areas where full implementation of ESD is likely to prove problematic relate to services where face-to-face contact is essential: work with the victims of crime; the processing of asylum-seekers; welfare-to-work interviews; transactions that involve the authentification of documents and so on. Progress varies dramatically across the types of service being delivered. Most of the services that are currently online are informational (for example how to apply for a passport). Apart from revenue collection transactions, such as self-assessment returns and VAT, so far there is little in the way of opportunities to undertake transactions online. Some examples of progress made across departments and services currently online are shown in Table 17.1 (reproduced from Comptroller and Auditor General, 2002b: 22).

So what in practice does ESD involve? A central notion in the development of ESD in the USA has been the concept of the single point of access or *portal* for government services (Dawes et al., 1999). In this model, services are listed in one place, a website or similar environment, which is easy to access and easy to use. Services are then presented according to which part of, or event in, a person's life they apply to. So, for example, all the services related to moving house, the birth of a child or experiencing crime are found together, regardless of which agency provides them. This idea has been copied and there is already a 'portal' for central government in England at www.ukonline.gov.uk. The organizational implications of this idea are potentially profound because:

People should not need to understand how government is organized, or to know which department or agency does what, or whether a function is exercised by

Table 17.1 Services available online by department as at November 2001

Department	No. of services online	Example
Department for the Environment, Food and Rural Affairs (DEFRA)	54	Cattle tracing system enabling reporting and tracing of cattle movements online: www.defra.gov.uk
Department of Transport, Local Government and the Regions (DTLGR)	45	Provision of information to motorists on issues such as learning to drive: www.motoring.gov.uk
Department for Education and Skills (DfES)	36	Provision of online services for teachers, for example advice on setting up after-school learning activities and clubs: www.standards.dfes.gov.uk
Home Office	29	Obtaining application forms for grants to reduce youth offending: www.youth-justice-based.gov.uk
Department of Trade and Industry (DTI)	32	The Small Business Service (SBS) website: www.businesslink.org and call centre 0845 600 0096 provide access to information and advice for small/medium enterprises available from the DTI and other organizations
Department of Health (DH)	14	Information about health care via a telephone service – NHS Direct: www.nhsdirect.nhs.gov.uk
Ministry of Defence	14	RAF website provides information on low-flying exercises
Foreign and Commonwealth Office	8	Obtaining application forms for visas
HM Treasury	6	A self-analysis kit for firms to find out how likely they are to be affected by the phasing out of national currencies in the euro area on www.euro.gov.uk
Department for Work and Pensions (DWP)	5	Advertising job vacancies from the Employment Service
Lord Chancellor's Department	4	Online issue of money claims
Department for Culture, Media and Sport	4	Information available online about lottery distribution bodies: www.culture.gov.uk
Department for International Development	2	Online ordering of publications and research material
Export Credits Guarantee Department	2	Provision of Export and Credits Guarantee Departments' services on www.ecgd.gov.uk
Others	19	Land Registry (1); Public Record Office (7); British Trade International (1); Ordnance Survey (7); and Office for National Statistics (3)
TOTAL	**274**	

Source: Comptroller and Auditor General (2002b: 22)

central or local government ... [rather] services [are organized] in ways that make sense to the customer. (Cabinet Office, 2000: 1)

This statement says much about the sorts of relationship between the statutory, voluntary and private sectors that government envisages. It is not intended simply to involve borrowing concepts and buying technology from the private sector, but it is also meant to involve close working relationships. Further, ESD is viewed as being linked to the wider policy objective of increasing public–private partnerships and voluntary and private sector involvement in the delivery of public services. ESD could eventually happen via private or voluntary sector portals, in cooperation and competition with one another. As another policy report puts it:

> Electronic delivery of government services offers enormous new opportunities for the private and voluntary sectors. There should be a new, mixed economy in the electronic delivery of government services in which the public, private and voluntary sectors can all play a role on the basis that what matters is what works rather than who does it. (Cabinet Office/PIU, 2000)

Models of computerized business administration and direct selling through e-commerce and telephone call centres underpin the basic concept of ESD. ESD starts with a network. Communication then has to be established between 'customers' and this network. Communication between the customer and network happens in two ways: 'assisted' or 'direct' contact. With *assisted* contact, the network is made available to counter staff, project staff, community workers and staff in call centres. These staff, whether they are mobile staff working in the community, behind a counter or answering a telephone, use the network in order to provide the services that the customers need (cf. telephone banking). Alternatively, people can choose to interact *directly* with the network for themselves, through the medium of a website or similar interactive system (cf. Internet banking). As conceptualized by Pleace and Quilgars (2002), in a basic ESD model (Figure 17.1) all the needs of service users are met through the same network. Some people are helped by staff who use the network with them or on their behalf (assisted contact) and other people use the network directly for themselves, through a website or other interactive service (self-service).

Self-service is anticipated to be best for *relatively simple* exchanges. Self-service systems would not be able to handle assessments or determinations which required complex interpretation or professional judgement (Johnson, 1999). Equally, just as people now sometimes need help filling in a form, some would need help filling in a network's version of a form and so could

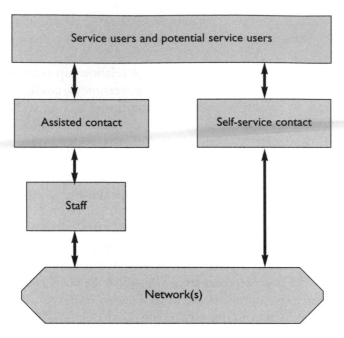

Figure 17.1 Basic model of electronic service delivery
Source: Pleace and Quilgars (2002)

not necessarily always use even relatively simple self-service facilities. Assisted contact would be employed whenever more complex procedures were required, or whenever someone needed assistance in arranging services because they were not able to do it for themselves. It is anticipated that outside agencies would also be able to access the network to provide support for people who were not able or willing to engage directly with the network.

Margetts and Dunleavy (2002) have developed a useful schematic overview of the main demand- and supply-side barriers to the implementation of e-government based upon this model of ESD. In relation to the likely demand for ESD of welfare, they recognize the importance of the role that *social exclusion* – the so-called 'digital divide' (Loader, 1998; DTI/PAT 15, 2000; Selwyn, 2002) – could play in fettering the development of ESD. Access to the Internet in the UK remains strongly socially patterned. Indeed, the patterning is such that those with the greatest need of welfare services are often the least likely to have access to the Internet. In the last quarter of 2001, 9.8 million households (39 per cent) in the UK could access the Internet from their homes (www.statistics.gov.uk). At the level of the individual, 46 per cent of adults had used the Internet in the last month and 56 per cent had used it at some time. Although rates of access in relation to gender are converging, significant differences remain in relation to both age and social class. Rates of access decrease with age: 80 per cent of those aged 16–24 have access compared to just 12 per cent of those aged 65 and over. The social class gradient is also dramatic. A full 78 per cent of households headed by a professional have access, falling to 53 per cent among households headed by someone with a skilled manual class background, falling again to just 27 per cent among households headed by someone from an unskilled manual social class background. But it is not only access to the Internet which is the issue (Hellawell, 2001).

Even when access is provided, patterns of use among different social groups are highly variable and there is some evidence that 'previously marginal groups may continue to be marginalized when they are connected' (Margetts and Dunleavy, 2002: 9). Some social groups may use the Internet primarily as a 'lean back' technology – as an entertainment medium in much the same way as they may consume TV or video. Others – what some have termed an emerging 'virtual middle class' (Burrows et al., 2000) – may use it more as a 'lean to' technology – as a virtual informational and reflexive resource which demands proactive engagement in order to obtain strategic advantage in the 'real' world (Burrows et al., 2000). Differing forms of engagement with the Internet mean that e-government may need to overcome what Margetts and Dunleavy (2002: 10) call the extreme *solemnity* of much existing provision (a function, as we shall discuss below, of a major supply-side barrier to e-government which relates to the dominant values of government organizations). For people who have an automatic association of the Internet with fun, games and entertainment, the 'conservatively designed … bureaucratic language … [and] … strict functionality' of much ESD may further discourage use.

Margetts and Dunleavy (2002) also identify a range of other factors which may influence demand. They point out that if e-government is to be successful, it must be based upon technological forms capable of being *domesticated*. By this they mean that the technologies that have become most successful and widely used are those which easily mesh with the everyday routines of citizens. This process of domestication certainly applies to TV and telephones and, most recently, mobile phones. In some sections of society (for example academia?), email might also be a candidate for such a domesticated technology. However, this is not yet the case for many web-based applications, although this may change as broadband access brings with it Internet connections which are constantly 'live'. At present, many e-government applications are structured in such a way as to encourage only episodic interactions with the technology – as in the case, described above, where portals are organized in relation to particular life events, for instance, which, by definition, means that they are unlikely to be used on an ongoing basis.

Linked to this issue of domestication is another – that of the importance of *transaction costs* in accessing welfare services electronically: gaining access to the Internet; finding the appropriate website; waiting for it to load; finding out how to interact with the site; putting right any mistakes; unfamiliarity with terminology and so on. These costs may, in reality, be very small but there is much evidence that even small, up-front transaction costs may stop many people from making an investment of time and energy that would pay them back many times over in the long term. Hitherto, there has been little attempt to balance such costs by providing any real *citizen benefits* for accessing services electronically. This contrasts markedly with the private sector where various encouragements have been developed in order to build demand for e-based services. So, for example, online banking generally offers marginally higher rates of interest for savers; online booksellers offer discounts and suggestions for new publications based upon patterns of existing sales; and so on. In relation to e-government, the opposite has sometimes happened and rather than offering clear citizen benefits, some forms of ESD have even generated 'negative incentives' – as has occurred in the USA where online tax returns have become unpopular because it has become clear that electronically filed forms have been scrutinized more thoroughly than those filed on paper.

Another demand-side barrier to the implementation of ESD relates to issues of *trust*. Many existing users of welfare services already possess low expectations of government services and where:

> individuals are accustomed to a conflictual, inflexible relationship with a government organization on paper, they are likely to expect that an electronic version of the organization will be the same. (Margetts and Dunleavy, 2002: 10)

Linked to this issue of trust is another, which relates to the manner in which much of the culture of the Internet is *exclusionary* to government. Given that government has come relatively late to the Internet, it has meant that many of its attempts to set up virtual structures in order to interact with its citizenry are ignored or little used because there already exist many other well-established non-governmental virtual communities and resources which are more trusted and often more attractive to users. The attempt by government to create a new formal virtual geography of the welfare state is being built upon virtual territories already densely populated by academia, self-help groups and commercial interests, antithetical, albeit in different ways, to such an imposition on 'their' spaces (see discussion below).

As well as there being barriers to the demand for e-government, there are also some major organizational barriers to the supply of ESD by government. Perhaps most fundamentally it is important not to underestimate the impact that a whole series of previous bad experiences of the introduction of ICTs has had on welfare organizations (Hudson, 1999, 2000): budgets have been overshot; few cost savings have been made; sometimes the technology installed failed to work as envisaged; jobs were lost and so on. Many core staff are thus approaching the development of ESD with a fatalistic attitude and a lack of any great enthusiasm. This is resulting in much ESD design and implementation being driven by a combination of internal IT departments and externally contracted private sector companies – neither perhaps being best placed to understand the needs of front-line welfare staff or the users of welfare services (see Pleace and Quilgars (2002) for an empirical examination of some of these issues in the early implementation of ESD).

The previous bad experience of the implementation of ICTs in welfare organizations is also sometimes reinforced by a lack of an ongoing familiarity with the Internet by many welfare professionals who do not have routine web access in their workplaces – some have even complained that they cannot get access to their own organization's website when at work (Margetts and Dunleavy, 2002: 7). This can lead to a lack of organizational demand for the technology which itself is sometimes further weakened by a staff concern about 'channel rivalry'. This refers to the (quite rational) fear that if ESD develops successfully, then other (non-e-based) channels of communication with government will be undermined and jobs will be lost. There are then clear organizational barriers to the supply of e-government services which can easily be rhetorically justified because of some of the demand-side barriers already discussed. A view can easily develop which says that 'our clients do not have access to the Internet and so won't use it so we won't develop an e-based service' and so on.

Although organizational factors such as these are important perhaps in the medium term, the main supply-side barriers to the development of ESD will relate more to issues of organizational *values* than to organizational *structures*. Margetts and Dunleavy (2002: 5–6) detail how some of the fundamental values of existing welfare organizations – formality, uniformity, robustness and hierarchy in particular – may work against the development of ESD. For instance, the widespread use of email is currently regarded by government as a phenomena that falls somewhere between an informal telephone call and a formal letter and yet 'if e-mail addresses are not seen as official, moves towards proactive service delivery ... will be almost impossible to implement' (Margetts and Dunleavy, 2002: 5).

The uniformity of current government service delivery and communication also presents problems for the implementation of ESD. One of the great strengths of the web is the manner in which populations can be segmented and targeted and services customized. There is no necessity to communicate with all citizens in the same way, yet the values of uniformity held by many welfare organizations push them away from experimenting with more flexible approaches.

The values of robustness also make electronic communications with government problematic on occasion. There is a perception within government that transactions with government must be particularly secure and, of course, in some areas this must be the case. However, the level of security demanded in even the most mundane of transactions means that the introduction of ESD could be more technically difficult and expensive than it might otherwise have been.

Governmental organizations also tend to be hierarchical and – almost by definition – bureaucratic; characteristics which do not articulate well with emerging networked forms of organizational life. There are myriad consequences of this hierarchical culture but particularly important for ESD is the way in which it discourages networked linkages between different web-based (re)sources. It often appears as if '.gov' existed as a self-contained entity when in reality the infinite expanses of '.org', '.ac', '.co', newsgroups, mailing lists and the rest – over which government has no/little control – are only a couple of mouse clicks away for users. For example, as Margetts and Dunleavy (2002: 6) point out in relation to health, the NHS

> health site www.nhs.uk does not make use of or even link to the numerous useful private sector health sites, such as www.patient.co.uk or even the excellent Web site of the British Medical Journal www.bmj.org – yet the whole relationship between doctors and patients is being challenged by citizen use of these and countless other sites.

Thus, although the e-government agenda continues apace, it must be recognized that there are very real barriers to its implementation. It must also be recognized that the informatization of formal welfare services is just one of a number of ways in which ICTs underpin the restructuring of welfare. At least as important is the role of ICTs in restructuring a range of social relations within civil society which condition the experience and delivery of social welfare. For instance, community informatics initiatives of various sorts (Keeble and Loader, 2001) harness the power of networked technologies to bring about a range of transformations in both physical and virtual community settings. At a more mundane level, though, the use of ICTs by individuals from the 'bottom up' may also have implications for existing patterns of welfare. This might particularly be the case in relation to the emergence of what might be termed 'virtual self-help' (VSH) (Pleace et al., 2003).

Social Policy and the Emergence of Virtual Self-help

The potential of computer networks to facilitate viable mutual support networks was perhaps first recognized in the early 1990s by medical researchers in the USA. Some early experiments were with people with HIV (Boberg et al., 1995) and cancer (Weinberg et al., 1995). However, as Denzin (1998) observes, positive cultural attitudes towards both technology and 'self-help' in the USA soon led individuals to begin setting up their own online self-help groups. Numerous studies have been conducted in the USA to examine VSH groups, for example people recovering from child abuse (Moursund, 1997), people with disabilities (Finn, 1999), and recovering alcoholics (King, 1994). As access to the Internet has spread, the nature of VSH has changed. Although it is still largely dominated by the concerns and perspectives of the citizens of the USA, its nature has begun to change as the cultural and ideological preferences and different institutional arrangements of other peoples residing elsewhere on the globe have begun to manifest themselves online. This means that, for example, as Internet access in Britain has increased, we have witnessed not just increased participation in existing USA-dominated systems of online self-help and support by people from Britain, but also the formation of new virtual spaces expressly designed to deal with the specificities of the British context (Burrows et al., 2000).

VSH takes place within four different virtual forums:

1. *Newsgroups* – probably the most important. Globally there are now in excess of 85,000 of these and a considerable number are devoted to VSH. UK-based examples include uk.people.disability, uk.people.support.depression and uk.people.support.cfs-me (Burrows et al., 2000: 102–3).

2. *email discussion or mailing lists*. A mailing list search engine such as Liszt suggests that some 100,000 such lists currently exist (http://www.liszt.com/).

3. *Internet relay chat (IRC) 'rooms'.* These allow individuals to hold the equivalent of a typed conversation within a shared virtual space. These synchronous forms of computer-mediated communication are less widely employed for VSH but examples certainly exist (Pleace et al., 2000).

4. Increasingly, a *website* that offers information on particular health or social care needs, links to other sites and web-based combinations of newsgroups, discussion lists or IRC rooms. In the UK, there are examples of such websites devoted to a range of health issues but also to topics such as bullying and mortgage repossession.

What consequences might these emerging systems of VSH have for social policy? First, although the rise of self-help groups is not a direct consequence of ICTs, the Internet has almost certainly accelerated the spread of such groups. The emergence of VSH has generated a large global space where a huge number of topics are debated independently of formal welfare institutions (and, indeed, as we discussed above, such spaces may even be exclusionary of many formal institutions). They provide a medium for sharing and exchanging information and ideas and, as such, form a prime site for the emergence of a new social politics of defensive and proactive engagement (Ellison, 2000). However, while these forums do in some ways comprise 'groups' or 'virtual communities', nevertheless they are simply the result of a collection of contributions from *individuals* and the scope and opportunity for any politics of collective resistance may be limited. Self-help groups are the descendants of an uneasy relationship between two ideologies of individualism and collectivism, where individualism is the dominant partner. It would appear that the format and nature of virtual groups are essentially about self-help rather than collective help, in that individuals seek out information and support or offer individualized responses to other participants. A second, but strongly related, issue is the salience and privileging of *personal experience and lay knowledge over 'expert' knowledge* within VSH. In the information age, traditional authority (such as the medical expert) is being replaced by multiple sources of authority. Clearly, the Internet expands the array of information sources dramatically on virtually every aspect of people's lives. But, as yet, we have little understanding of how and when people turn to the Internet for information and support and the relative weight they give to the sources of help which they access in that medium. Virtual communities offering online self-help undoubtedly do provide important sources of information and social support (Burrows et al., 2000; Nettleton et al., 2002). However, as we discuss below, they can also provide so much information and so many different perspectives on an issue that rather than assisting in the reflexive management of risk they can also induce anxiety. People are better informed but this does not necessarily mean that they are any more able to make the choices that they must make.

Critique of Information

One of the implicit assumptions of much policy discussion in relation to the new world of global information and communication networks and flows is that, other things being equal, the 'information-rich' will be ever more privileged over the 'information-poor'; talk of a *digital divide* is suggestive of a social chasm between those who have access to ICTs and those who do not. The suggestion that there will be an emergent *virtual middle class* implies that those who not only have access to the Internet, but also have the reflexive resources to act upon the information (derived from 'formal' e-government sources, 'informal' VSH resources or wherever) that they are able to assimilate from it, will be 'winners' in various social, political and economic arenas (Burrows and Nettleton, 2002; Slevin, 2000). But perhaps such a conceptualization of the relationship between information, reflexivity and welfare needs to questioned. And, indeed, this has begun to happen, most fundamentally perhaps in the recent work of Lash (2002) in his book *Critique of Information*.

Lash argues that reflexivity is becoming impossible in the information age. For him there is no longer any space for discursive or narrative knowledge, it has been displaced by informational knowledge. While discursive knowledge implies a unity, a set of beliefs, values and disciplinary underpinnings, informational knowledge, by contrast, has no unity – it is 'outside of a systematic conceptual framework' (2002: 3). This is not just due to the sheer proliferation of information and knowledge production per se, indeed Lash points out that information and knowledge may in fact be rationally produced within various sites or locales (by government, citizens, commercial organizations and so on) but it becomes irrational from the perspective of the user when the sheer quantity and variety of material is juxtaposed; multiple forms of information cannot be digested – let alone reflexively considered:

> look at the paradox of the information society ... how can such highly rational production result in the incredible irrationality of information overloads, misinformation, disinformation and out-of-control information. At stake is a *dis*informed society. The key to understanding this is to look at what is produced in information production not as information-rich goods and services, but as more or less out-of-control bytes of information. (Lash, 2002: 2)

While we may appear to be 'smartening up', the sheer proliferation of decontextualized information means that we are also experiencing a 'dumbing down'. The information that is being communicated by way of the new technologies may be experienced in a very different way to information gleaned from other sources which can be checked and cross-checked, discussed and reflected upon. We may have more and more information on matters that concern us, but, in the end, does it help our understanding? Does it improve our knowledge? Does it help us to feel more certain? Does it improve social outcomes? These are big questions with which to end – conceptual, theoretical, even philosophical questions about the very nature of the information age and the role of human agency within it (cf. Nettleton and Burrows, 2003). However, they are questions which will be evermore central to debates about the relationship between ICTs and social policy.

Further Reading

Burrows, R., Nettleton, S., Pleace, N., Loader, B. and Muncer, S. (2000) 'Virtual Community Care? Social Policy and the Emergence of Computer Mediated Social Support', *Information, Communication and Society*, **3**(1): 95–121.

Margetts, H. and Dunleavy, P. (2002) 'Cultural Barriers to e-Government', Academic Article HC 704-III in Support of National Audit Office, *Better Public Service Through e-Government*, London: Stationery Office.

Pleace, N. and Quilgars, D. (2002) *Social Housing, Social Care and Electronic Service Delivery*, York: Joseph Rowntree Foundation/York Publishing Services.

Slevin, J. (2000) *The Internet and Society*, Cambridge: Polity Press.

CHAPTER 18

Environmentalism and Social Policy

Tony Fitzpatrick

Social policy was slow to react to the challenge of environmentalism, despite the importance of early pioneers such as Illich (1973), Gorz (1983) and Robertson (1985). By the early 1990s, Green ideas had begun to influence academic debates about welfare (C. Pierson, 1991; Ferris, 1993), an influence that continued throughout the decade (Fitzpatrick, 1998; Trainer, 1998). With book-length analyses of environmentalism and social policy now readily available (Huby, 1998; Cahill, 2001; Cahill and Fitzpatrick, 2002; Fitzpatrick and Cahill, 2002a), it may seem as if the subject has finally arrived, yet its influence upon the practical business of policy making and welfare reform continues to be negligible, certainly in the UK. Is this due to weaknesses in the analysis, the neglect of politicians and other policy makers or the possibility that environmentalism demands far more radical changes to welfare systems than the current political orthodoxy is willing to contemplate?

This chapter reviews these questions by covering the following four areas. First, we outline the basic ideas of environmentalism. Second, we use those ideas to critique social policy. Third, we examine New Labour's record in this respect. Finally, we sketch the alternative approaches to that of New Labour's.

The Principle of Sustainability

Environmentalism might be thought of as the philosophy and politics of sustainability (Eckersley, 1992; Pepper, 1996; Dryzek, 1997; Barry, 1999; Dobson, 2000). Sustainability is a notoriously difficult idea to pin down. In its most famous definition, sustainability implies meeting 'the needs of the present without compromising the ability of future generations to meet

theirs' (Brundtland Commission, 1987: 8), yet this apparently simple definition raises many more questions than we have the space to consider here.
What do we mean by needs? How can the interests of present generations be
weighed against those of future ones? Does sustainability imply more
economic growth, less growth or something else entirely?

Essentially, environmentalists identify a conflict between what we demand
of the world and what the world is capable of supplying, both in terms of the
resources which are available to us and its ability to absorb the pollution
resulting from our use of those resources. If the demands we make are infinite, while the world possesses only a finite stock of resources and a finite
ability to absorb pollution, then ours is an unsustainable existence. Sustainability therefore implies reducing human demands to the point where this
conflict becomes less and less significant.

But by how far do demands have to be reduced? Most scientists agree that
carbon emissions have to decrease by significant amounts (anywhere between
60 per cent and 80 per cent by the middle of the century) if environmental
disaster is to be averted (Houghton et al., 2001). And even if we succeed in
doing so, a certain amount of global warming is already unavoidable (with
estimates ranging from $1.5°C$ to $10°C$) and, in fact, already visible: since
1980 we have experienced ten of the warmest years in recorded history. So
the consequences, in terms of drought, flooding, ecological migration and
transformations to the earth's weather system, are potentially disastrous. Yet
what changes to our societies and economies must we implement in order to
reduce emissions to that extent and manage the effects of rising temp-
eratures? This is where disagreement begins to kick in.

Material affluence is something that developed countries have long taken
for granted and there is resistance to the idea of reducing demands to any
great extent. Some insist that sustainability can be achieved without significant alterations to Western lifestyles or rates of economic growth and we
should not panic ourselves into imagining otherwise (Lomborg, 2001). This
position supports what might be called 'moderate sustainability', where the
emphasis is upon changing the finiteness of the physical world, for example
through the replacement of renewable resources, by finding substitutes for
non-renewable ones and searching for technological solutions to the problems of resource depletion and pollution. Many environmentalists, though,
argue that significant changes will be necessary to the ways in which we live,
work and consume (Dryzek and Scholsberg, 1998), a position that might be
termed 'strong sustainability'. So, in addition to measures just mentioned, we
must also revise the demands that we make on the world so that we consume
far less. This implies that rather than adapting the world to suit ourselves, we
adapt ourselves to meet the finiteness of nature

A further controversy concerns the means by which we are to achieve sustainability. Should we leave things to free-market forces, perhaps on the grounds that the price mechanism will preserve resources by making them more expensive (and so less in demand) as they become scarcer (Anderson and Leal, 1991)? Or should we adapt the existing blend of markets, state and non-state institutions towards environmental goals, a pragmatic strategy known as 'ecological modernization' (Hajer, 1995)? Or does sustainability require a much stronger role for the state, one that regards environmental justice as dependent upon the achievement of social and distributive justice (Pepper, 1993)? Or, finally, do we have to go 'beyond' both market and state approaches by creating autarkic communities (that is, local in orientation and entirely self-sufficient) (Sale, 1985)? These ideas are just a few among the many social prescriptions that environmentalists have adopted in their visions of a sustainable society.

We can see, then, that despite sustainability being an apparently simple idea, it gives rise to a complex and wide-ranging debate. Only a part of that debate has been sampled here; in reality, environmentalism stretches across a much wider range of disciplinary concerns: philosophy, politics, sociology, economics and geography, to name a few.

Critiques of Welfare

The disagreements and debates outlined above obviously affect the criticisms which can be made of social policies and welfare systems. Therefore, although we can identify a set of common themes, it must be remembered that different schools of environmental thought give differing emphases and interpretations to those themes. What, though, are the main criticisms which environmentalism wishes to make (cf. Fitzpatrick and Cahill, 2002b)?

First, and most obviously, it opposes social policies and welfare systems that are unsustainable and environmentalists agree that indiscriminate economic growth is at the heart of all unsustainable practices. With consumer capitalism fuelling demands whose appetites can never be fully satisfied, pressures are placed upon the planet's ecosystem which cannot continue indefinitely. Despite this, economic growth is one of the values of modern society which it is difficult to question and almost all political philosophies, environmentalism apart, derive from that value. For Marxists, the development of productive forces was the sine qua non of class conflict and so of a transition to a classless society, initially leading most Marxists to dismiss environmentalism as a bourgeois concern (Enzensberger, 1988), although this stance has now been replaced by a more considered position (Benton, 1996). So even those ideologies which have sought to challenge existing society buy into its 'productivism', that is, a belief that economic growth has to be the principal engine of progress and future well-being.

On these grounds, social policy leaves itself open to two forms of criticism by ecologists. One criticism is that existing welfare systems are dependent upon productivist practices that are ultimately unsustainable. Welfare and diswelfare are usually defined and measured according to distributive patterns which trace back to the logic of productivism. The Right, for instance, treat rising material prosperity as the central justification for capitalism and for free markets in particular, the job of social policies being to assist markets by maintaining social order and enforcing the disciplines which unregulated markets require. Many on the Left have thought it best to champion social justice by emphasizing a painless form of redistribution, where basic needs are met and the less well-off assisted, by directing ever-higher levels of growth in the appropriate directions. A modest amount of direct redistribution from rich to poor may be justifiable yet, by and large, social democrats have tried to improve the share of the poorest by increasing the overall stock of national resources. In short, productivism can be said to underpin all welfare regimes, whether on the political Right or Left.

Another criticism, therefore, is that social policies contribute to unsustainability. By perpetuating the ideologies of productivism, welfare systems only help to fuel more growth, regardless of the ecological consequences. One implication is that welfare reforms tend only to address what environmentalists regard as the surface symptoms of social problems and miss the fact that the roots of many problems lie in ecological degradation and injustice. For instance, environmentalists note the extent to which poor health is caused by industrial and postindustrial economies that place profits ahead of physical and mental well-being, a point missed by most health, housing, transport, urban and employment policies. Take one example. The welfare states that appeared in the middle of the 20th century were based upon male, full-time, full employment, for only if employment was high (and the numbers of benefit claimants low) could social expenditure be maintained at generous levels – the key assumption of Keynes and Beveridge. Indeed, state welfare seems to come under most attack when unemployment rises and tax rolls begin to fall. Yet, while welcoming the social benefits of full employment, and arguing that most ecological measures are or can be employment-friendly, environmentalists also point to the ecological damage to which most existing jobs contribute, whether directly or indirectly.

This leads to the second Green critique of social policy, that it is too heavily based upon wage-earning, whether as a source of material security, self-identity or social participation. The employment ethic is essential to modern society and so, in questioning it, ecologists may appear to be isolated cranks. Yet environmentalists are not quite as isolated as they first appear. Most are not arguing for the abolition of employment but for a recognition that security, identity and social participation derive from a far wider range of sources and activities than the current orthodoxy admits. In this respect, ecologists side with those feminists who redefine flexibility towards employment, unpaid work and leisure, and away from restrictive masculinist conceptions of economic well-being. Indeed, both ecologism and feminism argue that care is essential to well-being. Furthermore, environmentalists point out that the employment ethic has been undermining itself for several decades now. With the overall decline in employment levels, although some countries are obviously more successful in this respect than others, the social conditions of this ethic are fatally undermined (Gorz, 1989).

So rather than 'work' being equated with 'employment', we should recognize the wider spectrum of activities which are socially valuable. This most obviously includes 'care work', but may also encompass other forms of activity which are more creative and playful, or even rebellious. If a government is trying to build a bypass that is likely to destroy the local ecosystem, then who is contributing to society more: the unemployed protestors chaining themselves to trees or the underpaid security guards applying the bolt-cutters?

The third main critique made by environmentalists towards social policy concerns the degree of control and autonomy currently possessed by individuals. The allegation is that existing forms of social organization and welfare provision underestimate the extent to which citizens can be self-organizing. The state is interpreted largely as too distant and impersonal a set of institutions. Representative democracy is thought to encourage a passive, consumerist attitude towards the common good, one that minimizes the level of political participation and organizes participation around party machines that are top-heavy (Doherty and de Geus, 1996). The assumption is that although most people care about the environment (although see below), this concern has barely registered on the mainstream political agenda since the party system embodies a status quo that is immensely slow to respond to new developments. And even where the Greens have had some success (*die Grünen* in Germany, for instance), they have had to compromise to such an extent that their ideological distinctiveness is eclipsed.

In terms of social policy, this state centralization is thought to encourage the 'clientalization' of welfare, where well-being is something we receive from experts and bureaucrats, and rarely something that people collectively generate for and through themselves. The price of paternalism and basic needs satisfaction has been an overarching collectivism that allows little space for bottom-up provision. Greens therefore tend to support not an individualistic ethos of

Victorian self-help (since social justice is a necessary condition of decentralization), but a new welfare settlement where the state provides a universalistic
framework of regulation, accountability and basic service provision, but where
greater room is made for civic associations and policy communities (Offe,
1996) which would control funds and allow the 'recipients' of welfare to
become their own 'producers'. This is what Burns et al. (2003) call 'community self-help'. In short, Green social policies seem to require a greater degree
of decentralization and the emergence of a newly empowered 'welfare citizen'.

Yet the difficulty lies not only with the state but also with a market system
which is based upon the needs and demands of the most powerful economic
actors, by which is meant multinational and transnational corporations. In
particular, the chemical, car, nuclear and fossil fuel industries dominate the
market, establishing an oligopoly which actively resists environmental legislation and constantly tries to undermine the environmentalist case. It is the
influence of these actors upon political parties that is most worrying. By
being able to buy political power, they are able to undermine international
cooperative agreements.

These Green critiques of social policy – focusing upon growth, employment and centralization – are not meant to be exhaustive but they do capture
the basics of the Green challenge to social policy. However, it is salutary to
remind ourselves that the challenge is not all one-way: there is potentially
much that social policy has to teach environmentalism.

For instance, although it has its more utopian moments, the subject of
social policy is a reminder that to get to where we want to be, we have to start
from where we are. It is very easy to construct imaginary societies that would
be more desirable than our existing ones; the trick is to do so without ignoring
the problem of transition and whether we can realistically expect the present
to be transformed into that imaginary future. In short, utopianism has to be
tempered by pragmatism. As such, Greens are far better working with the
grain of existing welfare systems than supporting the dismantling of those
systems. Second, social policy can remind environmentalists not to apply too
generalized a critique to human destructiveness. At its worst, ecologism adopts
an anti-humanist stance that treats all humans as the same. Divisions between
rich and poor (both nations and individuals) make it clear that environmental
crises are more the product of a socioeconomic system biased towards inequalities rather than the product of humanity per se. The trick is to recognize why
environmental sustainability and distributive justice imply one another. Finally,
the basic material needs of all must be provided for through universalistic
provision. There is little point in preserving resources if the price is either
scarcity for all or health and security for some. Sustainability must imply transforming the world in order to serve human well-being. If ecologists regard

human and non-human well-being as irreconcilable, then they may only be repeating the underlying mistake of productivist welfare.

If environmentalism and social policy have much to teach each other, therefore, then are the lessons being learned at the level of government? We will address this question in the next section by outlining what has been happening in the UK over recent years.

New Labour, New Environment?

At the World Summits (Kyoto in 1997 and Johannesburg in 2002) on climate change, New Labour certainly knew how to talk the talk of environmentalism, yet even those broadly sympathetic to the New Labour project regard its environmental record as poor (Levett, 2001; Toynbee and Walker, 2001: Ch. 9) and there is little evidence of Green social policies.

New Labour supports the principle of sustainable development, for which it regards the maintenance of high and stable levels of growth and employment as essential. Its emphasis has been upon auditing (ensuring that ecological costs and benefits are taken into account), economic incentives (Green taxes, fines and emissions trading) and setting environmental targets. In 1999, it published 15 quality of life indicators that it promised would inform the full range of government policy, embracing a diverse set of economic, social and environmental factors. In its first term, the government's policies included:

- aiming to generate 10 per cent of UK electricity from renewable sources by 2010

- cutting VAT on insulation

- reducing VAT on domestic fuel from 8 to 5 per cent (benefiting poorer households although environmentally regressive)

- improving eco-taxation (introducing a fossil fuel levy on companies and increasing the landfill tax).

Furthermore, departments are required to integrate environmental concerns into their work, although this largely means reducing waste and energy use. The greening of the UK economy is therefore underway, at least partly, yet the government's discourse consists of injunctions to recycle rather than anything more fundamental.

On a global stage, New Labour announced its intention to reduce greenhouse gas emissions to 20 per cent below their 1990 levels by 2010, surpassing the targets set in Kyoto in 1997. Like most countries, it favours an emphasis upon emissions trading (where low polluting countries can sell credits to high polluting ones) and the provision of more carbon sinks to absorb greenhouse emissions – although carbon sinks cannot have an unlimited effectiveness. By and large, then, New Labour represents itself as taking Britain down the road towards a Green society and economy.

However, the assessment made by Green organizations is less congratulatory. New Labour has been accused of instinctively siding with corporate power (including firms promoting genetically modified food), developers and employers' organizations. It has operated with an economic conservatism that still ignores the importance of localized production and consumption and which fails to internalize environmental costs. This failure was symbolized towards the end of 2001 when it announced sweeping changes to planning procedures, ensuring that Green aims would be further marginalized in the design of large-scale projects, for example power stations, incinerators, roads and open-cast mines. Green campaigners are also critical of the government's lifting of restrictions on new gas-fired power stations.

New Labour's record on transport has been fairly disastrous (Grayling, 2002), despite the announcement in 2000 of a £180 billion programme for renewing Britain's transport infrastructure over ten years. By the end of its first term, the government had failed to reinvent a public sector ethos. Despite the growth in rail users, the private car still appears desirable, given the state of public transportation, symbolized by the incompetence of Railtrack which led to the semi-nationalization of the railways in 2001. At the end of 2002, the government announced a new road building programme that strongly contradicted its previous aim of shifting the emphasis from private to public forms of transport.

Nor has New Labour made rapid strides towards greater equality. By the 2001 general election, it seems that 'redistribution by stealth' had had some success, with the poorest groups experiencing a modest rise in their incomes, yet income inequality continued to widen (Howard et al., 2001). By the end of 2001, New Labour had still only made a dent in the figures for poverty and social exclusion, although some of its anti-poverty measures had still not had time to have an effect (Rahman et al., 2001). Why is this relevant to the environment? Because whereas poorer communities tend to act Green, for example by owning fewer cars, they tend not to think Green (Burningham and Thrush, 2001). So, greater equality may be the sine qua non of both social justice and sustainability. Indeed, New Labour may have contributed to a mistrust of politicians and government that, by 2000, had reduced the commitment of the British public to achieving environmental goals (Christie and Jarvis, 2001).

Green organizations are not entirely critical, praising the progress made in terms of eco-taxes, for example vehicle excise duty and tax allowances on environmentally friendly company cars, which are designed to make the polluter pay and so reduce incidents of pollution and/or raise revenue that can be used for environmental protection. Yet, even here, the environmental case is vulnerable to policy reversals, as demonstrated by New Labour's abandonment of automatic, above-inflation increases in fuel duty following the 2000 petrol protests. Indeed, New Labour has not established the link between eco-taxation and social equity, leaving eco-taxes to appear regressive and punitive. Additionally, Green organizations welcome the government's stated aim of addressing Third World poverty, but little progress has been made in terms of debt relief (ensuring that developing countries have fewer resources to address ecological problems), in terms of the West's over-consumption (with poorest countries suffering disproportionately from the resulting pollution) or in terms of global trade (with New Labour supporting a laissez-faire version of globalization).

Overall, the government's environmental record is unimpressively modest. Some, though, have insisted that New Labour's version of social democracy at least points in the direction of the kind of 'ecological modernization' that other nations have implemented (Jacobs, 1999; cf. Callaghan, 2000). Is this the correct approach to adopt or must we search elsewhere if we are to develop a Green welfare state?

Towards Green Social Policies

If New Labour's approach is largely inadequate, then what are the alternatives? How might environmentalism be allowed to shape social policies? There are basically two schools of thought that deserve mention. *Modernization* basically says that existing systems, relations, practices and institutions can and should be adapted for Green ends; *radicalization* says that a more fundamental restructuring of our societies and economies is needed. In this final section, we will pay more attention to the latter, not because it is necessarily the superior of the two (indeed, the schools overlap to a certain extent) but to help to redress the greater amount of attention that modernization has received.

Modernization

Modernization is a reformist and pragmatic doctrine that has five core themes (Mol and Sonnenfeld, 2000: 4–7):

1. Science and technology should be utilized more carefully than at present in order to prevent environmental problems at source. Modernization is therefore technocratic, although this does not necessarily imply a techno-logical determinism since the social context of technological innovation is equally important.

2. A mixed economy of markets, state agencies and civic actors is needed to ensure that ecological goals are pursued. This means bringing together representatives from business, government and Green social movements in order to find common ground.

3. The nation-state is being, and should be, relegated in importance. On one level, decentralized and bottom-up mechanisms of decision making, management and regulation are necessary; on another, these forms of governance must be coordinated on a supranational stage, through global forums and organizations.

4. Social movements must be accorded a greater role in decision making and agenda setting, although conversely this means that such social movements must eschew purely oppositional stances (an accusation often levelled at the anti-globalization and anti-capitalism movement, for instance).

5. The environment must not be regarded as being in competition with market forces and efficiency – a dichotomy perpetuated as much by Green fundamentalists as by anti-environmentalists – although markets certainly need regulating if social and ecological inequalities are to be avoided.

Such ideas have mainly been applied to the areas of economic policy, public policy and environmental management, rather than to social policy per se. This may be due to neglect or may simply reflect the view, held by many, that social policy is of secondary importance. It is health and health care that have arguably received most attention (although taxation and employment are also recognized as important) (cf. Weale et al., 2000). Health care systems have increasingly come to be labelled 'ill health systems', that is, as trying to relieve the symptoms of pollution, for instance, rather than preventing them at source. Therefore, a Green health system would be one fully integrated into policies regarding waste, pollution, urban planning, transport, food and risk manage-ment, reflecting the idea that ill health has social causes requiring socially inte-grative solutions. Green social policies, then, do not so much restructure welfare institutions as assimilate them across multiple dimensions of gover-nance: rather than confining policies to separate administrative boxes, modern-ization recommends a multiscalar approach which replaces boxes with much more complex and reflexive networks of decision making. One consequence of this is that both politicians and academics have to expand their view of what is and is not relevant to the subject of social policy, attending to issues that have traditionally been excluded, for example water and energy policy (Huby, 2002).

Radicalization

If modernization is essentially reformist, then radicalization is more ambitious regarding both the means and ends of social transformation. This does not mean that radicalization abandons reformism (Fitzpatrick with Caldwell, 2001) but it does mean that reformism need not be limited to modest and relatively conservative objectives. Therefore, although radicalization agrees with much of the above – especially the third point regarding localization and globalization – it regards modernization as the beginning rather than the end of social reorganization (Christoff, 1996; van der Heijden, 1999). Consequently, rather than burying welfare reform within a broader concern for economic and public policies, social policy comes much more to the foreground. This means that the radical Green critique is too wide-ranging for justice to be done for it here, so the discussion is limited to four key proposals: basic income; a greater role for the informal economy; working-time reductions; and a revolution in the tax system. Let us look at each of these in turn.

A *basic income* would be received by every man, women and child periodically (whether on a weekly, monthly or annual basis) as an unconditional right of citizenship, that is, without reference to marital or employment status, employment history or intention to seek employment (van Parijs, 1992, 1995; Fitzpatrick, 1999a). It would replace most of the benefits, tax reliefs and tax allowances that currently exist, and could be age-related, for example with a higher basic income for elderly people. Basic income therefore represents an alternative both to means testing and the social insurance principle.

Basic income has been defended from all parts of the ideological spectrum, although for different reasons and with different implications for its design and implementation (Fitzpatrick, 1999a). For those on the Right, it is the logical extension of a means-tested system. Some in the political Centre, such as Tony Atkinson (1996), argue that a basic income should not be received unconditionally but only by those who perform some socially useful activity. For those on the Left, basic income only makes sense as a precursor to a socialized economy. Some feminists have also supported the idea. Where do Green ideas fit into the debate? To what extent can a basic income be thought of as a Green social policy? There are three potential advantages that a basic income holds for Green welfare reforms (Fitzpatrick, 1999a: Ch. 9).

According to most Greens, as the discussion above makes clear, we should no longer equate 'well-being' with 'economic growth', implying that more sustainable forms of growth should be found. By being unconditional, a basic income suggests that there are ways of contributing to society other than through paid work. By being paid irrespective of job record and status, a basic income undercuts the employment ethic and so challenges the productivist assumptions which legitimate that ethic. For environmentalists, people should be opting out of the labour market: the fewer people who are actually contributing to growth, the more the brakes will be applied to such growth. In theory, the higher the basic income, the slower the rate of economic growth, although others point to the potential flaws in this argument.

The second major reason why many environmentalists support a basic income is because they hold it to embody an ethic of common ownership. Greens insist that the earth's resources should be thought of as held in common, so that being a global citizen means being a steward or a trustee whose duty it is to hand on the earth to the next generation of common owners. This means that a certain proportion of wealth (which ultimately derives from this common ownership) should be shared out unconditionally. Whereas the present transfer system provides most to those who contribute the most to environmentally damaging growth, a basic income would express and embody a communal egalitarianism.

The final reason why many Greens support a basic income is because it could reduce or eliminate poverty and unemployment traps and so would make part-time work and, depending upon its level, low-paid work more attractive. As part-time employment became more financially worthwhile, many people might take up the option of working part time and it is possible that an expansion in work-sharing activities and sabbaticals could result. In short, a basic income would provide a guaranteed minimum income for all (by repairing the holes in the benefit safety net), would not be a tax on jobs and would permit flexibility without being a charter for low-paid casualization.

However, there are also three principal reasons why Greens might not wish to support a basic income. First, although a basic income could have a role to play in a future ecological society, its ability to carry us forward into that society may be limited. The achievement of a Green society and economy is going to require a massive change in public consciousness and institutional reorganization, whereas a basic income might do no more than consolidate existing values, assumptions and habits (Dobson, 2000). The second Green objection concerns the unconditional nature of a basic income. On one level, it is true that a basic income would enable people to opt out of the 'employment society', with its ethos of competition and acquisition, and pursue other activities. The trouble is that there is no guarantee that these other activities will be environmentally friendly: perhaps they would merely be parasitic on the very productivism and materialism which Greens strenuously oppose. André Gorz (1992), for example, argues that although a guaranteed minimum income is a necessary condition for social participation, it is not a sufficient condition and, for a long time, Gorz insisted that the provision of a basic income to an individual should be conditional upon the performance of a minimum amount of work during his/her lifetime. The final objection states that there is a contradiction between the decentralization which Greens desire and the fact that a basic income would have to be administered centrally, for example to facilitate redistribution from rich areas to poor ones. If a Green society would need to be as localized and decentralized as possible, then a basic income may conflict with this objective.

The second recommendation made by Greens is for the *informal economy to play a greater role*. By the informal economy is meant the range of activities that contribute to social well-being but are not recognized by official measurements since they lie outside the formal economy of production, consumption and labour (Fitzpatrick, 1999b). This informal economy is also known as the 'third sector', that is, a 'region' of civil society that is not reducible to the public/state sector or to the private/market one. Some insist that the informal economy constitutes a site of welfare provision that is already important and one that could be made still more important in the future.

One example of informal exchange that has attracted much attention in recent years is local exchange and trading systems (LETS). LETS are schemes to encourage people to exchange goods and services within their local communities (Williams, 2002). Each LETS is a non-profit making network of local residents who trade goods and services with each other using a local currency. Each member advertises the skills he or she has to offer and/or the goods he or she has to sell, while being encouraged to buy skills and goods from other LETS' members. When a purchase is made, the relevant units of the local currency are transferred from the purchaser's account to that of the provider's. This local currency is issued by its members rather than a bank and so is potentially unlimited. Economic activity need no longer be restricted by a lack of money, no interest is payable and there is no incentive for people to accumulate savings as the money is worthless outside the group.

The attraction of LETS for Greens is that local currencies encourage local trading and therefore place less pressure upon national and international infrastructures (Barry, 1999: 163–4). They may be ways of promoting non-employment forms of work outside the formal economy and have also been championed as a way of alleviating inequity between the rich and poor. Williams (2002) has addressed the relevance of LETS to unemployment, stating that LETS can be viewed as a way of reducing social inequalities by encouraging the participation of the unemployed in informal work. The unemployed are able to trade their time in order to enhance their standard of living and improve their chances of finding work in the formal economy. LETS may also provide people with the opportunity to increase their stock of 'social capital', given that they are networks which are based upon, and seem to enhance, trust.

Environmentalists therefore recommend that more should be made of LETS and similar schemes, for example those based upon exchanges of time. Claus Offe, to take one example, encourages the growth of what he calls 'co-operation circles':

> our model of a 'co-operation circle' proposes that the collectivization of provision be organized neither in a communitarian nor in an administrative manner, but in the form of a market, albeit with two provisos. First, that the exchange of services should take place not through the medium of money, but through service vouchers valid only among members and only for the purpose of trade in services between a locally delimited number of households. Second, that the coming into being and maintenance of a market of this type, with nonconvertible currency, should be publicly subsidized, not financially, but through the provision of rooms, equipment, payments in kind, and human capital. (Offe, 1996: 142)

Offe is suggesting that a combination of cooperation circles and basic income (which he also supports) would help to carry us forward into an ecosocialist society, an alternative to the welfare capitalism of the 20th century.

The third Green proposal is for *systematic reductions in working time*. This objective has long attracted support from organized labour. Think of a society consisting of 100 people where there is 10 per cent unemployment, that is, 10 people not in paid work. If the other 90 individuals each spend 40 hours per week in employment, this adds up to a total of 3600 hours per week (90×40). The traditional strategy for addressing that unemployment would either consist of reducing the wages of the 90 (an approach favoured by the Right) or creating more jobs for the excluded 10, perhaps in the public sector (usually favoured by the Left). Since both strategies lead to well-documented problems, an alternative is to redistribute the amount of paid work available: instead of 90 people working for 40 hours, all 100 could work for 36 hours, leaving no one in unemployment.

In practice, things could not be that simple. There may be 'bottlenecks' of one form or another, meaning that the unemployment is not mopped up completely, and opponents point to an intractable feature of working-time reductions. If the 90 people continue to be paid the same gross wage after the reductions as they were before, this is equivalent to a wage rise that increases production costs which the employer will simply pass back to those 90 people in the form of higher prices. Alternatively, the wages of those 90 individuals could be reduced as an exchange for the extra free time they have gained, but this is something which most are likely to resist. However, a counterargument suggests that reductions could be implemented without these problems emerging, due to increases in productivity (Little, 2002).

The Left are attracted to working-time reductions since, with more people in employment, the power of labour is enhanced. For Greens, the attraction lies in taking the emphasis away from paid work (although there is an additional requirement to ensure that the jobs which remain are made more ecologically friendly), so freeing up time for the wider range of activities which, as we noted above, they regard as important for social and environmental well-being. Adrian Little (2002) emphasizes these points in his analysis of André Gorz, a long-standing proponent of working-time reductions (Gorz, 1999), although Little also notes the potential problems of such reductions for Greens; for example the possibility that they would divert time and energy away from more immediate problems of resource depletion and pollution.

The final recommendation is one that we mentioned earlier: *eco-taxation*. Yet, while eco-taxes are now widely regarded as acceptable, so long as their economic and social benefits can be demonstrated, Greens tend to go further than the current orthodoxy allows. This may or may not involve support for much higher levels of eco-taxation than presently exist but, perhaps more importantly, it involves a radical change in the source of taxation. Land is of key importance here. In a globalized era, many worry that the levels of taxation needed to maintain high levels of social expenditure are not going to be sustainable. The mobility of financial capital, in particular, makes capital flight and damaging currency speculation more of a problem; and the Internet may be a means of avoiding tax liabilities through the creation of 'offshore' accounts and by making taxable exchanges harder for authorities to detect. Arguably, one solution is to shift the burden of taxation towards land, with those who occupy the most and/or the wealthiest land having the heaviest liability; and because land does not move – although its value certainly alters – the problems generated by globalization and network technologies are partly (although not entirely) alleviated.

James Robertson (1994) once estimated that, based on 1990 values, the absence of a site-value tax on land might be costing up to £90 billion a year to UK taxpayers. If so, the amount of revenue that could be raised by taxing common resources more accurately would be immense: not only land but also energy, the environment's capacity to absorb pollution and waste, urban space, road, water and air traffic, water, the electromagnetic spectrum, genetic resources and the value arising from issuing new money (Robertson, 2002; cf. Fitzpatrick, 2002). Such revenue would fund not only high levels of social expenditure but also measures to create a sustainable society and economy, including basic income and working-time reductions.

Conclusion

At the beginning of this chapter we made the point that the environmental critique of social policy had barely registered with politicians and policy makers and we wondered whether this was due to analytical weakness, political ignorance or political conservatism. It may be that all these factors are relevant and readers are left to make up their own minds. However, we cannot help but feel that, if we are to develop Green social policies, the main challenge over the coming years will involve working out how to operate within the political orthodoxy while pushing it in directions that it does not yet wish to travel.

Further Reading

Cahill, M. (2002) *The Environment and Social Policy*, London: Routledge.
Cahill, M. and Fitzpatrick, T. (eds) (2002) *Environmental Issues and Social Welfare*, Oxford: Blackwell.
Fitzpatrick, T. and Cahill, M. (eds) (2002) *Environment and Welfare*, Basingstoke: Palgrave Macmillan.
Huby, M. (1998) *Social Policy and the Environment*, Buckingham: Open University Press.

CHAPTER 19

Genetics and Social Policy: New Science, Old Issues

TOM SHAKESPEARE

Previous editions of this volume, in common with most texts in the social policy field, have no entry for genetics in the index. There is some irony in this. A century ago, genetics – in the form of eugenics – was one of the dominant concerns of social policy. The 'science' of eugenics, espoused by Left and Right in Britain, mainstream opinion in the United States, the social democratic states of Scandinavia and thereafter by many countries throughout the world, dominated thinking about many social problems (Thom and Jennings, 1996). Pioneers of progressive thought – the Webbs, Marie Stopes, George Bernard Shaw, H.G. Wells, Richard Titmuss – were enthusiastic eugenists. Eugenics is part of the ancestry of many of the social sciences, for example responsible for key concepts and tools in statistics, as well as the origin of many health and social care professions.

This chapter will begin by summarizing recent developments in genetics, and the main medical applications which result from our new knowledge. The next section will explore some of the implications of these applications for the NHS. The penultimate section will look at the impacts of genetics on specific social groups, for example education and criminal justice. Finally, the chapter will conclude with a brief discussion of possible future policy challenges.

As the science discussion below illustrates, genetics is a rapidly changing field, and it is incautious to speculate about either the potential or the limitations of this science to change society. It has been said that people overestimate the short-term impact of genetics and underestimate the long-term impact of genetics. The media encourage us to think that genetics is changing our world in drastic ways, particularly with talk of designer babies. Recent analyses have encouraged this type of speculation (Silver, 1998; Fukuyama, 2002). Scientists retort that these developments will never be possible in these forms and that we should restrict our discussions to what is currently possible. But Barbara Katz Rothman makes a strong argument for considering future possibilities before they arise:

> The scientists quickly speak up: that isn't possible, they reassure us, you don't understand the genetics involved. Five years later, of course, that is possible, and then it is too late to decide whether or not to do it: we wake up to find it done. (Rothman, 1998: 37)

Genetics presents many challenges for analysts of social policy. One is the difficulty of prediction and the speed of change: by the time this chapter is published, it will certainly be out of date in drastic ways. A second is the steep learning curve in science. A third is the need to engage more closely with bioethics. A fourth may be the need to abandon some of our cherished assumptions about human differences and human nature. Once again, biology is coming to the fore as an issue in politics and social policy, this time with stronger scientific foundations than in the 19th and early 20th centuries. But the same issues of justice remain relevant if societies are to avoid the old dangers of increasing stigma, discrimination and inequality.

Overview of Recent Developments in Genetics

The implications of recent advances in the science of human genetics are more important than their current limited impact on clinical medicine and society. To read newspapers and listen to politicians and pundits would be to imagine that we were about to enter a utopia of longer lives and miracle cures, or else a brave new world of discrimination and eugenics. Yet both the promise and the threat of genetics have been overstated.

The momentum of genetic discovery has progressed with increasing rapidity, since James Watson and Francis Crick identified the double helix structure of the DNA molecule in 1953. A major impetus was provided by the US–UK Human Genome Project, which reported a rough draft in the year 2000, amidst much hype and after spending an estimated £3 billion. This means that the majority of the three billion 'letters' which make up our genes – estimated at about thirty thousand – have been transliterated. We know what some of the genes do. We have identified some of the mutations which cause genetic disease. But science is far from understanding the whole picture of how genes interact with each other to produce a phenotype, in other words, a living breathing organism. In particular, we still have very limited knowledge of the complex and multiple role of genes in contributing to the development of our brains and, by inference, our behaviours. While it is uncontroversial to observe that genes affect human behaviour, the details of scientific claims regarding that interaction are very much a subject for debate.

The potential benefits of genetic knowledge are various. First, science will be able to understand the molecular basis of both health and disease. Rather than classifying by symptoms or effects, medicine will increasingly proceed by understanding the different genetic changes in cells and proteins. As well as improving diagnosis, this will potentially improve drug discovery, because more targets for pharmaceutical action will be identified. Moreover, each individual differs minutely from every other human being, by approximately one genetic letter in every twelve hundred. This means that people react differently to drugs. In a cohort of people suffering a disease and prescribed a drug, some will react well and benefit, some will not benefit to the same extent while others may suffer side effects or 'adverse drug reactions'. Adverse drug reaction is the fourth largest cause of ill health in the US and leads to human suffering, as well as litigation and commercial damage to pharmaceutical companies. Specific drugs which act safely and effectively on specific groups of individuals should be a major spin-off of genetic knowledge.

Second, there is the promise of solutions to genetic disease which work at the genetic level. That is, where genes are missing or faulty, delivery of correct versions of the gene to the relevant organ system could rectify the problem. This 'gene therapy' has generated major hope and hyperbole over the past few decades. But despite considerable investment in therapies for conditions such as cystic fibrosis, there have been few unequivocal successes. In some cases, patients have died or suffered considerable adverse reaction in trials. However, one major breakthrough has occurred with the disease severe combined immune deficiency (SCID). In trials in Paris (May 2000), and the UK (April 2002), children with this disorder ('bubble children') seem to have been cured by gene therapy. The difficulties of getting the right gene to the right part of the body in the right quantity are not trivial. Existing techniques using virus vectors are clumsy and so far have been largely ineffectual. It is believed that ultimately success will result from the research, but it may be many decades before science has enough expertise to make gene therapy an everyday clinical reality.

Third, genetic knowledge coupled with reproductive technology promises new treatments through leading-edge research into stem cells and cloning. Here, defective organs or tissues may be replaced by tissues that have been engineered in laboratories. For example, embryonic stem cells have the potential to become any tissue in the body. Scientists are attempting to control differentiation of these cells, so that they can grow heart muscle, nerve cells or insulin-producing cells. If they eventually become successful, tissue banks might offer the hope of a cure to people with degenerative diseases such as Parkinson's, heart disease or diabetes. Therapeutic cloning builds on these stem cell approaches in order to ensure that the tissues produced are a genetic match for the patient, by inserting their own DNA via the somatic cell nuclear transfer technique. This same cloning technique might be used reproductively to engineer animals who either grow whole organs, or produce particular hormones and drugs in their milk, for treating human diseases. Needless to say, technical difficulties and ethical concerns abound in this area.

Finally, and more relevant at the current time, genetics gives patients the potential to know about their health risks and their danger of developing late-onset disease via genetic testing. *Diagnostic testing* is where people who are experiencing symptoms can have tests to identity their disease. *Predictive testing* allows people who are currently symptom-free to find out whether they are at risk of developing late-onset disease. In the latter case, knowledge may not lead to specific genetic or even medical solutions. It may allow prophylactic measures, such as change of diet for people at risk of heart disease, or even mastectomy for people at risk of breast cancer. It may also suggest possible future outcomes (for example onset of Huntington's disease in the four, fifth or sixth decade of life) which cannot be prevented. Single-gene disorders such as Huntington's disease are very rare. While there are more than four thousand such disorders, most occur only once in every ten or twenty thousand births. Multifactorial disorders – such as many cancers, heart disease, diabetes, Alzheimer's – are comparatively common. Genes contribute to the likelihood of developing such diseases. Knowing about your genetic make-up may give some predictive information about your future risks. However, understanding of the interaction of gene with gene, and genes with environment, is still incomplete.

Perhaps more controversial are those genetic tests which are connected with reproduction, due to the notorious histories of eugenics in Germany, Scandinavia, North America and many other countries in the first half of the 20th century. *Carrier testing* gives prospective parents information about recessive genes which they may be at risk of passing on to their children. Where a child gets the same recessive gene from each parent, serious diseases such as cystic fibrosis or sickle cell anaemia could result. *Prenatal genetic testing* might then be carried out during pregnancy to see if the fetus was affected. However, such testing is usually carried out only on families with a history of one of the rare single-gene disorders. *Prenatal screening* applies similar approaches to whole populations, identified either because of maternal age or some other risk factor, or because couples belong to an ethnic group with a high prevalence of a particular recessive disorder. However, very little *prenatal genetic screening* is currently available to the general population.

Most prenatal screening takes the form of ultrasound examination – which can show various fetal malformations and identify some genetic disorders – and maternal serum screening – which can highlight increased risk of Down syndrome and neural tube defects. The fifth and final form of testing is *neonatal testing* of children for inherited diseases. In conditions such as cystic fibrosis, early diagnosis and treatment can improve health outcomes. Yet where there are no treatments available, it is argued that testing might stigmatize children and infringe their autonomy (Clarke and Flinter, 1996).

In this section, the aim has been to give a briefing on the key terms and applications of genetic knowledge, as the basis for the discussion of social policy implications that follows. The intention is to show that the impact of genetics is still quite limited. Both advocates and opponents of genetic research and applications often overstate current possibilities. However, science is developing quickly. The gaps in our knowledge of gene–gene and gene–environment interaction will begin to be filled, partly through research such as the Icelandic and UK biobank initiatives. We will have a better understanding of how genes contribute both to somatic disease and personality, and advances in testing may make it easier and cheaper to do tests. In a few decades, individuals may be able to obtain a printout of hundreds of key genetic indicators very cheaply. During pregnancy, prospective parents may be able to look at a similar genetic profile of their developing fetus in the first trimester of pregnancy. Some will be able to afford pre-implantation genetic diagnosis and will be offered a choice from a selection of embryos in a petri dish, one or two of which would subsequently be implanted to produce a child not only free of major diseases and disease risks, but perhaps also selected for qualities of body or brain which might be advantageous. This is currently science fiction (Silver, 1998), but, in our lifetime, it may become science fact.

Implications for Health Care

Undoubtedly, genetics is having an increasing impact in the medical arena, which is likely to grow exponentially in years to come. This expanding role can be measured by increases in the numbers of people being referred for genetic testing. It is demonstrated by calls for an increased role for genetics in medical education. It is shown by an expansion in numbers of genetic counsellors and consultants in clinical genetics and by the increasing role that genetics plays in primary care.

It would be wrong to see these developments in purely technological terms. A focus on the scientific efficacy of tests and treatments, and the need for increased technical and scientific knowledge, can obscure the continuing importance of the art of medicine. Investment in genetic testing, for example, needs to be matched by investment in high-quality information to patients and effective counselling and other support services. Doctors and nurses need to know not just about molecular biology, but also about bioethics and psychology. This makes information, education and communication vital if the genomic revolution is truly to improve the delivery and experience of health care.

The financing of health care is a perennial issue in social policy. Previous editions of this volume have noted that health care inflation is higher than general inflation and increased investment in technological medicine has resulted in diminishing returns. The advent of genetic treatments may be an example of this trend. Diagnostic testing, prenatal screening, gene therapy and pharmacogenetics are all new possibilities which will have cost implications. Genetic knowledge creates a whole new class of patients, the presymptomatic healthy; along with the 'worried well', this huge group of people has the potential to overload primary care and specialist services.

However, advocates of genetics argue that new diagnostic techniques will have a rationalizing effect on medical care, which may contribute to major savings. For example, more precise molecular diagnosis may reduce the need for repeated tests to identify problems. Better prescribing of pharmaceuticals will not only reduce wasted or ineffectual medications, but should also reduce adverse drug reaction and consequent illness. Early identification of tumours and prophylactic measures such as mastectomy may save costly treatment regimes, as well as improve health outcomes.

A key area of potential saving would result if prospective parents terminated pregnancies affected by genetic diseases. One example is screening for Down syndrome, where approximately 90 per cent of women who have diagnostic tests terminate pregnancies which are found to be affected. Health economists and other medical professionals welcome this trend as an example of the potential benefits afforded by genetics to both the NHS and society at large. The discussion below will explore the extent to which the cost-effectiveness debate in prenatal screening risks returning society to the abuses of the eugenic past.

A second major saving would result if potential patients took action to avoid diseases to which they were predisposed. For example, people found to have alpha 1 antitrypsin disorder would be well advised to avoid smoking and polluted workplaces, because they have a susceptibility to lung disease. People with problems with cholesterol metabolism might avoid diets high in saturated fats. However, it would be simplistic to assume that 'forewarned is forearmed' and that genetic knowledge leads directly to gains for health promotion and behavioural change. It may be that knowledge of risk increases anxiety, but does not make people avoid diets, environments or behaviours that are harmful. The genetic nature of a diagnosis may serve to increase fatalism, due to the cultural assumptions that 'genetic equals pre-determined and inescapable'. Leading health psychologists report:

> The current evidence suggests that providing people with DNA derived inform-ation about risks to their health does not increase motivation to change behaviour beyond that achieved with non-genetic information. For some people, genetic information may even reduce motivation to change behaviour. (Marteau and Lerman, 2001: 1058)

In discussing the health care impact of new genetic knowledge, the commercialization of genetics is an important feature of the debate. This was underlined by the race to sequence the genome, which became a competition between the public collaborative effort led by the Wellcome Trust-funded Sanger Centre in the UK, and the private enterprise of the US corporation Celera, led by Craig Venter. Massive investment in gene discovery and patenting shows the commercial potential of genetic technology. While patenting of genes is permitted in the US, creating a 'gold rush' mentality, the UK and Europe are generally opposed to patents on DNA, as opposed to particular therapies or drugs resulting from research on genes. Many physi-cians have argued that biotechnology and pharmaceutical companies holding patents will use licensing arrangements to profit in the short term from diag-nostics. Potentially, the need to pay a fee for every genetic test would add massively to the NHS burden and reduce the likelihood of this knowledge benefiting the majority of patients. So far, the anticipated problems have not occurred, but anxieties remain.

In the post-genomic era, genetics and biotechnology are seen as key areas of commercial activity. The pharmaceutical industry is one of the few vigorous areas of UK manufacturing and is a key part of the economy. Prime Minister Blair has repeatedly called on UK science and capital to lead the world in reaping the commercial rewards of genetic research. The recent Department of Health/Department of Trade and Industry Genetic Knowledge Park Chal-lenge Fund was oriented towards exploiting the commercial potential of genetics, as well as improving NHS services and promoting public under-standing of science. The close commercial engagements which are envisaged in both academic molecular biology research and NHS diagnostic and other services are a source of concern to many scientists and clinicians.

Implications for Social Groups

Outside health care, genetics is only slowly beginning to have an impact on other areas of social policy. However, genetics has implications for issues such as criminal justice, education and social stratification. Abby Lippman (1994) has argued that a process of 'geneticization' leads to complex social problems being defined in terms of individual genetics. Inequality is legitimated, because the difficulties faced by socially excluded members of society are explained in terms of their own intellectual, physical or behavioural failures. We live in an age when genetic explanations have powerful resonances, and environmental explanations have been downplayed or discounted. Rather than seeking to improve social policy or remove social barriers, medicalization may lead to pharmaceutical or genetic solutions to problems ranging from disability to educational underachievement to criminality. At this stage, it is highly speculative to predict what scientific claims will lead to which future social policy outcomes. This section will look at the social groups on whom genetics is currently impacting, in order to start considering some possible effects of the new salience of biology.

Disabled people

Some of the loudest concerns about genetics have been expressed by disability rights groups, who have viewed prenatal screening as a new version of eugenics and fear a backlash against recent advances enjoyed by disabled people (Shakespeare, 1999). While the social model of disability has focused attention on barriers to the participation of people with impairments, a genetic approach redefines disability in individual terms. The increasing ability to diagnose conditions prenatally creates pressure for selective termination, which is regarded with horror by many disabled people. Those who support a woman's right to choose and parents' rights to genetic information still have major concerns about the lack of balanced information about disability, and the lack of support for women to continue pregnancies affected by disability. Prospective parents who are disabled face particular pressures to control their reproduction or avoid having children who inherit their conditions. Rhetoric about choice conceals the blame that is increasingly directed at people who refuse screening or knowingly bring disabled children into the world. Lack of support for disabled people and families means that the experience of having a disabled family member is more difficult than it need be and quality of life may be impaired because of poverty or lack of services. Arguments in favour of new screening programmes are made explicitly in terms of the savings to society from avoiding the birth of children with Down syndrome or other disabilities. All these factors are highly reminiscent of the bad old days of eugenics, and reinforce fears in the disability community that genetics is nothing but bad news. However, some disabled people also look forward to the promise of cures for degenerative conditions, for example gene therapy for cystic fibrosis, so it would be wrong to claim that there is unanimity about the impact of genetics. Whatever the perspectives of disabled people, their voices are rarely heard in policy debates on the new genetics, and this is an absence which urgently needs to be rectified: further research about the diverse views of disabled people is needed, together with research on how genetics changes perception of disability, and the potential for negative impacts on services for disabled people. It should be remembered that only 1 per cent of births are affected by congenital impairment, while approximately 12 per cent of the population are disabled. Genetics will not eliminate disabled people from society, but it might make their lives more difficult.

Women

Discussion of prenatal selection highlights the new pressures on women which may result from increasing availability of genetic information. Barbara Katz Rothman (1988) has written of the 'tentative pregnancy', where women become pregnant, but cannot bond with their child or look forward to parenthood until they have had a battery of tests in order to check that the baby is healthy. Every year, approximately 200 British women choose to terminate wanted pregnancies as a result of a diagnosis of fetal abnormality and many experience grief and guilt as a result. Even more women lose their wanted pregnancy as a result of miscarriages caused by invasive procedures such as amniocentesis and chorion villus sampling. These are the hidden costs of better reproductive technologies, which do not appear in the cost–benefit accounting of health economists.

The additional pressures and responsibilities which genetics creates for women do not end with prenatal testing. Because women continue to take more responsibility for looking after their families, they may feel particular pressure to look after their own health and take advantage of predictive testing to avoid the onset of disease. Research by Nina Hallowell (1999) into the psychological impact of testing for the BRCA1 and BRCA2 genes which are related to breast and ovarian cancer reveals that women often feel compelled to have these tests, because of feelings of responsibility to their families, and sometimes take prophylactic measures if they find that they are at high risk of developing cancer.

Finally, it should be mentioned that prenatal sex selection may become more widespread in future. While termination of female fetuses does occur in many parts of the world, with serious impacts on gender balance, it is rare in the United Kingdom, because it is only usually performed to avoid X-linked genetic disease. However, the new technique of pre-implantation genetic diagnosis allows couples to choose the sex of their potential child without resorting to the trauma of abortion. At the time of writing, regulatory authorities are about to consult widely on the acceptability of sex selection and many bioethicists believe that the technique should be permitted. Others argue that it will usually be boys who are preferred over girls and that this reflects and reinforces sexism.

Minority ethnic communities

Internationally, sex selection is associated with Asian countries such as India, China and Korea. Some UK commentators have claimed that opposition to sex selection is connected to racism, ethnocentricity and suspicion of the motives of minority ethnic couples seeking testing (Bradby, 1996: 309). This is only one of the ways in which genetic and reproductive technologies may be racialized. For example, each ethnic group is susceptible to different rare disorders. Among people of Asian or Mediterranean origin, thalassaemia is relatively common. Among people of African or Caribbean descent, sickle cell anaemia is a higher risk. Both these debilitating blood diseases can be detected prenatally and it is important to offer prospective parents the choice of screening. However, programmes to deal with these conditions have been associated with stigma and discrimination. The 1972 National Sickle Cell Anemia Control Act in the United States is an example of a policy which led to widespread problems for African-Americans who carried the sickle cell trait. All ethnic groups have their own pattern of susceptibility – among Caucasians, cystic fibrosis is comparatively common, for example – and it is important to ensure that the need for diagnosis and treatment does not lead to stigma and discrimination against either affected individuals or the entire ethnic group.

In designing services, it is important to ensure that issues of particular relevance to minority communities are not neglected. There are also dangers that stereotypes and ignorance will prevent programmes reaching those who need them, for example increasing numbers in the UK population are of a mixed ethnic background. People may appear to be white British, but may actually have grandparents originating in Africa, Asia or the Caribbean and are therefore at higher risk of specific genetic disorders associated with those populations (Anionwu and Atkin, 2001).

Conclusion

A fourth social group on whom genetics will increasingly impact is children. The increasing ability of parents to select the characteristics of their offspring may change the relationship which they have with them. If parents use sex selection to choose a son, intuitively they may be the sort of parents who rear their son in particularly gendered ways. If parents use pre-implantation genetic diagnosis to choose a baby who can donate chord blood or bone marrow to an existing child, they may think of that new baby differently, especially if that treatment is a failure. If the same technique is used to choose a baby with particular physical or intellectual advantages, the financial and emotional investments that the parents would have made in this child may lead to increased pressures for achievement or a particular career path.

This line of argument is speculative. But the debate about whether children should be tested for their susceptibility to genetic diseases, prior to their ability to consent for themselves, shows the controversies which already exist in this area. Genetics increasingly allows families and society to find out predictive information about children and this may increase pressure or stigma. For example, some children have dyslexia or other specific learning difficulties. Early diagnosis of this might be beneficial, as it could lead to targeted educational responses and better achievement. When it is considered that a high proportion of convicted criminals, in some studies, have undiagnosed dyslexia, the broader societal benefits of such a strategy may be clear.

But what about testing children for genes which contribute to overall intelligence? There is controversy over whether anything useful could be derived from genetic information, because genetic factors in intelligence will be multiple and complex. But if it was possible, it might be socially and individually corrosive. Parents might want to test embryos for such genes, to ensure a brighter child. Given that such technologies would be costly and unlikely to be available through public health systems, differential access might generate increased inequality.

Dyslexia is not the only educational impairment connected with criminality. In previous decades, spurious research has linked XYY males to greater propensities to violence and offending. There is a substantial programme of more scientifically reputable research tracing the genetics of antisocial behaviour. If this research results in robust findings, this could have major implications for criminal justice and the early prediction of susceptibility to subsequent offending behaviour, as well as obvious dangers of stigma, surveillance and human rights violations. The contemporary moral panic about paedophilia may be relevant here.

The mention of intelligence and criminality takes the argument back to the historical experience of eugenics with which this chapter began. But most scientific research in behavioural genetics is free of the obnoxious racism which characterized early 20th-century approaches to these issues and it cannot be rejected so easily. If some of the claims currently made about genetics, neuroscience and behaviour are subsequently verified, there will be major implications for social policy and our understandings of human action and the appropriate social response. Recent phenomena such as Prozac and Ritalin demonstrate the potential impacts on the lives of children and adults of pharmaceutical applications of these new insights.

None of this is to biologize social policy. However, biology has to be added to the other factors – cultural, social, familial – which influence human lives, and the social sciences have an urgent task to understand and engage with the challenge of genetics and neuroscience. We look forward to reading the results of this inquiry in subsequent editions of this volume.

Further Reading

Buchanan, A., Block, D., Daniels, N. and Wikler, D. (2000) *From Chance to Choice: Genetics and Justice,* Cambridge: Cambridge University Press.

Conrad, P. and Gabe, J. (eds) 1999) *Sociological Perspectives on the New Genetics,* Oxford: Blackwell.

Fukuyama, F. (2002) *Our Posthuman Future: Consequences of the Biotechnology Revolution,* London: Profile Books.

Kerry, A. and Shakespeare, T. (2002) *Genetic Politics,* Cheltenham: New Clarion Press.

Marteau, T. and Richards, M. (eds) (1996) *The Troubled Helix,* Cambridge: Cambridge University Press.

Petersen, A. and Bunton, R. (2002) *The New Genetics and the Public's Health,* London: Routledge.

New Labour, New Welfare State?

CHRIS PIERSON AND NICK ELLISON

Any survey of recent developments in British social policy is bound to be, in part, although only in part, a judgement upon the governing record of New Labour. As an exclusive interest in the actions of government gives way to a focus upon more complex networks of governance and in the context of Labour's own programme of constitutional devolution, it makes less sense than ever to see social policy as confined to the dispensations of a few key ministries within central government (on new modes of governance and changed patterns of delivery, see Peters this volume). In the course of this book, we have seen how private companies, voluntary and not-for-profit organizations have developed a whole series of new relationships with the public sector. Increasingly, government represents itself as the regulator rather than the provider of social services. Nonetheless, national government remains the single most important site of social *policy making* and welfare has been an area of intense policy activism for Labour since 1997. In this context, it is important to remind ourselves of just how extraordinary and recent has been the transformation of the electoral fortunes of the Labour Party (and, mirroring this, Britain's Conservatives). In 1997, Labour was a party that had not won a national election for more than 20 years. In a rapidly changing economy, its 'natural' electoral base seemed destined to wither away and with each electoral defeat there was a growing chorus which suggested that the party might be doomed to follow it. In the face of this recent history, Labour secured a stunning victory in 1997 and, almost more remarkably for those who had seen earlier Labour administrations fall apart, found itself returned with a barely-dented majority by a largely uninterested electorate in May 2001.

Of course, the party that returned from the political wilderness in 1997 was not the party that Margaret Thatcher's Conservatives had defeated in 1979 but the aggressively rebranded 'New' Labour of Tony Blair and his fellow 'modernizers' (Driver and Martell, 1998). New Labour was self-consciously different from the party that had preceded it and particularly from the demonic folk memory of what Old Labour had been. Friends and adversaries alike saw a change, not least in what had (alongside its ties to the trade unions) been the heartland of Labour's political identity, the welfare state. Many of these changes were explored in Part II of this book. Critics to the Left, and a few begrudging admirers to the Right, saw in New Labour's social policy reforms a continuation of the 'marketization' of welfare that had been the hallmark of the Conservative reform agenda after 1987. By contrast, supporters of the reform agenda drew attention to its sources in the 'new progressivism' of America's New Democrats, increasingly developing their own home-grown account of this politics fashioned around the idea of the 'third way' (most influentially, see Giddens, 1998, 2000).

Unfortunately, neither the supporters nor the detractors of New Labour's social policy have much interest in giving an accurate account of Labour's past experience with the welfare state. For advocates of the third way, the welfare state was part of the problematic heritage of 'old-style social democracy'. Paternalistic, patriarchal and inefficient, it 'create[d] almost as many problems as it resolve[d]' (Giddens, 1998: 16). For those who resisted the 'newness' of Labour, the welfare state was an expression of Labour's historic commitment to an inclusive social citizenship and greater social equality.

Neither of these views really does justice to Labour's lived experience. Certainly, the welfare state was never uniquely Labour's project. Nor was it the only route through which it sought to bring about social change. ('Industrial democracy' was however one ill-fated alternative; see Shaw, 1996). Tony Crosland, the arch post-war revisionist, while including the welfare state in his list of 'twelve socialist doctrines', was very clear that the welfare state could be just as much an instrument of conservative as progressive forces (Crosland, 1956: 49–50). And even where welfare was a part of Labour's programme for social reform, practising politicians were always concerned with the mundane issues of disincentives, effective management and, above all, cost. Even the NHS, the most sacred of all sacred cows in the Labour pantheon, was not quite immune to criticism (although extraordinarily difficult to reform).

Nonetheless, the welfare state did become a sort of shorthand for Labour's 'strategy of equality'. Although always marked by its New Liberal origins and repeatedly knocked off course, social policy (alongside a macroeconomic policy delivering full employment and economic growth) was seen by Labour as an instrument of incremental social change – gradually improving the quality of public services (including health care, education and housing). While markets should remain, as the maximizers of economic efficiency, growth and personal choice, they would no longer determine the life chances of ordinary citizens. In so far as Britain had a social democratic tradition, this was what it looked like. And in pursuing these strategies, at least until the mid-1970s, Labour clearly felt that it had not just the majority of its own working-class constituency but also much of post-war middle England on its side.

Of course, Labour had limited opportunities to put its welfare state commitment to the test. With some oversimplification, the history of post-war Labour governments (at least down to 1997) can be seen as one of serial disappointment. Elected in an atmosphere of expectation (at least in 1945 and 1964), Labour governments found their policy ambitions repeatedly frustrated by economic difficulties (not always of their own making). In any case, for most of the time, it was the Conservatives who had charge of the welfare state. Nonetheless, 'pre-New' Labour had a reasonably clear (if not entirely consistent) idea of what it wanted to do and a defensible account of why, if not quite socialist, theirs was a social policy with progressive intent.

The approach of New Labour is self-consciously different. Its supporters still speak of it as a party committed to a politics with progressive intent, in social policy as elsewhere (see Blair, 2001). But they insist that the circumstances for pursuing a successful progressive politics have changed decisively – so that the politics of progress now rest with the imperatives of the third way. The older politics of welfare may have been benign in intent, but it was flawed in its construction and perversely counterproductive in many of its outcomes. In any case, the social and political world within which welfare must now operate has been transformed. Globalization is often cited as the key process here but it is supplemented with evidence on the changing role of women, changing patterns of family formation, technological advance and a growing disaffection with mainstream politics and parties (see Reich, 1992; Cerny, 1995; Blair, 1998a; Giddens, 1998, 2000; see also Cerny and Evans this volume). In Giddens' formulation, the move from 'simple' to 'complex' modernity and the corresponding emergence of new forms of manufactured uncertainty (both social and environmental) vitiate the older forms of progressive politics. Above all, these changes made the 'old' forms of Centre-Left macroeconomic intervention and top-down welfare counterproductive.

Under these radically changed circumstances, progressives have to shift their aspirations from the defence of the welfare state to the active promotion of the 'competition state'. It is no longer possible for the state itself to guarantee the economic security and social protection of its citizens. Its new challenge is to legislate for flexibility and the enhancement of human capital in a symbiotic relationship with domestic civil society and an increasingly global business and financial community. The new agenda also requires a quite new dispensation for both governors and citizens. In welfare, what had once been seen as largely a technical issue or else a question of the state's responsibility for its citizens is increasingly recast as an issue of the moral responsibility of individuals to provide for their own (and their family's) well-being, supported by the state. 'Passive welfare' is no longer an option. Citizens have to be encouraged and enabled to be active entrepreneurs in the promotion of their own welfare. So, for example, the state moves from being the cashier of unemployment benefit to the enabler (not necessarily the provider) of the training that makes the unemployed 'job-ready'. It can also encourage participation in the workforce through supplementing low incomes (a minimum wage, earned income tax credits). The key aspiration is to build a 'social investment state' which will promote '*positive welfare*, to which individuals themselves contribute and which is functional for wealth creation' (Giddens, 1998: 117).

At the same time, New Labour's reforms have built in new forms of accountability. The welfare state of Old Labour was premised upon a trust in the competence and honesty of public servants (an extension of a still older ethic of civil service). But New Labour shares with its Conservative forerunners (and, so it supposes, the electorate) a mistrust of the integrity and capacity of those charged with delivering public services. Thus the public services are now replete with new forms of accountability – contracts, league tables, competition with other providers – which are supposed to make them consumer- rather than producer-focused. Although this means that there is some continuity with their neoliberal predecessors (whose reforms, particularly in the welfare area, were not, so it seems to the advocates of New Labour, all bad), this is not the welfare agenda of the New Right. The intention is not to leave all to their fates in an unmediated market economy, or to confine public provision to those who cannot afford a private alternative, but rather to maximize value for money and opportunities/outcomes for the ordinary users of public services. Maximizing public service outputs is a progressive politics because it increases opportunities for ordinary citizens who cannot afford to opt out into private alternatives. The more responsive public sector gives consumer powers to clients whose status is not determined by their ability to pay. The sense is that the state can still be concerned with redistribution and inclusiveness – but now through the reallocation of opportunities rather than financial resources.

The key figures of both academic and political advocacy of the third way insist that theirs is an unambiguously progressive project. Indeed, Blair (2001) claims to represent the historical tendency of progressives of *all* ages, with the temporary affiliation of these progressive forces to the labour movement being seen as a rather embarrassing historical accident. Indeed, modernizers articulate a 'world-historical' aspiration to reunite the 'liberal' and 'labour' wings of radical or progressive opinion whose division throughout the 20th century made this the century of conservatism. But can this New Labour welfare programme really be cast as a new form of progressivism adjusted to the changing needs of a new century?

There are certainly plenty who say that it cannot. Critics argue that, whether as a culpable act of betrayal or in the recognition that, for social democrats, 'the game is up', Labour's modernizers have abandoned even the mildly progressive aspirations of earlier generations of Labour politicians in favour of Thatcherism mark II (or III, depending upon the status one attributes to the Major interregnum). For these critics, social and economic change or the all-purpose 'imperatives of globalization' have been wheeled out to justify a strategy of more coercive labour markets ('flexibility'), deregulated public services ('consumer-responsiveness'), top-heavy regimes of accountability ('transparency') and privatization ('autonomy'), all of which belong firmly to the logic of neoliberalism. (Among the critics, see especially Levitas, 1998; Hay, 1999.) The attention lavished upon social exclusion is largely a device for drawing attention away from the failure to address poverty. The concern with equality of opportunity evidences a failure to take seriously the growing inequality of both income and outcomes. Privatization plus 'accountability' is simply a way of worsening the terms and conditions of workers in the public sector. In all these areas, New Labour has taken over more or less seamlessly the agenda of the Conservatives.

Despite these well-founded criticisms, it might still be possible to defend New Labour as the party of progress. Self-consciously pragmatic, New Labour asks to be judged by outcomes not aspirations. Much criticized for sticking to Conservative spending plans in its first two years in office, in its second period in power Labour has shown a real willingness to spend ('invest') in the public sector. Gordon Brown was frequently seen to have effected some redistribution 'by stealth' (despite 'prudence' and the ubiquitous commitment not to raise rates of personal taxation) but in the 2002 spending review he committed the government to quite substantial increases in public expenditure in the period down to 2006 (HM Treasury, 2002). The methodology of league tables may be hopelessly flawed, and the evidence of measurable improvements in standards similarly unreliable, but this does not alter the fact that more money has been made available to schools and hospitals. Nor can the government's claims about labour market reform be entirely dismissed. Certainly, the UK's comparatively good record in terms of employment has much to do with its already severely deregulated labour market – and there are plenty of claims that labour market programmes do comparatively little to raise levels of employment (see Finn this volume). But to some extent, New Labour just faces the same paradox that has dogged all social democratic forces – old or new – that is, that the benefits for its natural constituency among wage and salary earners, whether secured through employment or the social wage, have finally to be derived from the assets of an economy in which investment decisions are in private hands. Promoting economic growth and maximizing employment are seemingly the necessary premises of a progressive politics but they are conditional upon the success of economies beholden to international economic forces. Unless one is willing to pose a revolutionary challenge to existing economic forces (the rejection of which is one of the defining criteria of a social democratic politics), maximizing employability is in the interests of those with little or no investment capital. Of course, this is not a zero-sum game, which is why not all social democracies are the same. But it does suggest the real – as opposed to the conveniently imagined – limits that the processes of globalization (whether new or not) pose for domestic political actors. Nor is it actually clear that all the 'anti-progressive' measures are quite as they seem. It was Julian Le Grand (1982) who pointed out that the provision of services 'free at the point of delivery' is not always, in practice, a 'strategy for equality'. Some areas of welfare expenditure have always redistributed *upwards* (the funding of students in tertiary education is a good example) and it is at least possible that the movement away from universalism in such areas might seem like a step *forward*.

But if we are to buy this story about New Labour, welfare and the third way, we should see just how modest (if real) are its ambitions. For all its failings, the older Labour view had an account of how social policy could deliver incremental change which truly modified the outcomes that markets dictated. For advocates of the third way, the global economy and its distributional outcomes are largely 'given'. The third way seeks to operate in the area of policy discretion these global forces leave, with a view to maximizing the opportunities of its citizens. In many ways, it is a classical (and not necessarily unworthy) exercise in social democratic politics: accommodating to what are perceived to be unshiftable limits to policy making, making the best of a bad job and saying that it was what one wanted to do anyway. But it's not clear that this really adds up to a new politics for a new century.

References

Abbreviations used in the References

BMA	British Medical Association	DWP	Department of Work and
CEC	Commission of the European		Pensions
	Communities	HFMA	Healthcare Financial Management
CfIT	Commission for Integrated		Association
	Transport	IPPR	Institute for Public Policy
DETR	Department of the Environment,		Research
	Transport and the Regions	JPPAP	Joint Prison/Probation
DfEE	Department for Education and		Accreditation Panel
	Employment	NAO	National Audit Office
DfES	Department for Education and	NDTF	New Deal Task Force
	Skills	NHSE	National Health Service
DH	Department of Health		Executive
DoE	Department of the Environment	NRU	Neighbourhood Renewal Unit
DoT	Department of Transport	OECD	Organization for Economic
DRC	Disability Rights Commission		Co-operation and Development
DSS	Department of Social Security	OFSTED	Office for Standards in Education
DTI/PAT	Department of Trade and	ONS	Office for National Statistics
	Industry/Policy Action Team	SEU	Social Exclusion Unit
DTLGR	Department of Transport, Local	SSI	Social Services Inspectorate
	Government and the Regions	TUC	Trades Union Congress

Abbott, E. and Bompas, K. (1943) *The Woman Citizen and Social Security* (London: Mrs Bompas).

Abbott, D., Morris, J. and Ward, L. (2001) *Disabled Children and Residential Schools: A Study of Local Authority Policy and Practice* (Bristol: Norah Fry Research Centre, University of Bristol).

Abbott, S., Florin, D., Fulop, N. and Gillam, S. (2000) *Primary Care Groups and Trusts: Improving Health*, Interim Report (London: King's Fund).

Acheson, D. (1998) *Independent Inquiry into Inequalities in Health: Report* (London: Stationery Office).

Adams, J.G.U. (1990) 'Car Ownership Forecasting: Pull the Ladder Up, or Climb Back Down?', *Traffic Engineering and Control* 31(3): 136–41.

Age Concern (1999) *Values and Attitudes in an Ageing Society* (London: Age Concern).

Age Concern (2001) *Age Concern's Response to the Department of Health Consultation on the Single Assessment Process* (London: Age Concern).

Alcock, P., Craig, G., Lawless, P., Pearson, S. and Robinson, D. (1998) *Inclusive Regeneration: Local Authorities' Corporate Strategies for Tackling Disadvantage* (Centre for Regional Economic and Social Research, Sheffield: Sheffield Hallam University).

Alford, R.R. (1975) *Health Care Politics* (Chicago: University of Chicago Press).

All-Party Committee on Education (2002) *Report on Individual Learning Accounts* (London: House of Commons).

Allan, K. (2001) *Communication and Consultation: Exploring Ways for Staff to Involve People with Dementia in Developing Services* (Bristol: Policy Press).

Anderson, T. and Leal, D. (1991) *Free Market Environmentalism* (Columbia: Westview Press).

Anderton B., Riley R. and Young G. (2000) *New Deal for Young People: First Year Analysis of Implications for the Macroeconomy*, Employment Service, Research and Development Report, ESR 33 (Sheffield: ES).

Andrews, D.A., Zinger, I., Hoge, R.D. et al. (1990) 'Does Correctional Treatment Work? A Clinically Relevant and Psychologically Informed Meta-analysis', *Criminology*, **28**: 369–404.

Anionwu, E.N. and Atkin, K. (2001) *The Politics of Sickle Cell and Thalassaemia*, (Buckingham: Open University Press).

Armstrong, H. (1999) 'A New Vision for Housing in England', in T. Brown (ed.), *Stakeholder Housing* (London: Pluto Press).

Ashford, D.E. (1982) *British Dogmatism and French Pragmatism. Central–Local Policymak-*

351

ing in the Welfare State (London: Harper-Collins).

Atkin, J.M. and Black, P. (1997) 'Policy Perils of International Comparisons: The TIMMS Case', *Phi Delta Kappan* 79(1): 22–9.

Atkinson, A.B. (1998) 'Social Exclusion, Poverty and Unemployment', in A.B. Atkinson and J. Hills (eds), *Exclusion, Employment and Opportunity* (London: CASE, LSE).

Atkinson, R. (1995) 'Post-War Urban Policy in Britain: Changing Perceptions and Problems', *Policy Studies* 16(4): 6–17.

Atkinson, R. (1998) 'Countering Urban Social Exclusion: the Role of Community Participation and Partnership', in R. Griffiths (ed.), *Social Exclusion in Cities: the Urban Policy Challenge*, Occasional Paper No.3, University of the West of England, Faculty of the Built Environment (Bristol: University of the West of England).

Atkinson, R. (1999a) 'Urban Crisis: New Policies for the Next Century', in M. Chapman, and P. Allmendinger (eds), *Planning in the Millennium* (Chichester: J. Wiley).

Atkinson, R. (1999b) 'Countering Urban Social Exclusion: the Role of Community Participation in Urban Regeneration', in G. Haughton (ed.), *Community Economic Development* (London: Regional Studies Association/Stationery Office).

Atkinson, R. (1999c) 'Discourses of Partnership and Empowerment in Contemporary British Urban Regeneration', *Urban Studies* 36(1): 59–72.

Atkinson, R. (2000a) 'Narratives of the Inner City: The Construction of Urban Problems and Urban Policy in the Official Discourse of British Government, 1968–1998' *Critical Social Policy* 20(2): 211–32.

Atkinson, R. (2000b) 'Combating Social Exclusion in Europe: The New Urban Policy Challenge', *Urban Studies* 37(5/6): 1037–55.

Atkinson, R. and Cope, S. (1997) 'Community Participation and Urban Regeneration in Britain', in P. Hoggett (ed.), *Contested Communities* (Bristol: Policy Press).

Atkinson, R. and Davoudi, S. (2000) 'The Concept of Social Exclusion in the European Union: Context, Development and Possibilities', *Journal of Common Market Studies* 38(3): 427–48.

Atkinson, R. and Moon, G. (1994a) *Urban Policy in Britain: The City, the State and the Market* (Basingstoke: Macmillan – now Palgrave Macmillan).

Atkinson, R. and Moon, G. (1994b) 'The City Challenge Initiative: An Overview and Preliminary Assessment', *Regional Studies* 28: 94–7.

Atkinson, T. (1996) 'The Case for a Participation Income', *Political Quarterly*, 67(1): 67–70.

Audit Commission (1996) *Misspent Youth* (London: Audit Commission).

Audit Commission (1997) *The Coming of Age* (London: Audit Commission).

Auld Report (2001) *Report of the Review of the Criminal Courts of England and Wales* (London: Stationery Office).

Baer, K. (2000) *Reinventing Democrats: The Politics of Liberalism from Reagan to Clinton* (Kansas: University Press of Kansas).

Ball, S.J. (1999) 'Labour, Learning and the Economy: A "Policy Sociology" Perspective', *Cambridge Journal of Education* 29(2): 195–206.

Banks, O. (1955) *Parity and Prestige in English Secondary Education* (London: Routledge & Kegan Paul).

Bannerji, H. (1998) 'Politics and the Writing of History', in R. Roach Pierson and N. Chaudhuri (eds), *Nation, Empire, Colony: Historicising Gender and Race* (Bloomington: Indiana University Press).

Barber, M. (1996) *The Learning Game: Arguments for an Education Revolution* (London, Victor Gollancz).

Barber, M. (2002) 'High Expectations and Standards for All, No Matter What: The Leadership Challenge for a World Class Education Service', www.ncsl.org.uk/index.cfm?pageid=ev_auth_barber.

Barber, M. and J. Sebba (1999) 'Reflections on Progress Towards a World Class Education System', *Cambridge Journal of Education* 29(2): 183–94.

Bardach, E. (2000) *Getting Agencies to Work Together* (Washington, DC: Brookings Institute).

Barnes, M. (2001) 'Ending Child Poverty – Delivering on the Mandate?' *Poverty* 110: 103.

Barnes, M. and Sullivan, H. (2002) 'Building Capacity for Collaboration in English Health Action Zones', in C. Glendinning, M. Powell and K. Rummery (eds), *Partnerships, New Labour and the Governance of Welfare* (Bristol: Policy Press).

Barnett, A. (2000) 'Corporate Populism and Partyless Democracy', *New Left Review* 3: 80–9.

Barr, N. (2001) *The Welfare State as Piggy Bank* (Oxford: Oxford University Press).

Barry, J. (1999) *Rethinking Green Politics* (London: Sage).

Bartlett, W., Roberts, J.A. and Le Grand, J. (1998) *A Revolution in Social Policy Quasi-market Reforms in the 1990s* (Bristol: Policy Press).

Bauman, Z. (1998) *Work, Consumerism and the New Poor* (Buckingham: Open University Press).

Bayley, M. (1973) *Mental Handicap and Community Care* (London: Routledge & Kegan Paul).

BBC (2002) 'Blair Defiant Over Child Benefit Plan', 29 April, news.bbc.co.uk/hi/e...uk_politics/newsid_1957000/19957279.stm.

Bennett, C. (1997) 'Understanding Ripple Effects: The Cross National Adoption of Policy Instruments for Bureaucratic Accountability', *Governance* 1(3): 213–33.

Benton, T. (ed.) (1996) *The Greening of Marxism* (New York: Guilford Press).

Beresford, P. (2002) 'User Involvement in Research and Evaluation: Liberation or Regulation?', *Social Policy & Society* 1(2): 95–106.

Berthoud, R. (1998) *Disability Benefits: A Review of the Issues and Options for Reform* (York: Joseph Rowntree Foundation).

Beveridge, W. (1942) *Social Insurance and Allied Services*, Cmnd 6404 (London: HMSO).

Blair, T. (1996a) *New Britain – My Vision of a Young Country: A New Statesman Special Selection* (London: Fourth Estate).

Blair, T. (1996b) Speech to CPU Conference, 14 October, Cape Town.

Blair, T. (1997a) 'The 21st Century Welfare State', Speech by the Prime Minister the Rt Hon. Tony Blair MP to the Social Policy and Economic Performance Conference, 24 January, Amsterdam.

Blair, T. (1997b) Speech by the Prime Minister the Rt Hon. Tony Blair MP at the Aylesbury Estate, Southwark, Monday 2 June, London.

Blair, T. (1998a) *The Third Way: New Politics for the New Century* (London: Fabian Society).

Blair. T. (1998b) 'Building a Modern Welfare State', Speech by the Prime Minister the Rt Hon. Tony Blair MP, 15 January, Dudley, West Midlands.

Blair, T. (1999a) 'Beveridge Revisited: a Welfare State for the 21st Century' in R. Walker (ed.), *Ending Child Poverty* (Bristol: Policy Press)

Blair, T. (1999b) Speech by the Prime Minister the Rt Hon. Tony Blair MP to the National Association of Head Teachers. www.number10.gov.uk/public/info/releases/speeches/Speech_Display .asp?random= 4726&index=7.

Blair, T. (2000) Speech on the New Deal, 30 November, www.number10.gov.uk.

Blair, T. (2001) 'The Strong Society – Rights, Responsibilities and Reform', Speech by the Prime Minister the Rt Hon. Tony Blair MP, 30 May, Newport, Shropshire.

Blair, T. (2002a) 'A Britain in Which Nobody is Left Behind', Speech by the Prime Minister the Rt Hon. Tony Blair MP.

Blair, T. and Schroeder, G. (1999) *Europe: The Third Way – die Neue Mitte* (London: Labour Party and SPD).

Blundell, R. (2001) *Welfare to Work: Which Policies Work and Why?*, Keynes Lectures in Economics (London: University College and Institute for Fiscal Studies).

Blundell, R. and Walker, I. (2001) 'Working Families' Tax Credit: A Review of the Evidence, Issues and Prospects for Further Research', *Inland Revenue Analysis and Research*, Research Report, 1: 65.

BMA (1997) *Road Transport and Health* (London: BMA).

Boberg, E.W., Gustafson, D.H., Hawkins, R.P. et al. (1995) 'Development, Acceptance, and Use Patterns of a Computer Based Education', *Computers in Human Behaviour* 11(2): 289–311.

Bojke, C., Gravelle, H. and Wilkin, D. (2001) 'Is Bigger Better for Primary Care Groups and Trusts?' *British Medical Journal* 322: 599–602.

Bomberg, E. and J. Peterson (2000) 'Policy Transfer and Europeanization: Passing the Heineken Test?', *Queen's Papers on Europeanization*, The Institute of European Studies (Belfast: Queen's University Belfast). <www.qub.ac.uk/ies/onlinepapers/poe2.html>.

Bonjour, D., Dorsett, R., Knight, G. et al. (2001) *New Deal for Young People: National Survey of Participants: Stage 2*, Employment Service, Research and Development Report, ESR 45 (Sheffield: ES).

Bonoli, G. (2000) *The Politics of Pension Reform* (Cambridge: Cambridge University Press).

Bonoli, G., George, V. and Taylor-Gooby, P. (2000) *European Welfare Futures: Towards a Theory of Retrenchment* (Cambridge: Polity Press).

Bottoms, A.E. (1995) 'The Philosophy and Politics of Punishment and Sentencing', in C. Clarkson and R. Morgan (eds), *The Politics of Sentencing Reform* (Oxford: Oxford University Press).

Bradby, H. (1996) 'Genetics and Racism', in T.M. Marteau and M. Richards (eds), *The Troubled Helix* (Cambridge: Cambridge University Press).

Brah, A. (1996) *Cartographies of Diaspora* (London: Routledge).

Braun, D. and A. Busch (1999) *Public Policy and Political Ideas* (Cheltenham: Edward Elgar).

Brewer, M. and Gregg, P. (2001) 'Eradicating Child Poverty in Britain: Welfare Reform and Children Since 1997', Institute for Fiscal Studies Working Paper (London: Institute of Fiscal Studies).

Brewer, M., Clark, T. and Goodman, A. (2002) *The Government's Child Poverty Target: How much Progress has been Made?* (London: Institute for Fiscal Studies).

Brewer M., Clark T. and Myck M. (2001) *Credit Where It's Due? An Assessment of the New Tax Credits* (London: Institute for Fiscal Studies).

Brewer, T., Clarke, T. and Wakefield, M. (2002) *Social Security Under New Labour: What Did the Third Way Mean for Welfare Reform?* Institute of Fiscal Studies Working Paper (London: Institute for Fiscal Studies).

Brewster, C. and Teague, P. (1989) *European Community Social Policy: Its Impact on the UK* (London: Institute for Personnel Management).

Brooks, R. (2001) *Social Health Insurance: Working Paper* (London: IPPR).

Brooks, R., Regan. S. and Robinson, P. (2002) *A New Contract for Retirement* (London: IPPR).

Brown, P. and Scase, R. (1994) *Higher Education and Corporate Realities: Class, Culture and the Decline of Graduate Careers* (London: University College London Press).

Brown, P. and Scase, R. (1997) 'Universities and Employers: Rhetoric and Reality', in A. Smith and F. Webster (eds), *The Postmodern University?* (Buckingham: Open University Press).

Brundtland Commission (1987) *Our Common Future* (Oxford: Oxford University Press).

Burchardt, T. (1999) *The Evolution of Disability Benefits in the UK: Reweighting the Basket* (London: Centre for the Analysis of Social Exclusion, LSE).

Burchardt, T. and Hills, J. (1997) *Private Welfare Insurance and Social Security: Pushing at the Boundaries* (York: Joseph Rowntree Foundation).

Burningham, K. and Thrush, D. (2001) *Rainforests are a Long Way from Here* (York: Joseph Rowntree Foundation).

Burns, D., Williams, C. and Windebank, J. (2003) *Community Self-help* (Basingstoke: Palgrave Macmillan).

Burrows, R. (1997a) 'Virtual Culture, Urban Social Polarisation and Social Science Fiction' in B. Loader (ed.), *The Governance of Cyberspace* (London: Routledge).

Burrows, R. (1997b) *Contemporary Patterns of Residential Mobility* (York: Centre for Housing Policy).

Burrows, R. and Loader, B. (eds) (1994) *Towards a Post-Fordist Welfare State?* (London: Routledge).

Burrows, R. and Nettleton, S. (2002) 'Reflexive Modernization and the Emergence of Wired Self-help' in K. Renniger and W. Shumar (eds), *Building Virtual Communities: Learning and Change in Cyberspace* (New York: Cambridge University Press).

Burrows, R. and Rhodes, D. (1999) *The Geography of Misery* (York: Centre for Housing Policy, University of York).

Burrows, R., Nettleton, S., Pleace, N., Loader, B. and Muncer, S. (2000) 'Virtual Community Care? Social Policy and the Emergence of Computer Mediated Social Support', *Information, Communication and Society*, 3(1): 95–121.

Byrne, D. (1998) *Complexity Theory and the Social Sciences: An Introduction* (London: Routledge).

Byrne, D. (1999) *Social Exclusion* (Buckingham: Open University Press).

Cabinet Office (1996) *Government.direct: A Prospectus for the Electronic Delivery of Government Services* (London: Stationery Office).

Cabinet Office (1999) *Modernising Government*, Cmnd 4310 (London: Cabinet Office).

Cabinet Office (2000) *egovernment: A Strategic Framework for Public Services in the Information Age* (London: Cabinet Office).

Cabinet Office PIU (Performance and Innovation Unit) (2000) *e.gov: Electronic Government Services for the 21st Century* (London: Cabinet Office).

Cahill, M. 2001) *The Environment and Social Policy* (London: Routledge).

Cahill, M. and Fitzpatrick, T. (eds) (2002) *Environmental Issues and Social Welfare* (Oxford: Blackwell).

Callaghan, J. (2000) 'Environmental Politics, the New Left and the New Social Democracy', *Political Quarterly*, 71(3): 300–8.

Campbell, S., Wilkin, D. and Roland, M. (2001) 'Improving the Quality of Care Through Clinical Governance' *British Medical Journal* 322: 1580–2.

Carr, L. (2000) 'Enabling our Destruction?', *Coalition: The Magazine of the Greater Manchester Coalition of Disabled People*, August.

Castells, M. (1996) *The Information Age: Economy, Society and Culture I: The Rise of the Network Society* (Oxford: Blackwell).

Castells, M. (1997) *The Information Age: Economy, Society and Culture II: The Power of Identity* (Oxford: Blackwell).

Castells, M. (1998) *The Information Age: Economy, Society and Culture III: The End of the Millennium* (Oxford: Blackwell).

CEC (1993) *Growth, Competitiveness and Employment – The Challenges and Ways Forward into the 21st Century* (Luxembourg: CEC).

CEC (1995) *Equal Opportunities for Women and Men – Follow-up to the White Paper on Growth, Competitiveness and Employment* (Brussels: DGV).

CEC (1998) *Social Action Programme 1998–2000* (Brussels: EC).

CEC (2000a) *Report on Social Protection in Europe 1999.* Com (2000) 163 final. (Brussels: CEC).

CEC (2000b) *Communication from the Commission to the Council, the European Parliament, the Economic and Social Committee and the Committee of the Regions: Social Policy Agenda* (Brussels: CEC).

CEC (2000c) *Social Policy Agenda* (Brussels: CEC).

CEC (2001) *EU Employment and Social Policy, 1999–2001: Jobs, Cohesion and Productivity* (Brussels: EC).

Cerny, P.G. (1995) 'Globalization and the Changing Logic of Collective Action', *International Organization*, 49(4): 595–625.

Cerny, P.G. (2000). 'Restructuring the Political Arena: Globalization and the Paradoxes of the Competition State', in R.D. Germain (ed.), *Globalization and Its Critics: Perspectives from Political Economy* (Basingstoke: Macmillan – now Palgrave Macmillan).

Cerny, P.G. and Evans, M. (2000) 'New Labour, Globalization and the Competition State', Working Paper No. 70, Centre for European Studies, Harvard University.

CfIT (2001) *The CfIT Report 2001: Public Attitudes to Transport in England* (London: CfIT).

CfIT (2002) *CfIT's Initial Assessment of the Ten Year Transport Plan* (Londn: CfIT).

Charlton, B. (2000) 'The New Management of Scientific Knowledge in Medicine: a Change of Direction with Profound Implications', in A. Miles, J.R. Hampton and B. Hurwitz (eds), *NICE, CHI and the NHS Reforms* (London: Aesculapius Medical Press).

Chatrie, I. and Wright, P. (2000) *Public Strategies for the Information Society in Member States of the European Union* (Brussels: European Information Society Projects/EU).

Christie, I. and Jarvis, L. (2001) 'How Green are Our Values?', in A. Park, J. Curtice, K. Thomson et al. (eds), *British Social Attitudes: the 18th Report* (London: Sage).

Christoff, P. (1996) 'Ecological Modernisation, Ecological Modernities', *Environmental Politics*, 5(3): 476–500.

Cilliers, P. (1998) *Complexity and Postmodernism: Understanding Complex Systems* (London: Routledge).

Clark, T. (2001) 'Recent Pensions Policy and the Pension Credit', *Institute for Fiscal Studies, Briefing Note*, No. 17, www.ifs.org.uk.

Clarke, A. and Flinter, F. (1996) 'The Genetic Testing of Children: a Clinical Perspective', in T.M. Marteau and M. Richards (eds), *The Troubled Helix* (Cambridge: Cambridge University Press).

Clarke, J. and Glendinning, C. (2002) 'Partnership and the Remaking of Welfare Governance', in C. Glendinning, M. Powell and K. Rummery (eds), *Partnerships, New Labour and the Governance of Welfare* (Bristol: Policy Press).

Clarke, J. and Newman, J. (1997) *The Managerial State Power, Politics and Ideology in the Remaking of Social Welfare* (London: Sage).

Clayton, R. and Pontusson, J. (1998) 'Welfare-State Retrenchment Revisited: Entitlement Cuts, Public Sector Restructuring, and Inegalitarian Trends in Advanced Capitalist Societies', *World Politics*, 51(1): 67–98.

Cochrane, A., Clarke, J. and Gewirtz, S. (2001) *Comparing Welfare States*, 2nd edn (London: Sage).

Cole, I. and Furbey, R. (1994) *The Eclipse of Council Housing* (London: Routledge).

Commission on Public Private Partnerships (2001) *Building Better Partnerships* (London: IPPR).

Commission on Taxation and Citizenship (2000) *Paying for Progress: A New Politics of Tax for Public Spending* (London: Fabian Society).

Comptroller and Auditor General (2002a) *Widening Participation in Higher Education in England* (London: NAO).

Comptroller and Auditor General (2002b) *Better Public Services Through e-Government* (London: NAO).

Council of Europe (1998) *Gender Mainstreaming: Conceptual Framework, Methodology and Presentation of Good Practices.* Strasbourg (EG-S-MS (98) 2.

Cowan, D. and Marsh, A. (2001) *Two Steps Forward: Housing Policy into the New Millennium* (Bristol: Policy Press).

Cowles, M.G. and Risse, T. (2001) 'Transforming Europe: Conclusions' in M.G. Cowles, J. Caporaso and T. Risse (eds), *Transforming Europe: Europeanization and Domestic Change* (Ithaca: Cornell University Press).

Crawford, A. (2001) 'Joined up but Fragmented: Contradiction, Ambiguity and Ambivalence at the Heart of New Labour's Third Way', in R. Matthews and J. Pitts (eds), *Crime, Disorder and Community Safety* (London: Routledge).

Crompton, R. (ed.) (1999) *Restructuring Gender Relationships and Employment: The Decline of the Male Breadwinner* (Oxford: Oxford University Press).

Crosland, T. (1956) *The Future of Socialism* (London: Jonathan Cape).

Cunningham, S. (2000) *Disability, Oppression and Public Policy* (Keithley: Independent Living).

Daly, M. and Lewis, J. (1998) 'Introduction: Conceptualising Social Care in the Context of Welfare State Restructuring', in J. Lewis, (ed.), *Gender, Social Care and Welfare State Restructuring in Europe* (Aldershot: Ashgate).

Davies, H., Nutley, M. and Smith, P. (2000) *What Works? Evidence-based Policy and Practice in Public Services* (Bristol: Policy Press).

Dawes, S.S., Pardo, T.A. and DiCaterino, A. (1999) 'Crossing the Threshold: Practical Foundations for Government Services on The World Wide Web', *Journal of the American Society for Information Science* 50(4): 246–53.

Deacon, A. (2000) 'Learning from the US? The Influence of American Ideas upon "New Labour" Thinking on Welfare Reform', *Policy and Politics* 28(1): 5–18.

Deacon, A. (2002a) 'Echoes of Sir Keith: New Labour and the Cycle of Disadvantage' *Benefits* 10(3).

Deacon, A. (2002b) *Perspectives on Welfare: Ideas, Ideologies and Policy Debates* (Buckingham: Open University Press).

Deacon, A. (2003) 'Levelling the Playing Field, Activating the Players: New Labour and the Cycle of Disadvantage', *Policy and Politics* forthcoming.

De Groot, L. (1992) 'City Challenge: Competing in the Urban Regeneration Game', *Local Economy* 7: 196–209.

De La Porte, C., Pochet, P. and Room, G. (2001) 'Social Benchmarking, Policy Making and New Governance in the EU', *Journal of European Social Policy* 11(4): 291–307.

de Menil, G. (2002) 'Market and State Provision of Old-Age Security: An International Perspective', in J.D. Donahue and J.S. Nye (eds), *Market-Based Governance* (Washington, DC: Brookings Institute).

Deming, W.E. (2000) *The New Economics: For Industry, Government, Education.* (Cambridge, MA: MIT Press).

Denzin, N. (1998) 'In Search of the Inner Child: Co-dependency and Gender in a Cyberspace Community', in G. Bendelow and S. Williams (eds), *Emotions in Social Life* (London: Routledge).

DETR (1997a) *Regeneration Programmes – The Way Forward* (London: DETR).

DETR (1997b) *Single Regeneration Budget Challenge Fund Round 4: Supplementary Guidance* (London: DETR).

DETR (1997c) *National Road Traffic Forecasts (Great Britain)* (London: HMSO).

DETR (1997d) *Developing an Integrated Transport Policy: A Consultation Document* (London: DETR).

DETR (1998a) *A New Deal for Transport: Better for Everyone*, Cm 3950 (London: HMSO).

DETR (1998b) *Breaking the Logjam, The Government's Consultation Paper on Fighting Traffic Congestion and Pollution through Road User and Workplace Parking Charges* (London: DETR).

DETR (1999) *From Workhorse to Thoroughbred: A Better Role for Bus Travel* (London: DETR).

DETR (2000a) *Housing Policy Statement, The Way Forward for Housing* (London: Stationery Office).

DETR (2000b) *Co-ordination of Area-based Initiatives*, Research Working Paper (London: DETR).

DETR (2000c) *Collaboration and Co-ordination in Area-based Initiatives.* Second Research Working Paper (London: DETR).

DETR (2000d) *Our Towns and Cities: The Future. Delivering an Urban Renaissance*, Cm 4911 (London: HMSO).

DETR (2000e) *Local Strategic Partnerships* (London: DETR).

DETR (2000f) *Preparing Community Strategies. Government Guidance to Local Authorities* (London: DETR).

DETR (2000g) *Transport 2010, The 10 Year Plan*, TSO, July.

DETR (2000h) *Transport 2010, The Background Analysis*, TSO, July.

DETR/DSS (2000) *Quality and Choice: A Decent Home for All* (London: DETR/DSS).

DfEE (1997) *Excellence in Schools* (London: Stationery Office).

DfEE (2000) *New Deal Facts and the Future: 250,000 off Welfare and into Work* (London: DfEE).

DfEE (2001a) *Schools Achieving Success: Raising Standards, Promoting Diversity, Achieving Results* (Norwich: Stationery Office).

DfEE (2001b) *Toward Full Employment in a Modern Society, Secretary of State for Education and Employment*, Cm 5084, (London: Stationery Office).

DfES (1999) *Learning to Succeed: A New Framework for Post-16 Learning* (London: Stationery Office).

DfES (2001a) *Schools Achieving Success*. Government White Paper (London: HMSO).

DfES (2001b) 'Participation in Education, Training and Employment by 16–18 Year Olds in England: 1999 and 2000' www.dfes.gov.uk/statistics/DB/SFR/s0273/sfr30-2001.pdf.

DfT (2002) *Transport Statistics Great Britain* (London: Stationery Office).

DH (1991) *Getting it Right for Carers* (London: HMSO).

DH (1996a) *Primary Care: the Future* (London: HMSO).

DH (1996b) *Choice and Opportunity* (London: HMSO).

DH (1996c) *Primary Care: Delivering the Future* (London: HMSO).

DH (1997) 'Health Action Zones Envisaged as Co-operative NHS Partnerships' Press Release, 145, June.

DH (1998a) *Modernising Social Services* (London: HMSO).

DH (1998b) *Moving into the Mainstream: The Report of a National Inspection of Services for Adults with Learning Disabilities* (London: DH).

DH (1998c) *Modernising Mental Health Services* (London: DH).

DH (1999) *Community Care Statistics 1998* (London: DH).

DH (2000) *The NHS Plan: A Plan for Investment, a Plan for Reform* (London: Stationery Office).

DH (2001a) *Shifting the Balance of Power within the NHS. Securing Delivery* (London: DH).

DH (2001b) *Community Care Statistics 2001: Residential Personal Social Services for Adults, England* (London: DH).

DH (2001c) *Community Care Statistics 2000: Home Care/Home Help Services for Adults, England* (London: DH).

DH (2001d) *Modern Social Services: A Commitment to Deliver* (London: Stationery Office).

DH (2001e) *Fairer Charging Policies for Home Care and Other Non-residential Social Services – LAC 2001(32)* (London: DH).

DH (2001f) *Valuing People: A New Strategy for Learning Disability for the 21st Century* (London: Stationery Office).

DH (2001g) *Shifting the Balance of Power: the Next Steps* (www.doh.gov.uk/shiftingthebalance/nextsteps.html).

DH (2002a) *Fairer Charging: Practice Guidance* (London: DH).

DH (2002b) *Planning with People: Towards Person Centred Approaches* (London: DH).

DH (2002c) *Fair Access to Care Services: Policy and Practice Guidance* (London: DH).

Dignan, J. (1999) 'The Crime and Disorder Act and the Prospects for Restorative Justice', *Criminal Law Review*, 48–60.

Disability Rights Task Force (1999) *From Exclusion to Inclusion: A Report of the Disability Rights Task Force on Civil Rights for Disabled People* (London: Stationery Office/DfEE).

Dobson, A. (2000) *Green Political Thought*, 3rd edn (London: Routledge).

Docking, J.W. (ed.) (2000) *New Labour's Policies for Schools: Raising the Standard?* (London, David Fulton).

DoE (1977) *Policy for the Inner Cities*, Cmnd 6845, London: HMSO).

DoE (1987) *Housing: The Government's Proposals* (London: HMSO).

DoE (1993) *Bidding Guidance. A Guide to Funding from the Single Regeneration Budget* (London: DoE).

Doherty, B. and De Geus, M. (1996) *Democracy and Green Political Thought* (London: Routledge).

Dolowitz, D. (1998) *Learning from America: Policy Transfer and the Development of the British Workfare State* (Sussex: Academic Press).

Dolowitz, D. and Marsh, D. (1996) 'Who Learns What from Whom: A Review of the Policy Transfer Literature', *Political Studies* **44**(2): 343–57.

Donaldson, L. and Muir Gray, J.A. (1998) 'Clinical Governance: a Quality Duty for Health Organizations', *Quality in Health Care* 7 (Supplement), 37–44.

DoT (1989a) *National Road Traffic Forecasts (Great Britain)* (London: HMSO).

DoT (1989b) *Roads for Prosperity*, Cm 693 (London: HMSO).

DoT (1996) *Transport: The Way Forward, The Government's Green Paper on Transport* (London: HMSO).

Downes, D. and Morgan, R. (2002) 'The Skeletons in the Cupboard: The Politics of Law and Order at the Turn of the Millennium', in M. Maguire, R. Morgan, and R. Reiner (eds), *The Oxford Handbook of Criminology*, 3rd edn (Oxford: Clarendon Press).

Dowswell, T., Wilkin, D. and Banks-Smith, J. (2002) 'Nurses and Primary Care Groups: Their Experiences and Perceived Influence on Policy Development', *Journal of Advanced Nursing* 37(1): 35–42.

DRC (2002) *The Powers of the Commission* www.drc.org.uk/drc.

Driver, S. (2002) 'Frank Field's Fifteen Minutes' in A. Deacon (ed.), *Debating Pensions: Self Interest, Citizenship and the Common Good* (London: Civitas).

Driver, S. and Martell, L. (1998) *New Labour: Politics After Thatcherism* (Cambridge: Polity Press).

Driver, S. and Martell, L. (2000) 'Left, Right and the Third Way', *Policy and Politics* **28**(2): 147–61.

Dryzek, J. (1997) *The Politics of the Earth* (Oxford: Oxford University Press).

Dryzek, J. and Scholsberg, D. (eds) (1998) *Debating the Earth* (Oxford: Oxford University Press).

DSS (1998a) *New Ambitions for Our Country: A New Contract for Welfare*, Cm 3805 (London: HMSO).

DSS (1998b) *A New Contract for Welfare: Partnership in Pensions*, Cm 4179 (London: HMSO).

DSS (1998c) *A New Contract for Welfare: Support for Disabled People* (London: HMSO).

DSS (1999) *Opportunity for All*, Cm 4445 (London: HMSO).

DSS (2000) *The Changing Welfare State – Social Security Spending* (London: HMSO).

DTI/PA Team 15 (2000) *Closing the Digital Divide: Information and Communication Technologies in Deprived Areas* (London: DTI).

DTLGR (2000) *Housing Policy Statement; The Way Forward for Housing* (London: DTLGR).

DTLGR (2001) *Local Public Service Agreements, Annex A: The National Targets for Local PSAs* (London: DTLGR).

Duff, A. (1997) *The Treaty of Amsterdam: Text and Commentary* (London: Federal Trust).

Duncan, S. and Edwards, R. (1999) *Lone Mothers, Paid Work and Gendered Moral Rationalities* (Basingstoke: Macmillan – now Palgrave Macmillan).

DWP (2001) *New Deal: Next Phase – Towards Full Employment in a Modern Society* (London: Employment Service).

DWP (2002) *Pathways to Work: Helping People into Employment*, Cm 5690 (London: HMSO).

Dwyer, P. (1998) 'Conditional Citizens? Welfare Rights and Responsibilities in the Late 1990s', *Critical Social Policy* **18**(4): 493–517.

Dwyer, P. (2000) *Welfare Rights and Responsibilities* (Bristol: Policy Press).

Dwyer, P. and Heron, E. (1999) 'Doing the Right Thing' Labour and Welfare Reform: A New Moral Order? *Social Policy and Administration* **33**(1): 91–104.

Eckersley, R. (1992) *Environmentalism and Political Theory* (London: UCL Press).

Ellison, N. (1996) 'Consensus Here, Consensus There ... But Not Consensus Everywhere', in H. Jones and M. Kandiah (eds), *The Myth of Consensus: New Views on British History, 1945–64* (Basingstoke: Macmillan – now Palgrave Macmillan).

Ellison, N. (1999) 'Beyond Universalism and Particularism: Rethinking Contemporary Welfare Theory', *Critical Social Policy* **19**(1): 57–85.

Ellison, N. (2000) 'Proactive and Defensive Engagement: Social Citizenship in a Changing Public Sphere', *Sociological Research Online* **5**(3).

Elston, M.A. (1991) 'The Politics of Professional Power: Medicine in a Changing Health Service', in J. Gabe, M. Calnan and M. Bury (eds), *The Sociology of the Health Service* (London: Routledge).

Emmerson, C. and Leicester, A. (2000) *A Survey of the UK Benefits System, Institute for Fiscal Studies Briefing Note 13*, www.ifs.org.uk.

Employment Policy Institute (1998) *What Works? The New Deal for Young People* (London: Employment Policy Institute).

Employment Select Committee (1999) *The Performance and Future Role of the Employment Service, Seventh Report of the Education and Employment Committee, Session 1998–99*, Volumes I and II, HC 197–I&II (London: Stationery Office).

Engwicht, D. (1993) *Reclaiming Our Cities and Towns, Better Living with Less Traffic* (Philadelphia: New Society).

Ennew, C., Feighan, T. and Whynes, D. (1998) 'Entrepreneurial Activity in the Public Sector: Evidence from UK Primary Care', in P. Taylor-Gooby (ed.), *Choice and Public Policy* (Basingstoke: Macmillan – now Palgrave Macmillan).

Enzensberger, H.M. (1988) *Dreamers of the Absolute* (London: Radius).

Equal Opportunities Commission (2002) Facts About Women and Men, www.eoc.org.uk/cseng/research/factsgreatbritain.pdf.

Esping-Andersen, E. (1990) *The Three Worlds of Welfare Capitalism* (Cambridge: Polity Press).

Etzioni, A. (1995) *The Spirit of Community: The Reinvention of American Society* (New York: Touchstone/Simon & Schuster).

European Parliament (1998) *Health Care Systems in the EU: A Comparative Study, Directorate-General for Research*, Working Paper (Luxembourg: European Parliament).

Evans, M. (2000) *Welfare to Work and the Organisation of Opportunity: European and American*

Approaches and their Lessons for the UK (London: LSE, CASE Report 15).

Eve, R., Horsfall, S. and Lee, M. (eds) (1997) *Chaos, Complexity, and Sociology: Myths, Models, and Theories* (London: Sage).

Exworthy, M. (2001) 'Primary Care in the UK: Understanding the Dynamics of Devolution', *Health and Social Care in the Community*, 9(5): 266–78.

Exworthy, M. and Halford, S. (eds) (1999) *Professionals and the New Managerialism in the Public Sector* (Buckingham: Open University Press).

Fairclough, N. (2000) *New Labour, New Language?* (London: Routledge).

Fairleigh Committee (1971) *Better Services for the Mentally Handicapped* (London: HMSO).

Falkingham, J. and Hills, J. (1995) *The Dynamic of Welfare: The Welfare State and the Life-Cycle* (London: Prentice Hall).

Falkner, G. (1998) *EU Social Policy in the 1990s: Towards a Corporatist Policy Community* (London: Routledge).

Farrington, D.P. (1996) *Understanding and Preventing Youth Crime* (York: Joseph Rowntree Foundation).

Faulkner, D. (1996) *Darkness and Light: Justice, Crime and Management for Today* (London: Howard League).

Fawcett, H. (1995) 'The Privatization of Welfare: The Impact of Parties on the Public/Private Mix in Pension Provision', *West European Politics* 18: 140–69.

Ferrera, M. and Rhodes, M. (eds) (2000) *Recasting European Welfare States* (London: Frank Cass).

Ferris, J. (1993) 'Ecological Versus Social Rationality: Can There Be Green Social Policies?', in A. Dobson and P. Lucardie (eds), *The Politics of Nature* (London: Routledge).

Field, F. (2002) 'A Universal Protected Pension: Harnessing Self Interest to the Common Good', in A. Deacon (ed.), *Debating Pensions: Self Interest, Citizenship and the Common Good* (London: Civitas).

Finch, J. and Groves, D. (1983) *A Labour of Love: Women, Work and Caring* (London: Routledge & Kegan Paul).

Finn, J. (1999) 'An Exploration of Helping Processes in an Online Self-help Group Focussing on the Issues of Disability', *Health and Social Work* 24(3): 220–31.

Finn, D. and Blackmore, M. (2001) *Next Steps for Welfare Reform: Lessons from the New Deal for the Young Unemployed in Portsmouth* (Portsmouth: Portsmouth University).

Finn, D., Blackmore, M. and Nimmo, M. (1998) *Welfare to Work and the Long Term Unemployed* (London: Unemployment Unit).

FitzGerald, M., Hough, M., Joseph, I. and Qureshi, T. (2002) *Policing For London* (Cullompton: Willan).

Fitzpatrick, T. (1998) 'The Implications of Ecological Thought for Social Welfare', *Critical Social Policy* 18(1): 5–26.

Fitzpatrick, T. (1999a) *Freedom and Security* (Basingstoke: Macmillan – now Palgrave Macmillan).

Fitzpatrick, T. (1999b) 'New Welfare Associations: An Alternative Model of Well-being', in T. Jordan and A. Lent (eds), *Storming the Millennium* (London: Lawrence & Wishart).

Fitzpatrick, T. (2002) 'Green Democracy and Ecosocial Welfare', in T. Fitzpatrick and M. Cahill (eds), *Environment and Welfare* (Basingstoke: Palgrave Macmillan).

Fitzpatrick, T. and Cahill, M. (eds) (2002a) *Environment and Welfare* (Basingstoke: Palgrave Macmillan).

Fitzpatrick, T. and Cahill, M. (2002b) 'The New Environment of Welfare', in T. Fitzpatrick and M. Cahill (eds), *Environment and Welfare* (Basingstoke: Palgrave Macmillan).

Fitzpatrick, T. with Caldwell, C. (2001) 'Towards a Theory of Ecosocial Welfare: Radical Reformism and Local Currency Schemes', *Environmental Politics*, 10(2): 43–67.

Florin, D., Gillam, S., Abbott, A. and Fulop, N. (2002) 'The Object of the Exercise', *Health Service Journal* 17 January.

Ford, J. and Wilcox, S. (1994) *Affordable Housing, Low Incomes and the Flexible Labour Market* (London: National Federation of Housing Associations).

Ford, J. Burrows, R. and Nettleton, S. (2001) *Home Ownership and the Risk Society; A Social Analysis of Mortgage Arrears and Possessions* (Bristol: Policy Press).

Forrest, R. and Kearns. A. (1999) *Joined-up Places? Social Cohesion and Neighbourhood Regeneration* (York: Joseph Rowntree Foundation).

Forrest R. and Murie, A. (1988) *Selling the Welfare State: the Privatisation of Public Housing* (London: Routledge).

Forrest, R,. Murie, A and Williams, P. (1990) *Home Ownership* (London: Unwin).

Frazer, R. and Glick, G. (2000) *Out of Services: A Survey of Social Service Provision for Elderly and Disabled People in England* (London: RADAR).

Fukuyama, F. (2002) *Our Posthuman Future: Consequences of the Biotechnology Revolution* (London: Profile Books).

Gallie, D. and Paugam, S. (eds) (2000) *Welfare Regimes and the Experience of Unemployment in Europe* (Oxford: Oxford University Press).

Gallie, D. and Vogler, C. (1994) 'Labour Market Deprivation, Welfare and Collectivism' in D.

Gallie, C. Marsh and C. Vogler (eds), *Social Change and the Experience of Unemployment* (Oxford: Oxford University Press).

Garrett, G. (1998) *Partisan Politics in the Global Economy* (Cambridge: Cambridge University Press).

Gewirtz, S. (2001) 'Cloning the Blairs: New Labour's Programme for the Re-Socialization of Working-Class Parents', *Journal of Education Policy* 16(4): 365–77.

Geyer, R. (1998) 'Globalization and the (non-) Defence of the Welfare State', *West European Politics* 21(3): 77–103.

Geyer, R. (2000a) *Exploring European Social Policy* (Cambridge: Polity Press).

Geyer, R. (2000b) 'Can Mainstreaming Save EU Social Policy? The Cases of Gender, Disability and Elderly Policy', *Current Politics and Economics of Europe* 10(2): 127–46.

Geyer, R. (2001) 'Can European Union Social NGOs Co-operate to Promote EU Social Policy', *Journal of Social Policy* 30(3): 477–93.

Geyer, R. (2003) 'Beyond the Third Way: The Science of Complexity and the Politics of Choice', *British Journal of Politics and International Relations* forthcoming.

Geyer, R., Ingebritsen, C. and Moses, J. (eds) (2000) *Globalization, Europeanization, and the End of Scandinavian Social Democracy?* (Basingstoke: Macmillan – now Palgrave Macmillan).

Gibb, K. (2001) 'Helping with Housing Costs? Unravelling the Political Economy of Personal Subsidy', in D. Cowan and A. Marsh (eds), *Two Steps Forward: Housing Policy into the New Millennium* (Bristol: Policy Press).

Giddens, A. (1998) *The Third Way: The Renewal of Social Democracy* (Cambridge: Polity Press).

Giddens, A. (2000) *The Third Way and Its Critics* (Cambridge: Polity Press).

Gillam, S., Abbott, S. and Banks-Smith, J. (2001) 'Can Primary Care Groups and Trusts Improve Health?', *British Medical Journal* 323: 89–92.

Gilroy, P. (1987) *Ain't No Black in the Union Jack: the Cultural Politics of Race and Nation* (London: Hutchinson).

Glaister, S. (2001) *UK Transport Policy, 1997–2001*, Beesley Lectures on Regulation, 2 September, 2001 (London: The Royal Society of Arts).

Glaister, S. and Graham, D. (2000) *The Effect of Fuel Prices on Motorists* (London: AA Motoring Policy Unit and the UK Petroleum Industry Association).

Glendinning, C. (1998) 'From General Practice to Primary Care: Developments in Primary Health Services 1990–1998', in E. Brunsdon,

H. Dean and R. Woods (eds), *Social Policy Review 10* (London, Social Policy Association).

Glendinning, C. and Rummery, K. (forthcoming) 'Collaboration Between Primary Health and Social Care – From Policy to Practice in Developing Services for Older People', in A. Leathard (ed.), *Interprofessional Collaboration: from Policy to Practice in Health and Social Care* (London: Routledge).

Glendinning, C., Abbott, S. and Coleman, A. (2001) '"Bridging the Gap": New Relationships Between Primary Care Groups and Local Authorities', *Social Policy and Administration* 35(4): 411–25.

Glendinning, C., Powell, M. and Rummery, K. (eds) (2002) *Partnerships, New Labour and the Governance of Welfare* (Bristol: Policy Press).

Glennerster, H. (1995) *British Social Policy Since 1945* (Oxford: Blackwell).

Glennerster, H. (1997) *Paying for Welfare: Towards 2000* (London: Prentice Hall).

Glennerster, H. (1999a) 'A Third Way?', in H. Dean and R. Woods (eds), *Social Policy Review 11* (Luton: Social Policy Association).

Glennerster, H. (1999b) 'Which Welfare States are Most Likely to Survive?' *International Journal of Social Welfare* 8: 2–11.

Glennerster, H. (2001a) ' Social Policy' in A. Seldon (ed.), *The Blair Effect* (London: Little, Brown).

Glennerster, H. (2001b) *United Kingdom Education, 1997–2001* (London: Centre for Analysis of Social Exclusion, LSE).

Glennerster, H., Matsaganis, M., Owens, P. and Hancock, S. (1994) *Implementing GP Fundholding* (Buckingham: Open University Press).

Goode J., Callender, C. and Lister R. (1998) *Purse or Wallet? Gender Inequalities and Income Distribution within Families on Benefits* (London: Policy Studies Institute).

Goodin, R.E. (1985) *Protecting the Vulnerable. A Reanalysis of our Social Responsibilities* (Chicago: Chicago University Press).

Goodin, R.E. (2001) 'Work and Welfare: Towards a Post-productivist Welfare Regime', *British Journal of Political Science* 31: 13–39.

Goodin, R.E., Headey, B., Muffels, R. and Dirven, H.-J. (1999) *The Real Worlds of Welfare Capitalism* (Cambridge: Cambridge University Press).

Goodwin, P. (1992) 'A Review of New Demand Elasticities with Special Reference to Short- and Long term Effects of Price Changes', *Journal of Transport, Economics and Policy* 26(2): 155–69.

Goodwin, P. (2001) *Running to Stand Still? An Analysis of the Ten Year Plan for Transport* (London: Council for the Protection of Rural England).

Goodwin, P., Hallett, S., Kenny, F. and Stokes, G. (1991) *Transport: The New Realism*. Report to the Rees Jeffreys Road Fund, Transport Road Studies Unit Report 62X (Oxford: Transport Studies Unit, University of Oxford).

Gopinath, P. (1995) 'Preface' in G. Rodgers, C. Gore and J.B. Figueiredo (eds), *Social Exclusion: Rhetoric, Reality, Responses* (Geneva: International Institute for Labour Studies, ILO).

Gorard, S. and Taylor, C. (2001) 'The Composition of Specialist Schools in England: Track Record and Future Prospect', *School Leadership and Management* 21(4): 365–82.

Gorz, A. (1983) *Farewell to the Working Class* (London: Pluto Press).

Gorz, A. (1989) *Critique of Economic Reason* (London: Verso).

Gorz, A. (1992) 'On the Difference Between Society and Community and Why Basic Income Cannot by Itself Confer Full Membership of Either', in P. Van Parijs (ed.), *Arguing for Basic Income* (London: Verso).

Gorz, A. (1999) *Reclaiming Work: Beyond the Wage-based Society* (Cambridge: Polity Press).

Gould, P. (1998) *The Unfinished Revolution* (London: Abacus).

Graham, H. (1991) 'The Concept of Caring in Feminist Research: The Case of Domestic Service', *Sociology* 25(1): 61–78.

Graham, S. (1997) 'Liberalized Utilities, New Technologies and Urban Social Polarization: the UK Experience', *European Urban and Regional Studies* 4(2): 135–50.

Graham, S. (2000) 'Constructing Premium Networked Spaces: Reflections on Infrastructure Networks and Contemporary Urban Development', *International Journal of Urban and Regional Research* 24(1): 183–200.

Graham, S. and Marvin, S. (2001) *Splintering Urbanism: Networked Infrastructures, Technological Mobilities and the Urban Condition* (London: Routledge).

Gramsci, A. (1971) *Selections from the Prison Notebooks* (London: Lawrence & Wishart).

Gray A. (2001) 'We Want Good Jobs and More Pay': A Participants' Perspective on the New Deal', *Competition and Change* 5(4): 375–93.

Grayling, T. (2002) *Getting Back on Track* (London: IPPR).

Greater Manchester Low Pay Unit (1999) *Rhetoric and Reality: Young People and the New Deal* (Manchester: Greater Manchester Low Pay Unit).

Green D. (1999) *An End to Welfare Rights: The Rediscovery of Independence* (London: Institute of Economic Affairs).

Green Pedersen, C., van Kersbergen, K. and Hemerijck, A. (2001) 'Neo-liberalism, the "Third Way" or What? Recent Social Democratic Welfare Policies in Denmark and The Netherlands', *Journal of European Public Policy* 8(2): 307–25.

Greve, K. (1999) 'Creating Governance by Contract: Creating Public Private Partnerships in Denmark', in Y. Fortin and H. Van Hassel (eds), *Contracting in the New Public Management* (Amsterdam: IOS Press).

Hajer, M. (1995) *The Politics of Environmental Discourse* (Oxford: Oxford University Press).

Hall, S. (1985) 'Authoritarian Populism: A Reply', *New Left Review* 151: 115–24.

Hallowell, N. (1999) 'Doing the Right Thing: Genetic Risk and Responsibility', in P. Conrad and J. Gabe (eds), *Sociological Perspectives on the New Genetics* (Oxford: Blackwell).

Halpin, D. and Troyna, B. (1995) 'The Politics of Education Policy Borrowing', *Comparative Education* 31(3): 303.

Hantrais, L. (2000) *Social Policy in the European Union*, 2nd edn (Basingstoke: Macmillan – now Palgrave Macmillan).

Harris, M. and Rochester, C. (2000) *Voluntary Organizations and Social Policy in Britain* (Basingstoke: Palgrave – now Palgrave Macmillan).

Harrison, M. with Davis, C. (2001) *Housing, Social Policy and Difference: Disability, Ethnicity, Gender and Housing* (Bristol: Policy Press).

Hasluck, C. (2000) *Early Lessons from the Evaluation of the New Deal Programmes*, Employment Service, Research and Development Report, ESR 49 (Sheffield: ES).

Hasluck C. (2001) 'Lessons from the New Deal: Finding Work, Promoting Employability', *New Economy* 8(4): 230–4.

Hay, C. (1999) *The Political Economy of New Labour* (Manchester: Manchester University Press).

Hay, C. (2000) 'Globalization, Social Democracy and the Persistence of Partisan Politics: A Commentary on Garrett', *Review of International Political Economy* 7(1): 138–52.

Hay, C. (2001) 'Globalization, Economic Change and the Welfare State: The Vexatious Inquisition of Taxation', in R. Sykes, P. Prior and B. Palier (eds), *Globalization and European Welfare States* (Basingstoke: Palgrave – now Palgrave Macmillan).

Haynes, R.M. and Chalker, D.M. (1997) *World Class Elementary Schools: Agenda for Action* (Lancaster, PA: Technomic).

Heclo, H. (1974) *Modern Social Politics in Britain and Sweden* (New Haven, CT: Yale University Press).

Heiser, S. (2002) 'People with Dementia Reveal Their Views of Homecare', *Journal of Dementia Care* 10(1): 22–3.

Hellawell, S. (2001) *Beyond Access: ICT and Social Inclusion* (London: Fabian Society).

Help the Aged (2002) 'Closure of Care Home Crisis'. Press release, 18 March.

Henderson, G. and Karn, V. (1987) *Race, Class and State Housing: Inequality and the Allocation of Public Housing in Britain* (Aldershot: Gower).

Heron, E. (2001) 'Etzioni's Spirit of Communitarianism: Community Values and Welfare Realities in Blair's Britain', in R. Sykes, C. Bochel, and N. Ellison (eds), *Social Policy Review 13* (Bristol: Policy Press).

Hewitt, M. and Powell, M. (2002) *Welfare State and Welfare Change* (Buckingham: Open University Press).

Hewitt, P. and Gould, P. (1993) 'Lessons from America: Learning from Success – Labour and Clinton's New Democrats', *Renewal* 1(1): 45–51.

HFMA/NHSE (2001) *NHS Finance in the UK: Introductory Guide*, 5th edn (Bristol: NHSE and Healthcare Financial Management Association).

Hillman, M. (1986) 'Not a Carborne Democracy', in E. De Boer (ed.), *Transport Sociology* (London: Pergamon Press).

Hills, J. (1995) *Inquiry into Income and Wealth* (York: Joseph Rowntree Foundation).

Hills, J. (1998) *Thatcherism, New Labour and the Welfare State* (London: Centre for the Analysis of Social Exclusion, LSE).

Hills, J. (2000) *Taxation for the Enabling State* (London: Centre for the Analysis of Social Exclusion, LSE).

Hills, J. and Lelkes, O. (1999) 'Social Security, Selective Universalism and Patch-work Redistribution', in R. Jowell, J. Curtice, A. Park and K. Thompson (eds), *British Social Attitudes: the 16th Report: Who Shares New Labour Values?* (Aldershot: Ashgate).

Hills, J., Le Grand, J. and Piachaud, D. (eds) (2002) *Understanding Social Exclusion* (Oxford, Oxford University Press).

Hirst, P. and Thompson, G. (1999) *Globalization in Question*, 2nd edn (Cambridge: Polity Press).

HM Treasury (1999) *Tackling Poverty and Extending Opportunity: The Modernisation of Britain's Tax and Benefit System No 4* (London: HMSO).

HM Treasury (2000) *Government Interventions in Deprived Areas (GIDA) Cross-cutting Review, Spending Review 2000* (London: HM Treasury).

HM Treasury (2001a) *Tackling Child Poverty A Pre-Budget Report Document* (London: HMSO).

HM Treasury (2001b) *The Changing Welfare State: Employment Opportunity for All* (London: HM Treasury and DWP).

HM Treasury, *Budget 2002* (www.hm-treasury.gov.uk/budget).

HM Treasury (2002) *Spending Review 2002* (London: HMSO).

HMSO (1994) *Jobseeker's Allowance*, Cm 2687 (London: HMSO).

Hobcraft, J. (1998) *Intergenerational and Life-course Transmission of Social Exclusion: Influences of Childhood Poverty, Family Disruption and Contact with the Police* (London: CASE paper 15, LSE).

Hodson, D. and Maher, I. (2001) 'The Open Method as a New Mode of Governance', *Journal of Common Market Studies* 39(4): 719–46.

Holcomb, P. and Martinson, K. (2002) 'Putting Policy into Practice: Five Years of Welfare Reform', in A. Weil and K. Finegold (eds), *Welfare Reform: The Next Act* (Washington, DC: Urban Institute Press).

Hollway, W. and Jefferson, T. (2000) *Doing Qualitative Research Differently: Free Association, Narrative and the Interview Method* (London: Sage).

Home Office (1997a) *Getting to Grips with Crime* (London: Home Office).

Home Office (1997b) *No More Excuses* (London: Home Office).

Home Office (1998) *Joining Forces to Protect the Public* (London: Home Office).

Home Office (2001a) *Making Punishments Work: Report of a Review of the Sentencing Framework for England and Wales* (London: Home Office).

Home Office (2001b) *Policing A New Century: A Blueprint for Reform*, Cm 5326 (London: Home Office).

Home Office (2002) *Justice For All* (London: HMSO).

Hooghe, L. and Marks, G. (2001) *Multi-level Governance and European Integration* (Lanham: Rowman & Littlefield).

Hooghiemstra, E. (1997) 'Een-en tweeverdieners?', in M. Niphuis-Nell (ed.), *Sociale Atlas van de Vrouw, deel 4: Veranderingen in de Primaire Leefsfeer* (Rijswijk: Sociaal en Cultureel Planbureau).

Hope, T. (2001) 'Community Crime Prevention in Britain: A Strategic Overview', *Criminal Justice* 1(4): 421–39.

Houghton, J.T., Ding, Y., Griggs, D.J., Noguer, M., van der Linden, P.J. and D. Xiaosu (eds) (2001) *Climate Change 2001: The Scientific Basis, Intergovernmental Panel on Climate Change* (Cambridge: Cambridge University Press).

House of Commons Social Security Committee (1998) *Social Security Reforms: Lessons from the United States of America*, HC 82 (London: HMSO).

Howard, M., Garnham, A., Fimister, G. and Veit-Wilson, J. (2001) *Poverty: The Facts* (London: Child Poverty Action Group).

Hoyle, C. and Rose, D. (2001) 'Labour, Law and Order', *Political Quarterly* 72(1): 76–85.

Huber, E. and Stephens, J. (2001) *Development and Crisis of the Welfare State* (Chicago: Chicago University Press).

Huby, M. (1998) *Social Policy and the Environment* (Milton Keynes: Open University Press).

Huby, M. (2002) 'The Sustainable Use of Resources', in T. Fitzpatrick and M. Cahill (eds), *Environment and Welfare* (Basingstoke: Palgrave Macmillan).

Hudson, J. (1999) 'Informatization and Public Administration: A Political Science Perspective', *Information, Communication and Society* 2(3): 318–39.

Hudson, J. (2000) 'The Prospects for Information Age Government', in R. Burrows and N. Pleace (eds), *Wired Welfare? Essays on the Rhetoric and Reality of e-Social Policy* (York: Centre for Housing Policy, University of York).

Hudson, J. (2002) 'Digitizing the Structures of Government: The UK's Information Age Government Agenda', *Policy & Politics* 5: 15–33.

Hughes, G. and Lewis, G. (eds) (1998) *Unsettling Welfare: The Reconstruction of Social Policy* (London: Routledge).

Hunter, D. (1999) *Managing for Health: Implementing the New Health Agenda* (London: IPPR).

Hunter, D. (2001) 'Something Old, Something Borrowed, Something New', in I. Allen (ed.) *Social Care and Health. A New Deal?* (London: Policy Studies Institute).

Hutcheson, R. (2001) 'Bush to Push Faith-based Aid', *Philadelphia Inquirer* 26 January.

Hutton, W. (1995) *The State We're In* (London: Cape).

Illich, I. (1973) *Tools for Conviviality* (London: Marion Boyars).

Imrie, R. and Thomas, H. (1993) 'The Limits of Property-led Regeneration', *Environment and Planning C: Government and Policy* 11: 87–102.

Imrie, R. and Thomas, H. (eds) (1999) *British Urban Policy. An Evaluation of the Urban Development Corporations* (London: Sage).

Inland Revenue (2001) *New Tax Credits: Supporting Families, Making Work Pay and Tackling Poverty* (London: HMSO).

IPPR (2001) *Building Better Partnerships* (London: IPPR).

IPPR (2002) *A New Contract for Retirement* (London: IPPR).

Iversen, T. (2001) 'The Causes of Welfare State Expansion: Deindustrialization or Globalization?', *World Politics* 52 (April) 313–49.

Jacobs, M. (1999) *Environmental Modernisation* (London: Fabian Society).

Jeffs, T. and Spence, J. (2000) 'New Deal for Young People: Good Deal or Poor Deal', *Youth and Policy* 66: 34–62.

Jesson, D. (2002) *Value Added and the Benefits of Specialism* (London: Technology Colleges Trust).

Jessop, B. (1994) 'The Transition to post-Fordism and the Schumpeterian Workfare State', in R. Burrows and B. Loader (eds), *Towards a Post-Fordist Welfare State?* (London: Routlege).

Jessop, B. (2000) 'The State and the Contradictions of the Knowledge-Driven Economy' in J.R. Bryson, P.W. Daniels, N.D. Henry and J. Pollard (eds), *Knowledge, Space, Economy* (London: Routledge).

Jessop, B., Bonnett, K., Bromley, S. and Ling, T. (1988) *Thatcherism: A Tale of Two Nations* (Cambridge: Polity Press).

Johnson, P. (1999) 'Electronic Service Delivery: Achieving Accuracy and Consistency in Complex Transactions', *Australian Journal of Public Administration* 58(3): 66–71.

Jones Finer, C. and Nellis, M. (eds) (1998) *Crime and Social Exclusion* (Oxford: Blackwell).

Jones, T. (2001) 'Financing the NHS', in P. Merry (ed.), *Wellard's NHS Handbook 2001/02*, 16th edn (Sussex: JMH).

Jones, T. and Newburn, T. (1997) *Policing After the Act* (London: Policy Studies Institute).

Jordan, B. (1996) *A Theory of Poverty and Social Exclusion* (Cambridge: Polity Press).

Jordan, B. (1998) *The New Politics of Welfare* (London: Sage).

Joseph, K. (1972) 'The Cycle of Deprivation', Speech to Conference of Pre-School Playgroups Association, 29 June.

Joseph, K. (1974) 'Britain: a Decadent New Utopia', Speech, Birmingham 19 October, *Guardian*, 21 October.

Joseph Rowntree Foundation (1995) *Joseph Rowntree Foundation Inquiry into Income and Wealth* (York: Joseph Rowntree Foundation).

JPPAP (2001) *What Works: Towards Effective Practice* (London: JPPAP).

Kassim, H. and D. Hine (1998) 'Conclusion', in D. Hine and H. Kassim (eds) *Beyond the Market: The EU and National Social Policy* (London: Routledge).

Keeble, L. and Loader, B. (eds) (2001) *Community Informatics: Computer Mediated Social Networks* (London: Routledge).

Kemp, P. (1999) 'Housing Policy under New Labour' in T. Brown (ed.), *Stakeholder Housing* (London, Pluto Press).

Kemp. P. (2000) 'Housing Benefit and Welfare Retrenchment in Britain', *Journal of Social Policy*, **29**: 263–79.

Kemp, P., Wilcox, S. and Rhodes, D. (2002) *Housing Benefit Reform: Next Steps* (York: Joseph Rowntree Foundation).

Kempson, E., Ford, J. and Quilgars, D. (1999) *Unsafe Safety-nets* (York, Centre for Housing Policy, University of York).

Kennedy, H. (1997) *Learning Works; Widening Participation in Further Education* (Coventry: Further Education Funding Council).

Kennett, P. (1994) 'Exclusion, post-Fordism and the "New Europe"' in R. Brown and R. Crompton (eds), *Economic Restructuring and Social Exclusion* (London: UCL Press).

Kestenbaum, A. (1999) *What Price Independence? Independent Living and People with High Support Needs* (Bristol: Policy Press).

Kiel, L. and Elliot, E. (eds) (1997) *Chaos Theory in the Social Sciences: Foundations and Applications* (Ann Arbor: University of Michigan Press).

King, D. (1995) *Actively Seeking Work? The Politics of Unemployment and Welfare Policy in the United States and Great Britain* (Chicago: University of Chicago Press).

King, D. (1999) *In the Name of Liberalism: Illiberal Social Policy in the USA and Britain* (Oxford: Oxford University Press).

King, S. (1994) 'Analysis of Electronic Support Groups for Recovering Addicts', *Interpersonal Computing and Technology* 2(3): 47–56.

King's Fund/Audit Commission (1998) *Investing in Rehabilitation* (London: King's Fund).

King's Fund (2002) *Partnerships under Pressure* (London: King's Fund).

Kleinman, M. (2002) *A European Welfare State? European Union Social Policy in Context* (Basingstoke: Palgrave Macmillan).

Knight, J. and Brent, M. (1999) *Excluding Attitudes: Disabled People's Experience of Social Exclusion* (London: Leonard Cheshire).

Kotlikoff, L. (1992) *Generational Accounting. Knowing Who Pays, and When, for What we Spend* (New York: Free Press).

Kvist, J. and Thaulow, I. (2001) 'How Does "Flexicurity" apply to Denmark?', Paper given to EU COST A15, Budapest, 12–14 October.

Labour Party (1995) *A New Economic Future for Britain: Economic and Employment Opportunities for All, Final Report of the Economic Policy Commission* (London: Labour Party).

Labour Party (1996) *Tackling Youth Crime and Reforming Youth Justice* (London: Labour Party).

Land, H. (1980) 'The Family Wage', *Feminist Review* 6: 55–78.

Lash, S. (2002) *Critique of Information* (London: Sage).

Laurie, H. and Gershuny, J. (2000) 'Couples, Work and Money', in R. Berthoud and J. Gershuny (eds) *Seven Years in the Lives of British Families* (Bristol: Policy Press).

Lawless, P., Martin, R., and Hardy, S. (1998) *Unemployment and Social Exclusion* (London: Jessica Kingsley).

Layard, R. (1997) *What Labour Can Do* (London: Warner).

Layard, R., Nickell, S. and Jackman, R. (1991) *Unemployment: Macroeconomic Performance and the Labour Market* (Oxford: University Press).

Le Grand, J. (1998) 'The Third Way Begins with Cora', *New Statesman* 6 March: 26–7.

Le Grand, J., Mays, N. and Mulligan, J. (1998) *Learning from the NHS Internal Market: A Review of the Evidence* (London: King's Fund).

Leeds City Council and West Yorkshire Passenger Transport Authority (1991) *Leeds Transport Strategy*, February (Leeds: Leeds City Council).

Leese, B. and Bosanquet, N. (1995) 'Changes in General Practice and its Effects on Service Provision in Areas with Different Socio-economic Characteristics', *British Medical Journal*, **311**: 1256–67.

Legard, R. and Ritchie, J. (1999) *New Deal for Young Unemployed People: National Gateway*, Employment Service, Research and Development Report, ESR 16 (Sheffield: ES).

Leibfried, S. and Pierson, P. (eds.) (1995) *European Social Policy: Between Fragmentation and Integration* (Washington: Brookings Institute).

Levett, R. (2000) 'Economic Growth and Environmental Sustainability: the Prospects for Green Growth', *Local Economy* **15**(4): 352–4.

Levitas, R. (1998) *The Inclusive Society? Social Exclusion and New Labour* (Basingstoke: Macmillan – now Palgrave Macmillan).

Lewis, G. (ed.) (1998) *Forming Nation, Framing Welfare* (London: Routledge).

Lewis, G., Hughes, G. and Saraga, E. (2000) 'The Body of Social Policy: Social Policy and the Body', in L. McKie and N. Watson (eds), *Organising Bodies: Policy, Institutions and Work* (Basingstoke: Macmillan – now Palgrave Macmillan).

Lewis, J. (ed.) (1983) *Women's Welfare, Women's Rights* (London: Croom Helm).

Lewis, J. (1999) 'New Labour, Nouvelle Grande-Bretagne?' *Lien Social et Politiques* 41: 61–70.

Lewis, J. (2001) *Pictures of Welfare, Inaugural Lecture* (Oxford: Oxford University Press).

Lewis, J. and Sawyer, L. (2001) 'Rediscovering Community Care', series of articles published in *Homecare Professional* 7: Feb–July.

Lindblom, C.E. (1977) *Politics and Markets: The World's Political-Economic Systems* (New York: Basic Books).

Lippman, A. (1994) 'Prenatal Genetic Testing and Screening: Constructing Needs and Reinforcing Inequities', in A. Clarke (ed.), *Genetic Counselling: Practice and Principles* (London: Routledge).

Lipsey, M. (1992) 'Juvenile Delinquency Treatment: A Meta-analytic Enquiry into the Variability of Effects', in T. Cook, H. Cooper and D.S. Cordray (eds), *Meta-Analysis for Explanation: A Case-Book* (New York: Russell Sage).

Lipsky, M. (1980) *Street Level Bureaucracy: The Dilemmas of the Individual in Public Services* (New York: Russell Sage).

Lissenburgh, S. (2001) *New Deal the Long Term Unemployed Pilots: Quantitative Evaluation Using Stage 2 Survey*, Policy Studies Institute, Employment Service, Research and Development Report, ESR 81 (Sheffield: ES).

Lister, R. (1990) 'Women, Economic Dependency and Citizenship', *Journal of Social Policy* 19(4): 445–67.

Lister, R. (1998) 'From Equality to Social Inclusion: New Labour and the Welfare State', *Critical Social Policy* 18(2): 215–25.

Lister R, (2001) 'Doing Good by Stealth: the Politics of Poverty and Inequality Under New Labour', *New Economy* June 65–70.

Little, A. (2002) 'Working-Time Reductions', in T. Fitzpatrick and M. Cahill (eds), *Environment and Welfare* (Basingstoke: Palgrave Macmillan).

Loader, B. (1998) *The Cyberspace Divide: Equality, Agency and Policy in the Information Society* (London: Routledge).

Lodemel, I. and Trickey, H. (eds) (2000) *An Offer you can't Refuse. Workfare in International Perspective* (Bristol: Policy Press).

Lomborg, B. (2001) *The Skeptical Environmentalist* (Cambridge: Cambridge University Press).

Loynes, F. (2001) *The Rising Challenge: A Survey of Local Education Authorities on Educatiional Provision for Pupils with Autistic Spectrum Disorder* (London: All-Party Parliamentary Group on Autism).

Lunt, N., Atkin, L. and Hirst, M. (1997) 'Staying Single in the 1990s: Single Handed Practitioners in the New National Health Service', *Social Science and Medicine* 45: 341–9.

McCormick, J. (2001) 'Welfare and Wellbeing' *Political Quarterly* 72(1): 86–96.

McDonough, M. and Asvesta, M. (2002) 'Analysis of the Claimant Count by Age and Duration Including Clerical Claims', *Labour Market Trends* 110(7) (London: HMSO).

MacGregor, S. (1999) 'Welfare, Neo-Liberalism and New Paternalism', *Capital and Class* 967(2): 91–119.

McLaughlin, E., Trewsdale, J. and McCay, N. (2001) 'The Rise and Fall of the UK's First Tax Credit: the Working Families Tax Credit, 1998–2000', *Social Policy and Administration* 35(2): 163–80.

Macnicol, J. (1999) 'From "Problem Family" to "Underclass", 1945–95', in H. Fawcett and R. Lowe (eds), *Welfare Policy in Britain: the Road from 1945* (Basingstoke: Macmillan – now Palgrave Macmillan).

Macpherson, Sir William (1999) *The Stephen Lawrence Inquiry*, Cm 4262 (London: Stationery Office).

Mair, G. (2000) 'Credible accreditation?' *Probation Journal* 47: 268–71.

Malpass, P. and Murie, A. (1994) *Housing Policy and Practice* (Basingstoke: Macmillan – now Palgrave Macmillan).

Malpass, P. and Murie, A. (1999) *Housing Policy and Practice*, 5th edn (Basingstoke: Macmillan – now Palgrave Macmillan).

Mandelson, P. (1997) *Labour's Next Steps: Tackling Social Exclusion* (London: Fabian Society).

Mandelson, P. and Liddle, R. (1996) *The Blair Revolution* (London: Faber and Faber).

Margetts, H. and Dunleavy, P. (2002) 'Cultural Barriers to e-Government', Academic Article HC 704-III in Support of National Audit Office (NAO), *Better Public Service Through e-Government* (London: Stationery Office).

Marier, P. (2002) *Explaining Pension Reform: The Cases of France, Belgium Sweden and the United*

Kingdom, Ph.D. Dissertation Department of Political Science, University of Pittsburgh.

Marks, G., Hooghe, L. and Blank, K. (1996a) 'European Integration from the 1980s: State-Centric v. Multi-Level Governance', *Journal of Common Market Studies* 34(3): 341–78.

Marks, G., Nielsen, F., Ray, L. and Salk, J. (1996b) 'Competencies, Cracks and Conflicts: Regional Mobilization in the European Union' in G. Marks, F. Scharpf, P. Schmitter and W. Streeck (eds), *Governance in the European Union* (London: Sage).

Marks, G., Scharpf, F., Schmitter, P. and Streeck, W. (eds) (1996c) *Governance in the European Union* (London: Sage).

Marks, L. and Hunter, D. (1998) *The Development of Primary Care Groups: Policy into Practice* (Birmingham: NHS Confederation).

Marsh, A. (2000) 'Helping British Lone Parents Get and Keep Paid Work', Paper Delivered to Lone Parents and Employment Conference, University of Bath, 26–27 October.

Marshall, T. (2001) *Icteachers – A Revolution in Schooling?* www.spiked-online.com/Articles/00000002D1B9.htm.

Marshall, T.H. (1950) *Citizenship and Social Class* (Cambridge: Cambridge University Press).

Marteau, T.M. and Lerman, C. (2001) 'Genetic Risk and Behavioural Change', *British Medical Journal* 322: 1056–9.

Martin R., Nativel, C. and Sunley, P. (2001) 'Mapping the New Deal: Local Disparities in the Performance of Welfare-to-Work', *Transactions of the Institute of British Geographers* 26(4): 484–512.

Matza, D. (1971) 'Poverty and Disrepute', in R.K. Merton and R. Nisbet (eds), *Contemporary Social Problems*, 3rd edn (New York: Harcourt Brace Jovanovich).

May, P. (2002) 'Social Regulation', in L.M. Salamon (ed.), *Handbook of Policy Instruments* (New York: Oxford University Press).

Mays, N., Goodwin, N., Killoran, A. and Malbon, G. (1998) *Total Purchasing. A Step Towards Primary Care Groups* (London: King's Fund).

Mead, L. (1986) *Beyond Entitlement. The Social Obligations of Citizenship* (New York: Free Press).

Mead, L. (1997) *The New Paternalism. Supervisory Approaches to Poverty* (Washington, DC: Brookings Institute).

Melucci, A. (1980) 'The New Social Movements: a Theoretical Approach', *Social Science Information* 19(2): 41–56.

Menter, I., Muschamp, Y. and Nicholls, P. (1997) *Work and Identity in the Primary School* (Buckingham: Open University Press).

Merrington, S. and Stanley, S. (2000) 'Doubts About the What Works Initiative, *Probation Journal* 47: 272–5.

Meyer, M.H. (ed.) (2000) *Care Work, Gender, Class and the Welfare State* (New York: Routledge).

Millar, J. (2000) *Keeping Track of Welfare Reform: The New Deal Programmes* (York: Joseph Rowntree Foundation).

Millar, J. (2002) 'Adjusting Welfare Policies to Stimulate Job Entry: The Example of the United Kingdom', in H. Sarfarti and G. Bonoli (eds), *Labour Market and Social Protection: Reforms in International Perspective* (Aldershot: Ashgate).

Ministry of Transport (1963) *Traffic in Towns, a Study of the Long Term Problems of Traffic in Urban Areas* (the Buchanan Report) (London: HMSO).

Mintzberg, H. (1983) *Structures in Fives* (London: Prentice Hall).

Mirza, H.S. and Gillborn, D. (2000) *Educational Inequality: Mapping Race, Class and Gender: A Synthesis of Research Evidence* (London: OFSTED).

Mishra, R. (1999) *Globalization and the Welfare State* (London: Edward Elgar).

Mol, A. and Sonnenfeld, D. (2000) *Ecological Modernisation Around the World* (London: Frank Cass).

Moran, M. (2002) 'Understanding the Regulatory State', *British Journal of Political Science* 32(2): 391–413.

Morgan, R. and Newburn, T. (1997) *The Future of Policing* (Oxford: Oxford University Press).

Moriarty, M. (1977) 'Criminal Justice Policy-making: the View from the Home Office', in N. Walker (ed.), *Penal Policy Making in England* (Cambridge: Institute of Criminology).

Morris, E. (2002) 'Aim Higher', *Guardian*, 23 May.

Morris, J. (1993) *Independent Lives? Community Care and Disabled People* (Basingstoke: Macmillan – now Palgrave Macmillan).

Morris, J. (1999) *Hurtling Into a Void: Transition to Adulthood for Young Disabled People with Complex Health and Support Needs* (Brighton: Pavilion).

Morris, J. (2001) *That Kind of Life? Social Exclusion and Young Disabled People with High Levels of Support Needs* (London: Scope).

Morris, T. (2001) 'Crime and Penal Policy', in A. Seldon (ed.), *The Blair Effect* (London: Little, Brown).

Moursund, J. (1997) 'SANCTUARY: Social Support on the Internet' in J.E. Behar (ed.), *Mapping Cyberspace: Social Research on the Electronic Frontier* (United States: Dowling College Press).

Moynihan, D.P. (1969) *Maximum Feasible Misunderstanding* (New York: Free Press).

Mullins, D., Niner, P. and Riseborough, M. (1993) 'Large Scale Voluntary Transfers', in P. Malpass and R. Means (eds), *Implementing Housing Policy* (Buckingham: Open University Press).

Murie, A. and Nevin B. (2001) 'New Labour Transfers', in D. Cowan and A. Marsh (eds), *Two Steps Forward: Housing Policy into the New Millennium* (Bristol: Policy Press).

Murray, C. (1984) *Losing Ground. American Social Policy, 1950–1980* (New York: Basic Books).

Murray, C. (1990) *The Emerging British Underclass* (London: Institute of Economic Affairs).

Myles, J. and Pierson, P. (2001) 'The Comparative Political Economy of Pension Reform', in P. Pierson (ed.), *The New Politics of the Welfare State* (Cambridge: Cambridge University Press).

Myles, J. and Quadagno, J. (2001) 'Political Theories of the Welfare State', *Social Service Review* 76: 34–55.

NAO (2002a) *Better Public Service Through e-Government*, HC704-I (London: Stationery Office).

NAO (2002b) *Government on the Web II*, HC764 (London: Stationery Office).

NAO (2002c) *The New Deal for Young People, Report by the Comptroller and Auditor General* (London: NAO).

National Committee of Inquiry into Higher Education (1997) *Higher Education in the Learning Society* (London: HMSO).

National Council for One Parent Families (2001) *Lone Parents and Employment: The Facts* (London: National Council for One Parent Families).

NDTF (New Deal Task Force Working Group) (1998) *Meeting the Needs of Disadvantaged Young People* (London: NDTF).

Nellthorp, J. and Mackie, P.J. (2000) 'The UK Roads Review – a Hedonic Model of Decision Making', *Transport Policy* 7(2): 127–38.

Nettleton, S. and Burrows, R. (2003) 'E-scaped Medicine? Information, Reflexivity and Health', *Critical Social Policy*, Forthcoming.

Nettleton, S., Burrows, R., Pleace, N., Loader, B. and Muncer, S. (2002) 'The Reality of Virtual Social Support' in S. Woolgar (ed.), *Virtual Society?* (Oxford: Oxford University Press).

New Deal Task Force (1998) *Meeting the Needs of Disadvantaged Young People, A Report by the New Deal Task Force Working Group* (London: New Deal Task Force).

Newburn, T. (1998) 'Tackling Youth Crime and Reforming Youth Justice: The Origins and Nature of New Labour Policy', *Policy Studies* 19(3/4): 199–214.

Newburn, T. (2001) 'Community Safety and Policing: Some Implications of the Crime and Disorder Act 1998', in G. Hughes, E. McLaughlin and J. Muncie (eds), *Crime Prevention and Community Safety: New Directions* (London: Sage).

Newburn, T. (2002) 'Atlantic Crossings: "Policy Transfer" and Crime Control in the USA and Britain', *Punishment and Society* 4(2): 165–94.

Newman, J. (2001) *Modernising Governance: New Labour, Policy and Society* (London: Sage).

NHS (2001) *Shifting the Balance of Power: The Next Steps*, downloaded from www.doh.gov.uk/shiftingthebalance/nextsteps/htm.

NHSE (1994) *Developing NHS Purchasing and GP Fundholding*, EL(94)79 (Leeds: NHSE).

Norris, C., Moran, J. and Armstrong, G. (1998) 'Algorithmic Surveillance: The Future of Automated Visual Surveillance', in C. Norris, J. Moran and G. Armstrong (eds), *Surveillance, Closed Circuit Television and Social Control* (Aldershot: Ashgate).

North, N. and Peckham, S. (2001) 'Analysing Structural Interests in Primary Care Groups', *Social Policy and Administration* 35(4): 426–40.

NRU (2002) *Collaboration and Co-ordination in Area-Based Initiatives*, Research Report No.1 (London: NRU).

Oatley, N. (ed.) (1998) *Cities, Economic Competition and Urban Policy* (London: Paul Chapman).

O'Brien, M. and Penna, S. (1998) *Theorising Welfare: Enlightenment and Modern Society* (London: Sage).

O'Connor, W., Bruce, S. and Ritchie, J. (2000) *New Deal for Young People: National Follow-Through, National Centre for Social Research*, Employment Service, Research and Development Report, ESR 47 (Sheffield: ES).

O'Donnell, K. (2001) *New Deal Survey of Leavers to Unknown Destinations*, ORC International, Employment Service, Research and Development Report, ESR 63 (Sheffield: ES).

OECD (1994) *The Job Study* (Paris: OECD).

OECD (2000) *Economic Studies* 31 2000/2 (Paris: OECD).

OECD (2001) *Education at a Glance*, List of Indicator Tables www.oecd.org/EN/document/0,,EN-document-4-nodirectorate-no-27-22129-4,00.html.

Offe, C. (1996) *Modernity and the State* (Cambridge: Polity Press).

OFSTED (2001) Specialist Schools: An Evaluation of Progress www.ofsted.gov.uk/public/docs01/specialistschools.pdf.

Ohmae, K. (1995) *The End of the Nation-state: The Rise of Regional Economies* (London: HarperCollins).

Oliver, M.J. (1999) *Disabled People and the Inclusive Society: Or, the Times They Really Are Changing* www.independentliving.org.

ONS (2002) *Carers 2000* (London: Stationery Office).

Paris, C. (ed.) (2001) *Housing in Northern Ireland – and Comparisons with the Republic of Ireland* (Coventry: Chartered Institute of Housing).

Parry, G. (2001) 'Academic Snakes and Vocational Ladders', The Philip Jones Memorial Lecture (Leicester, NIACE).

Pascall, G. (1993) 'Citizenship – a Feminist Analysis', in G. Drover and P. Kerans (eds), *New Approaches to Welfare Theory* (Aldershot: Edward Elgar).

Pateman, C. (1988) 'The Patriarchal Welfare State', in A. Gutman (ed.), *Democracy and the Welfare State* (Princeton: Princeton University Press).

Pawson, H. (2000) *Local Authority Policy and Practice on Allocations, Transfers and Homelessness* (London: DETR).

Pensions Reform Group (2001) *Universal Protected Pension: Modernising Pensions for the Millennium* (London: Institute of Community Studies).

Pepper, D. (1993) *Eco-Socialism* (London: Routledge).

Pepper, D. (1996) *Modern Environmentalism* (London: Routledge).

Perry, J. (2001) 'The End of Council Housing?', in S. Wilcox (ed.), *UK Housing Review 2001/2* (London: Chartered Institute of Housing and Council of Mortgage Lenders).

Personal Social Services Research Unit (2001) *Demand for Long-term Care for Older People in England to 2031* (Canterbury: University of Kent).

Petchey, R. (1996) 'From Stableboys to Jockeys? The Prospects for a Primary Care-led NHS', in M. May, E. Brunsdon and G. Craig (eds), *Social Policy Review 8* (London: Social Policy Association, 1996).

Peters, B.G. (2001) *The Future of Governing*, 2nd edn (Lawrence: University Press of Kansas).

Peters, B.G. (forthcoming) *The Search for Coordination and Coherence: Horizontal Management in Government* (Lawrence: University Press of Kansas).

Piachaud, D. (2000) 'International Social Welfare and the Impact of Globalization'. Unpublished address.

Piachaud, D and Sutherland, H. (2000) 'Child Poverty and the New Labour Government', *Journal of Social Policy* 30(1): 95–118.

Pierson. C. (2001) *Hard Choices* (Cambridge: Polity Press).

Pierson, P. (1994) *Dismantling the Welfare State? Reagan, Thatcher, and the Politics of Retrenchment* (Cambridge: Cambridge University Press).

Pierson, P. (1996) 'The New Politics of the Welfare State', *World Politics*, 48(2): 143–79.

Pierson, P. (ed.) (2001) *The New Politics of the Welfare State* (Cambridge: Cambridge University Press).

PIU (Performance and Innovation Unit) (2000) *Reaching Out: The Role of Central Government at Regional and Local Level* (London: Performance and Innovation Unit, Cabinet Office).

Piven, F.F. and Cloward, R.A. (1972) *Regulating the Poor* (New York: Vintage).

Place, M. and Newbronner, E. (1999) *Roles, Functions and Costs of Primary Care Trusts; the Expected Costs of Managing a Primary Care Trust* (York: Health Economics Consortium).

Plant, R. (1998) *New Labour – A Third Way?* (London: European Policy Forum).

Plant, R. and Barry, N. (1990) *Citizenship and Rights in Thatcher's Britain. Two Views* (London: Institute of Economic Affairs).

Pleace, N. and Quilgars, D. (2002) *Housing.support.org.uk: Social Housing, Social Care and Electronic Service Delivery* (York: Joseph Rowntree Foundation/York Publishing Services).

Pleace, N., Burrows, R., Loader, B. Muncer, S. and Nettleton, S. (2000) 'On-Line with the Friends of Bill W: Social Support and the Net', *Sociological Research Online* 5(2), www.socresonline.org.uk/5/2/pleace.html.

Pleace, N., Burrows, R., Loader, B., Muncer, S. and Nettleton, S. (2003) 'From Self-Service Welfare to Virtual Self-help?' in E. Harlow and S. Webb (eds), *Caring Professions and Information Technology* (London: Jessica Kingsley).

Police Foundation/PSI (1994) *Inquiry into the Role and Responsibilities of the Police* (London: Police Foundation/Policy Studies Institute).

Powell, M. (ed.) (1999) *New Labour, New Welfare State?* (Bristol: Policy Press).

Powell, M. (2000) 'New Labour and the Third Way in the British Welfare State: A New and Distinctive Approach?' *Critical Social Policy* 20(1): 39–60.

Powell, M. and Exworthy, M. (2002) 'Partnerships, Quasi-networks and Social Policy', in. C. Glendenning, M. Powell and K. Rummery (eds), *Partnerships, New Labour and the Governance of Welfare* (Bristol: Policy Press).

Powell, M. and Hewitt, M. (1998) 'The End of the Welfare State?', *Social Policy and Administration* 32(1): 1–13.

Power, M. (1997) *The Audit Society* (Oxford: Oxford University Press).

Pratt, J. (1997) *Governing the Dangerous: Dangerousness, Law and Social Change* (Sydney: Federation Press).

Price, D. (2000) *Office of Hope: A History of the Employment Service* (London: Policy Studies Institute).

Pritchard, J. (2002) *Male Victims of Elder Abuse: Their Experiences and Needs* (London: Jessica Kingsley).

Putnam, R. (1988) 'Diplomacy and Domestic Politics', *International Organization* **42**: 427–61.

Putnam, R. (1993) *Making Democracy Work. Civic Traditions in Modern Italy* (Princeton: Princeton University Press).

Quayle, S. (1998) 'The "Drug Czar": A Triumph of Presentation Over Substance?' *Talking Politics* Winter: 87–92.

Raadschelders, J.C.N. and Toonen, T.A.J. (1999) 'Public Sector Reform for Building and Recasting the Welfare State: Experiences in Western Europe', *Research in Public Administration* **5**: 39–62.

RAC (2002) *Motoring Towards 2050* (London: RAC Foundation).

Radaelli, C. (2000) 'Policy Transfer in the European Union: Institutional Isomorphism as a Source of Legitimacy', *Governance* **13**(1): 24–43.

Rahman, M., Palmer, G. and Kenway, P. (2001) *Monitoring Poverty and Social Exclusion 2001* (York: Joseph Rowntree Foundation).

Raine, J. (2001) 'Modernizing Courts or Courting Modernization?' *Criminal Justice* **1**(1): 105–28.

Rake, K. (2000) 'Gender and New Labour's Social Policies', *Journal of Social Policy* **30**(2): 209–32.

Raynor, P. (2002) 'Community Penalties: Probation, Punishment and "What Works"', in M. Maguire, R. Morgan, and R. Reiner (eds), *The Oxford Handbook of Criminology*, 3rd edn (Oxford: Clarendon Press).

Raynor, P. and Vanstone, P. (2002) *Understanding Community Penalties: Probation, Policy and Social Change* (Buckingham: Open University Press).

Reich, R. (1991) *The Work of Nations* (New York: Simon & Schuster).

Reiger, E. and Leibfried, S. (1998) 'Welfare State Limits to Globalization', *Politics and Society* **26**(4): 363–90.

Renshaw, J. and Powell, H. (2001) *The Story So Far: Emerging Evidence of the Impact of the Reformed Youth Justice System*, Draft Report (London: Youth Justice Board).

Richards, S. and Raine, J. (2001) Criminal Justice and the Modernization Agenda, Unpublished paper for the IPPR Criminal Justice Forum.

Rihani, S. (2002) *Complex Systems Theory and Development Practice: Understanding Non-linear Realities* (London: Zed Books).

Riley, R. and Young, G. (2000) *The New Deal for Young People: Implications for Employment and the Public Finances*, National Institute for Social and Economic Research, Employment Service, Research and Development Report, ESR 62 (Sheffield: ES).

Roberts, K. (2001) *Class in Modern Britain* (Basingstoke: Palgrave – now Palgrave Macmillan).

Robertson, J. (1985) *Future Work* (London: Gower).

Robertson, J. (1994) *Benefits and Taxes: A Radical Strategy* (London: New Economics Foundation).

Robertson, J. (2002) 'Eco-Taxation in a Green Society', in T. Fitzpatrick and M. Cahill (eds), *Environment and Welfare* (Basingstoke: Palgrave Macmillan).

Robinson, P. (2000) 'Active Labour-market Policies: a Case of Evidence-based Policy Making?', *Oxford Review of Economic Policy* **16**(1): 13–26.

Robinson, P. (2001) *Time to Choose Justice* (London: Institute for Public Policy Research).

Rodrik, D. (1998) 'Why Do More Open Economies have Bigger Government?', *Journal of Political Economy* **106**(5): 997–1032.

Rogers, R. and Power, A. (2000) *Cities for a Small Country* (London: Faber and Faber).

Roland, M. and Shapiro, J. (eds) (1998) *Specialist Outreach Clinics in General Practice* (Manchester: National Primary Care Research and Development Centre and Oxford: Radcliffe Medical Press).

Room, G. (1992) *National Policies to Combat Social Exclusion, Second Annual Report of the EC Observatory on Policies to Combat Social Exclusion* (Brussels: European Commission).

Room, G. (1995) *Beyond the Threshold* (Bristol: Policy Press).

Rose, R. (1993) *Lesson-drawing in Public Policy. A Guide to Learning Across Time and Space* (New Jersey: Chatham House).

Ross, F. (2002) 'Social Policy', in G. Peele, C.J. Bailey, B. Cain and B.G. Peters (eds), *Developments in American Politics, 4* (Basingstoke: Palgrave Macmillan).

Rothman, B.K. (1988) *The Tentative Pregnancy: Amniocentesis and the Sexual Politics of Motherhood* (London: Pandora).

Rothman, B.K. (1998) *Genetic Maps and Human Imaginations* (New York: WW Norton).

Royal Commission on Environmental Pollution (1994) *Transport and the Environment* (London: HMSO).

Royal Commission on Long Term Care (1999) *With Respect to Old Age: Long Term Care – Rights and Responsibilities* (London: Stationery Office).

Rubery, J., Smith, M. and Fagan, C. (1998) 'National Working-Time Regimes and Equal Opportunities', *Feminist Economics* **4**(1): 71–101.

Ruggie, J.G. (1982) 'International Regimes, Transactions, and Change: Embedded Liberalism in the Postwar Economic Order', *International Organization* **36**(2): 379–415.

Rummery, K. (2002) 'Towards a Theory of Welfare Partnerships', in C. Glendinning, M. Powell and K. Rummery (eds), *Partnerships, New Labour and the Governance of Welfare* (Bristol: Policy Press).

Rustin, M. (1994) 'Flexibility in Higher Education', in R. Burrows and B. Loader (eds), *Towards a Post-Fordist Welfare State?* (London: Routledge).

Ryan, T. (1998) *The Cost of Opportunity: Purchasing Strategies in the Housing and Support Arrangements of People with Learning Difficulties* (London: Values into Action).

Sainsbury Centre for Mental Health (2001) *Cultural Sensitivity Audit Tool for Mental Health Services* (London: SCMH).

Salamon, L.M. (2002) 'Introduction', in L.M. Salamon (ed.) *Handbook of Policy Instruments* (New York: Oxford University Press).

Sale, K. (1985) *Dwellers in the Land: The Bioregional Vision* (San Francisco: Sierra Club).

Saunders, T., Stone, V. and Candy, C. (2001) *The Impact of the 26 Week Sanctioning Regime*, Employment Service, Research and Development Report, ESR 100 (Sheffield: ES).

Savage, S., Charman, S. and Cope, S. (2000) *Policing and the Power of Persuasion: The Changing Role of the Association of Chief Police Officers* (London: Blackstone Press).

Scharpf, F.W. and V.A. Schmidt (2000) *Welfare and Work in the Open Economy* (Oxford: Oxford University Press).

Secretary of State for Health (1997) *The New NHS: Modern, Dependable*, Cm 3807 (London: HMSO).

Secretary of State for Health (1998) *Our Healthier Nation: A Contract for Health*, Cm 3852 (London: HMSO).

Selwyn, N. (2002) '"E-stablishing" an Inclusive Society? Technology, Social Exclusion and UK Government Policy-making', *Journal of Social Policy* **31**(1): 1–20.

SEU (1998) *Bringing Britain Together: A National Strategy for Neighbourhood Renewal*, Report by the Social Exclusion Unit, Cm 4045 (London: HMSO).

SEU (2001) *A New Commitment to Neighbourhood Renewal. National Strategy Action Plan* (London: SEU).

SEU (2002) *Making the Connections: Transport and Social Exclusion – Interim Findings from the Social Exclusion Unit* (London: Cabinet Office).

Shakespeare, T. (1999) '"Losing the Plot?": Medical and Activist Discourses of Contemporary Genetics and Disability', *Sociology of Health and Illness*, **21**(5): 669–88.

Shaw, E. (1996) *The Labour Party Since 1979* (London: Routledge).

Sibley, D. (1995) *Geographies of Exclusion* (London: Routledge).

Silver, L. (1998) *Remaking Eden: Cloning and Beyond in a Brave New World* (London: Weidenfeld & Nicholson).

Sinfield, A. (2001) 'Managing Social Security for What?', in D. Pieters (ed.), *Confidence and Changes: Managing Social Protection in the New Millennium* (Amsterdam: Kluwer Academic).

Slevin, J. (2000) *The Internet and Society* (Cambridge: Polity Press).

Smith, D. (2000) 'Corporatism and the New Youth Justice', in B. Goldson (ed.), *The New Youth Justice* (Lyme Regis: Russell House).

Smith, D. and Ray, J. (eds) (1993) *The 1992 Project and the Future of Integration in Europe* (New York: Sharpe).

Smith, R., Stirling, T. and Williams, P. (2000) *Housing in Wales: The Policy Agenda in an Era of Devolution* (Coventry: Chartered Institute of Housing).

Smith, S., Munro, M. and Ford, J. (2002) *Flexible Mortgages* (London: Office of the Deputy Prime Minister/Council of Mortgage Lenders).

Somerville, P. (2001) 'The Allocation of Social Housing: Allocating Housing – or "Letting" People Choose?', in D. Cowan, and A. Marsh (eds), *Two Steps Forward: Housing Policy into the New Millennium* (Bristol: Policy Press).

Sorenson, E. (1997) 'Democracy and Empowerment', *Public Administration* **75**: 553–67.

Soskice, D. (1999) 'Divergent Production Regimes: Coordination and Uncoordinated Market Economies in the 1980s and 1990s', in H. Kitschelt, P. Lange, G. Marks and J.D. Stephens (eds), *Continuity and Change in Contemporary Capitalism* (Cambridge: Cambridge University Press).

SSI (1991) *Getting the Message Across: A Guide to Developing and Communicating Policies, Prin-*

ciples and Procedures on Assessment (London: HMSO).

Stokoe, R. (2001) *Keep Taking the Medicine: Antipsychotics and the Over-medication of Older People, Causes and Consequences* (London: Liberal Democratic Party).

Stone, D. (1999) 'Learning Lessons and Transferring Policy across Time, Space and Disciplines', *Politics* **19**(1): 51–9.

Strange, S. (1996) *The Retreat of the State* (Cambridge: Cambridge University Press).

Swank, D. (1998) 'Funding the Welfare State: Globalization and the Taxation of Business in Advanced Market Economies', *Political Studies* **46**(4): 671–92.

Sweeney, K. and McMahon, D. (1998) 'The Effect of Jobseeker's Allowance on the Claimant Count', *Labour Market Trends* **106**(4): 195–203.

Sykes, R. and Alcock, P. (eds) (1998) *Developments in European Social Policy: Convergence and Diversity* (Bristol: Policy Press).

Taylor, M. (2001) 'Too Early to Say? New Labour's First Term', *Political Quarterly* **72**(1): 5–18.

Taylor-Gooby, P. (ed.) (2001) *Welfare States Under Pressure* (London: Sage).

Thair, T. and Risdon, A. (1999) 'Women in the Labour Market: Results from the Spring 1998 LFS', *Labour Market Trends* **107**: 103–27.

Thelen, K. and Steinmo, S. (1992) 'Historical Institutionalism in Comparative Politics', in S. Steinmo and F. Longstreth (eds), *Structuring Politics: Historical Institutionalism in Comparative Analysis* (Cambridge: Cambridge University Press).

Thom, D. and Jennings, M. (1996) 'Human Pedigree and the "Best Stock" from Eugenics to Genetics?', in T. Marteau and M.P.M. Richards (eds), *The Troubled Helix: Social and Psychological Implications of the New Human Genetics* (Cambridge; Cambridge University Press).

Thomas, A. and Griffiths, R. (2002) *Early Findings from Lone Parent Personal Adviser Meetings: Qualitative Research with Clients and Case Studies on Delivery*, Employment Service, Research and Development Report, ESR 132 (Sheffield: ES).

Thompson, N. (1996) 'Supply Side Socialism: The Political Economy of New Labour', *New Left Review* **216**: 37–54.

Thomson, D. (1991) *Selfish Generations? How Welfare States Grow Old* (Wellington, NZ: Bridget Williams Books).

Tight M., Bristow, A., Page, M. and Milne, D. (2000) *Transport – A Vision for the Future, A Report of the Rees Jeffreys Road Fund* (London: Landor Press).

Tobin, T. (2002) 'Called to Account', *Health Service Journal*, 17 January: 22–3.

Tomlinson, S. (2001) *Education in a Post-Welfare Society* (Buckingham: Open University Press).

Tonry, M. and Rex, S. (2002) 'Reconsidering Sentencing and Punishment in England and Wales', in S. Rex and M. Tonry (eds), *Reform and Punishment: The Future of Sentencing* (Cullompton: Willan).

Torfing, J. (1999) 'Workfare with Welfare: Recent Reforms of the Danish Welfare State', *Journal of European Social Policy* **9**(1): 5–28.

Touraine, A. (1981) *The Voice and The Eye: An Analysis of Social Movements* (Cambridge: Cambridge University Press).

Toynbee, P. and Walker, D. (2001) *Did Things Get Better? An Audit of Labour's Successes and Failures* (London: Penguin).

Trainer, F.E. (1998) 'The Significance of the Limits to Growth for the Discussion of Social Policy', *International Journal of Sociology and Social Policy* **18**(11/12): 36–60.

Transport, Local Government and the Regions (TLGR) Select Committee (2002) *Eighth Report, Ten Year Plan for Transport* (London: House of Commons).

Trickey, H., Kellard, K., Walker, R., Ashworth, K. and Smith, A. (1998) *Unemployment and Jobseeking Two Years On*, DSS Research Report No. 87 (London: DSS).

Troup, Sir. E. (1925) *The Home Office* (London: G.P. Putnam's and Sons).

TUC (1998) *Comments on the Green Paper on Welfare Reform* (London: Trades Union Congress).

TUC (2002) *Labour Market Programmes*, No. 46 in the TUC Welfare Reform Series (London: Trades Union Congress).

Turok, I. (1992) 'Property-led Urban Regeneration:Panacea or Placebo?', *Environment and Planning A*, **24**: 361–79.

Turok, I. and Webster, D. (1998) 'The New Deal: Jeopardised by the Geography of Unemployment?', *Local Economy* **12**(4): 309–29.

Unwin, L. (2002) '21st Century Vocational Education. What Would Dickens Think?' Unpublished Inaugural Lecture (University of Leicester, 21 May).

Urban Task Force (1999) *Towards an Urban Renaissance*, Final Report of the Urban Task Force Chaired by Lord Rogers of Riverside (London: E. and F.N. Spon).

Urry, J. (2000a) *Sociology Beyond Societies: Mobilities for the Twenty-First Century* (London: Routledge).

Urry, J. (2000b) 'Mobile Sociology', *British Journal of Sociology* **51**(1): 185–203.

VanDerhei, J. and Copeland, C. (2002) 'The Changing Face of Private Retirement Programmes', in P. Edelman, D.L. Salisbury and P.J. Larsen (eds), *The Future of Social Insurance* (Washington, DC: National Academy of Social Insurance).

Van der Heijden, H. (1999) 'Environmental Movements, Ecological Modernisation and Political Opportunity Structures', *Environmental Politics* 8(1): 199–221.

Van Oorschot, W. (2001) 'Welfare Reform, Welfare Outcomes, Activation and Flexicurity Policies in The Netherlands', paper given to EU COST A15, Budapest, 12–14 October.

Van Parijs, P. (ed.) (1992) *Arguing for Basic Income* (London: Verso).

Van Parijs, P. (1995) *Real Freedom for All* (Oxford: Oxford University Press).

Vinzant, J.C. and Crothers, L. (1998) *Street-level Leadership: Discretion and Legitimacy in Front-Line Public Services* (Washington, DC: Georgetown University Press).

Visser, J. and Hemerijck, A.C. (1997) *'A Dutch Miracle': Job Growth, Welfare Reform and Corporatism in The Netherlands* (Amsterdam: Amsterdam University Press).

Walby, S. and Greenwell, J. (1994) 'Managing the National Health Service', in J. Clarke, A. Cochrane and E. McLaughlin (eds), *Managing Social Policy* (London: Sage).

Walker, A. and Walker, C. (eds) (1997) *Britain Divided: The Growth of Social Exclusion in the 1980s and 1990s* (London: Child Poverty Action Group).

Walker, R. (1998) 'The Americanization of British Welfare: a Case Study of Policy Transfer', *Focus* 19(3): 32–40.

Walker, R. and Howard, M. (2000) *The Making of a Welfare Class? Benefit Receipt in Britain* (Bristol: Policy Press).

Walsh, K. and Stewart, J. (1992) 'Change in the Management of Public Services', *Public Administration* 70: 499–518.

Wanless, D. (2001) *Securing our Future Health: Taking a Long-term View*, Interim Report (London: HM Treasury).

Ward, H. (2002) 'Key Stage 2 Test Spotlight Falls on Headteachers', *Times Education Supplement*, 27 September.

Warren, T. (2000) 'Diverse Breadwinner Models: A Couple-based Analysis of Gendered Working Time in Britain and Denmark', *Journal of European Social Policy* 10(4): 349–71.

Watson, D. and Bourne, R. (2001) 'Can We Be Equal and Excellent Too? The New Labour Stewardship of UK Higher Education' Occasional Paper, Education Research Centre, University of Brighton (Brighton: University of Brighton).

Weale, A., Pridham, G., Cini, M., Konstadakopulos, D., Porter, M. and Flynn, B. (2000) *Environmental Governance in Europe* (Oxford: Oxford University Press).

Webster, F. (2002) *Theories of the Information Society*, 2nd edn (London: Routledge).

Weinberg, N., Schmale, J., Uken, J. and Wessel, K. (1995) 'Online Help: Cancer Patients Participate in a Computer Mediated Support Group', *Health and Social Work* 21(1): 24–9.

Wells, W. (2000) 'From Restart to the New Deal in the United Kingdom', in *Labour Market Policies and the Public Employment Service*, OECD Proceedings (Paris: OECD).

White, M. and Riley, R. (2002) *Findings from the Macro Evaluation of the New Deal for Young People*, Research Report No 168 (London: DWP).

White, S. (1998) 'Interpreting the Third Way: Not One Road But Many', *Renewal* 6(2): 17–30.

Whitty, G. (2001) 'Education, Social Class and Social Exclusion', *Journal of Education Policy* 16(4): 287–95.

Wilcox, S. (ed.) (2001) *Housing Finance Review, 2001/2002* (York: Joseph Rowntree Foundation/Chartered Institute of Housing and Council of Mortgage Lenders).

Wilcox, S. (ed.) (2002) *UK Housing Review, 2002/2003* (York: Joseph Rowntree Foundation/Chartered Institute of Housing and Council of Mortgage Lenders).

Wiliam, D. (2001) *Level Best? Levels of Attainment in National Curriculum Assessment* (London: Association of Teachers and Lecturers).

Wilkin, D. and Glendinning, C. (2002) '"Modernising" Primary Healthcare in the UK – the Role of Primary Care Groups and Trusts', in R. Sykes, C. Bochel and N. Ellison (eds) *Social Policy Review 14* (Bristol: Policy Press).

Wilkin, D., Gillam, S. and Smith, K. (2001) 'Tackling Organizational Change in the NHS', *British Medical Journal* 322: 1464–7.

Williams, C.C. (2002) 'The Social Economy and Local Exchange and Trading Schemes (LETS)', in T. Fitzpatrick and M. Cahill (eds), *Environment and Welfare* (Basingstoke: Palgrave Macmillan).

Williamson, O.E. (1985) *The Economic Institutions of Capitalism: Firms, Markets, Relational Contracting* (New York: Free Press).

Wilson, E. (1977) *Women and the Welfare State* (London: Tavistock).

Wilson, J. and Kelling, G. (1982) 'Broken Windows', *Atlantic Monthly* March, pp. 29–38.

Wilson, W.J. (1996) *When Work Disappears* (New York: Alfred A Knopf).

Women's Freedom League (1943) *Women's Bulletin* (29 January).

Work and Pensions Select Committee (2002) *'One' Pilots: Lessons for Jobcentre Plus*, Work and Pensions Committee, House of Commons, HC 426, (London: Stationery Office).

Working Brief (2002) *Working Brief*, Issue 130 (London: Centre for Economic and Social Inclusion).

Yeatman, A. (1994) *Postmodern Revisionings of the Political* (London: Routledge).

Young, J. (1999) *The Exclusive Society* (London: Sage).

Index